Founders of
Comic Fandom

FOUNDERS OF COMIC FANDOM

*Profiles of 90 Publishers, Dealers,
Collectors, Writers, Artists and
Other Luminaries of the
1950s and 1960s*

Bill Schelly

McFarland & Company, Inc., Publishers
Jefferson, North Carolina, and London

The essay "A Brief History of Comic Fandom"
appeared in longer form in the *Comics Buyer's Guide 1996 Annual,* under the
title "Comics Fandom Marks Its 35th Anniversary."
© 1995 Krause Publications, used with permission.
Uncredited quotations in this book have been drawn
from interviews conducted by the author from 1992 to 2009.

LIBRARY OF CONGRESS CATALOGUING-IN-PUBLICATION DATA
Schelly, Bill.
Founders of comic fandom : profiles of 90 publishers, dealers,
collectors, writers, artists and other luminaries of the
1950s and 1960s / Bill Schelly.
p.   cm.
Includes bibliographical references and index.

ISBN 978-0-7864-4347-5
softcover : 50# alkaline paper ∞

1. Cartoonists—United States—Biography.
2. Comic books, strips, etc.—Collectors and collecting—United States—Biography.
3. Comic book fans—United States—Biography.
4. Comic books, strips, etc.—Publishing—United States—History—20th century.
5. Comic books, strips, etc.—United States—History and criticism.
I. Title.
PN6725.S369   2010   741.5'9730922—dc22   [B]   2010024735

British Library cataloguing data are available

Front cover photograph by Bill Schelly

Manufactured in the United States of America

*McFarland & Company, Inc., Publishers
Box 611, Jefferson, North Carolina 28640
www.mcfarlandpub.com*

To the hundreds of fans who contributed
so much to getting comic fandom started,
too many to be named individually in this book.
Your efforts and contributions are
remembered and appreciated.

TABLE OF CONTENTS

V. Writers 109

VI. Artists 135

VII. Active Fans and Collectors 168

VIII. Professionals 189

ACKNOWLEDGMENTS

I would like to acknowledge the contributions of the following individuals, living and dead, and two newspapers, that directly or indirectly contributed to the information in *Founders of Comic Fandom*:

Marty Arbunich, Jean Bails, Jerry Bails, Michael Barrier, Roy Bonario, Lance "Doc" Boucher, Charles N. Brown, Bernie Bubnis, Richard Buckler, Bob Butts, Aaron Caplan, Vincent Davis, Bill DuBay, Mark Evanier, John Fantucchio, Ronn Foss, Rudi Franke, Brent Frankenhoff, Paul Gambaccini, Jeff Gelb, Don Glut, Janice Green, Richard "Grass" Green, Merlin Haas, Krista Hanley, Claude Held, Dave Herring, Steve Herring, Roger Hill, Alan Hutchinson, Larry Ivie, Robert Jennings, David Kaler, Steve Kelez, Richard Kyle, Stan Landman, Larry Lattanzi, Richard Lupoff, Patricia Lupoff, Tom McGeehan, *The Miami Herald*, Raymond Miller, Rick Norwood, Bob Overstreet, Ron Parker, Steve Perrin, Bud Plant, Howard Rogofsky, Derrill Rothermich, *The Rutland Herald*, Howard Siegel, Gerry Sorek, Bill Spicer, Larry Stark, Bhob Stewart, Hugh Surratt, Bill Thailing, Roy Thomas, Mike Tuohey, Fred Von Bernewitz, Mike Vosburg, Len Wein, Alan Weiss, Biljo White, Ted White, Malcolm Willits, Marvin Wolfman, Glen Wooten and John Wright.

Special thanks also go to John Benson for his series of articles on the EC fanzines of the 1950s that appeared in his magazine *Squa Tront*. The entries in this book on the participants in EC fandom relied significantly on Benson's research, expertise and writings. Thanks also go to Gary Brown, Michelle Nolan, Richard Olson and Jim Rossow for help on certain entries, and to Jim Korkis for helping with the proofreading of the manuscript.

Finally, I would like to acknowledge *Alter Ego* magazine from TwoMorrows Publishing as a source for some of the quotes herein, which originally appeared in my "Comic Fandom Archive" features in *AE* from 1998 to 2009.

Preface

Over the past 20 years, I have been researching the beginnings of comic fandom, the grassroots movement of the 1950s and 1960s that brought fans of comic books and strips together. Fandom was a way for fans to share their interest with others of like mind, find information about the objects of their fascination, and locate back issues to fill the gaps in their collections. My research, which included interviews and correspondence with most of the Big Name Fans of that era, resulted in *The Golden Age of Comic Fandom* (Hamster Press, 1995), the first book dedicated to chronicling that bygone era.

Just as comic fandom has been partly dedicated to the identification and appreciation of the creators who made the comics, so this book is dedicated to giving recognition to the energetic fans who did so much to get comicdom rolling in the 1950s and 1960s. Considering the hundreds of folks who were active in those early days, it wasn't easy to decide which fans would be represented in this book. The criteria that I used to select the 90 individuals are as follows:

First, the individual's achievements or efforts toward helping establish fandom had to take place during the formative years, roughly 1952 to 1970. By 1970, with the publication of the *Overstreet Comic Book Price Guide* and San Diego's Golden State Comic-Con, I contend that fandom had been founded. By then, all the major facets of comicdom were in place: the fanzines, the comicons, the reference guides, and just about everything associated with it.

Second, the fan's efforts needed to be visible to others. Essentially, it means that the fan should be a well-known fan, not one who participated mainly behind the scenes. Most of the founders were leaders: editors, chairmen, creators, entrepreneurs or organizers.

Third, the person had to be active in generally more than one kind of category. Though the people I profile have categorized as "Indexers," "Dealers," Convention Organizers," and so on, you'll discover that nearly everyone accomplished things that fit in more than one category.

It has been a subjective process. I would like to stress that these individuals aren't the only ones who contributed to the founding of fandom. What about, you may ask, fans like Bruce Hamilton, Gary Groth, Sol Davidson, Russ Cochran, Parley Holman, Bob Barrett, Alex Almaraz, Mike Friedrich, Mickey Schwaberow, James V. Taurasi, Bob K. Greene, Marc D. Nadel, Frank H. Nuessel, Murray Bischoff, Paul Seydor, Jeremy Barry, Dick Memorich, Tony Isabella, Dwight Decker, L. L. Simpson, Larry Raybourne, Joe Sarno, Ken Krueger, Ken Mitchell and so many other familiar names? The answer is that there simply wasn't enough space. The logical solution, of course, is to put together a second book. If enough people buy and enjoy this one, then perhaps another can be produced. I stand ready, willing and able.

INTRODUCTION: A BRIEF HISTORY OF COMIC FANDOM

Confronted with the spectacle of the throngs of comics fans at the major comic book conventions of today, it's almost inconceivable that there could have been a time when there was no comic fandom.

Yet, when John Fitzgerald Kennedy was sworn into the presidency in January 1961, comic fandom as it is known today didn't exist. There were no comicons, no comic book specialty stores, no comics trade publications, and no price guides. There was no special place for the comic art collector and fan to link up with others who were also interested. Comic book and comic strip collecting was, for the most part, a solitary pursuit.

Today, fans worry about burning issues like crowd control at the big conventions and the industry's ongoing boom-and-bust cycles. In 1960, the questions were far more basic: "How do I find someone with whom I can share my hobby? How long have comic books been published? What were they like in the past? Where do I find back issues? Are my comics worth saving, or should I throw them away when I'm done with them? If I keep them, how can I store them?"

There were no easy answers, until a disparate group of energetic, talented—even visionary—souls scattered across the United States made up their minds to bring collectors together to answer those questions.

Not that there weren't fans of comic art before 1961 who had similar unanswered questions. There were many of them. For fans to come together to form a cohesive fandom, the first prerequisite was a central meeting place. No such rallying point exclusively for comics fans emerged in the 1940s, though a few isolated comics fanzines did see print. David Kyle's *Fantasy World* (1936), Phil Bronson's *Scienti-Comics* (1940) and Malcolm Willits' *The Comics Collector's News* (1947) were like lonely little satellites looking for an orbit. Though the science fiction fanzines of the era, like James V. Taurasi's *Fantasy News* and *Fantasy Times*, often ran comic book news, it wasn't until the 1950s that fanzines devoted exclusively to comics gained a foothold. Led by titles like *The EC Fan Bulletin* and *Hoohah!*, a handful of amateur journals devoted to Bill Gaines' line of fabulous EC comic books, like *Weird Science* and *Tales from the Crypt*, were the first significant fanzines devoted exclusively to comic books. Even after the advent of the Comics Code Authority in 1955 and the subsequent death of EC comics, these stalwart fans kept the faith with publications devoted to *Mad* magazine (the only surviving EC publication) and the work of Harvey Kurtzman and other EC alumni.

To fully appreciate the events of 1961, we have to look at a memorable event in the prior September that catalyzed an upsurge in comics interest. At the 1960 World Science Fiction Convention in Pittsburgh over the Labor Day weekend, two SF fans named Dick and Pat Lupoff created a sensation when they appeared at the masquerade as Captain and Mary Marvel, the only superheroes in a field of as many as fifty costumers. Dick recalled, "We didn't win a prize, because they were not great costumes, but everyone just clustered around and wanted to talk about the costumes and the characters they were based on." At the same PittCon, the Lupoffs were distributing the 100 copies of their new fanzine *Xero*, which contained an article on Captain Marvel by Dick called "The Big Red Cheese," the first in a series dubbed "All in Color for a Dime."

Sharing the limelight in the ballroom that night in 1960 were two other fans with whom the Lupoffs would eventually become close friends: Don Thompson and Maggie Curtis. Later, in the pages of *Xero* #2, Hal Lynch wrote, "At the PittCon, I met up with Don Thompson, who told me of his desire to start a comics fandom." Soon Don and Maggie announced their intention to launch a fanzine devoted to comic strips and books called *Comic Art*.

In "Re-Birth," an article in *Comic Art* #1 (spring 1961), Dick Lupoff wrote, " 'All in Color for a Dime' has been the most letter-provoking feature of *Xero*.... All of this activity means something, and, unless I'm one very lousy inducer, it means that there is a great amount of interest in comic books, that it has been rolling along, usually unpublicized, showing through only occasionally in science fiction fandom and other peripheral areas of activity. Now, maybe Charles Fort would say that the Fall of 1960 was comic book time and that first article in *Xero* had nothing to do with the revival of interest. Certainly I would not claim that 'The Big Red Cheese' created the interest. But I do believe that the article served as a catalyst for all the latent interest which had been trying so long to break through to the surface."

Events happened quickly after that fateful Labor Day weekend in 1960, for it developed that the science-fiction double-fans who also loved comics were soon to be joined by a contingent of fans energized by the advent of the Silver Age superhero revivals in mainstream comic books (or, as it was known at the time, the Second Heroic Age of Comics). No one was more central to this part of the comic fan movement than a college professor in Detroit, Michigan: Jerry G. Bails, Ph.D.

Supporting the superhero revivals from DC (and other publishers) was the stated mission of Bails' *Alter-Ego* (which dropped the hyphen after the first four issues). The appearance of *A-E* #1 in March 1961 is often cited as the moment modern comic fandom was born, because it was sent free to the readers in DC letter columns, as well as to addresses Jerry found in *Xero* and other fanzines, in a concerted effort to instigate such a movement. In *Brave and the Bold* #35, the second issue to feature a re-tooled Hawkman for a new generation of readers, Schwartz printed full addresses with each letter, and continued this practice in the letter columns in the other books that he edited. Schwartz recognized that the older readers drawn to his titles might wish to correspond, as SF fans had done through addresses found in the "Discussions" lettercol of Hugo Gernsback's *Amazing Stories*. Schwartz, who had been a founding member of SF fandom in the late 1930s, surely must have known that facilitating contacts among readers could lead to some sort of fandom especially for comics fans.

In any case, a cursory examination of those letter columns in *Flash*, *Justice League of America*, and the other Schwartz-edited titles reveals that a large percentage of those enthusiastic writers were drawn into the giddy world of comicdom. The same holds true for the "Fantastic Four Fan Page," which was the only letter column in Marvel comics for some time. Beginning in *Fantastic Four* #3 in early 1962, Stan Lee printed letters (with full addresses) from dozens of fans who would play key roles in comic fandom. These letterwriters formed the beginning of Jerry Bails' huge mailing list, either receiving sample copies of one of his fanzines or an information sheet about them.

Untold numbers of old-time comics fans came out of the woodwork in 1961 and 1962 when they saw early issues of *Alter-Ego*, its sister publications, and the other fanzines of the day. Some of them were the double-fans who were well known in the ranks of SF fandom, but many more were new to this sort of thing—and delighted to get in touch with other comics enthusiasts through the U.S. Postal Service that reached fans from across the country as well as far-flung continents. These fans came from all walks of life: mail carriers, ambulance attendants, reporters, commercial artists, musicians, businessmen and college students. While many of the rank and file of this fledgling fan movement were from the Baby Boom generation, many were considerably older. And this older contingent provided an important steadying influence.

Where there is a gathering of comic book fans, a dealer hoping to capitalize on a market for back issues cannot be far away. In fact, early issues of *The Comicollector* carried ads from some dealers who had been around for years. Claude Held and Bill Thailing were two of them. Others with advertisements in the first issue of *CC* were John McGeehan, Red's Book Shop, Paul Seydor and Frank H. Nuessel. Soon, a fan named Gordon Belljohn (G. B.) Love introduced a competing adzine called *The Rocket's Blast*, and the trading and selling of old comics took center stage. For some, perhaps a majority of collectors, the treasures listed in the pages of *CC* and *RB* made those advertising publications the main attraction of fandom.

How did a collector choose from among the thousands of back issues in the ads? Where did a collector look for details about comics of the past? A collector couldn't go to the local library for that kind of data since no books on the subject existed. A collector couldn't find informative articles on comics in the periodicals of the day. Thus, fans gratefully taped their nickels, dimes and quarters to a piece of notebook paper and sent their hard-earned cash off to any fanzine editor who offered informative, intelligent articles and indexes.

Fans with an indexing bent devoted untold hours to gathering data to make up the first lists, such as Fred von Bernewitz's *Complete EC Checklist,* Jerry Bails' *All-Star* and DC indexes (assisted by Howard Keltner), Don and Maggie Thompson's *Dell Special Number Series* list, and the McGeehan brothers' many "House of Info" checklists. Raymond Miller wrote dozens of articles providing specific information about various costumed heroes and heroines of the 1940s, often accompanied by carefully traced illustrations. In most cases, younger fans' first exposure to the Golden Age of comics came through the pages of the early fanzines. This, in turn, fed into the market for old comics and put smiles on the faces of dealers as well as hard-earned coins in their coffers.

The year 1963 saw a virtual explosion of fanzines of all types, often printed on spirit duplicators, which were hand operated and produced copies in distinctive purple ink. Their circulations were small, often fewer than 100 copies, but these publications were avidly read, collected and traded. Anyone who wanted to participate could see his or her name in print, if only in the many letter columns. A sensational milestone was reached in 1964, when *The Rocket's Blast* and *The Comicollector* merged into the powerhouse adzine of the decade known as *RBCC*.

Another important amateur publication was launched in 1964, though with little fanfare: *Capa-alpha*, the first amateur press alliance (apa) for fans of comic books and strips. An apa, modeled after the form in SF fandom, called for a limited roster of participants to print a pre-determined number of their own contributions each month, send them all to a central mailer, and then receive back a thick mailing containing all the individual mini-zines from other contributors stapled together in one magazine-sized package. It proved a popular, durable formula in comic fandom and outlived Jerry Bails' tenure at the helm, when Don and Maggie Thompson assumed the CM spot.

An important phenomenon of the early 1960s was the emergence of stores that devoted a part of their operations to the stockpiling and selling of vintage comic books. They were usually located in large metropolitan areas. One of the most significant was the AbleMan

Book Store in Hamtramck, Michigan. Tom Altschuler's store was a normal bookstore downstairs, and a collector's dream upstairs. A customer had to be invited into the second floor sanctorum; those ushered in were treated to the spectacle of stacks of old comic books, movie magazines, pulp mags, Big Little Books and much more. Detroit fans met one another as they examined AbleMan's stock, and soon were informally meeting there on Saturdays to forage for treasures and discuss their hobby.

The Cherokee Book Store on Hollywood Boulevard was one of the earliest used-book stores to specialize in comics, beginning around 1962. It was also one of the most fondly remembered. Though owner Burt Blum wasn't a comics fan, per se, he presided over one of the most impressive stocks of Golden Age comics in the country. The other major comic book source in Hollywood was Collectors Book Store, run by Malcolm Willits and Leonard Brown.

While fanzines featuring articles and ads were perhaps the most popular, an important quotient of fan publishing revolved around amateur comic strips. Exemplary early efforts by talented amateur writers and artists such as Roy Thomas, Ronn Foss, Biljo White, Mike Vosburg, Steve Perrin, Richard "Grass" Green, Alan Weiss and Steve Gerber captured the imagination of fans who, after all, had a fairly limited selection of comics at the newsstand from which to choose. In the first half of the decade, Marvel published fewer than a dozen monthly superhero titles, and DC/National didn't have many more. Fans cheerfully paid for fanzines featuring amateur characters like The Eclipse (*Alter Ego*), Doctor Weird, The Eye and The Human Cat (*Star-Studded Comics*) and, in an EC vein, work by Bill Spicer, D. Bruce Berry, and Landon Chesney (*Fantasy Illustrated*).

Amateur writers and artists worked late into the night to produce these labors of love, which were genuinely popular with many fans. Sometimes their visions were as compelling

Rick Durell (left) and proprietor Burt Blum in the legendary Cherokee Book Store in Hollywood, California, ca. 1965.

as those of the pros, and their talent was undeniable. Soon, a few of them (such as E. Nelson Bridwell and Roy Thomas) broke into the ranks of the pros, but it would be several more years before the wall between the amateurs and the pros would crumble.

In a letter to Jerry Bails on October 25, 1961, Roy Thomas wrote, "I just had a crazy idea and thought it might be worth something. Your self-appointed #1 idea man was just thinking that *Alter Ego* ... should add a new feature: The Alter Ego Award, based on the Academy Award system. Maybe you could get prominent collectors ... to form a committee to nominate the candidates for the award (which I suggest be called an Alley after both *Alter Ego* and Alley Oop, who, living in prehistoric times, is the earliest possible adventure hero)." Thomas dubbed the proposed nominating committee "the Academy." Roy's suggestion was adopted, and Jerry conducted the first Alley Award poll for works appearing in 1961. All winners in the original ten categories were (predictably) Schwartz-edited titles, with *Justice League of America* winning the Best Regularly Published Comic Book category. The Alley Award poll proved popular but the Academy of Comic Book Fans and Collectors, less so. Some chafed at what was perceived to be an attempt to organize or even control comicdom, and, after several years of internal squabbling and few accomplishments, the Academy collapsed for lack of interest.

In 1962, Jerry Bails pointed out, "Comics fandom will not be a fandom in its own right until it holds its own convention." When the *Who's Who in Comic Fandom* (1964) was published, over 1,600 fans were involved in comicdom in some fashion. (See Appendix.) The

Fans attending the 1964 Alley Tally Party at Jerry Bails' house. Left to right: Don Glut, Bob Butts, Larry Raybourne, Russ Keeler, Alex Almaraz, Jerry Bails, Jim Rossow (head turned), Robert K. Greene. Kneeling: Ronn Foss (as Rocketman), Mike Tuohey.

desire to get together with other collectors and pros was strong and getting stronger, as evidenced by a growing number of fan meetings, conclaves and regional cons. Finally, an enterprising 16-year-old named Bernie Bubnis stuck his neck out and organized the first New York Comicon in 1964. Although it lasted only four hours, with about 50 fans in attendance, Bubnis's con has traditionally been considered the first real comics convention, perhaps because of the presence of representatives from Marvel (Steve Ditko and Flo Steinberg) and the number of well-known fans and dealers in attendance. Years later, Bubnis commented, "I had no conception of how to organize a comicon. I was just too young. I did it, because I thought someone should."

Events had crowded together thick and fast in the first half of the decade, as fans seemed to be trying to make up for lost time. In retrospect, it's possible to identify 1965 as the year when it all came together. The comic fandom movement had gained a momentum all its own that would propel it even without the nurturing guidance of its founders. All the tributaries had flowed together into a single rushing river.

In 1965, comicons took large leaps forward. Detroit-area fans pulled out all the stops to launch the Detroit Triple Fan Fair, which brought together fans and collectors of fantasy literature, films, and comic art. It was a huge success and might have overshadowed the New York Comicon held just a few days later, except that the event in the Big Apple also proved to be a hit with the estimated 200 fans in attendance.

Organizer Dave Kaler was able to use his contacts in New York at DC and Marvel to ensure this first "Academy Con" in the Big Apple had an impressive guest list. The line-up of pros on hand included Gardner Fox, Otto Binder, Bill Finger, Mort Weisinger, Jim Warren and Gil Kane, as well as Kaler's friend and roommate, Roy Thomas. In 1966, New York offered two major comics conventions. The first, hosted by John Benson, had Jack Kirby as the guest of honor; the second Kaler con featured the first appearance of Stan Lee at such an event.

Starting in 1968, Phil Seuling helmed the New York cons, which were held around the July Fourth holiday. Other areas of the country caught the "comicon bug," most notably hotbeds of fan activity like the Dallas-Houston connection (the Southwestern Cons) and the St. Louis area (the Gateway Cons).

Other events, besides the advent of the comic convention, mark 1965 as the watershed year. The hobby of comic collecting garnered unprecedented attention outside its relatively small circle of practitioners. One of the earliest media articles appeared in the *New York Times* in December 1964, headlined "Old Comic Books Soar in Value." Shortly after it appeared, Jerry Bails was contacted by a reporter from the same newspaper for a follow-up story; this piece included Bails' name and the fact that he was a professor at Wayne State University. This second article was reprinted in scores of newspapers across the country. As Jerry ruefully recalled, "The word was out that some kooky professor in Detroit was an avid [comics] collector."

In turn, Bails invited a number of Detroit area fans to meet with *Newsweek* reporter Hugh McCann in a round-robin interview. The famous (or infamous) article, "Superfans and Batmaniacs," appeared in *Newsweek* on February 15, 1965. While basically accurate, the magazine adopted a snide tone at times, referring to fans as "the comic cultists."

After receiving national exposure, Bails wrote that "not a day has passed since that I haven't been bugged by a reporter wanting to get in on the bandwagon." Other fans were also finding smug reporters on the other end of their phone lines. Suddenly comics fans, who had craved recognition for their hobby, discovered that attention was not always a good thing. The stories invariably focused on the "incredible sums" that old comics could command. (At the time, it was said, one might pay the astronomical amount of $75 for a copy of *Action*

Fan gathering in 1965. Top row, left to right: Glen Johnson, Rick Durell, John McGeehan, Eugene Henderson, Bill Spicer. Front row, left to right: Bob Foster, Chuck McCleary, Richard Kyle, Mike Royer.

#1!) As *Time, The New Yorker, Newsweek* (again), and others gave fandom exposure, fans began noticing prices for old comics escalating at a faster pace than ever before. There was no mystery about what was happening. More and more people were beginning to see comics as an investment. People who knew absolutely nothing about the hobby found out that old comic books could be valuable. Some, like a recent high school graduate named Howard Rogofsky, were able to move into selling vintage comics full-time. The trend had begun that would transform comics into legitimate, insurable collectibles. Despite the negatives that would inevitably come with that change, there could be no doubt that it was necessary to move in that direction if comic books were to be valued and preserved.

The next step was to reach agreement on uniform grading standards. Toward that end, Bill Spicer and Jerry Bails teamed up to produce *The Guidebook to Comics Fandom*. It offered a grading system consisting of Mint, Near Mint, Very Good, Good, Fair and Poor. The descriptions of the grades are close to current definitions, with the exception of Near Mint, which is expected to fill in the entire area between Mint and Very Good. (Fine and Very Fine would not appear for some time.)

Interest in comics of the past offered enough commercial enticement for Crown Publishers to release Jules Feiffer's *The Great Comic Book Heroes* late in the year. Excerpted earlier in *Playboy*, it was the first collection of classic superhero stories of the 1940s in book form, somehow managing to bring material owned by DC, Marvel, Fiction House, Fawcett and Will Eisner together under one cover. For fans who couldn't afford the escalating prices of Golden Age classics, Feiffer's book was an unexpected blessing.

Comic book conventions played an extremely important role—perhaps, ultimately, more important than the fanzines—in the maturing of comic fandom. They introduced collectors to worlds outside their immediate limited parochial interests. Cons exposed fans, not just to American comic strips, but European and other foreign comics, silent films like *Metropolis* and *The Phantom of the Opera* (in the pre-video and DVD era), the collecting worlds of pulp magazines and Big Little Books, and much more. Cons hastened the speed of fan contacts, which had previously been only as fast as the U.S. mails and the urge to write. Cons also exposed fans to the comic book professionals who created the objects of their fascination.

For their part, the pros were flattered by the attention. If collectors had spent years with their hobby in relative isolation, pros, too, had long accepted their lot of writing and drawing works for hire considered of little or no value in the tight compartments of their home studios and a few scattered offices in Manhattan. Meeting the denizens of comic fandom, many of them well-educated, literate, and, if nothing else, enthusiastic, gave pros a badly needed shot in the arm. More than that, it opened their eyes to future possibilities. Fandom, initially shrugged off and deprecated by many professional publishers, was clearly a growing phenomenon. As comicdom grew, it became clear to some of the pros that a demand existed for their work outside the strict confines of New York publishers. There might even be some money to be made in this small, but hungry, market.

In 1966, when Wally Wood launched *Witzend*, he wrote, "The existence of fandom gave the necessary impetus to our faint hearts, and so we want to say to all you horny-handed, ink-stained editor-publishers, demon reviewers and wild-eyed mimeograph machinists, rustling out there in the underbrush.... You have shown us the way! We are eternally grateful ... unless we lose our shirts!" Wood's small-press publication was a pioneer effort in creative ownership.

Before long, an increasing number of established pro artists dug into their files for unpublished material. A series of slick, thick, and high-priced prozines (magazines sold like fanzines but consisting mainly of professional work) began to emerge in the latter part of the decade, with one major calling card: irresistible art by pros and near-pros. All were printed via professional photo-offset. Soon the worthy but less-impressive fanzines (many printed via ditto or mimeograph) fell by the wayside, as fans switched their fanzine buying power to the prozines.

If 1965 was the year when the architects of comic fandom could be confident that the movement was now self-sustaining, 1970 was the year when the face of fandom was forever changed by a number of major developments in the publishing world.

The *Steranko History of Comics* was a for-profit project marketed to comicdom by a popular professional. It had originally been proposed to Marvel by Jim Steranko as *Stan Lee's History of Comics*, but when Steranko severed his connections with Marvel, he re-conceived the book and it became the first publication of his new Supergraphics company. The two volumes that were produced went a long way toward providing fans with a handy, fairly comprehensive reference to the Golden Age of comics.

An important source of reprinted comic art began in 1970 with Woody Gelman's Nostalgia Press. Gelman (who had written and drawn funny-animal comics for DC) soon edited a wide-ranging assortment of cartoon collections, newspaper strip reprints, and even underground comix (in addition to his other general-interest nostalgia books). His catalog sported a cover by underground cartoonist R. Crumb. Perhaps the most high-profile endeavor from Nostalgia Press was *The EC Horror Library* (1972), a hardbound collection of 23 EC stories in full color.

One of the early mainstream books about comics was *All in Color for a Dime*, edited by Dick Lupoff and Don Thompson, collecting and augmenting the original articles from Lupoff's fanzine *Xero*.

G. B. Love's *Rocket's Blast-Comicollector* found a major new competitor, when a young man named Alan Light in East Moline, Illinois, launched an adzine called *The Buyer's Guide for Comic Fandom*. "I remember holding my breath to see if G. B. Love would publish my ad, since I was an obvious competitor out to take business away from him," Light recalled later. "That ad was critical to my success." Love did print the vital two-page ad for *TBG* #1 in *RBCC* #76 (December 1970). The first issue of Light's fanzine was mailed in February 1971, at no charge to recipients. Two of the most popular columns in *TBG* in the coming years were "Beautiful Balloons" by Don and Maggie Thompson, and "Fit to Print" by Cat Yronwode.

Perhaps the most significant event of 1970, with the most far reaching implications, was the appearance of the first *Overstreet Comic Book Price Guide*. Bob Overstreet recalled, "I had price lists from practically every dealer from the early 1960s. So I went through everything I had, compiling a list of titles. [Jerry] Bails had just published his *Collector's Guide to the First Heroic Age*, which ... proved to be a tremendous source of information. The 1930s stuff, the romance comics, everything from the late 1940s up, the funny animals, I had to pick up myself. That's what went into the initial *Price Guide*." The first edition was not complete or without errors, but, as an index, it was a tremendous achievement. The guide sold well, and it was soon apparent that the demand would be sufficient for periodic updates.

What were some of the prices in that first edition? *Action* #1 was listed at $250 in Fine condition. *Amazing Fantasy* #15 came in at $16 in Mint condition. *X-Men* #1 was $6. Although fans and dealers had a love-hate attitude toward the *Comic Book Price Guide*, it immediately proved itself to be an essential reference book for any serious comic book collector.

How many fans were involved in 1960s fandom? That's a tough question, because there was no census of comicdom taken. But if one considers that *RBCC* reached a peak circulation of 2,500 copies per issue by 1970, and the New York Comicon posted attendance figures of 2,000 participants in 1969, then it's reasonable to estimate that there were about 10,000 to 15,000 fans in and out of fandom during the decade.

Of course, comic fandom continued to grow unabated throughout the following decades. Fanzines, conventions, dealers all flourished, though a new generation of fans came forward to carry the torch. Perhaps the most dramatic change was the number of fans who graduated from the ranks of comicdom into pro comics. Old-time pros (Mort Weisinger, for example) were reaching retirement age, and comic book publishers were beginning to see the need to bring in fresh talent. When new blood was needed, fandom was the logical place to find it.

E. Nelson Bridwell, Archie Goodwin and Roy Thomas had been the earliest success stories, but eventually the list expanded to include Rich Buckler, John Byrne, Dave Cockrum, Richard Corben, Kerry Gammill, Steve Gerber, Dave Gibbons, Don Glut, Sam Grainger, Mark Gruenwald, Rick Hoberg, Klaus Janson, Jeff Jones, Al Milgrom, Frank Miller, Doug Moench, Don Newton, Jerry Ordway, Neal Pozner, Don Rosa, Jim Starlin, Joe Staton, Mike Vosburg, Len Wein, Alan Weiss, Marv Wolfman and John Workman.

Let's not forget Stephen King. Yes, the writer of *The Shining* and many other best sellers of horror fiction got his start in comic fandom. A short story by King was published in Mike

Fan groups such as "The Illegitimate Sons of Superman" (TISOS) proliferated in the mid-to-late 1960s. At the 1967 New York Comicon, standing left to right: Pat Yanchus, Len Wein, Andy Yanchus, Ron Fradkin, Eliot Wagner, Marv Wolfman, Rich Rubenfeld. Sitting: Mark Hanerfeld, Stan Landman.

Garrett's obscure fanzine *Comics Review*, then reprinted more widely in Marv Wolfman's *Stories of Suspense* in the mid–1960s.

While *RBCC* ended its 21-year run with #153 in 1981, and *The Comic Reader* published its final issue shortly thereafter, the adzine and newszine have survived in the form of *Comics Buyer's Guide*, a direct descendant of the fanzine world, as well as new Internet counterparts like eBay and other auction sites.

Comics apa *Capa-alpha* is still going strong, celebrating 45 years of continuous monthly mailings. In the fanzine arena, *K-a* (as it's abbreviated) is the last survivor of that halcyon era. Apas have kept the spirit of fannish publishing alive, though many of them have now migrated to the Internet, or been supplanted by newsgroups.

The first San Diego Comic-Con (then San Diego's Golden State Comic-Con) made the scene August 1–3, 1970, at the U.S. Grand Hotel. Shel Dorf, one of the originators of the Detroit Triple Fan-Fair, had moved to San Diego by 1969. "I was bored out of my gourd, and they had a lot of science-fiction conventions around San Diego, but no comics conventions," Dorf remembered. So, with the help of Ken Krueger, Richard Alf, and others, Shel started what has become the premiere comics con in the world, and seems in danger of outgrowing its hometown convention center, with attendance well over the 100,000 mark in recent years.

For the average comic book fan and collector, perhaps the single most obvious outgrowth of comic fandom is the comic book specialty store and the direct market that supplies it. Though they did not precisely and wholly grow out of fandom, comics shops might never have come into existence if comicdom hadn't come together in the 1960s. Many original retail outlets were hippie head shops, but a good proportion (like Cherokee, AbleMan, and Collectors Book Store) did have their roots in the comic book fan movement. The man who finally convinced DC Comics (and later Marvel) to sell direct to retailers was long-time fan and dealer Phil Seuling.

As for the quest for respectability that motivated Jerry Bails, Richard Kyle, Don and Maggie Thompson, Rick Weingroff and others, one only has to enter a Barnes and Noble bookstore to find that now the "graphic novels" and "comics history" categories are well-established. As for society as a whole, one need only look at the stratospheric success of comic book–based films such as *The Dark Knight Returns*, *Spider-Man* and *Iron Man* to see that the four-color heroes of the past have been accepted as fitting subjects for popular entertainment. Today, an adult can read a comic book on the bus, and not feel embarrassed as the early comic fans did.

Fandom's founders did their job well. The contemporary collector now has an incredible wealth of products, services, resources, and events to enhance his or her enjoyment of the medium. Fancy, upscale reprint editions exist for virtually every type of Golden Age and Silver Age comic book, and there are black and white "economy priced" editions, which any budget-minded collector can afford. Moreover, the off-brand Golden Age comics in public domain are widely available on a plethora of web sites or CDs, providing unprecedented access to comic books of the past that are too rare for the average collector to afford.

What a difference 50 years makes!

FANDOM TIMELINE

1952—Ted White publishes *The Story of Superman* (titled *The Facts Behind Superman* in subsequent revised editions), perhaps the first comics fanzine devoted to the study of a comic book character. The only edition circulated beyond family and friends was published in 1953 (possibly early 1954).

1953—Bhob Stewart's *The EC Fan Bulletin* is published in April, marking the beginning of EC fandom.

1955—First edition of the *Complete EC Index* is published.

September 1960 (Labor Day weekend)—Richard and Pat Lupoff appear at the SF WorldCon as Captain and Mary Marvel, and distribute copies of *Xero* #1 (with the "All in Color For a Dime" article devoted to the Marvel Family).

March 28, 1961—*Alter-Ego* #1 printed, and mailed by month's end. First comic book fanzine inspired by and founded to promote the return of the costumed heroes at DC and other comic book companies.

April 1961—*Comic Art* #1.

September 1961—*The Comicollector* #1, first all-comics adzine.

December 1961—*The Rocket's Blast* #1.

January 1962—*All-Star Index*, the first index to superhero comics of the 1940s.

June 1962—First Alley Awards poll.

1963—Ronn Foss, Roy Thomas and Jerry Bails visit fans in other cities.

March 20 & 21, 1964—Alley Tally Party at Jerry Bails' home, the first sizable gathering of comic fans.

April 1964—*The Rocket's Blast* and *The Comicollector* merge into one adzine, *RBCC* #29.

June 1964—*Who's Who in Comic Fandom* is published.

July 27, 1964—First New York Comicon, organized by Bernie Bubnis; *Batmania* #1 is published.

February 1965—"Superfans and Batmaniacs" article appears in *Newsweek*, first national magazine to discuss comic fandom.

July 1965—First Detroit Triple Fan Fair; second New York Comicon; these were considered the first "full service" comic book conventions, with most of the elements that would be henceforth considered standard for a true comicon, and drew fans from remote distances.

1965—*Guidebook to Comics Fandom* is published.

January 1966—*Batman* TV show debuts.

August 1967—*Squa Tront* #1 is published.

July 1968—First New York Comicon chaired by Phil Seuling.

August 1, 1970—First San Diego Comic-Con.

1970—*Overstreet Comic Book Price Guide* published; *The Buyer's Guide for Comic Fandom* begins.

GLOSSARY

In any hobby, a specialized vocabulary is established over time. In comic fandom, there are many such terms, often adopted from science fiction fandom which came before. Below are such words that are used frequently in this book.

adzine—amateur magazine, usually published frequently, that exists primarily to publish "for sale" and "wanted" advertisements from dealers, collectors, fanzine editors and others.

apa—amateur press alliance (or association), where each member contributes (and generally prints) a pre-determined number of his/her own fanzine, possibly as short as a single sheet; then a central mailer makes up collections of all the fanzines (also called apazines) and mails a complete set to each member.

Big Name Fan—member of fandom who, through dint of accomplishments, became widely known and respected. (Usually capitalized.)

comic fandom (or comics fandom)—a group of people who enjoy and often collect comic books and related items, who generally honor certain fair practices, who come together for conventions, who have their own publications, and who often attempt to raise the consciousness of non-members about the inherent value of the sequential art medium. Some prefer the term "comics fandom," but the terms are used interchangeably.

comicon—contraction of "comic fan convention."

comicdom—contraction of "comic fandom."

crudzine—a fanzine with nothing of interest or value, poorly written and/or illustrated, and often badly printed; often produced by younger fans.

dealer—anyone who buys something at one price, and attempts to sell it for a profit.

ditto—a hand printing process using a spirit duplicator; the purple printing gradually gets lighter, until after about 200 copies, it becomes illegible; blue, black, green and red ditto masters were used to print multi-colored pages.

double-fan—member of more than one fandom, such as superhero and SF fandom.

fandom—any group of people with a common interest that come together to appreciate that interest.

fan-ed—fanzine editor.

fannish—having to do with the fans themselves, rather than the professional comic books.

fanzine—term for amateur publications; contraction of "fan magazine," invented ca. 1941 by Louis Russell Chauvenet, a deaf science fiction fan; alternate term is "fanmag" or "fanmag."

The Golden Age of Comics—Comic books published roughly from 1938 to 1945, beginning with the first appearance of Superman in *Action Comics* #1, and ending roughly at the end of World War II.

grading—the art of determining the condition of any item, most often a specific comic book; basic grading terms in descending order are Mint, Near Mint, Very Fine, Fine, Very Good, Good, Fair and Poor.

hecto—hectograph printing, a rudimentary and time-consuming process that appeared similar to ditto printing, though it could produce far fewer copies than spirit duplication.

illo—illustration.

issue—the latest in a sequence of periodicals; refers not to a specific comic book (for example) but all comic books with the same title and number.

letter column—section in a periodical that prints letters from readers, usually about prior issues; sometimes abbreviated as "lettercol."

mimeo—mimeographic printing, which uses a mimeograph machine with a perforated drum, that is coated with ink on the inside; when special mimeograph stencils are affixed to the drum, which have been typed or drawn upon, the ink is forced through openings in the stencils and, as the drum is rotated, rolled onto the surface of individual sheets; most often the ink and printing is black, though other color inks (most often red and blue) can be used.

panel—boxes containing the story images on a comic book page, or in a comic strip.

photo-offset (or lithographic printing)—professional lithographic printing, where pages were photographed, then etched into plates which were affixed to a printing press.

pro—a professional in the comics industry; usually a writer, artist or editor, but refers to any professional.

prozine—A fan publication produced by professionals in the comics industry, and filled mainly with work by professionals. Term invented by Louis Russell Chauvenet.

pulp—the cheap paper used to print comic books, similar to the paper used in newspapers; or, a magazine format popular from the 1920s to the 1950s, popularly known as "pulp magazines."

RBCC—Abbreviation for the unwieldy fanzine title *Rocket's Blast-Comicollector,* the leading adzine of the 1960s.

SF—science fiction.

The Silver Age of Comics—period of time when comic books were published generally considered to have begun with the return of the Flash in *Showcase* #4 (1956) and ended around 1970. ("The Bronze Age of Comics" followed.)

zine—Abbreviation for "fanzine."

Section I: Indexers

The sequential numbering of comic books fostered their collectibility in many ways. The fact that there was a *Superman* #100 indicated that there was an historical background to the character, and that there were past issues. If a reader liked an issue of *Superman* a lot, he or she might try to collect #1 through #99 to add to their stack of new issues, bought off the rack. He or she might wonder what Superman had been like in his early days, and who created him. Were Lois, Perry and Jimmy in the first issue, or if they came along later, in what issues did they first appear?

In 1953, there was literally nowhere to look for such information. There were no price guides, no comic art collections in universities, no books or other publications that offered elucidation. There was only the obscure and difficult to obtain *The Facts Behind Superman*, a postcard-sized amateur publication in which Ted White and Ronnie Graham pooled all their knowledge about the Man of Steel. A collector would have had to be extremely lucky to find a copy, however, because there were most likely only 35 copies of that fanzine printed. Furthermore, to hear of its existence, a person would most likely have had to be active in SF fandom, or perhaps be in touch with Ted White through a letter column in one of the professional SF magazines that were being published at the time.

EC fans were lucky because they only had to wait until 1955 to purchase Fred von Bernewitz's *Complete EC Checklist*, which was prepared with the cooperation of the publisher William Gaines. Those fans who craved data about the comics of the 1940s were on their own.

Many a fan desperately searched dusty used bookstores for back issues that later research proved were never published. Comic books often changed titles in mid-numbering, so as not to incur another registration fee for second-class mailing privileges. In the wild and wacky world of comic books, it wasn't unheard of for two consecutive issues to use the same number, or for a number to be skipped. Often, early adventures of a favored character began in the back pages of another comic book, but where and when was the often unanswered question. Dell's *Four Color* series, begun in 1939, had over 600 issues by the mid–1950s, featuring a mix of all their licensed properties within the same numbering sequence. Figuring out what issues to look for was a collector's nightmare. This lack of knowledge was like a great yawning chasm, which had to be crossed before the hobby could really take off.

No publisher thought it was financially worthwhile to hire someone to research the history of comic books, so it fell to individual collectors to do the work. Certainly, many fans kept their own painstakingly constructed lists of existing comic books, and early collectors may have traded their lists to other aficionados, if they knew of them. Not surprisingly, one of those knowledgeable fans lived in the publishing capital of America, New York City. His name was Larry Ivie.

With the rise of general comic fandom, opening communication between fans across the country and around the world, the pooling of data could begin. Certain fans, through whatever personality quirk, particularly enjoyed seeking out such information and indexing it. Others liked circulating non-profit publications that carried the embryonic checklists and compilations of available information to others, which accelerated the accumulation of still more data.

The indexing function could be deemed the most important activity of fandom, which is why this is the first section of *Founders of Comic Fandom*. These were the enthusiasts who, among whatever other roles they played in early fandom, were the ones with a passion for gathering and indexing data. Their efforts began compiling and fleshing out an outline of an entire industry's historical output. By the end of the 1960s, due to their efforts (and that of others like them) much of that job would be completed.

Jerry Bails
(1933–2006)

Jerry Bails is sometimes referred to as "the father of comic fandom" because he laid the foundation for an ongoing comic fandom: creating the fanzines *Alter-Ego*, *The Comic Reader*, *The Comicollector*, starting *Capa-alpha*, and spearheading a drive to establish the Academy of Comic-Book Fans and Collectors, an organization that was formed in part to promote the idea that there was nothing inherently childish about the sequential art medium or comic books. In addition, Bails published some of the earliest indexes of comic book data, and hosted the first sizable gathering of comic fans, a sort of "proto-comicon."

Jerry Gwin Bails was born in 1933 and grew up in Kansas City, Missouri, where his father ran a pool hall called "Bails Recreation." Jerry saw his first copy of *All-Star Comics* with #6, which began his lifelong affection for the Justice Society of America. Jerry got polio when he was ten years old during the epidemic of 1943, but recovered fully. He was a physically active youth who opted out of group activities like organized sports. From an early age, Bails not only enjoyed reading, but he loved storytelling and drawing. In school, he did layouts and artwork for the school newspaper and yearbook, and might have pursued a career along those lines if he hadn't had an equal or greater affinity for the sciences. Math came easily to him, and he ended up a high honors student at Westport High. Jerry graduated in 1951, a few months after his beloved JSA had died, with the metamorphosis of *All-Star Comics* into *All-Star Western* that spring.

Bails entered a period of minimal interest in comics during the 1950s, as he

Jerry Bails

concentrated on college. He attended the University of Kansas City, and married his high school sweetheart, Sondra, in 1953 at age 20. After attaining a Bachelor of Science degree in Physics in 1955, he went on to attend the University of Chicago for a semester but returned to the University of Kansas City to finish his Master's degree in Math, and then a Doctorate in Natural Science. By 1960, Jerry and Sondra had moved to Detroit, where he had accepted a position as an Assistant Professor of Natural Science at Montieth College, part of Wayne State University.

During the 1950s, Jerry's avocation had become astronomy, but his love of comics hadn't vanished. In 1953, he entered into a correspondence with Gardner Fox, writer of the Justice Society of America and many other features published at DC Comics. They discussed the JSA, and Jerry made it known that he was rebuilding his personal collection of *All-Star*. Some time in the late 1950s, Fox sold Bails his bound volumes of *All-Star* for a total of $75. Bails wrote, "Gardner Fox was a most generous and compassionate man and it is clear to me that he had influenced my basic values through the vehicle of the Justice Society. He made a big difference to me." Attempting to elaborate on this in later life, Jerry said, "No group today is quite like the original JSA. The Justice Society was an egalitarian group of psychologically mature adults, not a pack of adolescent neurotics who needed a father-figure to keep them in line. While the JSA did elect a chairman, the chairman never bossed around the other members. In my youth, I didn't fantasize about being a kid with super-powers who was able to get away with murder and mayhem. I fantasized about being an adult superhero capable of putting the world in right order."

Bails kept an eye on the newsstands, and noticed the Flash revival in *Showcase* #13 which appeared around January 1958. The sight of that comic book on the stands excited him, for it raised the possibility of further revivals, including his beloved JSA. Two years later, after the Flash and Green Lantern had their own magazines, the Justice Society was back in its new incarnation: The Justice League of America. The team's revival in *Brave and Bold* #28 hit the newsstands at the very end of 1959, and the JLA were given their own title shortly after Jerry had moved to Detroit. Immediately, Bails began thinking of ways to support and encourage this exciting development. Unexpectedly, the young professor received a letter in July 1960 from a comic book fan and JSA enthusiast finishing college in Missouri. That fan was Roy Thomas, who was given Jerry's address by Gardner Fox. Though Jerry didn't want to sell the *All-Star* comics that he had purchased from Gardner, he immediately wrote an enthusiastic response, enclosing dog-eared duplicate copies of *All-Star* #4 through 6, the first Roy had ever seen of those issues. This generosity on Bails' part cemented their friendship.

Thomas and Bails began a long and voluminous correspondence, each writing two or three letters a week to each other, with queries and responses often crossing in the mail. Jerry penned numerous letters to DC letter columns, sometimes under pseudonyms. In August, Bails wrote to Fox suggesting a revival of the Atom, since Hawkman was slated to make his debut in December. He and Roy concocted an idea for a revived Atom in a letter to editor Julius Schwartz in early December. In January 1961, Schwartz responded that by sheer coincidence, he and his staff had been planning their own Atom revival. About this time, Jerry was thinking about publishing a JLA newsletter that he would distribute to contacts made through the letter pages in Julie's comics. Schwartz had decided, toward the end of 1960, to begin running complete addresses in his letter columns. Fortunately, Jerry was asked to visit and lecture at Adelphi College on Long Island, which gave him the opportunity to visit Schwartz at the DC office in New York City. When Bails broached the subject of a JLA newsletter to Julie Schwartz, he received an entirely positive response, for such amateur publications were well known to Julie. With his amateur publishing background, Schwartz may have seen Jerry and Roy as something of successors or counterparts to himself and Mort Weisinger, in terms of their fannish pursuits. It was Julie who told Jerry that amateur magazines and newsletters were called fanzines, and showed him copies of Richard and Pat Lupoff's SF zine *Xero*. Bails also had lunch with Gardner Fox on this visit. When he returned to Detroit, Jerry wrote to Roy: "I know now (for sure) that I want to bring out a 'fanzine' devoted to the Great Revival of the costumed heroes. I even have what I consider to be a brilliant title and format. It will be called *Alter-ego* [sic]."

Jerry began building up a mailing list of people who would receive *Alter-Ego* #1 free of charge. The first issue, twenty-two pages long, was printed on a desk-top spirit duplicator. The cover featured Roy's parody of the *JLA*, known as the Bestest League of America. Inside the fanzine, after the contents page was "A Matter of Policy," the brief editorial which announced, "This is the first issue of *Alter-Ego*, a new comic fanzine devoted to the revival of the costumed heroes." From there, Bails launched into four pages of pro news in a feature called "On the Drawing Board." It carried advance word of the forthcoming "Flash of Two Worlds" story (*Flash* #123), which brought back the Golden Age Flash. Next was "The Wiles of the Wizard, Portrait of a Villain," Jerry's two-page JSA–related article. On pages 10 through 12, Roy Thomas presented the first part of his "Reincarnation of the Spectre," which proposed a new version of the Spectre as a man divided into two characters representing good and evil, ego and id: the Spectre and Count Dis. Then came "Merciful Minerva: The Story of Wonder Woman," followed by the first five-page chapter of "The Bestest League of America" by Thomas. The members of the *BLA* were Wondrous Woman, the Cash, Aquariuman, S'amm S'mith, Lean Arrow and the Green Trashcan. By March 28, 1961, *Alter-Ego* #1 was completed, with copies mailed by the month's end.

The response to *Alter-Ego* was immediate and explosive. Bails had clearly tapped into an un-met need of comic book fans and collectors, a magazine such enthusiasts could call their own. (The Thompsons' *Comic Art*, published about this time or shortly thereafter, ignited similar interest among the mainly SF fans who received it.) Jerry sent out the entire print run (estimated at 200 copies) in short order, including a number of truncated copies which were missing the BLA comic strip. He and Roy (upon whom he'd conferred the equal status of "editor") immediately launched into producing a second issue, which would appear in June, and then a third which saw print in the fall of 1961.

It quickly became apparent that "Wanted" and "For Sale" advertisements would fit better in a separate publication which could see print more often than *A-E*. Thus was born *The Comicollector*, which Bails published beginning in September 1961. The "On the Drawing Board" segment of *A-E* would break out as a separate news sheet with #4 (October 7, 1961), and from there gradually add pages until it was a fanzine rather than a sheet. As for *Alter-Ego* itself, issues #2 and #3 offered the last two chapters of Roy's Bestest League of America strip, as well as introducing a letter column called "Conversations." Early letter writers were such fans as Steve Gerber, Dale Christman, Harry Thomas, Ted White, Larry Ivie, Bill Sarill, Ronnie Graham and Irving Glassman. *A-E* #3 featured Jerry's only major article to ever appear in the fanzine, "The Light of the Green Lantern."

Jerry Bails had a fiery urgency, an almost messianic fervor, in his effort to support the superhero revivals of the era he dubbed "The Second Heroic Age of Comics." That support was, indeed, the avowed mission of *Alter-Ego*. Excitement crackled through its pages (and those of its spin-offs), a result of Jerry's almost breathless "what's next?" attitude about upcoming revivals. His enthusiasm was contagious, and helped his recruitment efforts catch fire across the country (and around the world) within a very short time. He produced a magazine that was decidedly down to earth (even a little "gosh-wow," in Ted White's words). Bails was on a crusade to bring as many people into fandom as possible, since it would further the goals of *Alter-Ego*. It was Bails who had the organizational skill, desire and vision to lay the groundwork for an ongoing comic fandom. Don and Maggie Thompson later wrote, "*Alter-Ego's* editors were trying to get it distributed to the largest possible number of fans—thus earning its reputation as a seminal point in comics fandom. We tried [with *Comic Art*], as did Dick and Pat Lupoff with *Xero*, to keep our circulation as small as possible," to save work. Had Jerry Bails not come along when he did, quite probably someone else would have come up with the idea of a comics fanzine devoted to the resurgence of the superheroes. Jerry himself acknowledged, "Had there been no Jerry or Roy or Don or Maggie, someone else would surely have come up with the idea." In the following years, one thing did become clear: fans with Bails' vision and organizational ability were rare.

All the furious fanzine publishing of 1961 should not obscure the fact that at least 50 percent of Bails' "mission" was to collect data on comics of the past. Jerry knew that information was the key to any collecting hobby; moreover, he was the type of person who felt the behind-the-scenes creators should be credited for their achievements, and be accorded commensurate appreciation. As early as 1945, he had set out to record artists on strips in a spiral notebook. He had learned to recognize such favorites as the work of Joe Kubert, Alex Toth and Lee Elias. While Jerry's first published efforts along these lines were *The Authoritative Index to All-Star Comics* and *The Authoritative Index to DC Comics* (1963), co-authored with Howard Keltner, Bails was also busy behind the scenes researching the framework of all comic books published during what Dick Lupoff had called their "Golden Age," a term that stuck. Toward that end, Jerry networked intensively with others of similar bent, such as Howard Keltner, Raymond Miller, Bill Thailing, Don and Maggie Thompson, Fred von Bernewitz and many others. This research became the basis of a truncated list of Golden Age comics that appeared in the *Guidebook to Comics Fandom*, and came to fruition in full form with Jerry's self-published *Collector's Guide: The First Heroic Age* in 1969. In turn, the *Collector's Guide* provided a framework for Bob Overstreet who was then working on his comic book price guide. Later still, from 1973 to 1976, Bails would co-edit *The Who's Who of American Comic Books* with Hames Ware, which appeared in four volumes. Jerry's contributions to fandom as an indexer were immense, since he provided the foundation for so much additional information and research in later years.

In 1963, Jerry worked to write a charter for a fan organization, inspired by Roy's mentioning in a letter (written on October 25, 1961) that an "academy" of fans could annually select nominees for an "Alter Ego Award." Bails immediately envisioned something more ambitious, an Academy of Comic-Book Arts and Sciences. As for the awards, Jerry carried the ball on that as well, and they were called the "Alley Awards" and Alley Oop was the mascot. The first nominating ballot was distributed in 1962 to the 20 original members of the Academy. They were Jerry Bails, Bob Barron, Len Brown, Dale Christman, Wendell Davis, Rick Durell, Don Foote, Ronn Foss, Irving Glassman, Ron Haydock, Howard Keltner, Ed Lahmann, Dick Lupoff, Douglas Marden, Raymond Miller, Frank Neussel, Fred Norwood, Roy Thomas, Don Thompson, and Biljo White. Bails wrote and published a proposed charter, after seeking input from others, and it was mailed to 92 active fans. In a cover letter, Bails announced that he had changed the name of the organization to "The Academy of Comic-Book Fans and Collectors," which he felt was less pretentious and more accurate. The charter, which was resoundingly ratified, stated that the Academy would conduct the Alley Awards, publish *The Comic Reader* (formerly *On the Drawing Board*), endorse a Code of Fair Practice in the selling and trading of comic books, publish a directory of comic fans, encourage the formation of local chapters, endorse other fan organizations, assist in the effort to establish an annual comicon, and encourage participation in these functions by industry professionals. General membership in the Academy was free, and would be automatically conferred on those who voted in the annual Alley Awards poll. The charter established the position of Executive Secretary (which Jerry would hold, at first) and took steps toward setting up an elective Executive Board. Now, in its masthead, *The Comic Reader* was referred to as the "Official Newsletter of the Academy of Comic-Book Fans & Collectors."

Jerry Bails was a visionary, but was willing to pass along his responsibilities as soon as someone came along who was capable of assuming them. He passed *The Comicollector* and *Alter-Ego* to Ronn Foss, and *The Comic Reader* to Glen Johnson. It wasn't long before Paul Gambaccini became the Executive Secretary of the Academy. Meanwhile, Jerry was deeply involved in photographing old comic book covers and selling photo-sets, as well as microfilming entire Golden Age comics. He borrowed many comics from collectors just long enough to microfilm them, an activity that consumed much of his time in 1963 and 1964.

In March 1964, Jerry held what has come to be known as the Alley Tally Party, publishing an invitation in *Dateline: Comicdom*, the newszine Ronn Foss had established for fanzine editors and active contributors in 1963. Recipients of the fanzine (there were about 50) were "cordially invited to attend the Tally Party to count the votes in the Alley Poll. Date: March 21–22; place: home of JGBails, 22529 Karem Ct., Warren, Mich. RSVP. Particulars will be sent to those who can make it." All told, 19 fans showed up for what is considered the first sizable gathering of comics fans. They were Alex Almaraz, Dick Andersen, Edwin Aprill Jr., Bob Butts, Ronn Foss, Don Glut, Grass Green, Keith Greene, Fred Jackson, Russ Keeler, Chuck Moss, Larry Raybourne, Jim Rossow, Gerry Sorek, Don Thompson and Maggie Thompson, Mike Tuohey, Mike Vosburg and Jerry himself. Chuck Moss had come from farthest away, hailing from Nebraska, and the Cleveland fans (Larry, Russ, Don and Maggie) had come a good distance as well. In addition to tallying the awards for 1963, they showed one another original art, Golden Age comics and other rarities, passed around copies of their fanzines and solicited contributions for future issues, and discussed the future of fandom—including their desire for a regional or national comicon.

Also in 1964, Jerry was responsible for two more publications. The first was the *Who's Who in Comic Fandom*, with the first edition typed by Larry Lattanzi; a supplement a few months later added to the list of fandom addresses considerably. A staggering 1,683 addresses were listed, mainly drawn from Bails' personal mailing list. (See Appendix.) Then, in August, Bails launched the first comics apa (amateur press alliance) called *Capa-alpha*, which gathered together pre-printed contributions from its members and sent out the collated bundles to each of them. The concept, as with virtually everything else Jerry introduced, wasn't new—apas had long been established in SF fandom—but it worked like a charm, and proved to be long-lasting. *Capa-alpha* continues many decades later to the present day in print form.

Toward the end of 1964, a few articles appeared (in the *New York Times* and elsewhere) talking about the high prices that were being commanded by "those old funny books." This led to reporters hearing about a college professor in Detroit who was a ringleader of the comic book collectors, and telephoning Bails for quotes and other information. In early 1965, Bails was contacted by *Newsweek* reporter Hugh McCann who wanted to interview him in Jerry's Detroit home. Jerry invited fans to join in the interview, including Shel Dorf, Marvin Giles, Eugene Seger, Bob Brosch, Gary Crowdus, Dennis Kawicki and Carl Lundgren. To the reporter, no doubt curious as to why adults would be interested in something like comic books, Jerry explained, "They say that men in our society frequently make a total break from their childhood. I see no reason, if you enjoy something as a youngster, why you should ever lose that enjoyment." The resulting article, "Superfans and Batmaniacs," appeared in *Newsweek* on February 15, 1965. The tone of the article was, at times, snide and condescending, while the information it contained was basically accurate. Bails had mixed feelings about it, and avoided subsequent interviews by reporters who obviously had their own agenda.

In 1965, Bails was also on the organizing committee, along with those who had been in his living room for the *Newsweek* interview, for the Detroit Triple Fan Fair, a convention for fans of comic books and strips, fantasy literature and film. However, difficulties in his personal life were overtaking Bails, and for a time caused him to pull back almost entirely from fannish pursuits. His wife, Sondra, was deeply depressed after their son was born. Her problems increased over the next several years. Eventually, the two were divorced. This painful period meant that fandom heard little from Jerry after his appearance at the 1965 New York Comicon.

Gradually, Bails built a new life with the woman who became his second wife, Jean, and began publishing data in the form of a fanzine called *The Panelologist*. (Jerry was enamored with this term to describe a fan of comic art, but it was too awkward to pronounce to be widely accepted.) This activity represented the prelude to the publication of his *Collector's Guide: The First Heroic Age* (1969), his most ambitious data project yet. This publication, which sported a cover by Richard Buckler, was greeted warmly by fandom. From there, he launched into compiling and publishing the *Who's Who in American Comic Books* with Hames Ware.

In later life, Jerry adapted to the personal computer and Internet revolutions with alacrity, as one would expect of a science professor, and he became extremely active in newsgroups on various topics. His politics, which were generally on the far left, bespoke his deep concern for humanity, and for the obligations of citizens to one another and to their country (just like his heroes in the JSA). For him, environmentalism was one of the most important issues of all; he wrote a book on that subject called *Coming Clean*, which he used in his classrooms but never pursued getting published professionally.

Jerry Bails retired from teaching in 1996, and now was able to devote himself fully to his family and his avocations. Jerry attended the Fandom Reunion 1997 held in Chicago during the Chicago Comicon, meeting up again with Roy Thomas (whom he had seen sporadically over the years), as well as 31 others, such as Howard Keltner, Jay Lynch, Jerry Ordway, Maggie Thompson, Grass Green, Ken Tesar, Bob Butts, Bob Beerbohm, Jim Rossow and Bill Schelly. When *Alter Ego* was revived by Roy Thomas at TwoMorrows Publishing, Bails was pleased, read each issue avidly, and often wrote letters to Roy with corrections and thoughts on various articles and interviews. The magazine celebrated Jerry's 70th birthday (*AE* #25, June 2003) with a series of articles about the uberfan's contributions to fandom over the years.

As Jerry and Jean passed their 35th wedding anniversary, his health was clearly deteriorating. He became more and more homebound in his last years, as he suffered a series of heart attacks and other ailments. Nevertheless, he remained very active on the Internet in both newsgroups and the volume of his email correspondence.

Then, on November 23, 2006 (Thanksgiving Day), Jerry Bails passed away in his sleep. Fandom had lost its key founder, and the larger world had lost an exceptional member of the human race and community. He was survived by his wife, Jean, three children, and several grandchildren. A tribute to his passing appeared in *Alter Ego* #68 (May 2007).

Among comics-related things, Jerry would want to be remembered most for his efforts identifying and indexing comic book writers and artists, which became his massive life's work, *Who's Who in American Comic Books*. While the *Who's Who* is unquestionably the centerpiece of his legacy, Jerry Bails will be remembered as far more than an inexhaustible indexer. He'll be remembered as an instigator with vision whose energies and ideas on behalf of comic books and comic book fans in the early 1960s justify giving him the sobriquet "the father of comic fandom."

Larry Ivie
(b. 1936)

Larry Ivie was one of the most active comics fans of the late 1950s. His creation of "The Comics Library" during that time was emblematic of the depth of his knowledge about the history of the comic book and strip medium, and provided a starting point for research into the history of comics. He wrote and published articles about comics in his fanzine *Concept* (1956–1959) and contributed to other EC and post–EC fanzines such as *Hoohah!*.

Larry Ivie was born in January 1936 in Salt Lake City, Utah. His father was a biology instructor at the University of Utah. Larry began reading comics from the beginning of World War II, and became a fan of the fiction of Edgar Rice Burroughs as a teenager. Unlike many others, he managed to save many of his Golden Age comic books through his high school years. His favorite artists were Reed Crandall, Hal Foster and Alex Raymond. An artist with considerable potential, Ivie read in an EC comic book of the Cartoonists and Illustrators School (C&I) located in New York City. He moved to Manhattan in the summer of 1955, finding an apartment at 230 East 26th Street. Notwithstanding the fact that he was a bit older than the central cohorts of EC fans except one (Larry Stark), Ivie didn't enter EC fandom as such until he met Archie Goodwin at C&I. Before long, Larry had drawn a cover for *Hoohah!* #5 (July 1956) for Goodwin's pal, Ron Parker.

Larry Ivie

Ivie himself was an EC fan, and had started a project in 1955 called *The EC Story*, a complete scrapbook of EC history including photos, story excerpts, the EC Fan-Addict bulletins, and other items. When he became active in EC fandom, he found that much of this material was already in the hands of the other EC followers, some having appeared in one form or another in the EC fanzines. However, Larry's collection of Golden Age comic books and comic strips from the 1930s and 1940s was a treasure trove of reference material on the history of comics before EC. (He had a complete run of "The Spirit" and nearly all of the comics by Carl Barks, just for starters.) Ivie recognized his collection's value and published the following statement in his fanzine *Concept* #3 (February 1957) which is sort of a manifesto for what he grandly called "The Comics Library":

The main source of reference for comic fans ... is the Comics Library. This collection is owned by this magazine, and includes contributions (including original artwork) from many of the top individuals in the comics field. We hope that this library will someday become the basis for not only permanent preservation of all comic work, but for hardbound reproduction of the "classics" in this field. We know this will be done *someday* ... for the children of yesterday, and of today, as they begin to run the world, will *demand* another look at their childhood fantasies, and will eventually come to look on them as what they are—a true form of twentieth century folklore. As Krazy Kat and Buster Brown were to one generation, so will Superman and Camilla be to the next—only *more* so. All ... will eventually land in the History books; until that day, however, we will print as much as we possibly can, for those interested, in *Concept.*

Larry Ivie utilized his library as the basis for articles on Superman and other comic book characters in *Concept,* though the fanzine's emphasis tilted more toward science fiction articles, reviews and fiction. More significantly, Ivie's Manhattan series of walk-up apartments—filled with stacks of comics, magazines, and other related material—were meccas for virtually everyone active in 1950s fandom who lived within geographic proximity. When Fred von Bernewitz moved to New York City, he became Ivie's roommate for a period of time. John Benson's early trips from Philadelphia in 1957 and years following to visit Larry and peruse his collection were typical of many others. In addition, Ivie's mailbox was frequently filled with requests for comic book and comic strip data. While not a hardcore data-indexer, he was a source of information to nearly all the earliest fans who were obsessed with gathering and coordinating such data. He was the closest thing to an authority on comics that was available in the 1950s.

Ivie's great disappointment was that DC Comics wasn't interested in his proposed revival of the Justice Society of America, to be called the Justice Legion of the World, which would be made up of the sons and daughters of the original JSA. His "new version" of the Atom appeared on the cover of *Xero #5.* One of Larry's passions was for the masquerade competitions that were a part of the annual World Science Fiction Convention. He played Batman to Les Gerber's Robin at the 1962 ChiCon, the same event when members of the Los Angeles Science Fiction Society made their appearance as the Justice Society of America.

Larry Ivie remained a ubiquitous denizen of New York fandom and publishing into the 1960s, working for *Castle of Frankenstein* magazine, attending the first 1964 comicon in the city, and appearing as an expert on old comics at later cons. He edited and published *Monsters and Heroes,* his own black-and-white nationally distributed magazine in the mid to late 1960s, which included coverage of the masquerades held at the New York comicons of that era. Ivie was involved in the creation of the T.H.U.N.D.E.R. Agents for Tower Comics.

In 1970 Larry moved to California to take care of his aging grandparents. Since then, he has worked on various personal and freelance projects, including a commissioned history of comic books, still in progress. In later years, he painted new covers and provided editorial material for a revival of *Castle of Frankenstein* magazine, and has contributed to *Alter Ego* magazine and other publications to the present day.

Howard Keltner
(1928–1998)

A founding member of the Academy of Comic-Book Arts and Sciences in 1962, Howard Keltner was a passionate indexer whose focus was on the super- and costumed-hero comic books of the Golden Age of comics. As editor/publisher of *Star-Studded Comics* (along with Buddy Saunders and Larry Herndon), Keltner created the popular amateur hero Doctor Weird. He contributed heavily to all of Jerry Bails' fanzines and his articles on the history of comic books were widely published, in *Alter-Ego*, *RBCC* and elsewhere.

Starting in 1953, John Howard Keltner of Gainesville, Texas, began indexing the comics in his own collection. When he discovered other comics fans who were doing the same thing, notably Jerry Bails and Raymond Miller in the early 1960s, Howard began pooling information with them, in an effort to create an index on the contents of every Golden Age comic book. This *Golden Age Comic Book Index* would become his life's work. In the process, he was credited with making significant contributions to virtually every other major index of the day. For example, Keltner received co-credit on Jerry Bails' *DC Index* in 1963. He was a major source of data for Bails' *Collector's Guide: The First Heroic Age* (1969), which provided a basis for much of the information that was used to create the *Overstreet Comic Book Price Guide* the following year.

Howard incorporated his data into various articles he penned for the fanzines of the day. Perhaps best known was his "MLJ Leads the Way" article in *Alter-Ego* #4 (1962), which recounted the careers of MLJ's nine leading costumed characters from the early 1940s, including the Wizard, the Shield, Steel Sterling and the Black Hood. He also wrote a number of pieces for G. B. Love's fanzines. In 1964, Keltner became a founding member of *Capa-alpha*, contributing pages to the first mailing along with John McGeehan, Paul Gambaccini, Al Kuhfeld and others.

Keltner also possessed art talent, using it to create covers, illustrations and comic strips. His style was characterized by an attention to detail, and an ability to create pleasing artwork in the ditto medium. He drew a number of covers for the early issues of *The Rocket's Blast*, *Capa-alpha*, and others. Keltner illustrated Raymond Miller's "Black Scorpion" strip in *Fighting Hero Comics* #4.

Howard Keltner

In addition to his contributions as a researcher, indexer and writer of informative articles, as well as being an able artist, Howard Keltner was a co-editor and publisher of one of the most celebrated fanzines of the 1960s, *Star-Studded Comics*. Keltner along with partners Larry Herndon and Buddy Saunders launched the venerable amateur comic strip zine in June 1963, and it ran for 18 impressive issues, through the summer of 1972.

Of all the amateur superheroes introduced in the pages of *Star-Studded*, one of the most popular—and the one who appeared in the most issues—was Keltner's Doctor Weird. In a 1990s interview, Howard recalled, "From the moment I first laid eyes on the cover of *Blue Ribbon Comics* #15, Mr. Justice was my favorite character. Doctor Weird was created very soon after that. For years I drew stories of him in pencil on typing paper, all crude, of course. Even though he was an out-and-out copy of the Mr. Justice concept, a supernatural hero engaged in combat with supernatural foes, I gave him a different origin and didn't copy any of the Mr. Justice stories."

The six-page origin strip in *SSC* #1 was written and drawn solely by Keltner. The art, in particular, was a stand-out in its day: extremely neat and meticulous, it bore an attention to detail that was rare among ditto strips. "Introducing Doctor Weird" tells the story of futuristic time traveler Dr. Rex Ward, who leaves his beloved wife, Erla, in 2013 to travel back to 1963. As he exits his time machine, Ward is killed by two burglars in the home where he has materialized. Yet his spirit is denied entrance to heaven. A disembodied voice proclaims, "You have died before you were born, and such cannot be. You must return to Earth, there to remain for the next fifty years, whereupon you will be allowed to cross the gulfs to your final resting place." In the interim, Rex Ward is given supernatural powers to combat evil. This the newly named Dr. Weird does, tossing the car containing the burglars who killed him off a cliff, grimly muttering, "It's better that such vermin do not exist!"

The twelve strips and prose stories featuring the "Golden Ghost" (as Dr. Weird was called) were written and drawn by some of the best in fandom. Besides Keltner himself, some of those creative fans were Al Kuhfeld, Phil Liebfred, Alan Weiss, Landon Chesney, Raymond Miller, George R. R. Martin, George Metzger, Mickey Schwaberow, Rudi Franke and Jim Starlin. Keltner also wrote scripts for Powerman and Astral Man, and drew three of the fanzine's covers.

In the summer of 1972, just shy of its tenth anniversary, *Star-Studded Comics* finally ceased publication. During its ten year run, *SSC* had published 58 comic strips. *Star-Studded* #18 (the final issue) featured an epic sword and sorcery adventure, "Jabberwacky" by Steve Fritz; Dr. Weird in "The Miracle" by Jim Starlin and Howard Keltner; "Double Jeopardy" by Dennis Fugitake; and "Un-Man" by Dave Cockrum. With that final issue, an era in fan publishing ended. "There were several factors," Keltner explained. "Many of our contributors had turned pro, and it was getting difficult to obtain good material. Larry and Buddy were nine years older and were looking around for other things to do. The fellow who was acting as our publisher [Joe Bob Williams] was losing some of his initial enthusiasm. We realized the fire was going out, so we shook hands and went our separate ways." The members of the trio parted on friendly terms, and all moved on to new fan projects.

In later years, Howard Keltner collaborated with Grass Green on numerous comic strips, with Green penciling and Keltner inking. "Grass taught me how to ink," Keltner remembered. "I really hadn't known what I was doing until we collaborated on Human Cat and Wildman strips in the 1970s. I learned how to use a brush, and that made all the difference." When arthritis limited his hand control, Keltner moved into oil painting, and became extremely adept at it.

In 1997, though ailing from cancer, Howard and his wife, Reva, attended the Fandom Reunion in Chicago, where he met his long-time friends and collaborators Jerry Bails and Grass Green for the first and only time. He succumbed to kidney and liver failure on July 29, 1998. Howard's massive *Golden Age Comic Books Index*, his life's work as an indexer, was published posthumously by his longtime friend Bob Klein. The rights to the Doctor Weird character were purchased from Howard by Gary Carlson and Edward DeGeorge, and the character subsequently appeared in issues of *Big Bang Comics*, and his own self-titled comic book.

John McGeehan
(1940–1980)

John McGeehan was known for creating "The House of Info" (in concert with his younger brother Tom), an archive that collected all manner of data about comic books, comic fanzines, pulp magazines, old radio shows, comics-related newspaper articles, comic strips, fantastic films, Edgar Rice Burroughs, and more.

John McGeehan was born in San Diego on February 25, 1940. By the time comic fandom was growing in the early 1960s, John McGeehan was an adult who worked in his family's shoe repair business in Santa Ana, California. As a teenager, the dark-haired, bespectacled McGeehan became an ERB enthusiast and collector, as did his younger brother Tom (who looked enough like him to be a twin). John was already aware of fanzines in the late 1950s, such as *The Fantasy Collector* (established in 1958), *ERB-dom* (1960) and Jiro Tomyama's little-known comics-related fanzine *Plague* (1960). Therefore, he heard about Jerry Bails' *Alter-Ego* early, and was a reader from the first issue in 1961.

Like many indexers, John McGeehan's drive to collect and collate data about his interests seemed inexhaustible, and was the defining characteristic of his involvement in comic fandom. Because John and Tom had income from the shoe shop, they were able to indulge their hobby-ism, doing so with tremendous energy and enthusiasm. They had a penchant for creating checklists for every conceivable aspect of their interests, which (beyond their basic ERB enthusiasm) encompassed Walt Disney comics, syndicated comic strips, Marvel comics, television series, Flash Gordon, Buck Rogers, old-time radio shows and so on. They named their archives "The House of Info," which became the name of their apa-zine for comics apa *Capa-alpha* (*K-a*). The McGeehan brothers were founding members of the amateur press alliance. John's first piece to appear in the apa's first mailing was titled "Info Bits, Comments, and Just Plain Gab."

Others endeavored to gather data in the same areas as the McGeehans, but in one area the McGeehans stood head and shoulders above the rest, and that was their documentation of fanzine publishing. Every fanzine editor could count on an order from John McGeehan, who in the early days purchased four copies of all fanzines related to comics and/or Edgar Rice Burroughs. In the late 1960s, with the explosion in the number of fanzines being published, the House of Info reduced their orders from four to two copies per zine. They published lists of their latest fanzine acquisitions (often in *The Comic Reader*), with the mailing address and price, a brief description, and a rating of "1" to "5," with "5" being the best.

It is largely because of "The House of Info" that researchers know how many

John McGeehan

fanzines were published in this era. By October 16, 1966, John and Tom knew of 192 different comic-slanted fanzines with a total of 724 issues, and owned 695 of them. Breaking down the numbers, 90 of these zines were active at the time, 90 were defunct, and 12 were one-shots long out of print. In October 20, 1972, John stated that he had documented the publication of 680 different comics-slanted amateur publications since March 1961. Of these 680 publications, there were a total of over 2,900 different issues. However, in mid-summer 1972, "The House of Info" had issued a 20-page "Fanzine for Sale" list, which in itself is a collectible item. It seems the McGeehans decided to sell their extra fanzine copies, not only to raise money but to reduce the amount of room it took to store them.

Although full-fledged comicons didn't get started in California until 1970, there were significant fan-meets in earlier years. The earliest recorded one occurred on May 28, 1964, at the home of Russ Manning. John McGeehan was there, along with Richard Kyle, Rick Durell, Glen Johnson and Bill Spicer. A photo of the six fans became well-known, since it appeared in *Fantasy Illustrated, Star-Studded Comics* and elsewhere.

In 1972, John's father, Joseph, retired from his shoe repair shop, leaving John and Tom to take full charge. The brothers continued with their contributions to *Capa-alpha*. John was an avid reader of Marvel Comics until his death in 1980. For reasons unknown to his family and friends, John McGeehan took his own life on November 28, 1980.

Tom McGeehan

(b. 1943)

Tom McGeehan, along with his brother John, created "The House of Info" in the early 1960s, an umbrella title for their archive of lists, files, index cards and other records of data amassed by the indefatigable duo who were inveterate indexers of the first order.

Thomas McGeehan was born in San Diego on February 2, 1943. As the younger sibling, Tom was perhaps less known to fandom than John. It seemed that John took the lead, typical of an older brother, but "The House of Info" was a roughly equal accomplishment by them both. Certainly their interests ran parallel, with both being ERB fans and thoroughly enthusiastic about the field of a comic art and fantasy literature.

Tom's major publishing efforts appeared in comics apa *Capa-alpha* (*K-a*) of which he was a founding member in 1964 along with his brother John, Dan Alderson, Jerry Bails, David Castronuovo, Paul Gambaccini, Margaret Gemignani, Glenn Goggin, Pete Jack-

Tom McGeehan

son, Bob Jennings, Dave Kaler, Howard Keltner, John Koch, Al Kuhfeld, Richard Kyle, Dick Memorich, Marc Nadel, Pete Phillips, Bill Placzek and Duncan Robertson. He contributed a seemingly endless stream of data sheets, check lists and opinion columns. There were reprints of obscure articles about comics that appeared in newspapers, commentary on newsstand distribution in Santa Ana, checklists on the publishing history of Zorro, the line-up of comic strips appearing in specific newspapers, lists of fanzines with occasional reviews, et al. Tom was especially fascinated with tape recorders, and the process of tape recording old-time radio shows and other programs from the radio with the best possible sound quality. The McGeehans' contributions to *K-a* were always printed in black mimeograph ink on white paper. The white paper became a sort of trademark, in a publication where most of the other members used colored paper and often multi-colored ditto printing. It was "black-and-white all the way" for "The House of Info."

After John's passing in 1980, Tom continued his membership in *Capa-alpha*, and has maintained it to the present day. While he no longer reads comics, he is a cinema enthusiast, and has written hundreds—perhaps thousands—of movie reviews for the edification of the members of the amateur press alliance. He is the only founding member who remains active, some 45 years after the alliance's inception.

Raymond Miller

(b. 1931)

Raymond Miller was perhaps early fandom's most widely published authority on the Golden Age of comics, having created scores of features and articles that appeared in *RBCC*

Raymond Miller

throughout the 1960s, as well as numerous other popular fanzines. Though he was a fan of EC and comics of the Silver Age, he was primarily interested in writing about comic books published from 1938 to 1946.

Miller was born in 1931, which made him of prime comic book buying age during the 1940s. He grew up in Vandergrift, Pennsylvania, a small town not far from Pittsburgh. He bought his first copy of *Captain Marvel Adventures* in early 1943 (#18, the one featuring the introduction of Mary Marvel), and soon was purchasing as many comic books as he could afford. "In those days, you didn't need a comic book store," he recalled in an interview that appeared in *Comics Buyer's Guide* #1167 in 1996. "You could buy comics at newsstands, drug stores, grocery stores, five-and-dime stores. I must have had access to at least ten different places to buy comics in a town of nine thousand people. Now that I think back on it, I often wonder where I got the money to buy what I did." In the post-war period, he bought every Fiction House title, along with *Batman* and *Superman*, *Phantom Lady*, *Blue Beetle* and many others. He collected all the Fawcett westerns and, in the early 1950s, all the EC comics. He kept his comic books in neat stacks on shelves, and never loaned them to friends. Today he still has over 30 books that he originally bought between 1943 and 1945.

For many years, Miller knew of no one else who collected comic books, nor of any source for back issues. This changed in 1959 when he managed to link up with Dean Newman of Bard, California. In September of 1960, Newman told Miller about a dealer in old comics named Bill Thailing who lived in Cleveland, Ohio. By the time Raymond caught up to the Ohioan, the dealer's selling prices generally ran from 25 cents to $1.50 for a Golden Age comic. The prime comics before 1943 commanded a stiffer price, $1.75, $2 or higher. He was selling *Batman* #1 for $3. Raymond bought as many of these rarities as he could afford, though he was never flush with funds.

Miller and Thailing constantly traded data about Golden Age comics. Raymond began compiling his own data with information he obtained not only from Bill Thailing, but from an emerging roster of correspondents who became known to him through *Alter-Ego*, *The Comicollector* and *The Rocket's Blast* beginning in 1961 when the fanzines came long. These included veteran collectors M. C. Goodwin, Jerry Bails, Howard Keltner, Dick Hoffman, Kenny Heineman, Rick Durell, Hames Ware, Richard O'Brien, Don Rosa and Don Foote, among many others. Miller discovered that he not only liked compiling comic book data for himself and his correspondents, but enjoyed sharing that data with others in the form of articles written for the amateur publications. Perhaps the first to feature Raymond's work was G. B. Love's *The Rocket's Blast*, beginning a writer-publisher relationship that put the collector's efforts before a readership that constituted just about every active fan in those days.

Raymond Miller contributed countless articles and pin-ups on the Golden Age heroes to *RBCC* as well as Gordon Love's other fanzines. Miller's artwork was essentially traced from the vintage comics themselves, but this was necessary because the earliest fanzines couldn't reproduce images from the actual comics. Miller authored the first *Rocket's Blast Special* on Timely Comics, issues of *The Illustrated Comic Collector's Handbook*, and *The Golden Age*. But he didn't restrict his fan efforts to those fanzines from G. B. Love. Miller tirelessly created features for many other fan publications, including *The Comicollector* (before it merged with *The Rocket's Blast*), Bob Jennings' *Comic World* and many others. Eventually, he settled down and concentrated on regular "Information Center" columns for *RBCC*, which the magazine continued running until Raymond gave them up in the mid–1970s. (He only stopped when he had to take fulltime care of his ailing mother.)

Raymond Miller became one of the main disseminators of information on comic books published before 1950, a contribution of inestimable importance to fandom. One of his most significant pieces was the first long history of Will Eisner's career, which appeared in *Sense of Wonder* #11 (1972). He was a major source of data for Jerry Bails, Howard Keltner and Michelle Nolan when they were planning various seminal indexes that saw print in the 1960s and early 1970s.

Over the ensuing years, Raymond Miller has stopped buying new comic books, but still treasures and enjoys his collection of Golden Age goodies. "I like to display my comics, for my pleasure, once a year," he said. "I have a big piece of plywood that holds eighteen comic books and, right after New Year's, I set up my board and display eighteen comics a day." Raymond considers these comics his "old friends," which remind him of the 1940s, the era when so many of the characters who remain popular today were introduced.

Michelle Nolan

(b. 1948)

Michelle Nolan researched and published three key indexes: the *Nedor Comics Index* (1968), *Timely Comics Index* (1969) and *MLJ Comics Index* (1969). She was a partner in the pioneering Seven Sons Comic Shop in San Jose, which opened in 1968.

Michelle Nolan was born February 1, 1948, in San Jose, California, and spent her childhood in both the Bay Area and Northwest Washington State. Her father, Phil Nolan, was a Certified Life Underwriter and a noted horseracing player at Bay Meadows in San Mateo, California. Michelle's mother, Jean, was a medical technologist and professional artist. Michelle credits her parents with inspiring her love of comics and writing. Unlike many parents of the 1950s era, Phil and Jean Nolan didn't discourage the reading of comic books, as long as prose books were also included.

Michelle's first comic book purchase—at the urging of Phil Nolan following a day at the beach in 1956—was *Mystery in Space* #32 (June–July 1956). Thus was a life-long love of comics collecting begun. At the age of eight, Nolan began collecting old comics as well as new issues, regularly scouring three second-hand bookstores and finding such gems as *Superboy* #1, *All Star Comics* #57 and *Green Lantern* #35, each for a nickel in the 1950s. Nolan began making notes about everything encountered in old comics, showing an early bent for research which led to her becoming a comics historian.

Michelle discovered organized fandom in 1964 via *RBCC*. Nolan's first convention was a one-day affair hosted by Rudi Franke in Oakland, California, in January 1966. At age 19 in 1967, she made the first of more than three dozen trips around the United States, meeting as many comic collectors and dealers as possible and becoming friends with New York convention impresarios Phil and Carole Seuling. Nolan assisted the Seulings with the major New York conventions from 1969 through 1972.

Nolan's research led to three ground-breaking issue-by-issue indexes of Golden Age comic book companies, inspired by Fred von Bernewitz's earlier EC Index. Nolan released the *Nedor Comics Index* (with a cover drawn by Rudi Franke) in 1968, and the *Timely Comics Index* and *MLJ Comics Index* in 1969. (The Timely and MLJ indexes have been reprinted by *Alter Ego* magazine.) Michelle also compiled a 25-page *Golden Age Super Hero Index* in May 1968, although the genuinely ground-breaking general superhero index was released in 1969 by Jerry Bails and Howard Keltner. Nolan distributed more than 500 copies of each index, paying for the comics collecting hobby and travels with the profits. They are still being sold at comics shows and on eBay at many multiples of the original one-dollar price.

Michelle Nolan was one of seven partners in 1968 with the comic book store Seven Sons Comics Shop, which opened at 40 E. San Fernando Street in downtown San Jose, California, on March 3, 1968. (It's now a parking lot.) Nolan signed the business license for the store. The other partners were Bud Plant, John Barrett, Jim Buser, Tom Tallmon, Al Castle and Frank Scadina. The historic retail business opened during a period when back-issue comics were sold only in used book and magazine stores, such as the Cherokee Book Shop in Los Angeles, and other stores with a variety of used merchandise. Since 1968 was several years before Phil Seuling created the Direct Market in the mid–1970s, new comics could not yet be obtained for sale in the store. However, Seven Sons was the first store that sold only comic books, albeit of the used variety.

Nolan attended the first San Diego Comic-Con show in March 1970, and contributed much data for the original *Overstreet Comic Book Price Guide* in 1970. A 1970 graduate of San Jose State University with a major in U.S. history, Michelle has published more than

10,000 newspaper and magazines stories in more than four decades as a journalist, covering human-interest features, pop culture and sports. She has written more than five hundred comics-related features for magazines such as *Comic Book Marketplace, Comics Buyer's Guide, Alter Ego, Comic Book Artist* and Comics Guaranty Corporation's newsletter. She wrote 100 consecutive "Nolan's Notebook" columns for *Comic Book Marketplace* from 1993 to 2005. She has contributed to dozens of books and wrote the ground-breaking book *Love on the Racks: A History of American Romance Comics*, published by McFarland in 2008.

Nolan's son, Ray Nolan, teaches history at Fort Hays State University in Hays, Kansas. Ray played baseball as an infielder for the University of Redlands in Southern California until graduation in 1998 with a degree in U.S. History, and formerly coached baseball at Colby (Kansas) Community College.

Bob Overstreet
(b. 1938)

Bob Overstreet is best known as the editor and publisher of the *Overstreet Comic Book Price Guide*, the dominant guidebook to comic book values that was been updated annually since 1970. Others had published price guides before him, but he had the vision to realize how important such a publication would be for the hobby, and the tenacity to produce some-thing vastly superior to what had come before. Overstreet was also an artistic collaborator with Landon Chesney, inking Chesney's pencils on amateur comic strip features that appeared in *Fantasy Illustrated* and *Voice of Comicdom*.

Robert M. Overstreet encountered a serious comic book enthusiast when his family moved to Cleveland Tennessee, and he began attending eighth grade at Arnold School. It was there he met Landon Chesney, a gifted artist and a rabid fan of EC comics. Upon viewing the treasures in Landon's neat stack of ECs, Bob became equally enthusiastic about the comic book publishing company's titles (*Tales from the Crypt, Vault of Horror, Shock Suspenstories, Mad*, et al.) This was in the early 1950s when EC was at their creative zenith, two-and-a-half years before the advent of the Comics Code Authority, which signaled the end of the "New Trend." Overstreet's first EC bought off the stands was *Crime Suspenstories* #11 (June–July 1952).

Bob Overstreet

After the death throes of EC comics, and Chesney's induction into the U. S. Air Force, Overstreet assumed his interest in comics was over. However, with Landon's return, and the rise of comic fandom on a national scale in the early 1960s, the two friends decided to finally craft their own version of the ultimate EC comic strip. To create "A Study in Horror," which appeared in Bill Spicer's *Fantasy Illustrated* #3 (1964), Landon and Bob called on their teenage fascination with photography. Many of the panels, portrayed with chiaroscuro lighting effects, were based on photos they took of each other. Overstreet proved to be an able inker, and the finished strip was highly effective. (It was reprinted in color in the *Overstreet Comic Book Price Guide* #30 in 2000.) Bob also inked Chesney's pencils on an episode of "The Cloak" that saw print in *Voice of Comicdom* in 1965.

Upon joining the fan movement, Overstreet set about completing his EC comic book collection, then branched out into seeking other vintage comic books. Soon he realized that purchasing decisions about early comics were difficult to make without a source of information about their contents, as well as some idea of their rarity. He collected the indexes produced by Jerry Bails, Howard Keltner, Michelle Nolan and others. As for the issue of rarity and prices, an early attempt at a price guide in 1965—*The Argosy Price Guide*—proved virtually worthless. However, it suggested the idea of a such a guide, reminding Bob of the coin price guides he had seen as a teenager. In a 1978 interview in *Collector's Dream Magazine*, Bob recalled, "Back in the 1950s I used to be in coins, and I remember the impact *Yeoman's Red Book* had on me and how it helped me to learn the market. Using that as a model, I typed up some rough ideas of what I thought a price guide for comics should look like. I went to Bob Jennings, who was publishing *Comic World* in Nashville, and asked him if he thought it would be a good idea. Bob didn't think it was a good idea; he didn't think it would work." Unfazed, Overstreet enlisted the aid of Jerry Bails, who had conceived such a project early on.

At the round table discussion which ended the 1964 Alley Tally Party at his home, Bails had discussed the need for an all-encompassing index, and also introduced the idea that such an index could be the basis for a comic book price guide. Jerry's heart was not in the perplexing task of assigning comic book values, and even if he could publish such a price guide, who would take on the endeavor of publishing updated and corrected editions as they became necessary? Then, out of the blue, he heard from Bob Overstreet. Bails wrote, "Without knowing anything about my work on a price guide, Bob contacted me. I don't recall if he asked for my help or was just announcing his plans, but I was happy to turn over what I'd done, because I had other projects that interested me more. He was delighted to accept my help, but he took the ball and ran with it. I think he did a remarkably fine job."

Overstreet used price lists from nearly all the dealers in fandom at the time as a starting point, as well as fan-produced indexes. Jerry Bails had just published his *Collector's Guide to the First Heroic Age*, which listed all the Golden Age heroes and which comics they appeared in, and which proved to be a tremendous source of information. "Probably the *Price Guide* wouldn't have been possible if Bails hadn't published that source book," Bob acknowledged, "but Bails only listed the 1940s hero comics. The 1930s stuff, the romance comics, everything from the late 1940s up, the funny animals, I had to pick up myself. I pulled all this information out of all the dealer lists that I had. That's what went into the initial *Price Guide*." Jerry Bails, whose name offered the ultimate in fan prestige, would be Associate Editor of the first edition. The editorial material from the *Guidebook to Comics Fandom* (written by Bails) under the umbrella title "America's Four-Color Pastime" was incorporated into the new guide, with the blessing of Bails and Spicer. One significant advance was the addition of the grading category "Fine" (FN) between Mint and Very Good. (Near Mint was added to the 1972 price guide grading definitions.)

The first edition of the *Overstreet Comic Book Price Guide* (November 1970) had 218 pages of listings, and a total of 244 printed pages, from cover to cover. It was digest-sized, with wrap-around saddle-stitched binding (quite awkward, for the number of pages) and sold for five dollars per copy. (The pre-publication price was three dollars and fifty cents.) Overstreet's introduction read, in part, "The comic book market from the early to the late 1960s was very unstable. Prices were increasing so rapidly in all categories during that period, that the debut of a Price Guide was impractical. However, the market seems to have stabilized over the past two years, making it now possible to have a realistic, dependable price guide. In the past there has been a lot of confusion as to pricing books by condition. It is my sincere hope that the *Price Guide* will help in this regard. Everyone connected with the publication of this book advocates the collecting of comic books for fun and pleasure, as well as nostalgia, art, and cultural values. Second to this is investment, which, if wisely placed in the best quality books ... will yield dividends over the long term."

The first edition of the *Comic Book Price Guide* was not complete or without errors (quite the opposite), but as an index, it was a tremendous achievement. The guide sold well, and it was soon apparent that the demand would be sufficient for periodically updated editions. The first edition was reprinted in 1971 with only the color of the cover (blue) changed. In the coming years, the number of pages dedicated to listings increased continually. Overstreet turned out to be a remarkably reliable publisher, and one who was committed to the essential task of maintaining and improving the data in the guide.

Bob Overstreet had no control over the way the information in the guide would be used. In the hands of the unsophisticated (or unscrupulous) reader, the Mint price was often quoted—despite the actual condition of the comic book in question. The guide's existence meant that even "the little kid down the block" would have a way of assigning values to the stack of comics that his parents had saved through the years. Opportunities for windfall deals began to evaporate. The guide made it easier for anyone to become a dealer (instead of just active researchers who loved and appreciated the books). Both collectors and dealers seemed to have a love-hate relationship with the guide. Ironically, though Overstreet had waited until the market seemed to have stabilized, the publication of the guide probably had the effect of pushing prices upward.

What were some of the prices listed in that first edition of the guide? *Action* #1 was $250 in Fine condition ... *Amazing Fantasy* #15 came in at $16 in Mint ... *X-Men* #1 was $6 in Mint ... and so on. Most fans welcomed the guide, but there were many who felt it led to inflated prices. The prices *were* higher than they had been, but hardly unrealistic at the time. If sales are the measure of the need and interest in the price guide, then it's clear Bob Overstreet's book filled a necessary gap. About 1,800 copies of the first edition were sold. According to Overstreet, the second edition garnered sales approaching four thousand copies. By the sixth edition in the late 1970s, the print run had topped 40,000 copies.

The *Overstreet Comic Book Price Guide* continues to be published (in various formats) to the present day, with the 39th edition in 2009 (from Gemstone Publishing) containing 1,120 pages. Over the years, its purview has expanded to cover the entire history of the American comics publication as far back as the Victorian Age and Platinum Age. Each edition also covers promotional comics and Big Little Books, and continually updates new publications and market reports that cover the prior year of market activity.

Fred von Bernewitz
(b. 1938)

Fred Von Bernewitz will first and foremost be remembered by comic book fans and historians as the writer, editor and publisher of *The Complete EC Checklist*, with the first of several editions appearing in 1955. It is the first-known fanzine devoted solely to a checklist of the entire output of one comic book publisher. He also contributed articles and cartoons to several of the EC fanzines of the 1950s.

Fred von Bernewitz grew up in Silver Springs, Maryland, a suburb of Washington D.C. His father was a technical photographer. A science fiction fan from an early age, Fred most likely first came into contact with SF fan Ted White through a letter column in a newsstand SF magazine. Though they lived about 13 miles apart (Ted in Falls Church, Virginia), they probably first met in person at a meeting of the Washington Science Fiction Association (WSFA) in 1953, held roughly equidistant between their homes.

Von Bernewitz was also a comic book fan, especially of Captain Marvel and other Fawcett titles, the work of Walt Kelly and (though he didn't know his name then) Carl Barks. White was heavily into DC comics, as evidenced by his *The Facts Behind Superman* fanzine. Soon they shared their mutual enthusiasm for EC, especially *Weird Science*, *Weird Fantasy* and *Mad*, but also the others. When Fred began receiving the early EC fanzines, such as Mike May's *EC Fan Journal*, he particularly noticed fans' efforts to create checklists of certain EC titles. Realizing that a complete EC checklist would be even more useful, he decided to take on the task himself.

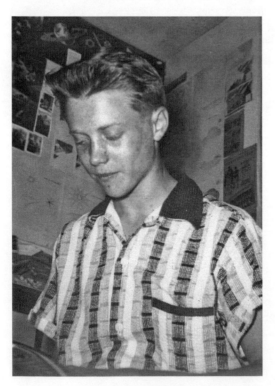

Fred von Bernewitz

Since Fred owned only a percentage of the EC output, he couldn't have accomplished the job without the help of other EC Fan-Addicts. He added information from published checklists in the fanzines to what he could glean from his own collection, then solicited information from perhaps a dozen others, including Larry Stark, Ted White and Mike May. He also received information from EC artist George Evans. *The Complete EC Checklist*, with cover art by Fred himself, appeared in mid–1955 in a print run of 50 copies. It was printed by Ted White's mimeo service, and sold for 25 cents. The $5\frac{1}{2} \times 8\frac{1}{2}$ booklet, consisting of 56 pages, required just one four-cent stamp to be sent via third class mail. It contained listings for all the New Trend titles in their entirety except for *Panic*. The 50 copies of the EC checklist were soon gone, after gratis copies to EC and contributors were distributed, and Bill Gaines' cash order for an additional 16 copies was fulfilled. After receiving a raft of orders from a plug in *Incredible Science Fiction* #33 (which appeared in the fall of 1955), an additional 200 copies were printed in January 1956, differing from the original only insofar as certain errors were corrected. In March 1958, its 24-four-page *Supplement* was produced, with the data on the New Direction and Picto-Fiction titles. In all, 250 copies of the *Supplement* were printed, and were sold for ten cents each.

Fred's fannish activity took on a new dimension when he and Ted White went north in the days after Christmas in 1955 to visit Larry Stark in New Jersey. The three of them then trekked into Manhattan, lugging a 25-pound tape recorder, to interview Bill Gaines and gather additional data on the Pre-Trend titles for an ultimate version of the checklist. The three prominent EC fans were accorded VIP treatment in the EC offices, and later wrote a serialized account of this visit called "We're Off to EC" that appeared in *Hoohah!* #4 and #5 (1956). Bill Gaines was most effusive in his appreciation for the EC checklist, and offered another small sum to help Fred defray costs of the project, or perhaps toward his fans' stated plan to publish a new version that would include the New Trend titles. In 1963, after many delays, and in order to make it as perfect as possible, Fred finally published *The Full Edition of the Complete EC Checklist*. This incredible amount of effort was put into a publication with an estimated print run of 200 copies. Such was the fannish spirit of the day, exemplified by pioneering indexer von Bernewitz.

Out of his appreciation for the checklist, Bill Gaines subsequently hired Fred von Bernewitz to produce periodic indexes to *Mad* magazine on an ongoing basis. In *Squa Tront* #8, John Benson described them: "The first issue covered *Mad* 1 through 64 and appeared in September 1961 (with a second printing on cheaper paper in February 1962). Issues 65– 88 were covered in #2, dated July 1964, which also had summary data for the entire run. The third issue, in July 1971, indexed issues 89–136; it was so bulky that it came in two parts. All features were cross-referenced by artist, writer and titles, and reprints were referenced by original source. Sergio Aragonés did an original cover for the third issue. All issues of *The Mad Checklist* were 8½ × 11 inches and mimeographed, with probable print runs of about 250 copies."

In 1970 and 1974, Fred allowed Joe Vucenic to publish new editions of *The Complete EC Checklist*, further disseminating his research for the benefit of the large number of EC fans who desired such information at this time. The checklist reached its ultimate incarnation in 2000, when Grant Geissman and Fred von Bernewitz teamed up to produce the slick hardcover and softcover editions of *Tales of Terror! The EC Companion*, co-published by Gemstone Publishing and Fantagraphics Books. The checklist data was supplemented with full-color reproductions of the comic book covers, and a great many additional features, including a transcript of the meeting/interview in the EC offices with Bill Gaines, Fred von Bernewitz, Larry Stark and Ted White.

As an adult, Fred moved to New York City and became a professional film editor (collaborating with Robert Downey and others), and worked as a movie theater manager. Several of the films he worked on received awards.

SECTION II: DEALERS

The kind of fans who had the interest and energy to found a fandom for those who appreciated comic art weren't just casual readers of comic books or newspaper strips. Casual readers purchased comics off the newsstands to read once or twice, and then passed them on to a friend, or—horror of horrors—threw them away. Some fans enjoyed reading the comic strips in their daily or Sunday newspaper, but never thought of clipping or saving them.

The fans profiled in this book are the ones who were also collectors. Some, perhaps, collected only to the extent that they saved their favorite comics as they bought them off the stands, or read them in the newspaper. Most were also seeking to add back issues or older strips to their collections. One way was to obtain them from friends and acquaintances that had stacks of older issues, the proverbial "kid that lived down the block." Another was to find someone who had back issues for sale.

For the purposes of this book, the term "dealer" is used for anyone selling back issues of comic books and/or strips for more than he paid for them. In other words, selling them for a profit.

In the 1950s and early 1960s, before comics received any respect, or were thought to have much resale value, the dealers were few. Other than a couple of pioneering dealers who are profiled here, and a few dealers in SF and Edgar Rice Burroughs collectibles who carried some comics on the side, the main hope for finding those desired items was the used bookstore.

Every large city in America had at least several, or perhaps a dozen or more, stores that sold used books and magazines. Often, in the course of buying collections for resale, they would be offered other ephemera such as movie press kits, pulp magazines and comic books. Most, probably the majority, didn't bother with comic books because they took up space that could be better used to display higher-ticket items. Generally, it was felt that a used comic book that sold originally for ten cents would sell for less, not more, usually two-for-a-nickel. This wasn't attractive to a store owner unless he had a lot of space. Then, there was also the reluctance of some stores to carry comic books, which could only attract unruly boys who didn't have much money to spend.

Nevertheless, there were some who did carry comic books, in various quantities. Perhaps one or two stores in each city had a substantial number of them, usually stacked on tables in random order. In a few cities, there were stores that went further, carrying lots of comic books, as well as related items like Big Little Books, Sunday newspaper sections, and pulp magazines. Shops like the AbleMan Book Shop in Hamtramck, Michigan (see entry for convention organizer Shel Dorf) had a whole second floor devoted to such material. Often, these stores got more into comics because the owner himself was a fan.

Used bookstores were nothing like the comic book specialty stores that came later. They tended to be dark and dusty places, and were often somewhat haphazardly organized. Sometimes there were stacks of unfiled books or magazines one had to step around, and one sometimes had to rummage through boxes of magazines and comics that were under the main display tables. Of course, that was part of the fun. One never knew what treasures awaited in this or that disparate box or shelf.

As the 1960s arrived, and with the advent of fanzines such as *Comic Art, Alter-Ego* and *The Comicollector*, mail order dealers sprang up around the country. As the fanzines proliferated, they now had the perfect place to advertise their wares, and reach a readership that was hungry—nay, desperate—for them. Some of them became prominent, by dint of the amount of their stock, and the frequency and size of their ads and/or mailing lists. Though a number of these best-known dealers are profiled here, there were dozens more very successful and well known back-issue dealers of comic books. Most of them entered the marketplace in the mid to late 1960s, or the 1970s. By then, *RBCC* had reached a circulation of 800 or more subscribers. At that point, fandom had already been founded.

Burt Blum
(b. circa 1945)

Comic book collectors who experienced the enchantment of Burt Blum's loft on the second floor of Hollywood's Cherokee Book Store in the 1960s were spoiled for life. Such fortunate collectors are sadly aware there's nothing left in the world like the four-color paradise over which Blum presided for more than a decade at 6607 Hollywood Boulevard.

In the era before the Bob Overstreet *Comic Book Price Guide* first appeared in 1970 and changed comic collecting forever, Burt Blum was one of the closest things to a *de facto* price guide available. Long before the Internet and eBay, even well before *The Buyer's Guide for Comic Fandom* began to become a long-running comic book advertising marketplace in 1971, Blum was a wise 20-something arbiter of values, even though he himself was neither comic collector nor historian. Fate, however, placed him in charge of what was then the world's largest assortment of truly collectible old comics available for public perusal.

Jack Blum founded Cherokee Books in 1949. The huge store, a classic second-hand book emporium with hundreds of thousands of paper goods, was in the perfect place at the perfect time to amass untold thousands of comic books for resale, beginning in the early 1960s, less than three decades after the first modern American comics were published. About the time the *Batman* television show debuted in 1966 and provided a huge jump-start for pop culture collectibles, along with the interest sparked by the Silver Age of Comics and the unique Marvel Comics icons-to-be, the millions of residents in Los Angeles County provided an ideal base of both buyers and sellers for Burt Blum's comic book loft treasures. Eventually, Cherokee would stake a claim as the first store to sell early comic books in nice condition as collectibles, not just five-cent items. The Blums may well have been correct about their claim, although used bookstores had been selling second-hand comics and pulps for a nickel apiece for many years. By 1966, Burt could boast an inventory of 50,000 comics covering the entire first three decades of comic book publishing history.

Cherokee was located in an old Spanish architecture building that looked something like a Moorish temple, with a huge two-story–tall front room. It was across the street from the famous Frederick's of Hollywood. One stepped from the bright sunshine into a darkened temple of old books. To see Blum, collectors would seek permission of his father, Jack, the store owner who was stationed downstairs and would always let customers know if Burt was "in" or "out." If the news was good, collectors could either look for cheap comics in the dozens of boxes outside Burt's "inner sanctum," or enter the hallowed place itself and find out if Burt's prices on unmarked merchandise matched the collector's idea of what the books were worth.

Malcolm Willits, who teamed with Leonard Brown to open the Collectors Book Store in the same Hollywood Boulevard neighborhood in 1965, expressed this viewpoint to Steve Duin, co-author of *Comics Between the Panels* (1996): "[Burt's] father put him in charge of the comics to keep him out of trouble. Burt was a good guy, but he didn't like comic books and he didn't like comic book collectors. He liked to sit up there and vegetate. He was stone lazy; he'd sit up there like a bump on a log. People were stealing from him right and left. We'd tell kids to go down there and tell them what to swipe."

Many collectors who grew up in California have Burt Blum stories. Comics fan and fanzine publisher Rob Gluckson recalled that treasures could be found even among the cheap comics at Cherokee. "Since Burt didn't really read comics, he didn't recognize most artists. You could find Williamson, Wood and Ditko stories that would make an otherwise dog title worth a couple of dollars. We pored through those boxes for buried gold. I once found a mint comic with Frank Frazetta's first work for comics in that outer room. Burt would look at my pile of a hundred or so comics gleaned from the outer room, flip through it, notice perhaps a few good titles, EC-style art ... smile knowingly, and charge me between five and 20 cents a book. He couldn't be bothered with pricing them individually."

Comics historian Mark Evanier blogged on December 8, 2008, about first seeing Burt's comic loft when Evanier was 13 in 1965, and how noted Southern California collectors such as Rick Durell first encouraged Cherokee to find collectible comics for resale at collectors' prices. "I never bought many comics at Cherokee," Evanier said. "I couldn't stand the little game of humbling yourself before Burt to ask the price of a comic you wanted. The prices were often steep and you felt like a pauper if you declined the deal. Some fans I knew had developed a cozy enough relationship with Blum that he was willing to haggle a little ... but he could also turn on you, decide you weren't a serious customer and order you off the premises. But it was an interesting place to be, even if the cramped quarters weren't conducive to hanging around. You might meet someone famous (I met Jules Feiffer there) and you might make friends with a fellow lover of fine comics. You might also see the second act of the following drama: A kid would come in and spend, say, 15 dollars for a copy of *Batman* #4 from 1941. A few days later, the kid would be back with the comic ... dragged there crying and screaming by a father who'd accuse Burt of cheating his son and demand a refund. I wasn't there that often but I saw it happen at least twice, and a friend of mine who worked there estimated it as a twice-monthly occurrence." The creation of the *Overstreet Comic Book Price Guide* helped eliminate such complaints, but it also exponentially increased the desire of collectors to find either investments or bargains. It wasn't too long before the Cherokee Book Store's "good stuff" couldn't easily be replaced the way it had been in the early and mid–1960s.

Comic book collector and historian Michelle Nolan recently expressed a different view of Burt Blum and Cherokee Books. "People had told me Burt could be intimidating, because he was always wary of shoplifters for good reason and he didn't want people just hanging out, but he always treated me very well," Nolan remembered. She began making the 800-mile round trip from the Bay Area to buy comics from Blum in the mid–1960s in the company of younger collectors such as Bud Plant. "Some people didn't like the fact you had to ask Burt for prices on the books in his 'inner sanctum' but that never bothered me. Other people didn't like that the organization was somewhat lacking and it wasn't always easy to get to the titles or types of comics you really wanted. But if Burt priced a comic too high for my budget, I would just move on to others, because there were always an unlimited number of comics to look at and to buy. Perhaps my memories of being Burt's customer are good because he could see I not only had a little money to spend, but I was also genuinely interested in the comics and their history. I can remember spending three dollars, five dollars or ten dollars on Golden Age comics in an era when that was considered a lot of money to spend on individual old comics that weren't iconic first issues or didn't feature still-current characters like Batman or Captain America. But Burt's prices usually seemed fair, if not bargains, and the best part was that you could actually see and hold the books. In those days, so many of the dealers who advertised nationally in fanzines like *RBCC* would sometimes send out ratty books and call them 'good' as long as they were complete. With Burt, you always knew what you were getting. I must have bought several hundred Golden Age comics from him, and I remember it as a positive experience."

In the late 1970s, when most of the high-value comics had been bought up from the nation's used bookstores, Blum founded his own store, the Santa Monica Trading Company, and sold vintage magazines and books for 25 years before closing in 2002. "Things have changed," he told the weekly *Santa Monica Mirror* for a story about the store's much-lamented demise. "Customers used to come in and buy things. Now regardless of whether I have something or not, they will say, 'Oh, let me check the price on the Internet.'" Blum told the newspaper he still recalled selling a copy of *Superman* #1 for $20, which 40 years earlier had been considered an outrageous price for a comic book, even a first issue printed in 1939. It wasn't long, however, before the price jumped to $100, in large part thanks to East Coast mail-order dealers.

San Diego's Jackie Estrada, for many years an official at Comic-Con International, told Duin about what a treat a visit to Cherokee always was. "In the hallway we'd find Barks comics and Little Lulus in the ten cents-apiece or three-for-a-quarter bins. We'd load up on a hundred comics at a time. But then one trip, I think it was in 1968, we walked into the comics hallway and—no bins. Suddenly, everything was individually priced in boxes in Burt's inner sanctum. I guess that's when comics collecting—especially Barks—must've really caught on."

Leonard Brown

(1943–2007)

Leonard Brown (not the Leonard Brown who worked for Tower Comics or Topps) was a comic book and Big Little Book fan who co-owned Collectors Book Store in Hollywood, California, with partner Malcolm Willits. Collectors Book Store was one of a handful of retail outlets in the country that carried a large stock of back issues.

Leonard Brown grew up in Long Beach, California, home of several used bookstores and one fantastic old comic book shop. He was a collector in the 1950s before it was fashionable because he loved old comic books, especially the Disney comics.

He had just progressed to the point of running a couple of ads for old comic books in the local newspaper when he met Richard Olson, an equally intense collector from the other side of town. They both immediately recognized a kindred spirit, and became partners in 1959. Their business cards were placed on the bulletin boards of nearly every market in Southern California. In those days, people were happy to get a few extra dollars for that stack of old comic books that had been in their closet for years, and the young partnership flourished. At Leonard's insistence, they pioneered the emphasis on quality. They were also the first to sell books in plastic holders, which the customers loved.

Each year their stock grew, but not as rapidly, and Leonard saw the need for a store. He felt it was important for people to have a place to go to sell their books as it was already clear that there was a market for old comic books but that the supply was not endless. Olson was finishing college and wanted to go to grad school, but fate intervened and Leonard met Malcolm Willits, who was clearly another passionate collector. Leonard and Malcolm opened Collectors Bookstore in 1965 on Wilcox Avenue just off of Hollywood Blvd., the first store dedicated to selling movie and comic collectibles. Other used bookstores generally had no more than a box or two of tattered old comic books; however, also unlike other used bookstores, Collectors Book Store had a nearby competitor in the form of the Cherokee Book Store, also in Hollywood. Cherokee had an excellent inventory of rare books, and on their second floor the owner's son, Burt Blum, presided over a large number of old comic books. Although Burt knew nothing about old comics to begin with, it is to his credit that he learned. And with the financial support of a very successful store downstairs, he was in a nice position.

At Collectors Bookstore, Malcolm handled the movie material, Leonard handled the comics and related ephemera, and the store did well. They moved on to Hollywood Blvd. and added a new book section and changed the store's name to Bennett's Books. This was a disaster and was short lived. Collectibles were increasing in price almost daily and, with their immense inventory, they were soon able to move into a large old bank building on Hollywood Boulevard and actually became a tourist attraction. Leonard kept the best comics in the nicest condition in the vault and tried not to sell them except to good customers because he could tell he was no longer able to replace stock for pennies a book. His customers became very faithful because Leonard knew his material, was totally honest, and became a friend to many of them.

Along the way, Leonard put out the first comic book catalog, started a monthly auction, and added original art to their inventory. He and Malcolm also hired some of the great artists of the Golden Age to recreate some of their best covers, and in the case of Floyd Gottfredson, to create a set of 24 paintings based on his classic newspaper strips. What many people don't know about Leonard is that he had a heart of gold. If a young boy came in and couldn't afford something, Leonard would sometimes give it to him. If a child bought ten old Sunday pages, Leonard would give him a hundred of them if he felt the kid really loved the material. In short, Leonard was a true collector who was among the first to find a way to let his hobby become his career.

Leonard Brown died in 2007 of mesothelioma, the cancer associated with asbestos, even though he couldn't remember working with it.

Claude Held

(b. 1926)

Of the sellers of old comic books in the early 1960s, the one whose roots as a dealer reach back the furthest was Claude Held. He began stockpiling comics in the 1940s, and began including comics on his ongoing lists of fantasy books and magazines in the mid to late 1950s.

Claude Held grew up on Fountain Street in Buffalo, New York, in the 1930s. He and his best friend, Ken Krueger, became fans of the science fiction pulps of the day, such as *Thrilling Wonder Stories*. As early as 1939 or 1940, it occurred to young Claude that he could sell back issues of the pulps through the mail. He was about 16 years old when he created his first real "for sale" list, the first of 100s that Held would produce over the next 50 years.

After serving a hitch in the Navy, Claude was discharged in 1946, and went to the University of Buffalo. Since his classes were in the morning, he decided to open a bookstore on the corner of Utica, near Jefferson. "The comics started from that," Held recalled in an interview that appeared in *Alter Ego* #23 (April 2003). "One day this guy who'd just gotten out of the Army pulled up his car outside my store ... and said to me, 'Do you buy comics?' I said, 'Yeah.' He said, 'What do you pay?' And I said, 'A dollar a hundred.' He says, 'Okay,' and he went and parked his car a block or so down the street. When he came back, he had these two stacks. He brought them in the store, and then he turned around and started out. I asked him, 'Where are you going?' He said, 'To get some more.' By the time he was done, he'd brought in some 1,700 comics. I didn't have a helluva lot of dough.... I wound up getting the 1,700 comics for $15. It was fantastic because all of the early DC's, the *More Funs*, all that type of stuff was in there." This windfall, along with the other comics Held had acquired until then, gave him what he needed to make a "go" of the bookstore.

When Claude began selling comics via mail order in the late 1950s, adding them to his lists of science fiction and fantasy collectibles, many of the buyers were outraged that he would charge 50 cents or a dollar for a pre–1940 comic book. At the dawn of the new decade, Held finally began putting out lists of mostly comic books. His lists pre-dated those of Phil Seuling and Howard Rogofsky, who became prominent dealers in the 1960s. Claude's ad on the back cover of *The Comicollector* #1 (September 1961), read: "For sale: Thousands of old comics & Big Little Books dating back to 1933. Free price lists are available upon request. I will buy collections of pre–1945 comics." The ad was accompanied by the "*Alter-Ego* Seal of Approval," apparently affixed because editor Jerry Bails had had positive dealings with Held.

How did Held grade comics in those early days? "It was a graduated scale," he explained. "It went, Mint, and then it went Near Mint, and then Very Fine, and then Fine. That's the way I tried to grade things. Things were a lot looser then than they are today. I didn't think [grading] was a problem back then. People could always return stuff if they didn't like it." Held issued hundreds of lists in the 1960s, providing a source of back issues to the many fans who poured into comicdom during that period of time. His prices weren't the cheapest, but they were reasonable, and he had a reputation for fair and honest dealing.

Though he made a lot of money in comics over the years, Claude decided to focus on coins and stamps by the late 1970s, so he sold his remaining comic book stock to Gary Dolgoff. He com-

Claude Held (left) with unidentified fan.

mented, "As it turned out, I would have been much better staying in the comics and forgetting about stamps! Stamps have gone down, comics have gone up." Held retained his own collection of Golden Age comics, mostly the ones that reprinted the comic strips of the 1930s and 1940s, such as *King Comics*, *Ace Comics*, *Tip Top Comics*, *Super Comics* and *Popular Comics*. In the 1990s, he sold mainly classic comic strips saved from old newspapers, such as "Tarzan," "Flash Gordon," "Terry and the Pirates," "Prince Valiant" and many more.

Bud Plant
(b. 1952)

Bud Plant, comic book stores, and comic conventions all sprouted and grew together at the same time. Few comic art enthusiasts have had a more visionary and entrepreneurial impact on the hobby than Plant, and no mail-order merchandiser has sold more books about comics and comic art than he has over four decades.

He has owned Bud Plant Comic Art (now Bud's Art Books) since the firm began as a home-based business in 1970. He soon co-founded the nation's first comic book store chain, and, in tandem with Direct Market creator Phil Seuling, helped foster and distribute independent comics and fan projects. In the early 1980s, Plant became one of the key national distributors who helped make Seuling's concepts viable instead of seeing comic books suffer the fate of the pulp magazines two decades earlier.

Bud grew up on the east side of San Jose, California, long before the South Bay Area's emergence as the heart of Silicon Valley. The family home wasn't far from the famed, huge San Jose Flea Market where he began to collect back issues as a 13-year-old in 1965. Several

other collectors, some a little older and some a little younger, on the west, south and north sides of San Jose soon became fast friends with Bud, including John Barrett, Jim Vadeboncoeur, Jr., Michelle Nolan, Dick Swan, Jim Buser and Tom Tallmon. The result became a thriving comics fan community. Bud linked up with this group through another collector, Jim Leal, whom Bud encountered at the large Twice Read Books used-book store in downtown San Jose, where they would hunt out old comics, both the nickel sort and the emerging collectibles for a buck, circa 1965. Bud began acquiring mail-order comics from advertisements in the *Rockets Blast-Comic Collector* fanzine in 1965.

Plant was 16 years old and a sophomore in high school when he and Nolan, then a sophomore at nearby San José State University, along with Bud's teen-age buddies Barrett and Buser plus Tallmon and Frank

Bud Plant

Scadina, pooled their limited funds and not-so-limited collections of extra old comics to open what some feel was the earliest comics-only store in America. They called it the Seven Sons Comic Shop, which opened in March 1968 at a hole-in-the-wall rental at 40 E. San Fernando in the heart of downtown San Jose. The idea was to make a little money and add a lot of comic books to their collections, and the store worked well on both counts. The owners, however, were all still high school or college students except for Scadina, and they grew weary of taking turns running the store. By the start of the next school year, they sold out to Scadina, who soon changed the name of the store to Marvel Galaxy and moved to a new location.

Plant and Barrett returned in 1969 with another downtown San Jose store, Comic World, about a block away from the first store, in partnership with Buser and Swan. That year, they also attended their first comic convention, driving all the way to Houston, and their early experiences in wheeling and dealing turned out to be good business preparation for their founding of the first store in the Comics and Comix chain in 1972. The chain featured stores in Berkeley and San Jose, and quickly added Palo Alto, San Francisco, Sacramento and a couple of other locations. Michelle Nolan, who had begun assisting Phil Seuling with the 1969 New York Comicon, introduced fledgling business partners Plant and Barrett to Seuling when they went to New York to sell comics at Seuling's show in 1970, which was the same year Plant began the home-based business that quickly blossomed into Bud Plant Comic Art.

In a two-part series for *Alter Ego* #47 and #48 (April and May 2005), Bud recalled how those 1969–70 conventions were great business training: "We bought comics coming and going (from that first convention in Houston in 1969). First, we went to Hollywood and Los Angeles. We even went to Bond Street Books, where we got really good deals on Disney comics. We got *Walt Disney's Comics and Stories* and *Donald Duck* comics for something like 25 or 50 cents each. We found out when we took them to Texas we could sell them for a buck, or buck and a quarter. We returned to San Jose with a car jammed full of different comics than the ones we came with. We decided to open up another shop." That shop was Comic World. Bud's friends were amazed at the energy and business acumen of these teenagers.

"Bud was obviously a great young businessman and just a natural entrepreneur," said Nolan. "He also had the best taste in art of any of us, along with Jim Vadeboncoeur. Plus, Bud quickly built a reputation for honesty, from his teen years on, and it didn't take people long to know that here was a born bookman, plus someone they could trust. He was also one of the first guys, if not the first, to see the expanded retail potential of underground comix in the late 1960s. Bud made good money buying them wholesale and selling them retail at all the shows he attended. It was kind of amazing—he was selling them before he was legally supposed to be reading them! He and John Barrett would always have to make sure their display could be quickly taken off the table if needed, but today it seems like a pretty innocent thing."

Bud vividly remembered meeting the famed Seuling and participating in his first New York convention in 1970. When asked about his convention experiences, Bud recalled in the *Alter Ego* interview, "For some reason, I can remember the dollar figures. We made $450 at Multi-Con in Oklahoma City and $750 in New York.... We were actually able to make money in New York with the books that were left over from Oklahoma City. But we spent every penny we had while we were in New York (the first time). For one thing, Phil Seuling had DC original art pages. He had *Our Army at War* and *Our Fighting Forces* drawn by Joe Kubert and Russ Heath. And I think he was selling them for five bucks apiece. We spent every penny we had and we came back to California owing Seuling about 500 bucks. What blows me away is that Phil didn't know us from Adam before then, and he let us traipse off to California, trusting that we would pay him. I had never had credit before in my life!"

Not long after Plant's graduation from San José State University with a degree in business in 1975, he relocated to Grass Valley in the Sierra Nevada foothills. By this time, he needed a warehouse to house his rapidly expanding business, which included the sale of books related to comics and comic art, along with underground comix. At the same time, Bud and his original partner, the late John Barrett, were expanding the Comics and Comix chain. Bud and three others—Jim Vadeboncoueur, Al Davoren and Pat Price—created Promethian Enterprises in 1969 to publish the first fanzine that melded work by leading underground and mainstream artists. There were five issues through 1975, with Rick Griffin providing the first two covers and Robert Crumb the third. "In 1975, we published the first interview with Robert Crumb," Bud said. "Al Davoren had the underground comix connections and helped make it all possible."

In 1988, Plant sold his comic book distributorship to Steve Geppi at Diamond, allowing Bud to focus on Bud Plant Comic Art, which had long since become a stable presence at major conventions around the country. At about the same time, Plant and Vadeboncoeur formed Bud Plant Illustrated Books, which became a leading catalog outlet for fine used books for some 15 years until the Internet made the catalog business unprofitable. Bud also loves outdoor recreation and in the beautiful surroundings of Grass Valley he helped raise his two children, Alison and Philip, and his two step-children, Ena and Meadow.

Bud and his life partner, bookseller Anne Hutchison, now appear with merchandise at book and comic conventions all over the country, in addition to the major shows he does with the staff at Bud's Art Books. Bud remains a noted and enthusiastic collector of comics, books, original art, pulps and other items related to illustration.

Howard Rogofsky
(b. 1946)

Howard Rogofsky was the first full-time dealer of old comic books, and was highly controversial primarily because his prices tended to be higher than his competitors.

A New Yorker by birth, young Rogofsky's favorite comic book character was Plastic Man, who was still being published by Quality Comics in the early 1950s. He also loved any comic book featuring knights, Robin Hood or King Arthur. Rogofsky was living with his parents in Queens when he saw his first fanzines in 1960, one of them probably *The Fantasy Collector*, which listed people selling comic books. He wrote some of those fans in search of back issues of *Plastic Man*. One of them was Biljo White of Columbia, Missouri, who was the first person to sell an old comic to Howard. Soon Rogofsky decided to try selling comic books himself. His first advertisement appeared in White's *Komix Illustrated* #2 (September 1962). In *KI* #3, Biljo included an entry on Howard in the "Profiles on Collectors" series, which revealed the 16-year-old's favorite comic book creator to be Jack Cole, and his favorite current comic book *Justice League of America*.

Rogofsky's early advertisements met with success, for fans were desperate to find back issues, and his mail order business took off. His father was supportive, sometimes providing short-term loans to purchase "finds" of rare comics that could be quickly turned for a profit. In those days, he made incredible deals, such as trading three *Lone Ranger* comic books for a run of *Action* #1 to 232. Until a spate of articles appeared in 1964 and 1965, no one knew that the old comics in one's attic could be worth a lot of money; they were often seen as worthless, and the sellers were happy to receive anything a dealer like Rogofsky offered.

Howard had attended the 1964 New York Comicon organized by Bernie Bubnis, and appeared regularly at subsequent comicons in the city, but participated in fandom primarily as a businessman. In 1965, he graduated from high school. In an interview in *Comic Book Marketplace* #18 (1992), Rogofsky explained, "After I graduated from high school … I was accepted at college in the technology area, but I decided not to go. I just kept selling through the mail, except that I did it full time." Other major dealers, like Phil Seuling, had regular full-time jobs. As far as is known, Rogofsky was the first full-time dealer of old comic books. Howard's mother, Mildred, typed every one of his lists from 1962 to 1992; she worked as her son dictated, each page taking up to eight

Howard Rogofsky

hours. According to Howard, he grossed $15,000 in 1965, and $60,000 the following year. Rogofsky never looked back. His ads appeared in most issues of *RBCC* throughout the decade, and he would send his pre-printed list to any fanzine publisher who would include it in his latest issue. Rogofsky also began advertising in Marvel Comics, and when the *Overstreet Comic Book Price Guide* began appearing annually, Howard's large ads were always prominent.

Rogofsky's policies as a dealer were not popular with some fans. First, his prices, in general, were higher than those of his competitors. Second, he didn't grade comics individually (except to note if they were coverless), instead stating that the comics on his list "are complete and in very good condition unless otherwise stated." However, as the 1960s progressed, there were certainly dealers with higher prices, and Howard wasn't the only one to resist individual grading. In the early years, fans were so anxious to find the back issues they craved that condition wasn't so important as long as the book was complete and in reasonable shape. By 1970, this had changed, and Rogofsky's "tape is not a defect" policy was no longer acceptable.

In *CBM* #18, Howard stated, "I know there have been a few people over the years that didn't care for me. Maybe it was because I was making exceptional money off comic books. I would always tell them that if it wasn't for dealers turning up stuff and making a profit, there wouldn't be so much great material offered to collectors over the years. To me, a dealer is anybody who will sell something for more money than he paid for it. Lots of old-timers made money on comics. Jerry Bails had his own fanzine in which he advertised stuff and he also had ads to buy. Does that make him a dealer? Some say 'yes,' some say 'no.' I feel a dealer is anybody who makes a profit, and there is nothing wrong with that."

Howard's unwillingness to grade individually led him to de-emphasize comics, and move into other types of paper collectibles, such as selling *Playboy*, *TV Guide*, magazines, etc. He and his wife, Gail, who were married in 1965, have run their successful mail-order business to the present day. They live and operate out of the same house his parents moved into in 1955.

Bill Thailing
(1926–2003)

Bill Thailing is credited as the second major comic book dealer (after Claude Held) to sell back issues to members of fandom.

As a youth growing up in the 1930s, the first comic books William J. Thailing saw were those that reprinted non-hero newspaper comics. He was enamored with *King Comics*, *Ace Comics* and *Super Comics*, bringing him the syndicated strips that weren't in his local paper (the *Cleveland Plain Dealer*.) "Dick Tracy" was a particular favorite, and *Ace Comics* had the "Katzenjammer Kids" and "Prince Valiant." When original heroes came along, it wasn't Superman that caught Bill's attention, but Batman. DC characters became his favorites, as well as Timely comics such as *Marvel Mystery*.

Thailing served in MacArthur's army (which liberated the Philippine Islands in 1944 and 1945), and was discharged in 1946. His story was the familiar one of having his comics disposed of by his mother while he was away from home. When he returned, his interests had moved to the typical concerns of most young men, such as meeting girls and getting married. He did read *Other Worlds* and *Amazing Stories*, feeling he had "graduated" from comic books to science fiction. Then, in 1954, he had an epiphany. He explained:

Bill Thailing

> I was at a rummage sale of some kind and ran across some Big Little Books that I had fifteen years earlier, and it kind of hit me. They had these Big Little Books published by Whitman. Some Popeyes, some Flash Gordons, some Dick Tracys—and right away, I'm interested, all over again! Here I was pushing 30 years old, and thinking to myself, "Why not have the things I enjoyed when I was ten?" So the bug bit me, and I began collecting in earnest all over again. I was buying comic books in large lots, in order to get the things I wanted. In my readings of fantasy, I ran across science fiction readers that had comic books. I got in touch with other collectors and started trading and selling and sending out catalogs and getting

all excited about these things all over again like I did when I was a kid, on a little larger scale than trading with the neighborhood kids.

Bill Thailing never went as far as opening a book store; his dealing of comic books was strictly mail order, developing out of the trading and selling he did with individual correspondents. At first, he didn't even have a printed "comics for sale" list, merely including certain items in his handwritten letters, but eventually his dealing became more formalized. To him, it was less a business and more of a hobby and a labor of love.

Bill made many friendships in fandom over the years, not the least of them Raymond Miller, who got in touch with him in September 1960. He began selling old comics for 25 cents to $1.50 each, which gave Miller the basis for the many articles and other features he wrote for early issues of *The Rocket's Blast*, *The Comicollector* and other fanzines. Bill was also close to Don and Maggie Thompson, who also lived in Cleveland; he helped them obtain comics—often on loan—to research and write articles for their fanzine *Comic Art*. Thailing was a source of vintage comics to other writers as well, and indexers like Jerry Bails. Strange as it seems, Golden Age comic books were harder to find in the early 1960s than in later years, when the higher prices coaxed them out of attics, closets and basements.

Thailing's interest in comics was dwarfed by his love of railroading. "I worked 43 years for the railroad," he remembered. "My wife and I and the kids, we'd travel all over in trains. That was fun to do. In fact, one time I attended a comic book show in New York City back in the 60s, and actually pushed one of those huge dollies onto the baggage car, and the wife and I and the kids rode free, and the merchandise was carried in the baggage car, and right into Grand Central Station, and never even had to take a taxicab. Phil Seuling had his convention right there in one of the hotels right on Park Avenue. The New York Central owned the Commodore Hotel, I guess it was. That was very, very convenient. Phil Seuling was a nice man. He was a great influence on me. He was a great guy, that's all I can say about him."

Malcolm Willits
(b. 1934)

Malcolm Willits is best known as a historian of the works of Walt Disney, and conducted the first interview ever with Carl Barks. He was also a prominent comic book dealer, operating out of his Collectors Book Store in Hollywood, California, during the 1960s.

Malcolm was born in Portland, Oregon, in 1934. While growing up in Portland, he had a subscription to *Walt Disney's Comics and Stories*, and published a very early, crude comics fanzine. Of the early 1940s, Willits later wrote, "For me the comic books were merely a part of my life, not an all-consuming thing. They were so available one assumed their existence as a right. I do recall the privations of World War II hit me only when the comic books reduced their size and page counts to a point they seemed a shadow of their former selves. I could stand the rationing of food and clothing, since everyone still seemed to have more than they'd ever had anyway, but to see the comic books deteriorate was hard to take. They were done in by the paper shortages plus so many of their artists and their writers went off to war. The Golden Age was over, never to return."

In October 1947, Mal Willits and Jim Bradley started *The Comic Collector's News*, the only documented fanzine devoted exclusively to comic art in the 1940s. *CCN* featured rudimentary articles, advertisements and contests relating to comic books. Willits admitted, "Its real purpose was to enhance our own collections by making our wants more widely known." Their slogan was, "Your Comics are Valuable. Don't Throw Them Away." Over the next two or three years, several issues of *The Comic Collector's News* were published. In 1950, the duo launched a science fiction fanzine called *Destiny*. Even so, it included an occasional piece on animation or comics.

In late 1957, Willits had written to Disney and obtained the name of the "good duck artist." That information began a correspondence with Carl Barks, and the first ever Barks interview. At first, Barks thought Willits' fan letter was a hoax from a co-worker, for he couldn't believe anyone would take his work so seriously. (Don and Maggie discovered Barks' identity separately, in response to their query of Dell comics.) The eventual articles in *Comic Art* in 1968 introduced Barks to many comics fans who had never heard of him, and offered new areas of exploration and enjoyment to those who were getting a little tired of superheroes. From this point forward, Barks fandom grew by leaps and bounds.

In 1962, Malcolm had moved from Portland to Los Angeles to accept a teaching position, and met Leonard Brown (not the New York City–based pro comic writer by the same name in New York City) who was actively dealing comics while completing college. He advertised widely for old comic books, and accumulated several hundred boxes of comic books, old movie magazines, and old Sunday comic sections. Leonard suggested the two of them merge their holdings and open a store. They did, and called it Collectors Book Store when they opened in March of 1965. "Our store proved so successful that within ten months I was able to quit my tenured teaching position and join Leonard full-time. Our store encompassed three main fields: comic books, science fiction, and movie material. But it was definitely the comic books which carried us the first few years. Leonard put out the first real catalogue in the field in late 1965, a 36-page booklet which incorporated 21 separate collecting departments."

Collectors Book Store and the nearby Cherokee Book Store were important sources of

Malcolm Willits and Leonard Brown at the reception for the opening of Collectors Book Store, 1964.

vintage comic books within striking distance of Los Angeles. They also had mail-order operations. Collectors Book Store was known for its incredible inventory of high-grade comic book rarities (often many multiples of the same Golden Age issues)—and, the resultant upscale prices. It was not a place, like Cherokee, where kids could rummage around for ten cent comics; instead, it catered more to the collectors with a fair amount of cash, and the older, discriminating fans.

Malcolm developed into a writer with a strong humorous, iconoclastic bent not unlike Mark Twain in later years. His "Confessions of an Unrepentant Portland Comic Book Collector" appeared in the *Comic Fandom Reader* (Hamster Press, 2002). He wrote *The Wonderful Edison Time* (Hypostyle Hall, 1999), which appeared in a handsome hardcover volume designed by Scott Rubel with art by Toby Bluth. He also wrote the play *Shakespeare's Cat*, and published a book on the 1940 movie version of *The Thief of Bagdad* starring Sabu.

SECTION III: FANZINE PUBLISHERS

History can only tell the stories of those who leave their traces behind. In the case of comic fandom, there are no better examples of those "traces" than the surviving copies of the many amateur magazines—fanzines—devoted to the subject of comic art.

Somewhere around 2,500 different issues of these time capsules were produced between 1954 and 1970, and there were all types: general fanzines (genzines) which offer articles, features and indexes of comic books and strips; advertising fanzines (adzines) devoted mainly to the distribution of advertisements taken out by fans who wanted to sell, swap or buy back issues; newsletters, whose name is sufficiently descriptive; amateur comics, which published the efforts of talented fan writers, artists and editors; and any other type of format that could be concocted by innovative, passionate fans of the medium.

Perhaps, because copies of nearly every fanzine published have survived, and they contain such a wealth of information of value to historians—including all-important dates of important events, so vital to creating a timeline—some of the publishers and contributors to these labors of love may have been given undue prominence in the accounts that have surfaced in recent years. They give voice to those who have passed away in the ensuing decades, and can't give new interviews. As this introduction began, history can only be written when traces of the past exist.

The fan press offers those traces in abundance, and, significantly, they appear as frozen in time. Unlike interviews conducted much later, no memory is involved. The words and drawings on the pages are unchanged, though perhaps—in the case of ditto printing—somewhat faded. The atmosphere, the *zeitgeist*, of EC fandom of the 1950s, and general comic fandom of the 1960s, is captured undiluted.

As recently as the 1980s and early 1990s, old fan magazines like *Batmania, RBCC, Yancy Street Journal* and others could be purchased for as little as $5 or $10 each. When I re-entered fandom in 1991 and began researching the collective history, it involved rebuilding my long-gone zine collection from scratch. I was fortunate to have begun collecting them when I did, because by the late 1990s, prices began to go up. Way up! Some of this may be due to my book *The Golden Age of Comic Fandom* (Hamster Press, 1995), which rekindled interest in them, as did the several subsequent books that I wrote on the same subject. The Internet and the fact that anyone can have easy access to it is probably a greater factor. Bargains were hard to find when a new breed of monied, eager enthusiasts began sniping wars for fanzines on eBay.com and other auction sites.

The demand for these artifacts of a bygone age speaks to the importance they had for the Baby Boomers who made up the rank and file of fandom. Those of us who were there will always remember the thrill of finding the latest issue of a favorite fanzine in the mailbox. The daily postal delivery could bring much anticipated wonders to our hungry eyes and hearts, in those days when the mainstream world sneered at the objects of our fascination. The fanzines brought each of us a message: "You are not alone." There are others like us, who love the fabulous four-color medium, and who understand that graphic stories—sequential art, if you will—weren't intrinsically limited to childish interest and subject matter. The amateur publications helped bind us together and share our common dreams. Therefore, it's with great pleasure that this book offers portraits of a number of the most active and memorable fanzine editors and publishers. Those early fanzines really were labors of love, and often barely broke even or merely provided the funds for the next issue. They were the true pioneers who blazed the trials that led to our greater appreciation and knowledge of comic history and art.

Edwin Aprill, Jr.
(1928–1972)

One of the slightly older fans, an "ancient" 33 years old in 1961, Edwin M. Aprill, Jr. was best known for publishing a series of high-quality reprints of comic strips, beginning with "Buck Rogers." He also published *Cartoonist Showcase*, which featured current daily strips.

Ed lived 60 miles from Detroit, one of the main "hotbeds" of early fan activity, in Ann Arbor, Michigan. His full-time career was as a grade school art teacher in Ann Arbor, where he lived with his wife and daughters. His massive collection of original art from the comic strips was said to contain at least one example from all the major strips. According to one witness, he had Alex Raymond "Flash Gordon" and "Secret Agent X-9" pages, Hal Foster "Prince Valiant" pages, early "Krazy Kat" art, as well as dozens of pages of original comic book pages.

Often he hosted delegations of fans from Detroit, who were drawn by the opportunity to view the treasures in his basement sanctum. In *Graphic Story World* (V.2 N.2), Shel Dorf wrote, "Driving out the country roads, past farm houses and fields of crops, we'd turn into the driveway of his one-story brick home, and hearing the car Ed would bound out of the house with a big grin on his face…. We'd sit around … looking at old comics and studying the originals. Sometimes we'd trade items and … often he'd let us borrow books to read at home or to copy, and never gave it a second thought."

Aprill also made his way to the Motor City fairly often, and was in attendance at the legendary Alley Tally Party at Jerry Bails' home which was held March 21 and 22, 1964. This is considered the first sizable gathering of comic fans, with a total of 19 in attendance, though it soon would be outstripped by gatherings in Chicago, New York City and elsewhere.

Edwin Aprill, Jr.

In *Alter Ego* #5 (March 1965), an advertisement appeared announcing a publication that was "destined to become the most sought-after item in fandom!!" This was a limited numbered edition book reprinting "Buck Rogers in the 25th Century," a 68-page book that was on sale for the then-substantial price of $5 per copy ("mailed flat in an envelope"). This was an important, ambitious project which would prove to be a great success, and led to subsequent volumes in the same format, which Aprill called *Great Classic Newspaper Comic Strips* (abbreviated GCNCS). Later editions featured "The Spirit" dailies and other choice items. These inspired other publishers to put out collections of newspaper comic strips, such as Woody Gelman's Nostalgia Press hardcover reprinting of Alex Raymond's "Flash Gordon" in 1967.

Aprill launched *Cartoonist Showcase* in 1967, featuring current daily strips. It lasted into 1971, when it was superseded by the long-running daily strip publication *The Memononee Falls Gazette.*

Edwin Aprill, Jr., died tragically on February 3, 1972. On a winter morning, he was on his way to work when his car went out of control on an icy patch and hit a tree. Ed was survived by his wife, Joanne, and his daughters, Juliette and Sally. Aprill was a much-loved and respected collector whose publishing efforts ensured that quality vintage syndicated newspaper strips were available for appreciation and study to the rank and file of fandom, rather than be overshadowed by the comic book material that was so much a focus of comicdom's early days.

Marty Arbunich
(b. 1948)

Marty Arbunich was best known in fandom as editor and publisher of *The Yancy Street Journal*, fandom's first Marvel fanzine. He also played an editorial role and contributed to the other fanzines published by Golden Gate Features, a fannish consortium made up of Arbunich, Bill DuBay, Rudi Franke and Barry Bauman. These were *Fandom Presents*, *Fantasy Hero*, *Voice of Comicdom* and *All-Stars*. As such, Marty was an important figure in the very early years of comic fandom in California.

Martin Arbunich was born in November 1948 in San Francisco, California, the son of a mechanic for the Southern Pacific Railroad. When he entered first grade at St. Paul's Grammar School, he met Bill DuBay who became his best friend. One thing they had in common was their love of comic books from an early age. They discovered comic fandom after entering Sacred Heart High School in 1963. Bill, an aspiring artist, decided to publish a fanzine called *Fantasy Hero*, and enlisted Marty to write for it. This ignited Arbunich's abiding interest in publishing. As Marty later recalled, "Even though comics were interesting for me, what was even more interesting was the production end of it. Making something!"

Originally, Bill and Marty did most of their production work in Bill's bedroom, but when they acquired a ditto machine of their own, they set it up in the basement of Marty's house, establishing their own print shop. "We spent a lot of time down there, just grinding it out, with reams and reams of paper," Marty said. Somewhat to their own amazement, *Fantasy Hero* and its spinoffs were quite popular, and they had to provide a lot of copies to satisfy the demand.

The Yancy Street Journal began in ditto with #3 (continuing the numbering of *Comic Caper*), establishing several long-running columns. "The Timely Years" examined the Golden

Age comics featuring Sub-Mariner, Captain America, Human Torch and others; "Iz Zat So?" featured miscellaneous facts and news items from Marvel; "The Mystery of Marvel" offered Marty's reviews of the latest issues; and "Your Friendly Neighborhood Spider-Man" gave Bill DuBay a chance to discuss the latest issue of *Amazing Spider-Man* in some detail. Soon a regular readers' discussion column would hash over a particular topic each issue, and "Courageous Captain" discussed Captain America. This popular ongoing column, which debuted in #5, was written by Steve Perrin. Perrin was Marty and Bill's contact at San Francisco State College; they often met up with him to catch an episode of the movie serial *Adventures of Captain Marvel* when it was shown on campus. (Perrin had been in touch with them since the inception of *Fantasy Hero*.)

Marty Arbunich

The six ditto issues of *YSJ* were published in the space of one year, a remarkable record for any fanzine. Marty recalled, "We would set deadlines for ourselves … and we were good at crunching it away, and staying up until all hours until it was done." With #9, *YSJ* changed to the same photo-offset newspaper format as *Voice of Comicdom*, though it was Marty (not Bill) who did the lay-outs. *YSJ* offered a good mix of Marvel news, columns, and articles. The articles tended to be brief, but they were ably written and nicely augmented by photos, artwork and cover reproductions. It ended with issue #12 (January 1966) coinciding with the announcement that Steve Ditko was leaving the House of Ideas.

One highpoint of his years in fandom was Marty's contact with Ditko, which led to the Spider-Man artist drawing the cover for the fanzine *All-Stars*. It was done to order, to more or less represent the interior "Belle Star" strip by Ronn Foss, and is without question the most elaborate drawing Ditko—or virtually any comics pro—did for an amateur publication up to this time (1965). Arbunich still retains the original art, resisting all offers or the urge to put it up for auction.

By 1966, when Arbunich was graduating from high school, his interest shifted to the music scene that was flowering in San Francisco and across the country. He was paid to write for a British rock magazine, and ran the *Bay Area Entertainer* newspaper, based around the local entertainment scene in the early 1970s in San Francisco. Marty was the sort of person who thrived on running his own business. He started a record store in 1973, and expanded to three locations in the Bay Area, owning them until 1989. He also ran Solid Smoke Records, his own independent record label from 1977 until 1985, producing some 50 record albums.

In 1993, Arbunich founded the Eichler Network, based around the 11,000 mid-century modern Eichler homes in the Bay Area. Marty's original newsletter for the business has blossomed into *CA-Modern* magazine, which is delivered to some 30,000 people who live in MCM homes throughout California.

Gary Brown
(b. 1947)

Gary Brown was born February 25, 1947, in Cleveland, Ohio, the home of Superman's creators. His parents always encouraged reading and regularly bought him comic books to read, ranging from *Superman* to *Archie* to *Blackhawk* and a variety of Dell titles.

He started collecting comics in 1957 while living in Hialeah, Florida, when he bought a copy of *Action Comics* #226 (March) and was fascinated by it. While he had read comics previously, this kicked off his collecting DNA and he began buying them regularly.

His biggest thrill early on was having a poem published in *The Flash* #121 (June 1961), and winning the original Carmine Infantino artwork to the cover of *The Flash* #119.

He became involved in comics fandom in late 1965 while a freshman at the University of South Florida in Tampa/St. Petersburg. He and longtime friend Wayne DeWald had been making regular trips to Webb's City to buy comics and began sending away for fanzines like *The Comic Reader* and *Batmania*.

DeWald did two issues of a short letter zine called *Comic Comments* in 1966 and Brown joined in the fun with the third issue. In two or three issues, the free letter zine was a success and began receiving letters from fans like Roy Thomas, Jerry Bails, Glen Johnson, Rick Durell and Bob Butts. Brown and DeWald soon made contact with and met Alan Hutchinson, who contributed some of the best and funniest artwork in fandom to their fanzine and helped publish two issues of an article-based zine, *Gremlin*. In 1966, both Brown and DeWald joined *Capa-alpha*, the first comics oriented apa. Brown is still a contributing member 42 years later.

After college, Brown restarted *Comic Comments* in an all-offset form. After a dozen

Gary Brown

issues, he was contacted by Jim Steranko who brought Brown onboard for *Comixscene*, a new tabloid-sized magazine he was going to publish. Brown stayed with that publication for 12 issues.

Because he started out as a Superman fan, he's always collected the Man of Steel's comics, plus *Batman*, *Blackhawk* and the DC superheroes. He was there at the birth of Marvel, buying all the original comics off the newsstands. Over the years, his interests branched out to Carl Barks' work on the Disney ducks, EC, John Stanley's *Little Lulu*, Dan Spiegle's artwork and Al Williamson.

He was especially taken with the stories in *Little Archie* and not only has acquired a complete collection of that comic book title, but met and has become good friends with artists-writers Bob Bolling and Dexter Taylor, who worked on the stories.

He is a fan of musicians Jimmy Buffett and Harry Nilsson and continues to collect their albums. He also is a lifelong athlete and sports fans, following his beloved Cleveland Indians and Miami Dolphins.

He dropped out of fandom in 1979 after getting married, but maintained a presence in *Capa-alpha*. In 1985, he began collecting again and hasn't looked back. He writes articles for magazines like *Alter Ego* and *Comic Book Artist* and tries to maintain a monthly publication schedule of his *Capa-alpha* zine, *Ibid*. He also can be found looking through boxes of comic books at conventions and in comics stores.

He has worked as a journalist all of his life for such newspapers as *The Miami Herald*, *The Palm Beach Post* and the *Bradenton Herald*. He has been a city editor, news editor and Business News editor, in addition to a working reporter, copy editor and page designer over the years.

Brown has contributed some articles to several of the major comics companies, including the introduction to the first collection of *Little Archie* stories. He has two sons and lives with his ever-growing collection in Greenacres, Florida.

Larry Herndon
(ca. 1945–1982)

Of all the Big Name Fans who hailed from the Lone Star state, there was none bigger than diminutive Larry Herndon. Herndon was one of fandom's most prolific writers, fanzine editors and organizers. Beginning in 1962, he published a series of fanzines, with the best known being *Star-Studded Comics* (as a member of The Texas Trio) and *The Nostalgia News*.

One of the beautiful things about fandom was that physically challenged individuals could become giants in the fan community. G. B. Love was one example, and so was Larry

Larry Herndon

Herndon. Larry had muscular dystrophy, giving him limited use of his legs. Small of frame, and possessing genuine humility, Larry directed boundless energy toward all his fannish pursuits. He was greatly helped by the support he received from his parents (both school teachers), who helped him set up a comic book room and office in their modest home in Carrollton, Texas.

Larry Herndon jumped into the fanzine-publishing arena with a solid ditto fanzine called *Hero* in 1962, but it was when he teamed up with Howard Keltner and Buddy Saunders to launch *Star-Studded Comics* in 1963 that he made a big impact on early fandom. At the time, DC and Marvel were the only two professional comic book companies who focused on super- or costumed-heroes in a big way, and there was a great hunger among fans for more stories. Thus, when *Star-Studded* offered a roster of new heroes, many welcomed them with open arms. The heroes introduced in the first three issues of *SSC* were Doctor Weird, Powerman, The Defender, Astral Man, Blue Streak, Mr. Mystic, Changling and The Eye. The main character Larry Herndon originated for the fanzine was the Defender. Appearing in ten of *SSC*'s 18 issues, the Defender was in reality District Attorney Carl Reed. He received powers of super strength, the ability to fly and partial invulnerability by an alien named Val-lo, and vowed to use those powers to combat crime in ways not available to a D.A. Although the Defender's debut was a text story, with illustrations by Grass Green, the follow-up in *SSC* #2 was fully illustrated by Green and Keltner.

Though the first three ditto issues of *Star-Studded* offered above-average material, *SSC* really made its mark by switching to all-offset printing with #4, making it the first professionally printed fanzine devoted entirely to amateur heroes. This occurred in June 1964, and the issue unveiled the Liberty Legion, a team of the Trio's heroes: Doctor Weird, Changling, Mercury, Powerman, Astral Man and the Defender. Written by Herndon and Saunders, with chapters illustrated by the best of fandom (Foss, White, Green, Saunders and Keltner), it was a kind of ultimate achievement in amateur comic strips. The story was along the typical lines of the Justice Society and Justice League stories, with the group splitting up into two-person teams for the middle chapters, and only coming together at the beginning and end of the book-length tale.

In the course of writing many of the scripts for *Star-Studded Comics*, Herndon found himself collaborating with the best artists fandom had to offer. Some, like Ronn Foss, Grass Green, Biljo White, Mickey Schwaberow, Alan Hutchinson and Rudi Franke, were obviously highly-talented individuals, though they didn't go on to become important comic book professionals. But the superb Doctor Weird tale "The Curse of Skullwing!" teamed Herndon with future pro Alan Weiss, and Larry's Defender script "The Widow Worshippers!" was illustrated by Jim Starlin and Al Milgrom, who would become superstars in the Marvel firmament before long. Larry's "The House Where Terror Lived!" brought Herndon together with the young and talented Rich Buckler, just a few years before Buckler would become the regular artist of *The Fantastic Four*. And the Texan found himself in a posthumous collaboration with legendary pulp writer Robert E. Howard, when he adapted "Gods of the North" to comic strip form for *SSC* #14 (1968), with art by Steve Kelez and Alan Hutchinson. This strip had historical significance, for it was the first comic strip adaptation of the prose of Robert E. Howard, creator of Conan and Solomon Kane. Other folks to succeed in professional creative arenas whose work appeared in *Star-Studded Comics* were Roy Thomas, Sam Grainger, D. Bruce Berry, Dave Cockrum, Bill DuBay, Ron Harris, Gary Kato, Howard Waldrop and George R. R. Martin.

In addition to his love of comics, Larry Herndon was a fan of all areas of fantasy entertainment, from old-time serials to pulp magazines. He even published three issues of his own pulp-inspired fanzine, *Batwing*, in 1965, featuring a protagonist known as The Black Mask, obviously inspired by the venerable pulp magazine that had published the early work of Dashiell Hammett and so many other top writers in the detective and hard-boiled genre.

By 1966, Texas fandom decided it was time they had a comicon of their own, and launched the first Southwestern Con in Dallas, announcing that Dave Kaler would be the Pro Guest of Honor. Con chairman Larry Herndon organized the effort, and all were pleased when over 70 fans attended. Immediate plans were made for a follow-up in 1967, this time in Houston. That con drew 124 fans, and had the usual auctions, door prizes, film showings and much trading and selling. They decided to move the next one back to Dallas, with con chairman Tom Reamy handling it. Reamy brought his SF contacts to bear and Fritz Leiber was one of three pro writers attending. The 1968 Southwestern Con was the most impressive yet, with a separate film room and a program of guest speakers. At the time, everyone felt the figure of 160 registered attendees was huge.

Reports of the Southwesterncons, accompanied by numerous photographs, were highlights in later issues of *Star-Studded Comics*. Other highlights were Richard "Grass" Green's popular character Xal-Kor the Human Cat, who appeared in seven issues, and an adaptation of Gardner Fox's *Warrior of Llarn* by Roy Thomas and Sam Grainger. There were editions featuring Aussie fan John Ryan's "Bidgee" column, and a portfolio by Dave Cockrum. The later issues began moving from superhero stories to other genres, especially sword & sorcery. *SSC* also offered strips in the western, horror, war, humor and SF genres. Finally, after a total of 18 issues, the venerable fanzine ended its run in 1972.

Herndon, however, was far from finished from fanzine publishing. He had already branched out with *Remember When*, a general nostalgia fanzine, in 1971, and there was also *Yesterday's Comics* in 1973. The greatest impact was made by the *Nostalgia News*, which began as a regularly published progress report for Dallas's bid for the 1973 World SF convention, and morphed into an adzine with a purported circulation of 5,000 copies (for it catered to members of several fandoms). It was during this time that Larry sold a half-dozen scripts to Warren Publishing that appeared in the magazines *Creepy*, *Eerie* and *Vampirella*. Perhaps the most memorable story was his collaboration with John Severin on "Buffaloed" in *Creepy* #62 (1974).

Larry Herndon opened a nostalgia store, Remember When, in the 1970s, considered one of the first comic book retail stores in North Texas. However, the store sold not just comic books but vintage movie posters, books, paperbacks and pulp magazines. Larry's muscular dystrophy eventually took its toll, and he died in the autumn of 1982, leaving the store to his wife, Sharon.

Dave Herring

(b. 1946)

Dave Herring was the publisher and chief artist of the humor fanzine *Odd* (1964–1967), which featured contributions by his brother Steve, who was primarily a writer. Dave was especially skillful in his mastery of the ditto medium, the process that was used for all but the final issue of *Odd*.

The Herring family lived in Queens when Steve was born in 1943, but had moved to Brooklyn by 1946 when Dave was born. They grew up in Howard Beach. Their father, a native Brooklynite, worked for the New York Telephone Company at their substation near Coney Island. As young boys, the Herring brothers' college-educated mother encouraged their comic book reading by giving them subscriptions to *Walt Disney's Comics and Stories* and *Marge's Little Lulu*. Dave remembers his mother reading Little Lulu stories to him. The brothers also enjoyed *Superman* and other titles, but weren't especially captivated by comics until they discovered Harvey Kurtzman's *Mad*, while it was still in comic book form (probably in late 1953 or 1954, when they were both pre-teens). "It was witty and intelligent and we loved it!" Dave recalled in an interview in *Alter-Ego* #42 (2004).

Dave was already showing incipient signs of drawing ability. *Mad* undoubtedly fanned the flames of his cartooning aspirations. The younger Herring's favorite *Mad* artists were Bill Elder, Wally Wood and Jack Davis. Of the three, Dave's own artwork would come to most resemble that of Wood. The boys created their own knock-off of *Mad* that they called *Odd*. Both wrote and drew, though over a period of a couple of years—before the *Odd* fanzine appeared—it became apparent that Steve was a better writer than artist, and that Dave was a cartoonist of particular ability. Their earliest efforts at producing *Odd*, in 1957 and 1959, were of the pencil and crayon variety, with only one copy produced. Then came the discovery of comic fandom. (They never were aware of "spoof" fandom that had been a kind of an off-shoot from EC fandom in the late 1950s and early 1960s, with fanzines like *Wild* and *Smudge*.)

In the spring of 1964, when Dave was a senior at the High School of Art and Design in New York City, he met another comics fan named Marvin Wolfman. It was Wolfman who showed Herring examples of the fanzines being published at the time, such as *RBCC*, *Fighting Hero Comics* and others. Some had amateur comic strips, and Dave was especially drawn to those printed via spirit duplication, where a multi-colored effect could be achieved. He and Steve immediately decided to launch a run of *Odd* magazine to be printed and sold through *RBCC* to the members of the burgeoning comic fan movement.

Steve Herring, Jay Kinney and Dave Herring

Because they didn't own a ditto machine, which would cost $75 or more, *Odd* #1 and part of #2 were printed by the labor-intensive hectograph process, which resulted in very few copies being made of #1. The second issue was converted to ditto printing part of the way through, for the Herrings had scraped together the funds to buy a spirit duplicator, which could produce copies very quickly, and in larger numbers, than hectograph. This acquisition coincided with their family moving to Natick, Massachusetts, after Dave's high school graduation. All their fan publishing and related activity from *Odd* #3 onward occurred between the time of Dave's graduation to the time he was drafted into the U.S. Army and was shipped overseas to Vietnam in 1967.

The format of *Odd* was based on that of the *Mad* comic books: each issue consisted of two or three parodies of comic book or strip characters, along with some one-page gags, advertising parodies, and some text features, including an editorial (written in the jocular jargon familiar to readers of *Mad*) as well as a letter column. Often the strips were their own version of comics *Mad* had parodied, such as their "Souperman" in *Odd* #1. The subscription page in #1 had a typical *Odd* gag, showing a man flushing himself down the toilet, saying "Good bye cruel world! I missed the latest issue of *Odd* and I can't live without it!"

An example of *Odd* in full flower can by found in a rundown of the contents of #9 (May 1965) which consisted of 40 pages which sold for 20 cents per copy. The photo offset cover features the Fantastic Four as sideshow freaks drawn by Dave. The ditto interior begins with the editorial, followed by a letters page, then a "Mister Blister" strip written by Dave and drawn by Jay Kinney, "The Man From C.O.U.S.I.N.S." written by Marv Wolfman with art by Dave, cover parodies of "Defective Comics" and "The Amusing Spineless-Man," a three-page Captain Marvel parody strip by Steve Sabo, the "Fearsome Foursome" parody by Dave (where the FF meet the zine's mascot, the Odd Bomber), an article on *Mad* #8 including an excellent tracing of the cover by Dave, and a back cover featuring daily-type strips by Dave, Jay Kinney, Steve Sabo and Steve Herring (an episode of Steve's popular "Poor Mouses" feature). Jay Kinney not only contributed to *Odd*, but published his own similar fanzine *Nope*, which was printed on the Herrings' ditto machine.

The final issue of *Odd* was the only one printed by photo offset throughout, and was designed to be a sample that Dave could send to professional publishers in New York. "[#12] was our last issue primarily because it was time for me to get on with my life and find serious employment somewhere," he recalled in *Alter Ego*. "We wanted to go out with a bang. And in the back of my mind, one of the reasons for doing this was because—in my naïveté—I thought this would impress publishers and comic book companies and help me get a job somewhere. For the most part, I got nicely worded rejection letters." While Dave himself is self-deprecating ("I just wasn't that good; let's face it"), his talent is plainly evident in *Odd* #12, first with the excellent artwork on the "Lost in Space" parody, but also in "The Count" (scripted by Steve) which was very reminiscent of the *Mad* comic book strips like "Outer Sanctum."

Not long after *Odd* #12 was published, Dave was drafted in the U.S. Army and sent to Vietnam. After Dave's military discharge, he returned to the art field in 1969 with "Jonny Galaxie" in Gary Acord's *Wotta World*, and a few things of a more adult nature for the underground comix (appearing in *Pro Junior* and *Bizarre Sex*), but after that, he retired from fandom. He eventually worked fulltime in the art department of a newspaper which utilized his art ability to a degree. After that, he did graphics for a news magazine, and then became interested in computer graphics. This was the basis for his successful business doing graphics and web design, animation and other multimedia projects.

Steve Herring had more or less dropped out of being involved in the later issues of *Odd*, because he had gone off to Coe College in Cedar Rapids, Iowa. He later obtained a Bachelor's degree from Framingham State College. He has worked in the software world for his entire career, doing business and technical writing. "All very boring, not much opportunity for humor," Steve commented. "I have pursued a career in history, local history, and I've had the opportunity to write two books in that area, and I'm very proud and pleased to be able to do that and to contribute to my community." He has also dabbled in mystery writing, having had stories published in *Alfred Hitchcock Magazine*.

Today, Dave Herring makes his home in Ashland, Massachusetts, and Steve Herring lives in nearby Framingham. Neither of them reads comic books anymore.

Roger Hill
(b. 1948)

Roger Hill became known as co-originator with Jerry Weist of the fanzine *Squa Tront*, which brought a serious appreciation of EC Comics to fandom of the 1960s. *Squa Tront* was the most impressive EC fanzine published, due not only to its editorial matter, but its professional printing which allowed for the inclusion of rare art and photographs. *Squa Tront* published three never before published EC 3-D stories for the first time.

Wichita-born Roger Hill first exhibited the collecting impulse when he and his brother discovered Jack Davis's Topps gum cards, Bill Gaines' *Mad* magazine and Forry Ackerman's *Famous Monsters of Filmland* magazine all around the same time in 1959. In September 1963, he met Jerry Weist for the first time when Forry Ackerman came through Wichita as part of his famous 6,000 mile coast-to-coast trek from California to New York to meet *FM* readers and fans. At Ackerman's request, Weist had helped organize all the local Wichita fans ahead of time to meet at his home when Forry came through town. Unbeknownst to Hill, Weist had been publishing two monster fanzines, *Movieland Monsters* and *Nightmare,* and was president of the Forry Ackerman Fan Club. Roger had been contributing covers and interior artwork to an out-of-state monster fanzine called *The Monster Journal.* Weist and Hill became fast friends right away during Ackerman's visit.

In the field of comic books, Hill had discovered *Magnus Robot Fighter* and *Space Family Robinson* with their first issues and was buying pretty much any Gold Key comic with a painted cover. Soon after, he discovered *Amazing Spider-Man, Fantastic Four* and other Marvel and DC comic titles. Then, one fateful day, around 1964,

Jerry Weist and Roger Hill

Jerry showed him his first EC comic book. In *Squa Tront* #4 (1970), Roger wrote, "Jerry ... dropped by one day with the first EC that he or I had ever seen. It was a copy of *Panic* #7 and my first impression was that this EC comic really wasn't too great." Then Roger saw his first New Trend issue. "[Jerry] had just received in the mail *Haunt of Fear* #15 which he had bought from a fellow in Michigan. Wham!! The outstanding artwork and excellent story content of the EC comics hit me like a ton of bricks. Graham Ingels and Wally Wood became two of my all-time favorites." From that point on, Hill and Weist collected every EC comic book they could get their hands on, buying back issues from Phil Seuling, Bill Thailing and others. It wasn't until 1968 that Roger finally completed his EC collection, except for a few of the funny animal "Pre-Trend" titles.

Hill and Weist started getting involved in the burgeoning comics fandom movement in 1965. Unaware of the erstwhile EC fanzines of the 1950s, the first EC zine they saw was Rich Hauser's *Spa Fon*. A year or so after Jerry and Roger met (through a local used bookstore connection), they met another Wichita fan named Robert Barrett. Barrett, who was a little older than the boys, had been a long time Edgar Rice Burroughs and Frazetta collector. He informed them that EC artist Reed Crandall, then drawing comics for Tower and Warren Publications, was living in Wichita at the time. Hill and Weist were thrilled to discover an actual EC artist living in town. Since they were too young to drive, and didn't own cars yet, Barrett offered to pick them up and drive them over to Reed's place for a visit.

A few months later, when the *Spa Fon* editors—Rich Hauser, Helmut Mueller and Wally Reichert—came to town to visit, they all drove over for Crandall's place with Roger, Jerry and Bob. The group was able to watch Reed working on Flash Gordon art for King Features. Hill remembered, "We all had a great time, and after the *Spa Fon* boys left, we were all hyped up, and Jerry came up with his idea. He said, 'Let's do an EC fanzine. We'll call it *Squa Tront*!' Naturally, after *Spa Fon*, what else could you call it? In fact, we always kind of thought of *Spa Fon* as our sister publication." Roger, an aspiring artist, had already been working on a Wally Wood–influenced science fiction illustration to hang on his wall at home. When Jerry saw it, he said, "That's it! This will be the cover on our first issue of *Squa Tront*!" Bob Barrett hand-lettered the *Squa Tront* logo, wrote a contribution called "The Frazetta Collector," and provided other lettering for that first issue. Jerry got Reed Crandall involved also at some point providing art for the fanzine.

Jerry did most of the typing and layouts for that first issue, then from issue #2 on, Roger's mother volunteered to help out and took over that chore using an IBM typewriter that made it easier to justify the margins. When the first issue was finally ready to go, they had 500 copies printed up just in time to take to the 1967 World Science Fiction convention in New York City. Hal Foster and Frank Frazetta were lined up to be the guests of honor at the Edgar Rice Burroughs Dum-Dum meeting that year. (This was the annual get together of the Burroughs Bibliophiles that was held every year in conjunction with the World Con.) Frazetta brought most of his original paintings to the con for display only, but was selling "Johnny Comet" daily strip originals for $25, and Sunday pages for $75. This was also the first convention that Jeff Jones, Michael Kaluta and Bernie Wrightson attended, and the boys got to meet them, too. At that same convention, Roger and Jerry also met Phil Seuling, who was set up at a table selling pulps and comics. The highlight, however, was their special visit with Bill Gaines at the EC *Mad* offices. Bill invited the boys over to his penthouse apartment for the evening where they first viewed his sealed boxes of 12 copies each of every EC comic book ever published. Then it was out on the town for an Italian dinner and a special Bill Gaines tour of New York City in his gold-colored Cadillac. This included a brief stop in front of the old EC offices at 225 LaFayette Street.

Jerry and Roger were able to sell a lot of copies of *Squa Tront* #1, and before too long

Weist went back to press for a second edition of 500 more copies. Unlike the first edition, which had loose sheets stapled between a wraparound cover, this edition was saddle-stitched.

In due time, these Midwestern EC Fan-Addicts made contact with most of the former EC staff, and issues #2 through #4 were loaded with rare artwork and personal reminiscences, interviews, and opinion pieces. Roger did the first interview ever conducted with EC artist Johnny Craig. *Squa Tront* became a fanzine of the highest quality, not so much for the writing but because of the zine's intimate pieces on the lives of certain EC pros, and for the sheer quality of the artwork—much of it unseen before—that could be found within (and on) its covers. The material on Frank Frazetta and Harvey Kurtzman was especially outstanding. Hill served as "overseas correspondent" to the zine when he enlisted in the U.S. Navy after high school and wound up in Vietnam for 18 months. "We will always be indebted to Bill Gaines for letting us reproduce so much great EC art and other material in those issues," Hill recalled. "He was the most generous publisher we had ever met and gave us free rein on using EC copyrighted material. He was EC's biggest fan, and loved what we were doing with *Squa Tront*."

The four issues of *Squa Tront* published from 1967 to 1970 comprised a sterling achievement, but they were just the beginning of Roger's lifelong pursuit of writing and documenting the history of the comics. Today, he has a special interest in seeking out the history behind other comic artists who never received much public acclaim. He explained recently, "I've been working at a hectic pace for the past 20 years tracking down information on some of the more obscure horror comic artists and pulp artists who worked from the 1930s to the 1960s, and never received much recognition. I've managed to dig up a lot of important information that would otherwise have been lost to the ages, and will incorporate this information into various books I'm working on." Hill's other interests have gone far beyond those early years of collecting monster magazines and ECs. Today he's into space-related toys from the 1950s, horror and science fiction movie posters, lobby cards, pressbooks, stills, pulp magazines, sheet music, paperback books, gum cards, as well as all kinds of original book illustration and comic art. Roger recently collaborated with his old buddy Jerry Weist on writing an overview summary for a new book just published on the life and career of the "Dean of Science Fiction Artists," Frank R. Paul. He has also completed writing a book on comic artist illustrator Reed Crandall and is now involved with two other book projects, one on EC artist Johnny Craig, and the other on pulp illustrator and comic artist Matt Fox.

In 1985, Hill founded the *CFA-APA* (Comic and Fantasy Art Amateur Press Association) and served as Editor for the first five years and today remains an active member. In 1996 he organized and curated an exhibit of over 200 original pieces of comic art called "One Hundred Years of American Comics," which went on tour throughout Japan for a year. In more recent times, he wrote extensively for *Comic Book Marketplace* and *Alter Ego*, and was Art Director for the book on Wally Wood called *Against the Grain* published by TwoMorrows. His own *EC Fan-Addict Fanzine* (July 2004) brought back memories of *Squa Tront* in the 1960s. Roger Hill has projects in the works which will keep him busy, and contributing even more to fandom, for many years to come.

Robert Jennings

(b. 1943)

A popular fanzine publisher, Robert Jennings promoted the idea of longer articles about comic book characters and features. As he memorably put it, "If something is worth writing about, it's worth writing about at length and in detail." His publication, *Comic World*, lasted from 1963 to 1979, in three different phases. Jennings also wrote dozens of fanzine reviews for his own and other fan mags.

Bob Jennings (who was always known as Robert in his publications) was born in Nashville, Tennessee. His father was an entomologist in the Agriculture Department of the State of Tennessee. In 1959, at 16 years old, Jennings became active in science fiction fandom. It would be two more years before he became involved in comic fandom, after being shown a copy of *Alter-Ego* by a friend. Because his first fannish activity was in SF fandom, he was familiar with the traditions of that group, and brought some of those attitudes and practices to comicdom: outspokenness, a devotion to voluminous letter-writing, valuing long well-written articles, indirectly giving Jerry Bails the idea of an "apa" (amateur press alliance), and filling many a fanzine page with letters of comment and fanzine reviews.

By the end of 1962, Robert Jennings had published the first issue of *Comic World*, a mimeographed fan magazine devoted to articles and information about comics of the past, especially the Golden Age of Comics, as well as letters from readers and advertisements. By far the bulk of each issue was devoted to one long article, running 15 to 20 pages, in keeping with Jennings' espousal of such pieces. *CW* #1 actually featured two long articles: Bob's examination of the western hero The Ghost Rider, and Tom Fagan's article on The Black Canary. The next six issues, appearing over the next two years, offered similarly ambitious articles by Glen Johnson ("Skyman," "The Face" and "The Seven Soldiers of Victory"), Raymond Miller ("Captain Marvel Junior, the Early Years") and Jennings himself ("The Yellow Claw"). There were also articles on serials by Ron Haydock, horror comics by Jennings, and other secondary items. Almost as important as the articles, however, was the "Information Center" feature, where Jennings—with the help of other fans—attempted to answer questions about specific comic book runs, who wrote or drew a feature, and so forth. In 1963 and 1964, fans were struggling to get a handle on the multitude of back issues that were available to collect, and *Comic World* contributed significantly to the information pool.

By his own admission, Robert Jennings' fanzines had one continuing weakness. As he put it in a recent interview, "it's not for nothing that I was known as the 'King of the Typo.'" There were many and numerous spelling errors throughout *Comic World*. This flaw was especially frustrating for readers, who recognized the intelligence in the fanzine's printed matter, yet bemoaned the plethora of textual errata. Jennings was aware of this, and gradually improved. Fans' support for *Comic World* wasn't seriously jeopardized by this weakness; it always had a healthy circulation by fanzine standards.

Besides *Comic World* and its sister publication, an adzine Bob published called *The Comic Advertising Review*, Jennings' influence was felt in other corners of fandom. "I contributed to many other fanzines," he stated recently. "I also wrote tons of letters to fanzines, did review columns for fanzines, opinion sections for fanzines, helped lay out fanzines, helped edit and produce other fans' efforts, and encouraged people to publish and write for fanzines. Fanzines and letters were the heart of the hobby. I also wrote articles for some fanzines that never saw print, which was very frustrating." He regularly corresponded with DC editor Julius Schwartz, and pressured ACG editor Richard Hughes to put superheroes in *Adventures into the Unknown* (Nemesis) and *Forbidden Worlds* (Magicman).

The first era of *Comic World* ended in 1966 when Robert Jennings was inducted into the U.S. military. When he returned two years later, another Nashville-based fan, Harry Thomas, encouraged him to bring back the venerable fanzine. Thus, with covers drawn by Thomas, a new photo-offset version of *Comic World* picked up the number with #8, which appeared in November 1969. The first of these offered Bob's impressive 40-page article on Blackhawk, which was very well received across fandom. Jennings pumped out six more fine issues in rapid succession, until his job took him to Nashua, New Hampshire. Before leaving Tennessee, he had contributed a great deal of data to Bob Overstreet, a local fan who was putting together a comic book price guide. "I provided a lot of indexes and research material on companies, history, comics produced, issue runs and characters," Jennings recalled.

A demanding job and getting married kept Bob away from fanzine publishing for almost ten years, but somehow *Comic World* would not die. It returned for another eight issues, beginning in 1976. "The problem was that suddenly I had a shortage of writers," he remembered. "I wrote major parts of the next six issues. Harry Thomas came back on board with much new artwork, and I had a lot of help from Alan Hutchinson, an extremely talented artist and a clever cartoonist who I had met through the SFPA apa. I eventually found new dedicated fan writers. I also reprinted some of the articles from the original mimeographed issues which, to my astonishment, were selling for healthy amounts of money." This run continued up through 1979 when the final issue, *Comic World* #21, came off the presses. The zine ended because he had his hands full with a new collectible-oriented venture.

Jennings had been working for Proctor and Gamble, putting in a lot of hours, and found he had grown to hate it. He quit and opened a combination science fiction book store and comic book shop called the Fabulous Fiction Book Store. Running his own business kept him so busy that he was never able to get back to publishing again, though he always had plans for more issues. The store continued to the year 2000, when Jennings realized it was time to leave the brick-and-mortar shop behind, and continue the business via mail order only. "This turned out to be one of the smartest things I ever did," he declared recently.

As a collector, however, his interest has never waned. He has always collected multiple forms of popular media, especially science fiction literature, comic books, comic strips, old-time radio programs, dime novels, boys series books, and motion picture serials. He still buys and reads comic books, though he writes few letters of comment anymore. As he put it, "The Internet has opened up more lines of communication, but frankly it has not really helped open better communication. I find that there are many more jerks out there than ever, and comments often turn vitriolic very soon. On the other hand, more and better research on the history of comics and creators is being done these days. If comics as a literary form manage to survive, something I am no longer sure of, there will be a solid historical record for future generations to refer to."

G. B. Love

(1939–2001)

G. B. Love's *Rocket's Blast-Comicollector* played an incalculably important role in the founding and continuance of comicdom. *RBCC* was the meeting place of fandom, a juggernaut of an adzine that had something to interest everyone, including regular columns by some of the hobby's most knowledgeable fans and collectors. From Love's base in Miami,

Florida, he published the legendary fanzine for over 13 years, as well as dozens of other ancillary publications. From the mid–1970s until his passing, G. B. was a central figure in Houston fandom.

The year 1961 saw the birth of *Alter-Ego, Comic Art, The Comicollector* and *On the Drawing Board*, all fairly impressive publications in their day. Another amateur publication debuted that same year, one that would have at least as much importance for the fledgling fan movement: a brief four-page zine called *The Rocket's Blast*. Only six to eight copies of the first issue were produced, using carbon paper. There could have been no humbler beginning for this acorn which would one day grow into a mighty oak.

G. B. Love (left) with Howard Siegel.

The Rocket's Blast editor, Gordon Belljohn Love, was born in 1939 in Atlanta, Georgia. He became a comic fan early with his love for the original Captain Marvel comics in the 1940s. He dreamed of performing feats of derring-do, but, unlike other boys, even modest feats of physical prowess would remain outside his grasp. Love had had cerebral palsy since birth, when doctors found certain motor functions of his brain had been damaged.

"I was a little boy the first time I read comic books," Love told reporter John De Groot in an interview that appeared in *The Miami Herald* in 1971. "That's when comic books are magic. You're young. You're weak. You're smaller than anyone else. The whole world is bigger and stronger than you are. You have to deal with the neighborhood bully and a lot of giant adults. You read about superheroes. You fantasize. They're super-strong. They're all-powerful. You name it and a superhero has the power to do it … to achieve all that man has thought of in his wildest moments." His father, who worked at Royal Bakery in Miami, was quoted in that same article: "We came down [to Miami] about 12 years ago. I took [Gordon] around to the rehabilitation people and they gave him tests. They said there was just nothing they could do for him. Goodwill offered him a job for $25 a week, but he wouldn't take that."

G. B. Love had a great deal more to offer than charity make-work, even if his cerebral palsy made telephone communication an uphill battle, and he could only type by clutching a pencil in one hand and striking the keys of an electric typewriter with the eraser end, laboriously, one by one. In an interview done for *The Golden Age of Comic Fandom* in 1994, Love recounted the beginnings of his fanzine. "[In 1961] I was looking for something to occupy my time, and hoped to develop something that might eventually become profitable. My original idea was to combine SF and comics in a fanzine, but I quickly dropped the SF and concentrated on my first love, comic books. I picked the name *The Rocket's Blast* myself but I really don't remember how I came up with it." A letter from Love printed in *Mystery in Space* announced his intention to start a club and put out a newsletter. "At the time I produced the first issue of *RB*, I was unaware of anyone else trying it too. After I began publishing, I think the first fanzine I discovered was *Alter-Ego*." Love published under the aegis of "The S.F.C.A." This originally stood for "Science Fiction and Comic Association," but was changed to "South Florida Comic Association." In any case, it was merely the name of Love's company.

The Rocket's Blast was not, at first, primarily devoted to ads. The comics-oriented articles were generally brief and of variable quality. Some were profiles of Golden Age characters; others consisted of commentary on new comics. None of the first eight issues exceeded five legal-sized pages. When signs of interest in his publication surfaced, Gordon switched to mimeograph printing so that he could produce more copies; fewer than ten issues later, he switched again, this time to spirit duplicator, for it was a much friendlier medium for artists to use. By the 18th issue, the circulation had topped 200 copies per issue, and the ad content was definitely the dominant part of the mag. The reason was simple: Love demonstrated he was able to pump out issues frequently, often monthly or at least eight to ten times a year, which was far more frequently than any other amateur publication. This was because, for him, it was his "full-time job"; in fact, with the advertising revenue, it became modestly profitable. This further spurred him to keep the issues coming. Gaining notice for its frequency, advertisers recognized it as a way to reach the members of burgeoning fandom, thus *The Rocket's Blast* was transformed into an adzine with a few text features to provide a modicum of reading material. It proved to be a mix that worked well. When the print run grew beyond what was possible for ditto printing, Love switched back to mimeo for a few years, and finally to photo offset.

What really cemented RB's position was its merger with its only competitor, *The Comicollector*. The editorial reins of *The Comicollector* had passed from Jerry Bails (#1–6), Ronn Foss (#7–12) to Biljo White (#13–15). White was more of a creative soul, not temperamentally suited to the publication of an advertising zine. He approached G. B. Love with the idea of taking it over. Gordon merged it with *The Rocket's Blast,* and *The Rocket's Blast-Comicollector* was born. Since the title was rather ungainly, it became well known among fans as simply *RBCC.* Love also agreed to honor all *CC* subscriptions, thus absorbing *CC's* customer base. With #29 (April 1964), the first *RBCC* debuted, with the cover (of the Golden Age Daredevil by Saunders) sporting the blurb, "For the first time in fandom history you now get two of fandom's greatest zines for the price of only one." At first, even G. B. Love was daunted by the amount of work involved (simply the amount of printing and collating was staggering) and was forced to briefly go to a bi-monthly schedule. He remembered, "I usually worked on the *RBCC* from about 8 P.M. to about 2 or 3 A.M. I found I got more done working at night. I lived with my parents at the time and my set-up took about two-and-a-half rooms." Soon he returned to a five-week or monthly schedule. The circulation grew to 700, then 800, and in 1966 topped 1,000. By Love's own reckoning, he received 400 inquiries from a plug in *Justice League of America* #30 (September 1964).

To be sure, *RBCC* continued to have its shortcomings. Aside from the typos and strikeovers, Gordon Love did not have the finesse of a Foss or White. The layouts were functional, and no more than that. However, *RBCC* was dependable, the ads were readable, and there was enough in the way of columns and letters to provide some reading matter. Most fans subscribed to *RBCC,* and virtually every fanzine advertised in its pages. The switch to photo-offset printing by issue #50 (early 1967) relieved G. B. Love of the task of collating and stapling, for he had assembled the ditto and mimeo issues entirely on his own! Although he had the part-time assistance of his close friend Andy Warner, Love continued doing 95 percent of the work until 1970, when he hired James Van Hise as his Assistant Editor. (It wasn't just *RBCC,* either. The SFCA also published numerous fanzines, including *The Golden Age, the RBCC Specials, Fighting Hero Comics* and various specials and other mail-order offerings.)

Love was always trying to find ways to enlarge fandom. In 1965, he'd written an "Open Letter" to fans, asking them to list the addresses of newsstands and stores in their local area that carried comics, so that he could attempt to convince them to sell *RBCC* right next to the comics. This effort proved to be unsuccessful, but by dint of sheer effort, Love was able to push the envelope further. He was the first person in fandom to advertise in a Marvel comic book on their classified page. His ad was for *The Illustrated Comic Collectors Handbook* and it cost him about $350, a lot of money at the time. After Jerry Bails, G. B. Love deserves credit for bringing more people into comicdom in the 1960s than any other fan (though the efforts of others in this direction should not be denigrated). At the time, a few grumbled that Love was only interested in increasing the circulation of *RBCC*, but that automatically led to gains for fandom across the board since virtually every fanzine and fan organization advertised in its pages.

Perhaps as a result of the large circulation, *RBCC* attracted a staff of some of the most talented cover artists in fandom. By the time the conversion to photo-offset printing was complete, dazzling work began to appear by John G. Fantucchio, Don Newton, Berni Wright-son, Steve Fabian, Robert Kline and many others. Newton and Fantucchio, in particular, were mainstays.

In addition to his fanzine publishing, G. B. Love was active in the fan communities where he lived. He organized the first comic book conventions in South Florida, beginning in the late 1960s, in the Fireman's Hall in Coral Gables, and later at various American Legion Halls in Coconut Grove. Local comic fans Jim Van Hise, Andy Warner, John Ellis, and Rick McCoy (among others) helped. A frequent guest was former Captain Marvel artist C. C. Beck, who had retired to Miami. Then, after attending a comicon in Texas and finding great acceptance among the leading lights of Lone Star fandom, G. B. Love moved to Houston in 1974. He sold The S.F.C.A. to James Van Hise, who had worked with him for many years on the magazine. *RBCC* continued under Van Hise until 1981.

Love plunged into the larger fan community in Houston (which he described as "a real hotbed of fan activity"), and helped organize more conventions. With best friend Earl Blair Jr., Love launched *Trek: The Magazine for Star Trek Fans*. Later he co-edited a series of *Star Trek* books entitled *The Best of Trek*. That all this was accomplished by someone whose speech could be understood by few, who couldn't hold a pen to write his name, or walk with ease, is a tribute to Gordon Love's determination and love of fandom.

In November of 2000, G. B. Love was seriously injured in a car accident and never fully recovered. He died on January 17, 2001. He was 61 years old.

Dick Lupoff
(b. 1935)

An award-winning science fiction and mystery writer, Dick Lupoff (and his wife, Patricia) contributed greatly to the instigation of a fandom based on the superhero comic books of the 1940s. Their appearance as Captain and Mary Marvel at the 1960 World Science Fiction Convention excited interest in those erstwhile heroes, and their fanzine, *Xero*, launched the series "All in Color for a Dime," which was the first major attempt to chronicle Golden Age comic books.

Richard Allen Lupoff was born in Brooklyn, New York. His father, a Certified Public Accountant, found himself working in a food-processing business during the Depression and continued in that field most of his life. Dick grew up in the New York area. His mother passed away when the boy was beginning elementary school; since their father's job required a great deal of travel, Dick and his brother Jerrold were educated in boarding schools, including the Bordentown Military Institute, which Dick hated.

As a boy, Dick learned to read by reading comic books. He read the adventures of Captain Marvel from its beginning in *Whiz Comics*, and other superhero comics from the early 1940s from DC, Marvel, Fox and the rest. He was introduced to science fiction when he read Jules Verne's *20,000 Leagues Under the Sea*, and when he was given a copy of *Amazing Stories* in 1951, Lupoff discovered SF fandom from a column in the magazine. "I sent for some fanzines and was very taken with them, because I already had decided I wanted to be a writer," Dick recalled. "Once I saw these fanzines, they looked to me like a sort of halfway station between just schoolboy stuff that you write in your notebook and turn in for a grade, and real professional publications." Soon he was sending letters and articles to zine editors. He received his first taste of professional publishing when he provided prep school sports information to major papers such as the *New York Times,* the *New York Herald-Tribune,* the *Philadelphia Inquirer* and others. They paid by the column inch; a one-paragraph story would net the princely sum of 65 cents.

He received a degree in Journalism from the University of Miami in 1956, and then served two years in the Army. While stationed in Indianapolis, Dick met a college student named Patricia Loring on a blind date. (See entry for Pat Lupoff.) They were married in 1958, and were soon living in an apartment in New York City, where they became involved in an SF club called the Futurians. When a Futurians' picnic in a park was scuttled, due to dire warnings of an impending "rumble" by a member of a local gang, the incident inspired a four-page fan publication called *The Rumble.* After *The Rumble,* co-published by Walter Breen and Dick Lupoff, Dick and Pat thought it would be fun to publish their own fanzine. They decided to call it *Xero.*

Though *Xero* was ostensibly a science fiction fanzine, it was, in truth, a publication devoted to many aspects of popular culture. It covered areas of interest that were shared by many SF fans, including pulp fiction, movie serials, contemporary films, rock and roll, and most significantly, the history of comic books. The lengthiest feature in the first issue (which appeared in September 1960) was the first entry in a proposed series called "All in Color For a Dime," which was titled "The Big Red Cheese." In it, Dick Lupoff took a nostalgic look back at his discovery of Fawcett's Captain Marvel in *Whiz Comics* as a boy in Florida, and various aspects (written entirely from memory) of the often whimsical tales of the beloved character

(PHOTOGRAPH BY ANDREW PORTER)

Pat and Dick Lupoff

called by his nemesis Dr. Sivana "the Big Red Cheese." This article inspired a huge influx of letters from those who received the 90 copies of *Xero* #1 that were distributed by the Lupoffs at the 1960 World Science Fiction Convention in Pittsburgh. This reaction was undoubtedly amplified by their appearance costumed as Captain and Mary Marvel at the convention masquerade. The reaction to their appearance and "The Big Red Cheese" was volcanic, and the editors soon had volunteers lining up to write subsequent entries in the "All in Color For a Dime" series.

Those entries were "The Spawn of M. C. Gaines" by Ted White, "A Bunch of Swell Guys" by Jim Harmon, "O.K. Axis, Here We Come!" by Don Thompson, "The Several Soldiers of Victory" by Dick Lupoff, "Me to Your Leader Take" by Dick Ellington, "The Wild Ones" by Don Thompson, "The Education of Victor Fox" by Richard Kyle, "Captain Billy's Whiz-Gang" by Roy Thomas, and "Sparky Watts and the Big Shots" by Richard Kyle. In addition, there were several addenda and many letters published in response to the various articles. Taken together, the significance of "All in Color For a Dime" is simply this: the entries constituted the first concerted attempt to chronicle the history of the Golden Age of comic books. Incomplete as they were, and hardly comprehensive, these ten articles cemented the central role history must give to *Xero* in the founding of comic book fandom. Most of the entries were reprinted (in slightly revised form) in *All in Color For a Dime* (Arlington House, 1970), the first book devoted to the history of the medium. (A sequel followed titled *The Comic-Book Book.)*

Many other writers appeared in the pages of *Xero* in article or letter form, including Harlan Ellison, Roger Ebert and James Blish. When Captain Marvel scribe Otto Binder received a complimentary copy of *Xero* #1 with "The Big Red Cheese" he wrote a lengthy letter in response, with his own reflections on the experience of writing so many Marvel Family comic books. *Xero* also offered pieces that proved to be embryonic versions of later, much expanded works. Lin Carter's "Notes on Tolkien," for example, was enlarged into a book called *Understanding Tolkien and The Lord of the Rings.*

Xero ended with its 10th issue (in Spring 1963) because the magazine had grown to unwieldy proportions. "The actual page count was up ... around 100 per issue," Dick explained. "It was getting very elaborate. We were farming out printing jobs, and having gatefold artwork, and multi-colored mimeography, and so forth. It was a lot of work. We decided fairly early on, somewhere around the seventh issue, that we were going to cut it off." Lupoff also felt they had taken it as far as it could go unless they were prepared to publish it professionally. They weren't. Lupoff's dream of becoming a professional writer had not been forgotten, and Pat was pregnant with their second child.

Dick Lupoff broke into the professional book-writing field with *Edgar Rice Burroughs: Master of Adventure*, which grew out of his experience editing ERB books for Canaveral Press. After that came his first novel *One Million Centuries* (1967), then *Sacred Locomotive Flies* (1971) and *Into the Aether* (1974). Among his best-known books are *Circumpolar!* (1984) and *Countersolar!* (1985). He eventually wrote dozens of books, mainly in the science fiction and mystery fiction fields. His Hobart Lindsey and Marvia Plum murder mysteries, beginning with *The Comic Book Killer* (1988), have proved especially popular.

Of the experience publishing *Xero* from a personal standpoint, Dick Lupoff recently wrote, "As a hobby experience it was great fun, and winning the Hugo was a great thrill, but it was essentially equivalent to some kid who gets involved in hot-rod fandom and wins a golden trophy at a hot-rod show, or some hobby trout fisherman who wins the tournament for the biggest trout of the year. It's a thrill to win, I don't mean to deprecate that, but it's not a life-changing experience. It was fun. But that's all it was."

In terms of its influence on fandom, however, *Xero*'s legacy was mighty. Though Jerry

Bails had planned to publish an amateur newsletter about the revivals of the DC heroes before he saw *Xero* in February of 1961, the sight of the Lupoffs' first two or three issues inspired Bails to enlarge his vision for what became *Alter-Ego* #1. *Xero* also played a part in encouraging Don and Maggie Thompson to launch their own comics fanzine *Comic Art*, also published in 1961. The headline feature of *Comic Art* #1 was an essay by Dick Lupoff called "Re-Birth," which recounted his discovery of all the latent interest in comic books among science fiction fans and others. That same essay contains the earliest known instance of comic books' first great era being referred to as "their golden age."

Pat Lupoff
(b. 1937)

Pat Lupoff was Mary Marvel to her husband Dick's Captain Marvel at the 1960 World Science Fiction convention's masquerade, an appearance that inspired nostalgia for comics of the 1940s. As co-publisher of the legendary fanzine *Xero*, which launched "All in Color for a Dime," Pat contributed articles of her own, and edited the lengthy, star-studded letter columns that became an important part of each issue.

Born Patricia Enid Loring in 1937, she grew up in Manhattan. Her father was a lawyer who went into the metal fabrication business, and did very well with it. A voracious reader from an early age, she liked a wide variety of comic books. "I did love all the Captain Marvel comics," she remembered in a 1994 interview. "That was one thing that Dick and I had in common." She also enjoyed "Mary Jane and Sniffles" in *Dell Four-Color*, all the Walt Disney comics, and when she was older, *Classics Illustrated*.

Pat met Dick on a blind date when she was attending summer school in 1957 at Northwestern in Evanston, Illinois. Though she returned to Connecticut College in New London for the regular school year in the fall, Dick visited her, and they were married in August 1958. Shortly after their marriage, they moved to Manhattan, where they joined a science-fiction club, which led to their memorable appearance at the 1960 Worldcon.

Their costumes as the Marvels were hardly up to professional standards. The Mary Marvel costume was basically an oversized red T-shirt, with a yellow lightning bolt stitched on the front, and a yellow scarf around her waist. His was made up on red long johns, with the lightning bolt and sash and other crude accouterments. Their capes were pillowcases. They didn't win any prizes, but garnered the most attention from the onlookers, and made fannish history.

Pat remembers that there was a stigma against comics in those days, if one was an adult. "When we started *Xero*, my interest in comics sort of re-emerged.... Dick and I would go to the corner drug store to buy comics, and we'd make a big pretense of having a child, which at that point we didn't have—'This is for our little boy.' You know, nobody cared! We felt that we couldn't just buy them for ourselves."

Pat Lupoff shared her husband's enthusiasm for fandom and amateur publishing. In addition to her editorial role, she threw herself into the multitude of tasks involved in such an enterprise, and played a major role in *Xero*'s success. The birth of their first child, Kenneth, in 1961, did cut into her time for such things, but editorial efforts in producing the fanzine's voluminous letter columns (titled "Epistolary Intercourse") never flagged. It was she who chose and edited letters from prominent writers and fans such as James Blish, Richard Kyle,

Harlan Ellison, Anthony Boucher, Frederik Pohl, Marion Zimmer Bradley and Donald Wollheim, among many others. In her role as co-editor of *Xero*, Pat became the first female recipient of a Hugo award.

Though *Xero* ended with #10 in 1963, the Lupoffs' involvement in fandom continued. Their close friendship with SF and comics fans Don and Maggie Thompson, made during their earliest days in fandom, has endured to the present day, surviving Don's untimely passing in 1994.

Beginning in the early 1980s, Pat began working as a bookseller at Cody's Books in Berkeley, California. She worked her way up to the position of manager of the children's section, both buying and selling books, and built a small section of the store into a very successful operation. Following the closing of Cody's Books, Pat moved to a similar position at Dark Carnival Bookstore of the Imagination.

Ron Parker
(b. 1940)

Ron Parker was the editor and publisher of *Hoohah!*, described by John Benson in *Squa Tront* #8 as the "legendary fanzine that rose from a very humble beginning in November 1955 to become the best known—and the best—EC fanzine."

In October 1954, the Comics Code Authority was established. This meant the end of EC's horror and SF comics. In desperation, EC came up with its New Direction titles, but the line's days were numbered. The last EC fanzine begun while the publisher was in the comic book business was Ron Parker's *Hoohah!*, which was named after the title of the first story in the first issue of Harvey Kurtzman's *Mad*.

Ronald Parker was a sophomore in high school in Tulsa, Oklahoma, and already a confirmed EC fan, when he saw his first EC fanzine. It was *Potrzebie* #5 (August 1955), published by Larry Clowers of Hot Springs, Arkansas. Parker was immediately seized by the urge to publish his own fanzine, made practical when his parents bought him a mimeograph machine. The other key "enabler" to Ron's plans was his chance meeting of another EC fan named Archie Goodwin in a Tulsa used bookstore; Goodwin, three years Parker's senior, was a gifted cartoonist and writer who was about to begin the fall semester at the University of Oklahoma. After an admittedly crude *Hoohah!* #1, with a print run of fewer than 25 copies (with perhaps as few as six copies initially circulated), Parker was successful in gradually obtaining contributions from other EC fans.

Ron Parker

Hoohah! improved quickly. Despite having to be traced onto mimeo stencils, a difficult task, Archie Goodwin's covers were clever and amusing, and over the course of its ten issues (from 1955 to 1958) the zine presented topnotch work by nearly all the key members of EC fandom. After Goodwin had moved to New York City to attend the Cartoonists and Illustrators School, he brought fellow students Paul Davis and Larry Ivie into the fold, further enhancing the publication's visual offerings. E. Nelson Bridwell, a budding writer and cartoonist (who would become Mort Weisinger's assistant editor at DC Comics in the 1960s) sent Parker material which saw print, as did Ted White, Gene Kelly (not the dancer), Fred von Bernewitz, John Benson, Bhob Stewart and Bill Spicer. In addition to letters from most of its contributors, its letter column also printed missives from Larry Clowers, Buck Coulson, Alan Dodd (a British fan), Jim McCawley, Jr. and one Bill Gaines. A memorable essay in *Hoohah!* was Larry Stark's "Elegy" to EC, which is perhaps the best-known piece of writing to appear in any EC fanzine of the 1950s.

Like *Hoohah!*, other fanzines carried the torch for EC after its demise. Often the focus was on *Mad,* and the work of Harvey Kurtzman in *Trump, Humbug* and (later) *Help.* Some of the fanzines in this period were *Good Lord/Spoof* from Doug Brown (1957), *Frantic* from Joe Moser (1958); *EChhhh!* from Ken Winter (1959); *Squatront* (no relation to the later fanzine and spelled as one word) from Mike Britt (1959); *Fanfare* from Marty Pahls (1959); a number of titles from Sig Case and Gary Delain starting in 1958, including *Gamut;* John Benson's *Image,* which ran from January 1960 to 1962. In addition to their interest in Kurtzman and EC artists, these amateur publications included material on comic strips, paperbacks, movies and occasionally superhero comics.

In 1983, a highly informative history of *Hoohah!* by Ron Parker appeared in John Benson's *Squa Tront* #9, titled "The EC Fanzines Part 5: A Legend in its Time." Inspired by Benson's observation that *Hoohah!* was "one of the few EC fanzines that could bear extensive reprinting," and further urging by Benson, Parker began considering the idea of a compilation from those nearly impossible to find fanzines. (No more than 50 copies of any issue were distributed. Copies of *Hoohah!*, or, indeed, any of the early EC fanzines, are among the rarest collector's items in the world of comics fanzines.) *Hoohah! The Best of EC's Finest Fanzine,* published in 1984, showed that John Benson was right; the material proved that Parker's fanzine had offered much that was intelligent, charming, and humorous.

To quote from Ron's article in *Squa Tront* #9:

> There's one thing I'll always fondly recall from those days of stenciling, mimeographing, stapling and mailing out every copy. And that's the simple fact that everyone involved, whether it was Parker trying to pay his paper bill or Goodwin wondering where his next hot dog was coming from, Kelly stapling *Checklist* ads to telephone poles or Ivie and White wondering why the magazine's size kept changing; we all had one common purpose. And we were fortunate enough to experience EC when it was a living entity, and we had a lot of fun living with it, and a lot of pain dying with it. However briefly, EC was once ours.
>
> And we had fun.
>
> Oh God, how we did have fun...

Although Ron Parker has chiefly made his living as an accountant, writing continued to be an avocation. He sold scripts to Warren magazines *Creepy* and *Eerie,* and became a well-known columnist and editor of several prominent publications devoted to thoroughbred horse racing. His friend Archie Goodwin became an immensely successful comic book writer and editor for Warren Publishing, Marvel Comics and DC Comics until his demise in 1998.

At the time Ron published the *Hoohah!* reprint collection, he was living in Oakland, California. Today he makes his home in Paris, Kentucky, and works as the general manager of a local cemetery. His wife, Ellen, publishes a monthly newsletter on thoroughbred horses.

Derrill Rothermich

(b. 1945)

Derrill Rothermich was best known as the editor of *The Comic Reader* who assumed the publishing mantle from Jerry Bails' successor at the helm of that important fanzine, Glen Johnson.

Rothermich was born on February 15, 1945, in Fort Worth, Texas. Within a few months of his birth, his parents moved to St. Charles, Missouri, where Derrill grew up. A comic book fan from an early age, he became involved in fandom about the time he entered the University of Missouri in Rolla, Missouri, in 1963. Rothermich was a student at the School of Mines and Metallurgy. His collecting interest included almost all DC and Marvel comics.

During this time, Derrill met Roy Thomas, who was living nearby, and wrote a piece on the formative early days of Will Eisner's brainchild, Blackhawk, titled "When Hawkhood Was in Flower." Roy, who by this time had assumed the full editorial and publishing duties for *Alter Ego*, decided to rework Derrill's article. Thomas visited Biljo White in Columbia, Missouri, to consult White's collection of Golden Age *Blackhawk* and *Military Comics*. The rewritten article was published under both writers' names in *Alter Ego* #8 (March 1965), accompanied by artwork by Biljo White that included a spectacular cover featuring Blackhawk. Rothermich also penned a piece about the same time called "The Cult of Mercury" (about Flash imitators) for AE #10, which fell by the wayside by the time Roy pulled the tenth issue together in 1969.

When Glen Johnson became burned out on publishing *The Comic Reader*, Derrill Rothermich and his friend Jim King offered to take over. Their first issue was *TCR* #42 (October 1965), which was primarily different from the Johnson product because it was printed not by ditto but via photo offset. This printing process enabled the new publishers to produce many more copies than were possible by the spirit duplicator method, and also allowed for the reduction in print size which allowed the same material to fit into fewer pages, which saved on postage. (This helped keep the price down to 30 cents per copy.) It also allowed for the use of inked artwork and photographs, though photos in *TCR* would remain rare until much later. Rothermich was able to keep the issues coming over the next couple of years, offering news "on the drawing board" of upcoming pro comics by David Kaler, fanzine ratings by John McGeehan, and artwork by a panoply of fandom's best. Derrill shared a 1965 Alley Award with Glen Johnson for "On the Drawing Board" as "Best Regular Feature" in a fanzine (*TCR*). When Rothermich graduated from the University of Missouri, and entered the U.S. military, he passed the fanzine to Robert Schoenfeld, another Missourian.

Derrill ended up having a long military

Derrill Rothermich

career, beginning at Fort Bliss in El Paso, Texas, and then to South Korea, Germany and Saudi Arabia. His interest in comics in the 1970s expanded beyond DC and Marvel, but remained mostly in the superhero genre. Presently, Rothermich works at the El Paso Zoo.

Buddy Saunders
(b. 1947)

Buddy Saunders is a comic book dealer and retailer who was one of the most active fan publishers, artists and writers in comicdom from the beginning of the 1960s. Buddy was probably best known in those years as one-third of "The Texas Trio," along with Larry Herndon and Howard Keltner, who co-published *Star-Studded Comics*. The aspiring writer and artist contributed to numerous other fanzines, such as *RBCC* and *Fantasy Illustrated*, and was one of the earliest dealers in back-issue comic books.

Born Jakey (not Jake) Saunders in 1947, but known as Buddy as long as he can remember, Saunders was only 15 years old when he became a fan-editor with *The Comic Fan* #1 (July 1962). In those ditto pages, Buddy introduced what would become his premiere fan creation, "The Demon." The origin story begins when Dan Prat's friends are mysteriously killed while exploring caves. Prat comes across the underground sanctum of the ancient medieval sorcerer Geraldin. He discovers the secrets of the dead sorcerer and thus becomes the Demon. Saunders wrote, "My Demon, an ordinary man made extraordinary by his possession of supernatural lore, was an outgrowth of influences from the books I was reading (Lovecraft, etc.). More interesting and original was his primary enemy, the Chimera, a creature that sprang into being as the consequence of the Demon's own nightmares." The Demon bears a superficial resemblance to Marvel's Doctor Strange, but predates him by a year. After his origin in *The Comic Fan*, the Demon moved over to inaugurate *Fighting Hero Comics*, the first fanzine devoted entirely to amateur comic strips. He appeared in #1, #2, #6 and #9, and eventually also headlined strips in *Komix Illustrated* #7, #11 and #12, as well as *Fighting Hero Comics Special Edition* #1. In these early years, Buddy worked diligently on his artwork, and developed an effective, recognizable style that overshadowed an occasional deficiency in the area of anatomical accuracy. His work had energy and dramatic impact far superior to that of artists who drew better figures.

By the time *Fighting Hero Comics* had completed its twelve-issue run in 1964, it had been superseded by one of the most widely read and fondly remembered fanzines from the 1960s, *Star-Studded Comics*. Within a short period of time, *SSC* established itself as virtually the "official showcase" of the amateur

Buddy Saunders

superhero strip. It was published by Howard Keltner, Larry Herndon, and Buddy Saunders, known collectively as the Texas Trio. The first issue carried a September 1963 cover date, but was actually mailed in June.

Howard Keltner recalled, "I had noticed Buddy's artwork in *The Rocket's Blast* ... and noted that he lived only a short distance away from me [in Texas]. Then in late 1962, Larry [Herndon] wrote me requesting an article for his zine *Hero*. We were spending a lot of time writing letters to each other in early 1963. Larry finally suggested that we get together and really get acquainted, and since it was his idea we agreed to meet in his home in April."

"I was still too young to drive," Buddy Saunders remembered, "but I talked my mother into driving me to Carrollton where Larry lived with his folks. Larry's mom and dad were both school teachers and very nice." Herndon had a room toward the front of the house that was devoted solely to his comic collection. Neat stacks of comics were on shelves along the wall or in boxes. It was there, sitting around a folding card table in the house on Highland Drive that Larry and Buddy started talking about doing a fanzine together. Then Howard Keltner was welcomed into the comic book sanctum. Keltner, aptly described as "a real Southern gentleman," brought the perspective of a fan of Golden Age comics to the table. He was 15 years older than Buddy and Larry. "I was the last to arrive and one of the first things I learned was that they had already been discussing publishing an amateur strip zine," Keltner recalled. Right then and there, *Star-Studded Comics* was born, with Keltner suggesting the title. *Star-Studded Comics* #1 (June 1963) introduced Dr. Weird (art and story by Keltner), the Changling (story and art by Saunders), the Defender (by Herndon and Grass Green) and the Astral Man (by Tommy Fisher). Issue #2 added two more: Keltner's Powerman, and Saunders' Mercury. As the cast of characters grew, some of them inevitably stood out from the crowd. Buddy's cover for the second issue won an Alley Award for "Best Single Illustration—Cover."

The Texas Trio had the production of *SSC* extremely well organized. Herndon was the Circulation Editor and Head Writer, keeping track of orders, reading letters and writing scripts; Keltner was the Contributions Editor, handling contacts with their staff of writers and artists, and evaluating the work of up-and-coming talents; and Saunders served as Publishing Editor, liaison with the printer, and the one who colored the covers.

Buddy recalled, "It was a real challenge preparing color separations [for four-color offset printing] by crude estimation rather than via any sort of reliable color key. For example, if I wanted a light green, I'd blacken that area on the yellow overlay to get 100% yellow, then use a 20 or 30% screen on the blue overlay, and then hope the resulting green wasn't darker than I wanted. Usually, it turned out pretty close to what I wanted, and I still feel I was a pretty good colorist, especially given the crude system we were forced to work with. The thing I most remember about the Texas Trio was the excitement we always experienced on seeing the finished product." *Star-Studded* wasn't perfect. It was only as good as its contributors, which meant the offerings were uneven. Still, issue after issue, *SSC*'s batting average was higher than its peers, and it retained its popularity with fans until its final issue in 1972.

By the late 1960s, Saunders had come to terms with the fact that his artwork wasn't going to be able to reach professional standards, and turned his primary creative focus to his writing. In partnership with friend and fellow Texan Howard Waldrop, Buddy wrote a series of SF short stories that were published in *Galaxy* magazine. In 1974, they co-authored the book *The Texas-Israeli War: 1999*, and Saunders' short story "Back to the Stone Age" was nominated for a Nebula Award in 1976. He sold scripts to Warren Publishing for *Eerie* magazine, and horror stories to *Coven* magazine.

As the 1960s progressed, Buddy's comic book mail-order business flourished, and he opened the first of what would become a chain of comic book retail stores in North Texas called Lone Star Comics. The stores prospered, and, augmented by revenues brought in through a popular website (www.mycomicshop.com), have led to Saunders becoming one of the premiere comic book retailers and sellers in the country, a status he has maintained to the present day.

Bob Schoenfeld
(1949–2006)

Bob Schoenfeld was the St. Louis–based fanzine editor and publisher of *On the Drawing Board* and *Gosh Wow!,* two of the most essential fanzines in the mid to late 1960s, and is credited with discovering the writer-artist Vaughn Bodé.

Robert Schoenfeld became a prominent fan editor overnight, when the Golden Gate Comic Art Fan Club inherited the publishing mantle of *The Comic Reader*. Primarily designed to disseminate news of upcoming professional comic books and strips, *TCR* was founded by Jerry Bails in 1961. Because of the timely nature of the material, the publishing deadlines were more demanding than any other such amateur publications, and had a way of burning out editors. Bails handed the zine off to Glen Johnson, who found Derrill Rothermich to subsequently take its helm. Rothermich, a college student in Rolla, Missouri, published some excellent issues of *The Comic Reader* through late 1965 and 1966, and then was drafted into the Army. From him, presumably because he knew the St. Louis fans, the magazine passed to the Gateway City fan club. One of its most active members, as it turned out, was a slender, dark-haired teenager named Robert Schoenfeld.

Bob Schoenfeld

Bob jumped into the "lion's den" and soon proved his mettle as editor, perfecting the photo-offset look of *OTDB* at a time when professionally printed fanzines were few, and often bore a rudimentary appearance. In the editorial in *On the Drawing Board* #53 (October 1966), he wrote, "This is the first issue of *OTDB* to be completely in the hands of the Gateway Comic Art Fan Club, and we are very anxious to know your feelings [about] our effort. There are three people to thank for this. The first is Glen Johnson who supplied us with his old *TCR* subscription file, the second is Dave Kaler and the Academy for supplying the funds necessary to finance this, and the third is Ray Fisher, a club member who is doing our printing." He ended his first editorial by exhorting comics fans to expend more energy documenting the history of the medium. "The real superheroes are the artists and writers and their lives in the world of comics," Bob wrote. "We have to wake up today or we may find the past forever lost to us! Or, worse yet, persons only casually interested in comics may be producing the books we should be researching and working on right now!"

Over the next year, Bob saw to it that *On the Drawing Board* appeared near-monthly, and was a pulpit for many of the most active and vociferous comics fans. David Kaler, who had become Executive Secretary of the Academy of Comic Book Fans and Collectors, often contributed news of the New York pros, as well as Academy updates. As Kaler's contributions in this area faded, Mark Hanerfeld stepped into the function of providing such news. Others such as Bill Spicer, Bob Latona, John McGeehan and a cadre of letter writers kept the pages of the news-zine lively, and its circulation topped 500 copies per issue before long. True, Bob's grasp of spelling was often tenuous, and a lot of the material about the Academy was of marginal interest to some of the readership, but there was always plenty of news and information about professional comics to justify the price of 25 cents per issue (though this would go up) to any fan. Many of fandom's emerging new crop of amateur artists found a showcase in its pages; that's where folks like Alan Hutchinson, Jim Sullivan, Jim Gardner, Ken Keller, Rich Buckler and others gained prominence in the fan firmament. Schoenfeld also published his own general interest fanzine called *Gosh Wow!*, which was more or less to fill the gap left when *Alter Ego* was on hiatus. (*A/E* had last appeared in 1965.)

Though Bob (actually the Golden Gate Comic Art Fan Club) stopped publishing *On the Drawing Board* in 1968—it was revived as *The Comic Reader* that year by Mark Hanerfeld—he did publish the second issue of *Gosh Wow!* that summer, featuring the work of Vaughn Bodé. Schoenfeld's friend Robert Latona recently wrote, "Bob previewed his gift for promoting other people's talent with his discovery of Vaughn Bodé, fresh out of Syracuse University with wife, toddler son and head still screwed on more or less in place, handing out samples and originals at that year's St. Louiscon. Thinking back, I realize all Bodé's good work had already been done by then—Cheech Wizard, the lizards, and so forth—because I saw it all in St. Louis, and took a lot of it home with me. I don't think anyone would dispute that the discovery of Vaughn Bodé was entirely Bob's doing." (*Alter Ego* #72.) Latona and Schoenfeld attended the SCARP con in New York City together. That 1968 comicon, which stretched over five days, was the most impressive and well-attended gathering of comic fans yet, and Bob was in evidence in many of the photos taken there. The following summer saw Schoenfeld's last comics fanzine, *Gosh Wow!* #3, that was comprised mainly of an article with lots of photos of the SCARP Con, and a lengthy "Moondog" strip by George Metzger. It was a slim 36-page issue, but a fine capstone to Bob's three years as a prominent fanzine publisher. This ended his comics zine days. His contribution was a major one, filling an important function at a time when the ranks of fandom were growing by leaps and bounds.

Bob's interests went beyond comic art. In *On the Drawing Board* #63 (November 1967), one of the last issues of the zine published by Bob, his love of rock and roll music emerged. He wrote, "Off the subject here, I'd like to talk about something of personal interest—popular music. I've been a 'more or less' fan of rock & roll music for some time, but as of late I've gained a much more serious interest in view of several exciting (to me) events. To make it even more interesting I've discovered that many comic fans share my interest.... Mayhap a column or zine could be produced to cater to comic fans with this interest. I wouldn't mind hearing from other R&R enthusiasts, but be warned, if you're a Monkees fan you'd best forget it. Oh, yes, every rock & roll fan should be a regular reader of *Crawdaddy*—a magazine I've found to be the best bet for the rock-fan." By the early 1970s, Bob had fallen in love with reggae music and other musical idioms that originated from Jamaica. After visiting that Caribbean island in 1974 for the first time, that love led to his founding of Nighthawk

Records, one of the first U.S.-based independent labels to make a serious commitment to reggae. Nighthawk Records became the center of his creative energy for the rest of his life.

Beginning in the 1980s, Schoenfeld ended up producing several important Jamaican recording artists, and later co-edited (with Michael Turner) *Roots Knotty Roots*, a 716-page discography of Jamaican music that weighed three and a half pounds.

Bob Schoenfeld passed away "peacefully in his sleep" in 2004, not long after he conducted an auction of his mammoth collection of comic book fanzines.

Bill Spicer
(b. 1937)

A participant in EC fandom as a teenager, Bill Spicer became best known for publishing the fanzine *Fantasy Illustrated* beginning in 1964, which became even better known after its name was changed to *Graphic Story Magazine* with its eighth issue. Spicer was a writer-artist in his own right, but had few peers in fandom as an editor and publisher, and his ability to break down prose stories into comic book form proved to be central to his fanzine's success. In addition, he was a professional-caliber letterer who would make much of his living exercising that craft in later years.

As a comic fan in the early 1950s, Los Angeles-born William Spicer heard about EC fanzines either through the plug in *Weird Science* #20, or a plug in *Fantasy-Comics*. "I know I started receiving a few SF zines around 1951 or 1952 after seeing mentions of them in SF pulp mags," Bill wrote recently. "[I received] Malcolm Willits' photo-offset *Destiny*, vintage 1951, among others. These were my first exposure to fanzines per se, at about age 13." A budding artist, Bill drew a striking SF cover for the first real EC fanzine, Bhob Stewart's *The EC Fan Bulletin*, and one for Mike May's *The EC Fan Journal* about a year later. The intelligent stories and unmatched stable of artists at EC made a deep impression on him.

In 1961–1962, Bill became aware of the new fandom movement, and conceived of a fanzine that would carve out its own unique territory. Looking for artists, he ran a want ad in one of the SF fanzines of the period, most likely *The Fantasy Collector* or *Science Fiction Times*. Landon Chesney was one of several who responded, sending an illustration which ended up as the cover of issue #1. When asked to pinpoint his motivation for publishing *Fantasy Illustrated*, Spicer explained, "The big attraction of starting up a fanzine at that point, circa 1962, was the idea of having complete freedom to produce

Bill Spicer

just about any kind of comics stories, unconcerned with real-world commercial inconveniences like newsstand distribution and sales. At the time, I apparently fancied myself a minor league William Gaines and Harvey Kurtzman rolled into one." From the beginning, the all-offset *FI* (February 1964) delved into three of the four major genres of the EC New Trend stories: horror, SF, and parody. Also, like EC, the zine frequently adapted stories from other media to sequential art form.

One of the most highly praised strips was Spicer's two-part adaptation of Eando Binder's 1940s pulp magazine novella, "Adam Link's Vengeance." Drawn by professional artist and SF fan D. Bruce Berry, it was a stunning *tour de force*. James Warren was a subscriber to *FI*, and commissioned the Adam Link stories for *Creepy* (to be drawn by Joe Orlando) after seeing the Binder/Spicer/Berry adaptation. For that reason, Spicer's plans for more Adam Link strips had to be abandoned. It's too bad, because the *Creepy* version was much inferior to *FI*'s. Another early gem was the adaptation of Binder's pulp yarn "The Life Battery," which featured EC-like artwork of the highest caliber by Landon Chesney.

"*FI* probably owed as much if not more to science fiction fandom as it did to what constituted comic fandom at the time," Spicer recalled. "Considering the zine's title itself and an over-reliance on vintage SF adaptations, rather than going after a full line-up of original fan-written stories, it's still somewhat surprising that it was that popular. The prevailing mode of the day was costumed super heroes, as far as most comics zines were concerned." *Fantasy Illustrated* #1 had a press run of 500 copies, and Spicer managed to sell or otherwise circulate every copy within a couple of months.

About the time "Adam Link's Vengeance" was nominated in the "Best Fan Comic Strip" category of the 1964 Alley Awards (which it would win), Spicer was drafted into the job of laying out what was initially called the *Fandom Catalog*, designed as a comprehensive source of information about comic fandom for anyone interested. It would contain ads for prominent fanzines, and incorporate some of the material about the history of the fan movement from Jerry Bails' *Who's Who in Comic Fandom*. It was intended to introduce the steady stream of new fans who were hearing about comicdom via ads for fanzines and vintage comic books in Marvel Comics to the world of comic fandom. The *Catalog* would include a Grading Guide (which grew out of efforts to formulate a Code of Fair Practice for dealers and fans) in the first concerted attempt to establish grading standards.

Spicer developed a superlatively designed package, receiving the thousand copies back from the printer in time for distribution at the 1965 summer comicons. Now titled *The Guidebook to Comics Fandom*, it offered the following standard grading system: Mint, Near Mint, Very Good, Good, Fair and Poor. The descriptions of the grades are fairly close to current definitions, with the exception of Near Mint, which was expected to fill in the entire area between Mint and Very Good. (Fine would not appear for some time.) Unfortunately, professional comics seemed to have become more parsimonious in the number of plugs they would give fanzines about the time the *Guidebook* was completed. The expectation that pro comics would regularly publicize it went unfulfilled. However, even as a one-shot, it served a need for the new members of comicdom who found their way in through other paths.

The high quality of the comic strip features in *Fantasy Illustrated* continued to receive recognition. In 1965, the zine shared another Alley ("Best Fan Comic Strip") for Spicer's and Harry Habblitz's superb strip adaptation of Edgar Rice Burroughs "The End of Bukawai" in *FI* #3. In each of the three following years, *Fantasy Illustrated/Graphic Story Magazine* won Alleys for "Best Article/Strip Fanzine." Articles had begun appearing in the fourth issue, with Richard Kyle's "Graphic Story Review" column, and gradually became dominant, which was part of the reason for the title change. (*Fantasy Illustrated* no longer seemed to fit.) In the issues published up to the magazine's demise with #16 in 1974, Spicer published important interviews with Alex Toth (#10), Will Gould (#11), John Severin (#13), Gahan Wilson (#15) and Howard Nostrand (#16). *Graphic Story Magazine* #12 and #14 were devoted entirely to the work of Basil Wolverton. The letter columns were among the most interesting in all of fandom, featuring missives from a wide cross-section of articulate, intelligent fans.

GSM was then followed by several issues of *Fanfare*, a pop culture magazine which, while largely a departure from *GSM,* still had comics-oriented material that included substantial pieces on Charles Biro, Al Feldstein and, focusing on his early pulp magazine work, EC stalwart Graham Ingels.

In 1971, Bill Spicer (with partners Michael Moore and Fred Walker) formed the short-lived Los Angeles Comic Book Company to publish their version of underground comix, ending up with only one issue each of four titles: *Mickey Rat*, *L. A. Comics*, *Mutants of the Metropolis* and the full color *Weird Fantasies.* Three of the four books sold moderately well, but *Mutants* bombed in spectacular fashion and was a setback that played a major part in the undercapitalized company's reluctant decision to call it quits soon thereafter. Plus, the time for continuing with more comix wasn't right; undergrounds were already slumping in sales by 1973–74 and would not recover.

As a comics fan in the 1960s, Spicer's reading mainly consisted of Will Eisner's "The Spirit," Carl Barks' duck stories and John Stanley's stories of Little Lulu and Tubby. His collecting activities centered around the works of John Stanley and going after many pre-Trend EC issues. Having learned professional lettering techniques while working at an ad agency from 1955 to 1967, Bill became a comic book letterer for Western Publishing starting in 1967 (upon the recommendation of Mike Royer), which occupied him for the next 15 years. He has also lettered for Dark Horse (Paul Chadwick's *Concrete* and *The World Below* series), Another Rainbow (Disney), Fantagraphics, and from 1988 to 2005 a great deal of manga for Viz. In the 1980s, Spicer lettered two newspaper strips, "Conan the Barbarian" and "Rick O'Shay."

Bhob Stewart

(b. 1937)

Bhob Stewart was one of the key figures of EC comics fandom of the 1950s. He published the first EC fanzine, *The EC Fan Bulletin*, beginning in the summer of 1953. In 1954, he edited *Potrzebie* #1, considered the finest EC fanzine apart from *Hoohah!*, which came later. As a publisher, editor, writer and artist, he contributed to EC fandom across the board, and his seminal interview with Bernard Krigstein, conducted with John Benson, was published as the 28-page *Talk with B. Krigstein* (1963), bringing the level of discourse about comic art to a new level of sophistication.

When he was young, his family moved several times through the South and Southwest. He seems to have had publishing and writing in his blood, having created a weekly hand-written publication, *The Nutty Newspaper*, a compendium of juvenile features, jokes and cartoons, while he was in elementary school in Lexington, Mississippi. After moving to Kirbyville, Texas, in 1952, he began contributing to science fiction fanzines. Due to a vision problem, he could not see 3-D movies or comics, but after several experiments, he began creating science fiction and fantasy drawings in 3-D, teaming with Texas fan Bobby Gene Warner to publish *Fanciful*, the first 3-D fanzine. This led him to consider doing a publication devoted to EC comics.

In Benson's article, "The E.C. Fanzines, Part One" in *Squa Tront #5* (1974), Stewart recalled, "One day it hit me like a flash that I should be doing a fanzine—not about science fiction, since there were hundreds of them—but about the thing I was most inter- ested in, EC comics." The first issue came out in the

Bhob Stewart

(PHOTOGRAPH BY MARTIN JUKOVSKY)

summer of 1953, after an announcement in *Weird Science #20* (July–August 1953) brought 80 orders to Stewart's mailbox. It was printed via hectograph, a primitive printing process that had the virtue of being inexpensive. Up to 100 copies might be made, though 50 was the norm, and the printing process was labor-intensive. Among other features in *The EC Fan Bulletin* #1 was an account of the Fan-Vet Convention (also plugged in EC comics) on April 19, 1953, held by the Fantasy Veterans Association. The *Bulletin* carried a floor plan of the EC offices, the first of similar floor plans soon seen in other EC fanzines. *The EC Fan Bulletin* is considered the first true EC fanzine, because unlike James V. Taurasi's *Fantasy-Comics*, a newszine that had debuted a few months earlier, it was produced for comic book fans rather than science fiction fans, and it was about EC alone, covering their entire line. *Fantasy-Comics* was about SF comics from EC, Avon and other publishers.

There was only one more issue of Stewart's fanzine, about three months later, which sported a striking multi-colored cover with an outer space theme in the Feldstein tradition by EC reader Bill Spicer. Benefiting from Stewart's exposure to SF zines, *The EC Fan Bulletin* was a high-quality publication, with the second issue more professional than the first. The writing was literate, and at least some of the art was quite good. Puns throughout demonstrate the influence of both *Mad* and the GhouLunatics' banter in the EC horror comics. Although Stewart was unhappy with the limitations of hectograph printing and discontinued the fanzine, its publication proved influential. Seeing the first issue of *The EC Fan Bulletin*, EC publisher Bill Gaines was inspired to form the EC Fan-Addict Club, and he wrote to Stewart, appointing him Contributing Editor to the forthcoming official EC fan club newsletter, *The National E.C. Fan-Addict Club Bulletin*. Gaines' promotional newsletter ran five issues (November 1953 to December 1954), but Stewart's sole submission as Contributing Editor was never published.

In the wake of Bhob's publication, a number of other EC fanzines appeared. They were generally printed by ditto or mimeograph, and of variable quality. They included *EC World Press*, *The EC Slime Sheet*, *The Mad Melvin Newsletter*, *EC Scoop*, *The EC SF Mags Fanzine*, and *The EC Fan Journal*. A number of them sent reporters to visit EC's New York offices and printed trip reports; Bill Gaines always seemed willing to accommodate these enthusiastic efforts, and he spent time visiting with the fans in person or on the phone. News flowed freely into the pages of the fanzines. Influenced by his correspondence with Larry Stark, Bhob embarked on his first critical writing, an appreciation of Bernard Krigstein's EC stories and artwork, "B. Krigstein: An Evaluation and Defense," which was published in *The EC World Press* #4 (August 1954).

Meanwhile, the hue and cry against sex and violence in comic books rose to a fever pitch with the publication of Dr. Fredric Wertham's *Seduction of the Innocent* in 1954. In the book, Wertham stated, "Every medium of artistic and literary expression has developed professional critics ... the fact that comic books have grown to some 90 millions a month without developing such critics is one more indication that this industry functions in a cultural vacuum." Incensed by this statement, Stewart was determined to publish a new, more impressive EC fanzine with a higher level of criticism befitting the quality of the comic books involved and what he saw as the intrinsic potential of the medium. He envisioned it as a forum for critical essays by Larry Stark, EC's prolific "number one fan." As Bhob outlined it to Larry, rather than a fanzine, he wanted to create a "little magazine," the term then in use to describe literary journals.

The result was *Potrzebie*, a non sequitur from *Mad* (pronounced "pot-reez'-bie," according to Ted White). Using a postcard mimeo machine to produce 4" × 6" pages, White served as publisher for editors Stewart and Stark. The first issue (ca. June 1954) featured two long pieces by Stark, a couple of brief editorials and a few pages of ads, totaling 34 pages. As it turned out, it was the only issue of *Potrzebie* produced by the trio, due to the discouraging response to a plug in the *EC Fan-Addict Bulletin*. It seemed that the average age of the respondents was between nine and 13 years old, which dismayed White. Though Stewart had prepared much of #2, White set the stencils aside, only publishing them later in an SF apa. Without informing Stewart, he turned *Potrzebie* over to Texas fan Larry Clowers, who kept it going for several more issues.

In college, Stewart drew a weekly series of cartoons and comic strips for his college newspaper. Arriving in New York in 1960, he created several innovative three-page comic strip covers for White's SF fanzine, *Void*, and also became the art director (and later co-editor) for Dick Lupoff's Hugo Award-winning *Xero*.

Stewart's next major contribution to fandom, an even greater attempt to raise the level of discourse about the medium, was the lengthy, in-depth interview with Bernard Krigstein, conducted by Stewart and Benson. *Bhob Stewart and John Benson Talk with B. Krigstein* (1963) is a true milestone in the history of interviews with comic book professionals, who were, at that time, never interviewed at that length, and were rarely subjected to such probing questions about their artistic approaches, methods and goals.

In that decade and later, Bhob contributed to *Cavalier*, *The Realist*, *TV Guide* and other magazines. He invented the term "underground comix" in a panel discussion at the 1966 New York Comicon organized by Benson, and he also coined the word "flix" as the title for his 1980 film column in *Heavy Metal*. Bhob's love of EC was influential on some of his professional projects in subsequent years, such as his book *Against the Grain: Mad Artist Wallace Wood*, his underground comix book *Tales from the Fridge* (a collaboration with Russ Jones) and his negotiations with Bill Gaines in compiling Nostalgia Press's groundbreaking, full-color hardback, *EC Horror Comics of the 1950s*, plus his *Wacky Packages*, trading cards and other humor products for Topps Chewing Gum.

Bhob has been published by Marvel, Byron Preiss, Charlton and Warren. At DC Comics, he edited the *Mad Style Guide* and the first DC trading cards, *Cosmic Cards* and *Cosmic Teams*. He continues to write about popular culture and media. In 2005, he revived *Potrzebie* as a blog, where he occasionally posts his memoirs.

Don Thompson
(1935–1994)

Don Thompson was a comics and SF fan who co-founded (with his then-fiancée Maggie Curtis) the seminal fanzine *Comic Art* in 1961. A professional journalist, Thompson contributed two entries to the "All in Color For a Dime" series in *Xero*. His writing was accomplished, highly intelligent and occasionally acerbic. Don and Maggie Thompson were quintessential Big Name Fans.

Don and Maggie met in June 1957 at an SF picnic at the home of pulp magazine writer Basil Wells, with André Norton, Edmond Hamilton, Leigh Brackett and many others in attendance. In a 1992 interview, Don recalled, "I discovered … that one of these people was Betsy Curtis, who had written some very good stories for the magazines. And there was this annoying little fourteen-year-old kid running around. That was Maggie." While Don Thompson was a student at Penn State, he had been president of the SF society. A fan of the EC SF titles, and the Kurtzman humor books, he and Maggie found they had comics as a common interest. Don noticed *Humbug* #1 on sale shortly thereafter, and sent an extra copy to Maggie. "We started corresponding, and I visited her a few times," Don said. "[Our relationship] just kind of grew out of that."

One of their visits took place at the 1960 PittCon, the same SF convention where Dick and Pat Lupoff created a minor sensation when they appeared costumed as Captain and Mary Marvel. Don and Maggie shared the limelight at the masquerade with the Lupoffs and others. (The Thompsons and Lupoffs would soon become close friends.) They were appearing in a costumed group representing the Five Fannish Senses, with Maggie's family,

Left to right: Don and Maggie Thompson, with Roy Thomas.

and won the prize for "Best Group." "We got together at the banquet at the [convention] … and we talked with Hal Lynch and Will J. Jenkins. And we were talking about *comics*," Don remembered. "We had not seen *Xero*, which was being distributed at the convention. We said, 'There ought to be a fanzine about comics.'" Shortly thereafter, Hal Lynch corroborated this encounter with the Thompsons in the pages of *Xero*. "At the PittCon I met up with Don Thompson, who told me of his desire to start a comics fandom."

In January 1961, Don Thompson and Maggie Curtis sent out about 50 copies of a little one-sheet called *Harbinger*, a request for material for their projected fanzine about comics. Autumn after the PittCon, Maggie had begun her freshman year at Oberlin College, and Don found a job with *The Cleveland Press*. *Harbinger*, which presaged *Comic Art*, was printed on a mimeograph machine at Oberlin College. *Comic Art* saw the light of day in March or April. (There is no record of the exact publication date.) Don Thompson called it "a science fiction fanzine about comics." Much of the first issue was devoted to Dick Lupoff's article "Re-Birth," discussing the resurgence of interest in comics and the move to create a "general comics fandom." About the same time *Comic Art* #1 came out, Don Thompson's first entry in the "All in Color for a Dime" series in *Xero* appeared, in issue #4. It was "O.K. Axis, Here We Come!," a survey of the superhero comics published by Timely during World War II, accompanied by "illos swiped by Maggie Curtis." Don would add another chapter to the *Xero* series, "The Wild Ones," and ended up co-editing the book version of *All in Color for a Dime* with Dick Lupoff which appeared at the decade's end.

The year 1962 was a banner year for the Thompsons, for they were married in June, and produced the two best issues of *Comic Art* to date. *CA* #3 came out in April and #4 in December, with circulations of 200 to 250 copies, respectively. *Comic Art* #3 carried an article by Don Thompson on "Sam's Strip," and Dick Lupoff's "A Study in Scarlet," the first in a projected series (à la AICFAD) called "Also In This Issue…." Herb Beach named his choice for "The Top Ten of the Golden Era" (comic book creators, that is), and Larry Ivie appended a few thoughts of his own to the subject. (Beach's list of those who did the most for early comic books included Jerry Siegel, Joe Shuster, Bob Kane, C. C. Beck, Charles Biro, Gardner Fox, Carl Barks, Will Eisner, Charles Moulton and Fred Guardineer. The list showed comic fans' knowledge of the people behind the comics of that bygone era.) At the 1962 World Science Fiction Convention (ChiCon) masquerade, where a number of SF fans from Los Angeles dressed as members of the Justice Society of America, the Thompsons portrayed Fawcett's Ibis the Invincible and his female assistant Taia.

The cover of *Comic Art* #4 featured Ed Wheelan and his "Minute Movies," to go along with an article on the strip. That issue also had pieces on such diverse subjects as Sergio Aragones, Barbie, James Swinnerton and the Neal Adams' "Ben Casey" syndicated strip. *Comic Art* was genuinely unique in comicdom for its mix of intelligent, often provocative, articles.

Unfortunately (for its readers), 1962 was the last year more than one issue appeared. Due to a Cleveland newspaper strike, #5 wasn't published until 1964. Then, the final two issues were published at two-year intervals, in 1966 and 1968. Each issue had gotten thicker than the last, following a similar pattern as *Xero*. Issue #6 presented articles on Milton Caniff, "Pogo" and Jerry De Fuccio. Issue #7 weighed in at a whopping 76 pages, over half of them devoted to various pieces about Carl Barks, by Malcolm Willits, Michael Barrier and Barks himself. *Comic Art* #7 also included fiction by Harlan Ellison. There was no announcement of discontinuation; in fact, a next issue was promised. Another issue did not appear, and comicdom was the poorer for it. *Comic Art* had provided a unique forum for intelligent interaction between SF fandom and comicdom, and it was missed. Not that Don and Maggie had left fandom—far from it. They had two other major ongoing projects to keep them busy.

First was their Co-Central Mailer position for *Capa-alpha*, which they had assumed when Jerry Bails rather abruptly announced in *K-a* #20 (May 1966) that he was resigning as CM, thus suspending the apa. With no plan of succession in place, the Thompsons gamely picked up the ball, assuming the responsibility for keeping the amateur press association going. They had another publication, too—a little newsletter called *Newfangles*, which was devoted to keeping fans informed about the news in fans' personal lives. It was published more or less monthly, and would eventually inspire another fan to begin a monthly publication. That fan was Alan Light, and the fanzine was *The Buyer's Guide for Comic Fandom*. The Thompsons' "Beautiful Balloons" column became a regular feature, and eventually, when *TBG* was acquired by Krause Publications and renamed *Comics Buyer's Guide*, the Thompsons became its editors.

In May 1994, eleven years later, Don Thompson—who suffered from a variety of health problems—passed away in his sleep. Maggie has continued working for Krause Publications ever since.

Maggie Thompson
(b. 1942)

Writer, cartoonist, indexer and fanzine publisher Maggie Thompson was one of only three women whose activities in the early 1960s were central to the founding of comic fandom. (The other two were Pat Lupoff and Margaret Gemignani.) Along with her fiancé/husband Don Thompson, Maggie edited and published *Comic Art*, one of the earliest and most important fanzines of the 1960s.

Born Margaret Curtis, she was a second-generation fan. Her mother, Betsy, in addition to other writing, published a fanzine around 1950, when the Curtis family lived in Canton, New York. (Her father, Ed Curtis, was teaching at St. Lawrence University.) It was called *The Cricket*, a Pogo-esque pun on the word "critic." Maggie was an English major at Oberlin College, graduating with a B.A. in 1964.

Thompson was a full partner in *Comic Art* and *Newfangles*, contributing numerous cartoons and other art pieces, as well as editorial matter. Her writing was different from that of her husband: every bit as intelligent, yet not as acerbic. Maggie brought all her wide-ranging knowledge of popular culture to the task, and was accorded respect among fans commensurate with that shown toward Don.

When it was time for Jerry Bails to count the Alley Award ballots for 1963, Don and Maggie were among the 18 comic book fans who were invited to Bails' home in Detroit to help with the task. Aside from the business at hand at the Alley Tally Party, the Thompsons were particularly interested in the way Jerry had his comic books stored. "Don and I had seen Bill Thailing's collection," Maggie remembered. "But Jerry's was so carefully organized, in bags hanging from the ceiling, and I remember thinking, 'Can we adapt this for our own purposes?' Because there was no really good way to store and display the things."

Thompson was employed as an assistant children's librarian in the Cleveland Public Library system until mid–1966, when she quit to have children, Valerie and Stephen. She worked as a freelance writer and editor until the demise of *The Cleveland Press* in 1982. The following year, Don and Maggie moved to Iola, Wisconsin, to work for Krause Publications as co-editors of *Movie Collector's World* and *Comics Buyer's Guide*. *CBG* subsequently twice won the comic industry's Eisner Award for periodicals, and Maggie was the recipient of the Bob Clampett Humanitarian Award. She was also the first to be honored with the Friends of Lulu's "Women of Distinction" Award in 2004.

Mike Tuohey
(b. 1948)

Publisher of *Super-Hero*, and aid to Jerry Bails on *Alter-Ego* and other projects, Detroit fan Mike Tuohey was one of the earliest fans to be drawn into fandom as a result of Jerry Bails' efforts.

Michael Tuohey was born in Detroit, Michigan, in the era when television was just becoming widely popular. His father, Frank, was Director of Public Relations for Wayne State University in the city, and hosted a UHF-broadcast local TV interview show called "Spotlight" in the 1950s. The Tuoheys were early owners of television on their block. Mike was a rabid fan of *Captain Video*, *Crusader Rabbit* and *Adventures of Superman*, the latter serving to quicken his interest in comic books. While Francis and Gretchen Tuohey encouraged their sons' love of reading (*Tom Swift*, the *Hardy Boys*, Robert Louis Stevenson), they were initially reluctant to buy comic books for him. As Mike remembered, "My interest started at the time of the imposition of the Comics Code Authority, and they were concerned that they were trash or porno or both. Comic books were considered the literature of choice for idiots and backward adults." Certainly the nuns at his Catholic grade school snatched copies away from boys and girls who were foolish enough to bring them to school.

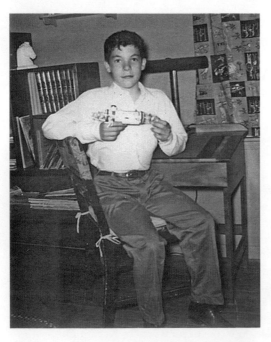

Mike Tuohey

Soon his parents relented, and Mike's father took an interest in his son's early attempts at creating his own comic strips. When he and his neighborhood friends put on plays in the basement, his mother sewed the costumes. Mike would be Superman or Batman, and his sister Bridget was Lois Lane. The boy avidly read the Sunday comics featuring "Flash Gordon," "The Phantom" and "Prince Valiant," and when he saw his first *Batman* comic book (which featured Bat-Hound), it was love at first sight. He was also drawn to the work of Jack Kirby on the character of the Green Arrow, *Adventures of the Fly*, and the pre-hero Marvel titles. As the 1950s drew to a close, he had become a comic book collector.

Then Tuohey read a letter in *Brave and Bold* #35 from Jerry Bails, who lived in Detroit. The 12-year-old looked up Bails' phone number in the city directory, worked up his nerve and phoned him in April 1961. Jerry, who was 27 years old at the time, told

Mike about his fanzine and sent him a truncated copy of *Alter-Ego* #1. They made arrangements to meet, and Mike's mother drove him the seven miles to Jerry's mother's house on Dale Street. Tuohey recalled, "We spent the afternoon looking at *All-Star* issues and other wonderful comic books from the 1940s and 1950s. I was thrilled. It was like Christmas." Subsequently, Mike would visit Jerry from time to time.

Initially, Mike's parents were a bit concerned about their 13-year-old son hanging around with a grown Monteith College professor. Later Tuohey found out that his father, who worked at Wayne State University (of which Monteith was a subsidiary college), did some checking up on Bails. Jerry passed muster, and as it turned out, proved to have a very positive effect on Mike's life. Bails recruited him to help with the production of *Alter-Ego* and his other fan projects. Tuohey folded flyers, affixing postage stamps, collating and stapling *A-E*, among other functions. In later life, Mike found the lessons in organization and producing a product helped him in his job. Jerry listed him in *Alter-Ego* #3 as a member of the "production staff," along with Don Foote and Gerry Sorek.

Having seen how it was done, Mike eventually began planning his own fanzine. The first issue of *Super-Hero* (Winter 1962–1963) was printed via hectograph in a run of just 20 copies. It was a humble beginning, but Mike had managed to achieve some good printing results for the hecto process, and published work by Ronn Foss, Alan Weiss and Tim Battersby. With *Super-Hero* #2 (Spring 1963), though, Tuohey leaped forward to produce a superb issue. Certainly, he benefited from receiving items for publication that Bails didn't feel were appropriate for *Alter-Ego*, and he gained access to Jerry's ditto machine which allowed for a better appearance and much larger print run. There's no denying that the final product was superior to most of the new fanzines that would appear on the scene in 1963. The cover by Grass Green featured Fighting American and Speedboy. Ted White contributed "A Partial Checklist of Artwork by Joe Simon and Jack Kirby," Roy Thomas did a one-page, 12-panel cartoon called "Capt. Cro-Magnon," Mike wrote an article on "Captain 3-D," Ken Tesar offered an original strip called "Thunderbird," Biljo White did a self-bio, there were short pieces on Speedboy and Yellow Claw, plus additional art by Mike Vosburg, Biljo White and Alan Weiss. Quite an issue, and one of which Mike is still justifiably proud.

Tuohey began gathering material for *Super-Hero* #3, but ran into a difficulty. Jerry had moved to 22529 Karem Court in Warren, Michigan, 17 miles from Mike's home. Tuohey could no longer get there by bicycle, and getting rides from his parents meant fewer visits. Without easy access to Bails' ditto machine, progress on the issue stalled and eventually Tuohey lost his enthusiasm. It would be finished and printed several years later by Richard Buckler, who took over the publishing of *Super-Hero* fully with the fourth issue.

Jerry's move to Warren was no barrier to Mike's attendance at the Alley Tally Party in March 1964. This event was intensely exciting for it offered the almost inconceivable thrill of meeting Big Name Fans from as far away as Ohio and Nebraska, some who had contributed to *Super-Hero*. As has been pointed out by Mike Vosburg, the 19 attendees tended to relate mostly (though not exclusively) with people their own age. So while Ed Aprill, Don and Maggie Thompson, Larry Raybourne and Jerry Bails were deep in discussion, Mike palled around with Jim Rossow, Bob Butts, Mike Vosburg and the younger set. Ronn and Grass, ever convivial and approachable, circulated among both groups. Still, everyone came together to tally the many ballots submitted in the 1963 Alley Awards Poll, which was the primary purpose of the gathering. The two-day Alley Tally Party is considered the first sizable gathering of the members of comic fandom.

Though Mike continued working on *Super-Hero* in a desultory fashion, and attended the Detroit Triple Fan Fair in 1965, his interest in fandom was waning. The experiences he was having in high school took precedence. Except for a brief return to hang out with Rich

Buckler to finish *Super-Hero* #3, Tuohey's involvement with fandom was over—for the time being.

High school graduation in 1966, attendance at Wayne State University (he received a B.A. in Psychology with a minor in English), his marriage to Susan Rahmel, and then a stint in the military (he was honorably discharged in 1972 as a conscientious objector) took center stage in Tuohey's life. He sold the bulk of his collection in 1971 to some dealers at the Triple Fan Fair. However, he occasionally picked up comic books from the stands over the ensuing years, such as Kirby's Fourth World titles. He was able to attend the 1983 San Diego Comic-Con, where he met Jack and Roz Kirby, and had the self described "great fanboy experience" standing a few feet away as Jack Kirby and Jerry Siegel embraced and renewed acquaintants after what must have been many years. Since then, Mike has been reading comics again and even doing a bit of collecting. Some of his favorites that kept him interested are comics with work by Frank Miller, Alan Moore and the Brothers Hernandez. In 1997, he and Jerry Bails met again at the Fandom Reunion held during the Chicago Comicon. Other Alley Tally attendees present were Maggie Thompson, Bob Butts, Jim Rossow and Grass Green.

Today, Mike is married (to Esther Romero, after the passing of his first wife) and his four children are grown. For the past 20 years, Tuohey has been an Informational Technology System Administrator. His current taste in comics gravitates to those written by Neil Gaiman, Brian Bendis, J. Michael Strazewski, Warren Ellis, Mike Millar and Geoff Johns. Tuohey said, "It is quite astonishing to me that today not only are there current stories of all the heroes from the '40s, '50s and '60s being published, but there are quality reprints of so much material and scholarly works outlining histories and biography of the creators. It's just wonderful."

Jerry Weist

(b. 1948)

(PHOTOGRAPH BY JIM GRAY)

Jerry Weist

Jerry Weist was editor and publisher of *Squa Tront*, sometimes referred to as the ultimate EC fanzine. *Squa Tront* brought in-depth information and appreciation of EC comics to fandom of the 1960s, and is credited for helping promote the career of Frank Frazetta.

Young Jerry Weist had a passion for monster movies and the monster magazines of the late 1950s and 1960s. Forrest J Ackerman—Uncle Forry—was the Pied Piper of this movement, with his *Famous Monsters of Filmland* the focal point for the interest in horror and fantasy films that was made possible by the television broadcasts of such films at that time. Weist and his buddy Roger Hill in Derby, Kansas, were snatching copies of *Famous Monsters* off the stands by the late 1950s. Jerry demonstrated a publishing urge early when he began putting out his own amateur versions of the monster mags, cranking out issues of *Nightmare* and *Movieland Monsters*, mimeographed efforts that he had completely written and drawn. When Ackerman was touring the country in order to meet with groups of his rabid followers, it was at the Weist home that he held court in the Wichita area.

Thus, an interest in EC—best known for *Tales from the Crypt* and *Vault of Horror*—seemed a logical progression for the teenager. Indeed, it was Jerry who showed Roger an EC comic book for the first time—*Panic #7*—which he had obtained from a dealer in Michigan. Before long, the boys were knee-deep in ECs of all genres, and thrilling over the appearance of a fanzine devoted solely to the erstwhile company: Rich Hauser's *Spa Fon*. The fanzine publisher in him immediately gave Weist the idea of putting out a sister zine about EC, which would be titled after the other form of alien expression used in EC science fiction comics, becoming *Squa Tront*. Weist was finishing high school, and planned a publication much superior to his earlier juvenile efforts, one that would even surpass the rather impressive *Spa Fon*.

Weist would serve as editor and publisher of *Squa Tront*, with Hill contributing both art and articles. Fellow Kansan Bob Barrett would co-edit, with a special emphasis on the works of Frank Frazetta. Chris Kettler was to be assistant editor, helping Jerry in whatever capacity was needed. Each brought different skills and areas of emphasis which, coupled with their shared passion for EC, helped achieve a high standard for the fanzine from the first issue. Roger, an aspiring artist, drew a cover to the first issue, inspired by Wally Wood's work for the EC science fiction comics, and he drafted his mother to work on the fanzine too. He recalled, "My mother did all the typing, on an IBM typewriter. She had access to an IBM typewriter because she was a secretary at a big corporation in Wichita for years. There was a way on there that you could justify your margins, and the type looked more professional than a regular typewriter." The first issue proved so successful that it went back to the printer for a second run. *Squa Tront #2* boasted a full color front cover by EC-alumnus Al Williamson, a back cover by Witchita-based Reed Crandall, and material by top fan artists Berni Wrightson and George Metzger.

For the third issue, published in 1969, Jerry came up with an incredibly ambitious package, with 80 pages of fabulous material highlighted by a stunning painting by Al Feldstein on the front cover, and a back cover featuring John Carter of Mars by Reed Crandall. The major features were a long article on the EC science fiction comics by Weist, a fascinating visit with the Frazettas at home by Barrett, a feature on Reed Crandall and a look at a proposed newspaper strip, "The Flying Swifts," by George Evans. The sheer size seems to have gotten away from Jerry, and he wrote in the editorial, "*Squa Tront* is dying. This issue will be the last—unless you want to see one more. My expenses for this issue amounts to a staggering $2,200. If this is not paid off in 30 days, then our hopes of putting out *Squa Tront* #4 ... are destroyed. The life or death of *Squa Tront* #4 lies in whether each and every one of you now reading this feels he can turn around and reorder #3 at its market price—$2.00 ... immediately!" In 1969, $2 for a fanzine was unheard of, though soon it would not be so unusual, as other fan editors realized that there was a market for a high-ticket publication if the production values, size and quality were top notch.

Fortunately, Weist was able to get his finances together sufficiently to produce another issue. *Squa Tront #4* was even more impressive than #3: 100 pages, with cover by Graham Ingels of the Old Witch, and much rare artwork by Harvey Kurtzman, George Evans, Al Williamson, Frank Frazetta, Roy G. Krenkel and others, plus complete strips by Bernard Krigstein and Reed Crandall. The issue extended the boundaries of its editorial purview to include fine works by non–EC artists such as Kenneth Smith, Richard Corben, Vaughn Bodé, George Metzger and Robert Kline. It was a fitting final issue, though fans greatly lamented its loss. However, by the mid–1970s, John Benson obtained Jerry's blessing to take over the title, publishing issues on an irregular schedule up to the present day. (The latest issues have been published by Fantagraphics Books.)

Jerry Weist now manages the famous Sotheby comic book auctions, which each year make news with the incredibly high prices that the rarest and most sought-after comic art items have commanded. His book *Bradbury: An Illustrated Life* (2003) was nominated for a Hugo Award for "Best Related Book," an award given annually by the World Science Fiction Convention for the best science fiction or fantasy works.

Ted White
(b. 1938)

One of the most interesting and ubiquitous of the double-fans in the 1950s and 1960s was Ted White, who went on from the amateur publishing field to become a novelist and editor of the professional SF magazines *Amazing* and *Fantastic*, as well as *Heavy Metal*. His fanzine one-shot, *The Facts Behind Superman* (1953), holds the distinction of being the earliest all-comics fanzine to publish a substantial prose history of a comic book character. White also acted as publisher of one of the best of the EC fanzines, *Potrzebie* #1 (1954), which presented editorial matter produced by Larry Stark and Bhob Stewart. In 1960, he wrote an entry in the famous "All in Color For a Dime" series of articles in *Xero*.

Theodore Edward White grew up in Falls Church, Virginia. "I'm sure that in many respects I was a typical comics fan," White later wrote in *Comic Art* #5 (1964). "From 1948 through 1953 or so, I relentlessly tracked down back issues of titles important to me ... by advertising on my school bulletin board and in the local paper, and repeatedly questioning all my friends. Every so often I'd stumble over a small hoard of needed comics, which I would then buy, trade for, or somehow wheedle from the owner." In 1952, White decided to create a fanzine called *The Story of Superman*. It was reprinted and revised four times, with the last one in late 1953 (or early 1954) renamed *The Facts Behind Superman*. Only the last edition was circulated beyond White's circle of friends, so the earlier ones might more properly be considered prototypes. Along with Eldon K. Everett and Ronald Graham, White wrote the 22-page treatment of the career of the Man of Steel, which sold for 10 cents. *The Facts Behind Superman* was printed on Ted's postcard mimeograph machine. While its size (4" × 6") and print run (probably no more than 35 copies) were

Ted White

modest, it represented the earliest known attempt to write an authoritative, in-depth article about a character created for comic books.

In *Squa Tront* #9 (1983), Ted remembered, "You know, I always had a foot in two different worlds back then. I was a comics fan—a very serious comics fan, written up by the Washington *Daily News* and the wire services as 'The Boy with Ten Thousand Comics'— but I was also a science fiction fan. Most SF fans looked down their noses at comics—and with some justification. After all, SF fandom had been given a bad name (as had SF itself) by the public media association of science fiction with 'Superman' and 'Buck Rogers,' which were very bad SF, irrespective of their merits as comics." White's SF fanzines included *Zip, Void* and *Stellar*.

When Bhob Stewart, whose *The EC Fan Bulletin #1* in April 1953 marked the beginning of EC fandom, decided to re-enter amateur publishing with a new, more impressive EC fanzine, Ted White acted as the publisher. Ted had formed his own mimeographing service called Qwertyuiop Press (named after the first line of alpha characters on the typewriter keyboard), and used his mimeo to print any number of EC and SF fanzines in the mid to late 1950s. White also became a contributor to Ron Parker's *Hoohah!*, writing critiques of EC's Picto-Fiction line, trip reports to the EC offices, and other miscellaneous pieces. His writing was concise, often humorous, occasionally acerbic, and always highly readable.

In 1959, at the age of 21, White moved from Falls Church, Virginia, to New York City with his first wife, Sylvia Dees White. The following year, the Whites were in attendance at the PittCon where the Lupoffs made their memorable appearance masquerading as Captain and Mary Marvel. Subsequently, after *Xero* and "All in Color For a Dime" were launched, White was the first to add another chapter to the AICFAD series. It was titled "The Spawn of M. C. Gaines." White began by discussing his devotion to collecting comics in the late 1940s and early 1950s, many which he had retained. "Comic books fascinate me," Ted wrote in *Xero* #2 (1960). "The way they were produced, the artists involved, the histories of the companies ... all this fascinates me." With that, White filled the next ten pages with an essential lesson in the history of DC Comics, beginning with an introduction to M. C. Gaines, whom he dubbed "The Father of Modern Comic Books."

As the 1960s progressed, it seemed that White's interest and involvement in comic fandom was crowded out by his focus on writing music criticism (for *Metronome* and *Jazz Guide*) and science fiction. His first professionally published story, "Phoenix," was written in collaboration with Marion Zimmer Bradley. White's first novel was *Invasion from 2500* (Monarch Books, 1964), a collaboration with Terry Carr using the pseudonym Norman Edwards. Ted went on to write many SF novels, and edited *Amazing* and *Fantastic*. He wrote a Captain America novel called *The Great Gold Steal* (Bantam, 1968). Despite his many achievements in the professional arena, White has always maintained that his fannish activities have meant the most to him, and it's fitting that he won a Hugo Award in 1968 for "Best Fan Writer."

SECTION IV:
CONVENTION ORGANIZERS

Science fiction conventions, which began in the late 1930s, were highly organized affairs from the very beginning. There was always a convention committee, with elected officials: a chairman or co-chairmen, secretary, treasurer, et al. It's fair to say that they took themselves quite seriously, and their approach to conventions was appropriately sober.

Comic book fans were a somewhat different lot—skewing younger, with plenty of teenagers, and extremely informal in their dress and demeanor—and the development of their conventions reflected their unpretentious natures.

Their earliest get-togethers, which might be deemed "proto-conventions," were highly spontaneous aggregations of as few as a half dozen participants to about twenty. Often planned no more than a few weeks in advance (or even a few days), with no set program other than perhaps the showing of an old movie serial, early gatherings in Los Angeles, Detroit, Chicago, San Francisco and a few other locales were lively, even rowdy affairs at times. The main activity was simply the showing, trading and selling of old comic books, and sometimes, original artwork. That, plus the opportunity for conversation with others of like mind, something exceedingly sweet to collectors who often experienced their hobby in relative isolation.

It wasn't long after the publication of *Alter-Ego* and *Comic Art* in 1961, and the influx of fans into what was laughingly, but somewhat appropriately, deemed "organized fandom," that people began wondering if a national comic book convention was feasible. Some, like Don and Maggie Thompson, and Richard and Patricia Lupoff, had attended SF cons, and knew such gatherings were do-able. But where? When? Would the first con be in the Midwest? Or New York City where the pros were, and might attend?

One of the initial difficulties was financial. High school students barely had enough money to keep up with their favorite 12-cent comic book titles, and few owned cars. How were they to afford a trip of any appreciable distance, especially if overnight accommodations were required? The adults in fandom were mainly in their twenties, a time when they were just beginning their lives after completing their education, and holding their first, often low-paying, jobs. Many were just starting families, and struggling to pay the bills. In general the standard of living in America in the early 1960s was lower than it is today. Plane travel was rare for working class and many middle class people, making cross-country treks more time consuming.

The leap to a national convention from smallish fan get-togethers was a big one, and was eventually bridged by an intermediate stage: regional conventions. The first was one held in New York City, sometimes billed as the "Tri-State Comicon" by organizer Bernie Bubnis. The Detroit Triple Fan Fair, which was only one-third about comics, was planned with the idea that it would draw from the Midwest and North Central states. Such regional conventions would continue even after the New York Comicon became recognized as the major, annual, national comic book convention. This recognition dawned in 1965, and became increasingly established in the latter part of that decade. By 1970, the Manhattan event had a rival on the opposite coast, in San Diego. Thus, the comicon grew from humble beginnings until there were two cons which could be called national in scope, along with many regional conventions in major population centers, such as Houston, St. Louis, Chicago, Miami, Detroit, even Oklahoma City.

The job of a convention organizer was a big one, not unlike planning a large wedding. It took organizational skill, financial and negotiating skills, and because one needs help, skill in dealing with all kinds of personalities. One must be a promoter, a spokesman, a ring leader and a master of ceremonies. As time went on, the organizer had to deal with matters of security and thievery as well. In the very beginning, convention organizers simply needed the desire to take on the task, the ability to raise enough money to rent a small venue, and some volunteers with varying abilities and a lot of enthusiasm to help out.

Despite the amount of work involved in mounting a comicon or nostalgia show, it was done by fans in addition to their other fannish activities. Some of the folks grouped under this heading contributed significantly in other ways to the world of fandom. Half of them were fanzine publishers. One of them was a major dealer. Perhaps they could have been classified in other sections of this book, but it was felt their efforts as convention organizers deserved to be spotlighted. Nevertheless, their entries don't de-emphasize their other often considerable contributions to the founding of comic fandom.

John Benson
(b. 1940)

John Benson organized a key New York comic book convention in 1966, the third two-day comicon ever, with Jack Kirby as Guest of Honor. He is also known for elevating the discussion of the comic book medium through the letters, articles, reviews and interviews he has contributed to the fanzines starting in the late 1950s. His interviews with key innovators in comics such as Gil Kane, Bernard Krigstein, Harvey Kurtzman and Will Eisner set a high standard. Yet Benson avows, "I'm not an intellectual. I've always been a child of popular culture."

John Benson spent most of his early years in the small towns of Mount Holly and Haddonfield, New Jersey, later moving to Philadelphia. His father was a printer and a Quaker theologian. As a youth, John was only an occasional reader of comics, mostly Dell titles. Then, when he was 12 years old (as he describes in an interview in *Alter Ego* #27, 2003), an older cousin "showed me the first four issues of *Mad* all at once, right after the fourth issue came out. That was the first popular culture thing that totally knocked me out. They were so strange and so different, and they were so perfect. They're whole, complete works of art ... totally organic. There was something about them that was mysterious. They were also so funny."

John continued his enthusiasm for *Mad* during a year in England in 1954–55, and on his return, while attending Westtown School, a Quaker boarding school, he bought some of the final ECs on the newsstands. One of these, *Incredible Science Fiction* #33, contained a plug for Fred von Bernewitz's *Complete EC Checklist*, which Benson immediately ordered. On February 4, 1956, he received Fred's acknowledgment, beginning a correspondence between the two that spanned some 100 letters. They met in person six months later, and it was Fred who introduced John, via correspondence, to Larry Ivie and directly or indirectly to the other players in EC fandom.

By the time Benson became active in EC fandom, Ron Parker's *Hoohah!* had become a very high quality publication, and the work in those pages by Archie Goodwin, Larry Ivie, Ted White, Larry Stark and others heightened Benson's interest. He contributed a very critical piece on the Feldstein-edited *Mad* magazine to *Hoohah!*, which highlighted the fact that Benson's strongest interest in EC comics was the work of Harvey Kurtzman. He recalled, "I considered myself an EC fan. But really, as I look back on it, the other EC comics were not material that I would have otherwise discovered or become interested in, if it hadn't been for Kurtzman." (*Alter Ego* #27) Nevertheless, he began ordering back issues of all the EC comics from several fans, paying between 15 and 50 cents each. His interest in comics broadened, and John not only developed an appreciation of the other EC artists, particularly Bernard Krigstein, but also reacquainted himself with the work of Will Eisner (he had read "The Spirit" in the Philadelphia *Bulletin*) and Carl Barks, both courtesy of Larry Ivie.

While attending Grinnell College, Benson published a fanzine of his own. The five issues of *Image* (1960–62) gave evidence of his increasing fascination with cinema, but contained plenty of comics-oriented material, including early interviews with Harvey Kurtzman, and even a report of a meeting with Will Eisner.

Starting in 1957 or 1958, John began a series of visits to New York City which continued until he moved there in 1963, cementing his friendships with Fred von Bernewitz, Larry Ivie and Bhob Stewart. In August 1962, Benson and Stewart—both admirers of the comic book artwork of Bernard Krigstein—interviewed Krigstein at length in the artist's home in Jamaica, Queens. In discussing his work on the comic book classic "Master Race" (*Impact* #1, 1955) and his other strips for EC, Krigstein proved to be remarkably articulate, and the resulting lengthy interview is surely the most extensive, penetrating and intelligent consideration of the sequential art form done up to that time—perhaps even to the present day. The resulting fanzine *Bhob Stewart and John Benson Talk with B. Krigstein* (ca. August 1963) is, therefore, a landmark publication in fandom history. Subsequently, Benson interviewed other industry giants, including Harvey Kurtzman (1965), Gil Kane (1967), Will Eisner (1969) and John Severin (1970). These saw print in fanzines like *Witzend*, *Graphic Story Magazine*, and *Alter Ego*, and in the case of Kurtzman as a stand-alone publication similar to the Krigstein one. In the sixties, Benson also contributed to *Castle of Frankenstein* magazine and wrote a few scripts for *Creepy* and *Eerie*.

A major contribution by Benson to the founding and development of comic fandom came in 1966, when he organized a comic

John Benson

book convention in New York City, the third two-day comicon ever (counting the Detroit Triple Fan Fair in 1965). If one considers the 1964 New York convention as a small preliminary event (since it lasted a mere four hours), David Kaler's 1965 "Academy Con" was the first comicon to establish the form of the "complete" convention that continued thereafter. When Kaler announced that he would not put on another convention, Benson, who had enjoyed the 1965 event, decided to keep comics conventions going and to put one on the following year. It was held July 23–24, 1966, with Jack Kirby as the Guest of Honor, and with film shows by Chris Steinbrunner. He enlisted the aid of his cohort from the science fiction Fanoclast group, Mike McInerney, and for the first time the expertise of SF fandom was applied to a comicon. There was a program booklet designed by Bill Pearson, with penciled panels by Jack Kirby on the front cover, and a back cover by Wallace Wood, drawn especially for the occasion. Golden Age artist Klaus Nordling made his only convention appearance, and there was a stunning display of original art for 15 to 20 prime DC comic book covers from the 1940s from the collection of Jerry Robinson. The con, which was held at the plush Park Sheraton Hotel, had a polished atmosphere throughout. One of the memorable moments was a debate between Leonard Darvin of the Comics Code and fan Don Thompson. Darvin told Ted White and Don Thompson that Bill Gaines should *thank* the Comics Code Authority for virtually driving him to create the magazine version of *Mad*, which had been Gaines' economic salvation. Ted White was livid! Other guests on hand included Wally Wood, Archie Goodwin, Gray Morrow, Otto Binder, Gil Kane, Dick Giordano, and Sal Trapani. Somewhere between 150 and 200 fans attended. As it turned out, David Kaler changed his mind and put on his own convention in August 1966 (though he did not inform Benson, who found out too late to cancel his), proving that comic fandom had grown to the point where it could support two full comicons within three weeks of each other.

When Phil Seuling took over the New York comicons in 1968 (along with an organization called SCARP—the Society for Comic Art Research and Preservation, Inc.—the first year), John Benson was part of the staff in the earlier years, co-producing the program books with Bill Pearson the first three years, transcribing and editing panel discussions for inclusion in subsequent programs, chairing panels and much more.

Benson published two issues of a general magazine about comics, *Panels* (1980–84) and currently edits the EC magazine *Squa Tront*. He edited and/or wrote many of the annotations for Russ Cochran's hardbound, slip-cased Complete EC Library, was a contributor to Ron Goulart's *Encyclopedia of American Comics*, and recently did the annotations for the Fantagraphics' slip-cased reprint of the Kurtzman magazine *Humbug*. He has contributed features about comics to many publications, including *The Comics Journal*, *Alter Ego*, and *The Cartoonist*, and recently edited two books about the St. John romance comics, *Romance without Tears* and *Confessions, Romances, Secrets, and Temptations* (both from Fantagraphics). John lives in Manhattan with his wife, Freidel.

Bernie Bubnis

(b. 1948)

Bernie Bubnis was an energetic SF and comic book fan who published a number of fanzines between 1962 and 1964. However, his most important contribution to the early years of fandom—a considerable one—was organizing the first New York Comicon in 1964.

By 1963, fans began discussing the possibility of a national comicon, or at least a regional one. Small local gatherings of handfuls of fans were happening with increasing frequency, with a key one at Biljo White's house in Columbia, Missouri. Jerry Bails, Roy Thomas and Biljo met for the first time in mid–1963. One of the key topics was the possibility of larger gatherings. Then, when Jerry Bails inaugurated the formation of the Academy of Comic-Book Fans and Collectors by circulating its official charter in September, he included assisting and supporting an annual comicon to the list of the Academy's functions. It was felt that the Academy would add respectability to fandom, thus gaining more credibility with the pros.

An effort to hold a regional con in Omaha in June had fallen through, but fans in the New York area began planning in earnest in November 1963. When George Pacinda, a major supplier of industry news to *The Comic Reader*, announced rather grandiose plans for an International Comicon to be held in New York City, fans were pleased, if a little skeptical. Enthusiasm seemed to dwindle when an attendance fee of $15—then a substantial sum—was mentioned. Soon it became clear that the committee was spinning its wheels, and nothing concrete was actually getting accomplished.

At this juncture, 16-year-old Bernie Bubnis (who had contributed to *The Rocket's Blast* #1 in 1961) decided to take matters into his own hands. In Ronn Foss's new "wire service" fanzine, *Dateline: Comicdom* #7 (February 1964), Bubnis wrote, "I know you'll probably make me play the part of heavy in the drama of putting on the Comicon, but I don't care what sort of criticism I get thrown at me—I'm going to take a crack at it. We need all the help and publicity we can swing. We've got to let fandom know that an organized group of fans are definitely putting on a plan to get this Con going."

Bubnis did his best to reduce expectations. He acknowledged that it wouldn't be anything like the grandiose convention that Pacinda had promised. He and his cohort, Ron Fradkin, decided to limit the con to one afternoon. It would be held on July 27, 1964, a Monday. This was selected because it was thought that they would have a better chance of gaining pro attendance from DC and Marvel, since it was a normal workday in Manhattan when such folks (especially editors) would already be downtown. It was held in the Workman's Circle Building on 4th Avenue, near Union Square.

Bernie Bubnis

On that day, fans were met at the door by Art Tripp, who gave each one a metal button two inches in diameter (red and blue lettering on a white field) emblazoned with the words, *"Comicon 1964."* Bubnis called the convention to order around 2:00 P.M. The program began with a question-and-answer session with Dave Twedt, an intern working at Marvel for the summer. As the several dozen fans in attendance peppered Twedt with questions, Steve Ditko arrived. One question Twedt hadn't answered was how much the writers and artists got paid. He referred the question to Steve Ditko, who declined to answer with a shake of the head.

Bubnis announced a break for refreshments, offering fans soda pop courtesy of local dealer Phil Seuling. Other dealers present were Don Foote, Howard Rogofsky, Claude Held,

Marc Nadel and Bill Thailing, but only Seuling and Foote had actual comics for sale. The others were armed only with their price lists. At one point, Malcolm Willits arrived with a box of comics for sale that included *Action* #1, *Captain America* #1 and *Superman* #1. Nearly all the attendees hailed from New York or New Jersey, though Ohio (Bill Thailing), Maryland (Rick Weingroff, Al Russell) and California (Tom Wilson, Mal Willits) had representatives. Others present were Paul Gambaccini, Dave Kaler, Margaret Gemignani and Dave Bibby.

In about an hour, Bubnis called the group to order for a presentation by Gold Key Lone Ranger artist Tom Gill, who set up two easels and entertained the group for 45 minutes. Then it was time to distribute the door prizes. Just about everyone in the group of 50 fans received something, usually a piece of original art. (Although no one from DC attended, editor Murray Boltinoff did contribute art for door prizes, and Julie Schwartz also supplied some pages.) The remainder of the time was spent with more swapping, gabbing and trading. Fans drifted out, and at 6:15 P.M., Bubnis declared the con closed.

Years later, Bernie Bubnis commented, "I had no conception of how to organize a comi-con. I was just too young. I probably had more respect for SF than comics, at the time. Of course, I had no idea that the 1964 comicon would mean anything, historically. I just did it because I thought *someone* should." In the 36-page souvenir booklet that was published after the event, Bubnis was self-effacing, and ran Rick Weingroff's rather pointed critique of the con. This and other post mortems talked about various shortcomings (lack of publicity, hard-to-find location, the weekday date, lack of pros, the stuffy room, etc.) but, in the final analysis, all gave due credit to Bubnis. If not for his efforts, the con would not have happened. The 1964 New York Comicon has traditionally been considered the first real comicon, perhaps because of the presence of three representatives from Marvel, and the number of well-known fans and dealers in attendance.

Bernie Bubnis continued reading comics into the early '70s but a stint in Vietnam, a return to college and then earning a living pulled him away from the hobby. He kept in touch by reading (and occasionally writing for) *RBCC*, and later *The Buyer's Guide for Comic Fandom*, even though he was no longer collecting or reading comics. He still reads *Comics Buyer's Guide* and marvels at the size of modern comicons.

Of those halcyon years, Bubnis recently wrote, "It pleases me to know I was somewhere there in the beginning. The 1964 Con may not have impressed anyone else, but I learned a lot about myself. I realized I could get things done and that thought helped me conquer a whole bunch of projects in my later life. I owe fandom a debt of gratitude. It helped a geeky, out-of-step, misfit take himself seriously. I am forever grateful. It was surely the best time of my life. Get me on the next time machine to the '60s!"

Shel Dorf

(1933–2009)

Comic strip enthusiast and artist, veteran interviewer and columnist, and co-founder of the Detroit Triple Fan Fair and the San Diego Comic-Con, Dorf's contributions to fandom are many. He is especially known for his keen appreciation of the professionals who created the comics; much of his involvement in fandom was to accord those creators their long overdue recognition.

Sheldon Dorf would later describe himself as a boy as painfully shy, retreating into his world of hobbies. He found solace in the pages of the popular comic strips of his youth, with "Dick Tracy" and "Terry and the Pirates" being his favorites. Growing up in the 1940s, he collected both the comics that reprinted newspaper strips (*Super Comics, Famous Funnies, Popular Comics, King Comics, Comics on Parade, Tip-Top*, etc.), and the superhero comics that became ubiquitous during World War II (especially *Dollman, Daredevil* and *Capt. Marvel Jr.*). Young Dorf showed a nascent art ability, which led him as a young man to find employment as a local commercial artist.

In 1963, he found AbleMan's Bookstore in Hamtramck, Michigan, which proved to be a pivotal event in his life. It was in Tom Altschuler's bookstore that he met other comic strip, comic book, and Big Little Book collectors. The nucleus of Detroit fandom would meet in that establishment every Saturday on an informal basis. AbleMan's was a large store which had the normal fare for such an establishment downstairs. However upstairs, where the public didn't have access, the place was crammed with Big Little Books, comic books, movie magazines and all manner of goodies. "He had beautiful stuff," Shel Dorf recalled wistfully. "One whole back wall was nothing but Big Little Books—10, 12 copies of each different title. For a fan, it was like you'd died and gone to heaven. I filled up a lot of gaps in my collection of old newspaper strips. Tom's attic was a real treasure trove."

After the invitation-only Alley Tally Party at Jerry Bails' house on March 21, 1964, Detroit fans were determined to throw a real fan-meet in the Motor City. This gathering was more like a swap-meet than a real convention and was held at the Hotel Tuller in downtown Detroit, and had as many movie fans as comics aficionados. There were several "short talks" by various fans with expertise on their subject. Shel Dorf's presentation was a talk on Edgar Rice Burroughs. This event was planned by two teenage fans, Dave Szurek and Bob Brosch. Some 70 fans and collectors attended.

A similar gathering in New York City on July 27, 1964, seemed to generate the first of a flood of newspaper articles on the comic book hobby. In early 1965, a *Newsweek* stringer contacted Jerry Bails for an interview. Bails contacted Dorf and a handful of other Detroit fans who went to Bails' home on January 16, 1965, for the round robin interview. Shel predictably emphasized the appreciation of newspaper comic strips, pointing out that Milton Caniff's work had been shown in museums, and was accepted by some as fine art. In the eventual article, "Superfans and Batmaniacs," which appeared in *Newsweek* the week of February 15, only Bails and Dorf were mentioned by name.

Shel Dorf

After the *Newsweek* reporter left, Dorf later recalled that the gathered fans began initial discussions that would lead to a larger comic convention in Detroit that year. It was decided that the convention would be aimed at fans of movies and fantasy literature, as well as comic art, so as to attract the largest gathering possible. It was recognized that many fans' interests overlapped into those areas, too. Someone, perhaps Dorf, came up with the name "Detroit Triple Fan Fair." The con committee of 12 was led by Chairman Shel Dorf (who designed the logo for it) and Co-chairman Carl Lundgren; also on board were Jerry Bails and Edwin Aprill, Jr. Another committee member, Gary Crowdus, was an aspiring filmmaker. Crowdus was a central member of the Midwest Film Society and had sponsored many movie showings in the recreation room in his home. He helped Dennis Kawicki handle the movie-division of the con. The Detroit Triple Fan Fair was held at the Embassy Hotel on July 24–25, 1965, and proved to be a great success. Over a dozen dealers brought thousands of comics, old movie magazines, stills and other collectibles. The program featured the showing of the original *The Phantom of the Opera* (1925) as well as movie serials and prominent speakers. The only thing missing was comics professionals, but everyone agreed it was still a great success, and the event spawned a series of annual Detroit comicons.

For a commercial artist, Shel found it tough going in Detroit, and decided to move to New York City in 1967 to pursue his art career. However, by 1969 he was living in San Diego, and helping to organize the push for an actual comicon in that city. Dorf, Richard Alf, Ken Krueger, Scott Shaw, and others pondered the possibility, but the hotels required money up front, and they had little to invest. They decided to test the waters with a mini-con, which was held on March 21, 1970. Its success was largely due to the support of Forrest J Ackerman. Ackerman was Special Guest of Honor. His fame brought in followers of *Famous Monsters of Filmland*. When asked how he was able to persuade a big name like Forry to attend a little mini-con, Dorf replied, "He had a lot of firsts to his career, and I asked him, 'Would you attend the first comicon in San Diego as our special guest?' He accepted, and paid for it out of his own pocket, too. It was Forry Ackerman's fame that actually put us on the map and started the San Diego comicon off." By putting on the one day mini-con, the committee was able to raise enough money to print fliers and to line up the three day convention.

San Diego's Golden State Comic-Con (as it was first known) was held August 1–3, 1970, at the U.S. Grant Hotel. Two of the most illustrious guests were Jack Kirby and Ray Bradbury. The program booklet boasted a beautiful two-color Kirby cover, a caricature of Bradbury by Caniff, and numerous sketches by Marvel and DC pros. While no one knew at the time, the San Diego Comicon would go on to become the premiere West Coast comicon, and then the leading comicon in the world. According to Dorf, the support of Kirby and Ackerman cannot be emphasized enough in terms of lending credibility to the con. Among his many contributions to comic fandom, it must be remembered that it was Shel who managed to coax Jerry Siegel into attending his first comicon in the mid–1970s, and started the ball rolling to get Siegel and Shuster some sort of financial compensation from DC Comics, publisher of the adventures of the duo's creation Superman.

In the 1970s, with all the connections he made as chairman of the San Diego Comicon, Dorf really came into his own. He became an inveterate interviewer and article-writer for industry fanzines and magazines. Shel conducted important interviews with such luminaries as Russ Manning, Wally Wood, Milton Caniff and many others. In 1977, he began an 11-year stint as letterer for Caniff's "Steve Canyon," though he hated lettering and the pay at first—$35 a week to do six dailies and a Sunday strip—was paltry. Later, Shel admitted that this assignment had many positive ramifications in his life. For one thing, it allowed him to intensify his friendship with Caniff. With the cartoonist's permission, Dorf taped many of their long telephone conversations. Eventually, those tapes were given to R. C. Harvey when he was writing the book *Meanwhile... : A Biography of Milton Caniff, Creator of Terry and the Pirates and Steve Canyon,* the definitive biography, published by Fantagraphics Books in 2007.

By the 1980s, Dorf's involvement with the San Diego Comi-Con gradually diminished, though he would always be a guest of the convention. He lamented how commercial it had become. Shel seemed more enthusiastic about the fan gatherings he held in his home each year, when friends were in San Diego for the con. His writing for the fan press flourished in the 1980s and 1990s, and he wrote for all the top publications of that genre, including *Comic Book Marketplace, Cartoonist Profiles, Comics Interview, Graphic Story World, The Comics Journal, Nemo, The Jack Kirby Collector, Alter Ego* and *Comic Buyer's Guide.* Dorf edited Blackthorne's series of "Dick Tracy" reprint comics. Shel Dorf passed away November 3, 2009, in Sharp Memorial Hospital in San Diego. His brother, Michael Dorf, was at his side.

David Kaler
(b. 1936)

Dave Kaler was a key figure in the advancement of the New York Comicon, which was considered a "national comicon" because it drew fans from all regions of the United States. Dave was the third Executive Secretary of the Academy of Comic Book Fans and Collectors, after Jerry Bails and Paul Gambaccini. He also regularly contributed news of the professional comics industry to *The Comic Reader.*

It's unclear exactly when David Kaler first became involved in comic fandom. As he tells it, he was so weak from a protracted illness that he couldn't concentrate on prose novels, so friends brought him comic books to read. Among those comic books were issues of *Showcase*

Flo Steinberg and David Kaler

with the new Flash and other heroes that contained letters from such notables as Jerry Bails and Roy Thomas. Dave wrote to Jerry to get more details about fanzines, and was thus introduced to fandom. Kaler's name is listed in the supplement to the *Who's Who in Comic Fandom,* so he was involved by spring of 1964. He attended the first New York comicon on July 27, 1964.

Kaler was 28 years old at the time, and working as a market researcher. When it became clear that someone new was needed to spearhead a full-fledged New York comicon in 1965, Dave volunteered. This convention was to have the imprimatur (and financial backing) of the Academy. It wasn't long before Kaler had become Executive Secretary of the organization, after Paul Gambaccini's one-year term. With the help of a crew of enthusiastic local fans, including Marv Wolfman, Len Wein, Mark Hanerfeld and Phil Seuling, Dave set about planning and publicizing the event.

He later recalled, "I got people like Jim Steranko [who had not yet begun working for Marvel Comics], and a whole group of people that I knew from DC and Marvel, who cooperated with me wonderfully." On July 31, 1965, fans converged on the Greenwich Village site of the Hotel Broadway Central, a fleabag hotel where a single room with a private bath cost $6, and a double was $8. Admission to the con was $5 for both days. Comicon II pulled in close to 200 fans, according to Tom Fagan's report in *The Golden Age* #2 (1966), which described the attendees as a curious mix of "well-dressed teenagers, and a few bearded and long-haired, others in T-shirts (Marvel shirts to be noted amongst them)." Jerry Bails acted as moderator of the first panel, featuring Gardner Fox and Otto Binder. It seems quite appropriate that they should be the first two big name pros to speak at a fan-sponsored event, given their participation in the earliest days of comicdom. When Bill Finger joined them, some fans were surprised to learn how instrumental he had been in the development of the characters of Batman and Robin. This was the first comic book convention to adopt most of the aspects of prior SF conventions: panel discussions, auctions, keynote speaker, a masquerade competition and more, including spanning more than one day. During the 1965 con's two days, fans scarcely had an opportunity to catch their breath, with the gaps between presentations being filled in with much buying and selling of rare back issues. This was the "blueprint" that was followed for subsequent New York cons, and Kaler was the first one to organize a comicon in this form. One very strange footnote to this comicon was that the Hotel Broadway Central collapsed for no apparent reason several years later.

In an interview with Dave Kaler in *Newsday* (November 4, 1965), when asked about the future of comic fandom, Dave responded prophetically, "No ones knows how long it will last, but the future is bright. More college students are finding that comics are interesting and not just trash. And so many children of the next generation will be reading comics without the stigma attached to it by today's adults." Fandom expressed its appreciation to Dave by giving him an Alley Award, when they voted the New York Comicon "Best Fan Project" in 1965.

In the post-comicon period, an exhausted Kaler told anyone who would listen that he would never helm another con. Local fan John Benson took him at his word, and began organizing for a New York con in 1966. Somewhere along the line, Dave changed his mind and decided to go forward with a follow-up to his 1965 gathering, so there ended up being two New York Comicons in the summer of 1966, one in July and another in August. Both were well attended and successful. At Kaler's con, Stan Lee made his first appearance at such an event, as Guest of Honor.

Dave chaired one more comicon in 1967, and then had finally had enough. By this time, he had broken into comics at Charlton as writer of Captain Atom (drawn by Steve Ditko), helped by the recommendation of his friend and roommate Roy Thomas. They shared a two-room apartment in east Greenwich Village with another young comics writer, Denny O'Neil. In addition to costumed heroes, Kaler wrote *Black Fury* as well as various hot-rod comics and romance comics for Charlton, then tried to follow editor Dick Giordano to DC Comics with limited success. He worked for Skywald on a revival of The Heap. Later he performed editorial functions for Woody Gelman at Nostalgia Press on books featuring Flash Gordon, Little Nemo and others.

Kaler's contributions to the fanzines consisted mainly of news items sent to the editors of *The Comic Reader/On the Drawing Board*, from 1965 to 1967. In the course of promoting the comicons, he made many contacts in professional comics, and was well positioned to obtain the latest news. Dave also wrote a column of "news and notes from the Academy of

Comic Art Collectors" called "Fandom Speaks" that appeared in King Comics in 1967. He passed the Executive Secretary position of the Academy of Comic Book Fans and Collectors on to Mark Hanerfeld, who became the publisher of *The Comic Reader* in 1968. The much-vaunted Academy had become moribund by that time, having accomplished all that it could.

Dave and his friend Bill Morse opened a comic book store called Adventure Bound, initially on Staten Island, then moved to Manhattan. Dave also worked for Supersnipe, another comic book store in Manhattan. His current whereabouts and welfare are unknown.

Phil Seuling
(1934–1984)

Brooklyn native Phil Seuling did much to popularize comic collecting as a hobby in the 1960s and 1970s, first as one of the nation's leading comic book dealers, beginning in the early 1960s when he was not yet 30 years old, and then as a convention impresario *par excellence,* starting when he co-hosted the New York show in 1968. Worried about the serious circulation and distribution problems afflicting the comics industry by the end of the Silver Age, he conceived of the Direct Market to serve a growing network of comic book stores in the mid–1970s. In partnership with other distributors, Seuling used his Seagate Distribution to help create a viable way for comics to survive despite ever-decreasing circulation figures.

Seuling, for many years an English teacher at Lafayette High School in Brooklyn, grew to love comics as a grade school student during World War II, and would often wax eloquent on that bygone era. Phil and his wife, Carole, and their daughters Gwen and Heather, quickly became well known to thousands of comic fans during the years of continual convention expansion from 1968 to 1974 in Manhattan. Seuling and Carole split in the latter stage of this historic period and later divorced.

Seuling was among the first to issue extensive price lists of Golden Age comics, beginning in 1962, when he was teaching at Lafayette High, not far from where he was born in the Bensonhurst neighborhood of Brooklyn. He was a Big Name Fan but sometimes, semi-humorously, complained that others received all the kudos. In *RBCC* #37 (1965), in his col-

Left to right: Carole Seuling, Otto Binder and Phil Seuling as Captain Marvel, at the 1965 New York Comicon.

umn "Seuling's Corner," Phil wrote, "When the writer from *Newsweek* called and interviewed me during a 45-minute telephone call, and when they borrowed my fanzines to examine, and when the photographer spent three hours at my place photographing covers of my books—naturally I was eager to see the completed article. It appeared in the February 15th issue (and the photographs came out well). So where did they give me credit? Only in a letter enclosed with a complimentary copy—not the article. So fame escapes me. But now CBS-TV has called and interviewed [me], and will visit my lair soon, so I still have a chance as the world's foremost authority on my own collection."

By the time he co-hosted the 1968 convention, Phil had produced 12 comprehensive price lists. His friendships with leading New York artists resulted in sketches on the covers of his lists from the likes of Jim Steranko, Al Williamson, Gray Morrow and Roy Krenkel. The cover of list #10 (Summer 1967) featured a nifty caricature of Phil along with the phrase, "Comic Book King." He would write a short message to customers at the top of his lists, such as this one for list #18, dated Spring 1972: "10 years of these comic book price lists and look at the size of this one! (It was 20 pages; *Batman* #5 was $35, *Fantastic Four* #1 was $35 and *Amazing Fantasy* #15 was $25.) Five years of comic conventions (including 1972) and this year it's five days long!"

In 1973, the year the third *Overstreet Comic Book Price Guide* appeared, Phil was still telling his customers, "All of my books are good or very good or excellent. But I cannot list condition of each copy. Therefore, I price them as if all were good, and you get the benefit if they are better than you bargained for. I refuse even to answer letters about the mint category, which I think is silliness." Phil became famed for saying, "Mint is a candy flavor, not a comic book condition." In earlier lists, Phil would proclaim, "I will not search out better condition (than good), which is unfair to others, and far too time-consuming."

Phil's first convention, sponsored by the short-lived Society for Comic Art Research and Preservation, Inc. (SCARP), and thus called the SCARP International Convention of Comic Art, was held on the entire top floor of New York's famed Statler-Hilton Hotel, 33rd Street and 7th Avenue, on July 4–7, 1968. Although significant comic book conventions had been held since 1964 in New York, as well as the Triple Fan Fair in Detroit, the 1968 New York show was by far the most important convention to date. To show how much influence Seuling had, Will Eisner contributed the program's cover and Al Williamson, Gray Morrow, Wally Wood, Roy G. Krenkel, Dan Adkins and Gil Kane donated art to the program booklet.

Phil wrote an essay for the program, "On Reading Comics in America, WW II," which was among the earliest writing about the influence of comic books on youth, following in the wake of Jules Feiffer's milestone, *The Great Comic Book Heroes*, in 1965. It read:

> Art exposes truth; the art I studied (in World War II comic books) gave me a clarity of vision I've long since experienced only through a few works of great insight and perception. War and politics and inter-personal relationships and the psyche—and so many more human problems— were far beyond my then young comprehension. Comics (books and strips both) became my teacher, reducing abstracts and complexities to learnable parts. The war and comics were formative influences; I've never been a subtle person. The war ended. So, for a while, did comics. Judging by my own experience and by well-known sales figures, readership fell to a fragment of what it had been. Their influence, though, never declined (but) increased rather as the world became less understandable and I looked to my "education" to assist me, now 12 years old, in handling a new world. It had been a time of inhumanity and savagery, not a time to grow up in. But I was given no other time. Study us who are in our thirties since we are assuming leadership of this world just about now. Study us to know how we think and why we act. (But) eliminate World War II and comics from your motivational research and we'll laugh at you.

The SCARP guests of honor in 1968 were Stan Lee and Burne Hogarth, and many of the leading comic artists who lived in the New York area attended. Phil's wife, Carole, chaired what was by far the most elaborate comics costume event ever held at a comic convention at that point. Phil followed up in 1969 with his first Seuling-owned show, an even more elaborate convention, held July 4–6, again on the entire eighteenth floor of the Statler-Hilton. His guests of honor were Hal Foster and Harvey Kurtzman, giving Seuling the reputation as a convention impresario of the first rank. In his first two conventions, he attracted four icons: the most influential of all comic book editors, the man who began the most iconic humor magazine in American history, and two of the finest comic-strip artists in the annals of an original American pop culture phenomenon.

"I was in awe of Phil's organizational and networking abilities," said Michelle Nolan, a friend and customer who drove from California's Bay Area to New York in 1969 to help Seuling with the convention. Phil didn't yet drive and used Nolan's 1964 Chevrolet to transport artwork and other convention staples. "Phil was a human dynamo unlike anything ever seen before or since in the comic book world. Anyone who ever met him would never forget him. People would sometimes get angry or frustrated with him because he wasn't one to suffer fools gladly, but he and his family and friends advanced the cause of comic collecting exponentially with those first two conventions in 1968 and 1969. I remember after the 1969 show was over, Phil celebrated at his apartment at the old-time fan-familiar address of 2883 West 12th Street, near Coney Island. He threw several thousand dollars in gate receipts into the air, letting out an ear-splitting whoop of joy that the show had been successful, both artistically and financially." What did it cost to attend the 1969 show in the Big Apple? A grand total of $3.50 for all three days. Dealer's tables were $10. Factoring in inflation, those figures are something like $20 and $75 today, still a bargain at anyone's major comic convention.

Watching all this develop was Paul Levitz, who was to work his way up the DC ladder to become publisher. Levitz has filled more roles in comic fandom and prodom alike than anyone else since he was a New York teenager in the 1960s. Perhaps nobody ever captured Seuling's spirit better than Levitz did in poetic fashion when he talked with co-author Steve Duin for the 1998 book *Between the Panels:* "The heart of understanding Phil as an individual is to understand Phil was an English teacher, a writer, a communicator, someone who loved words and ideas, and loved them in comics. He was the kind of person that if someone gave him pleasure, he desperately, urgently wanted to share it with other people to whom it would give pleasure, whether that was food, a comic book, the work of an artist, a conversation with an interesting person. You may or may not have known people like that in your life, who have a sheepdog like quality of wanting to bound in your lap and say, 'Look at this goddamn great bone I found in the backyard. Do you want to give it a chew?'"

Levitz continued, "Phil envisioned two things from which much of the shape of the business today flows. When [Jack] Kirby had disappeared from view, he talked Jack into coming back to New York for a comic convention as a 'guest of honor.' That had never been done in that fashion. He found Hal Foster and Will Eisner, who were unconnected to the mainstream of comic stuff, and pulled them back in. He got the publishers involved; he was the first person to reach out and say, 'You know, you ought to have a booth at a comic convention.' That was an extraordinarily radical concept 25 years ago."

Seuling continued his comic book conventions and year-round Sunday shows in the early 1980s, but he fell on hard times late in his life, losing his teaching job because of a controversial bust for selling underground comix to minors. When he died of a rare liver disease at age 50 in 1984, comic fandom was left with indelible memories of a unique, powerful and ground-breaking man.

SECTION V: WRITERS

Most hobbies need writers, especially when a hobby is focused on published works. Writers are necessary to convey information about those works, and to discuss the relative merits of the creative works being collected. In the fanzines that sprang up in the 1950s and 1960s, there were four main types of text features: (1) factual articles, (2) opinion pieces, (3) amateur fiction, and (4) letter columns. In addition, there was a great deal of miscellaneous writing that was needed, for various kinds of announcements, squibs, policy statements, calls for subscriptions, and more.

Many of fandom's scribes wrote on a juvenile level. Most of the text in the fanzines was, of course, simply serviceable. Nevertheless, a surprising number of the fanzines offered work by writers who possessed above-average ability. Some of these amateur wordsmiths stand out simply because they had better access to old comic books, virtually the only reference material in existence. Others offered perspectives and analysis that reflected above-average intelligence or understanding. While hordes of teenagers became fanzine publishers, nearly all of these better writers were adults.

The fans profiled in this section were primarily known for creating text features that were able to attract and hold the attention of the older fans that were such a necessary part of comicdom. In doing so, they received the kind of written responses that could make up an interesting letter column. They also implicitly conveyed the message that comic art was worthy of an adult's attention, and that the fanzines were worth their subscription dollars. After all, older fans tended to have more money than teenagers, and were able to support some of the higher-priced publishing endeavors that came out of fandom.

We hasten to add that many of the folks included in other sections of this book were above-average writers. Malcolm Willits, Gary Brown, Larry Herndon, Steve Herring, Dick Lupoff, Bill Spicer, Bhob Stewart, Don Thompson, Maggie Thompson, Ted White, John Benson, Bob Butts, Mark Evanier, Don Glut, Rick Norwood and Marv Wolfman (among others) could have fit here, if they didn't have even stronger claims for falling into another category. However, the 12 individuals in this section—11 men and one woman—are those whose ability to puts words on a page was their strongest claim to fame. Fandom would have been a much poorer place without them.

Michael Barrier

(b. 1940)

Michael Barrier published *Funnyworld*, the fanzine dedicated to animation and comic art, and was one of the most articulate, well-informed writers in comicdom on the subject of animated movies, cartoons and comic art in general.

Michael Barrier was born June 15, 1940, in Little Rock, Arkansas, where he now lives after a lapse of almost 30 years. On his web site, Barrier sheds light on his early years: "Like almost anyone else, I was first attracted to animation and the comics when I was a child. My interest was unusually intense—I published my own hectographed comic book for several years—and, to my surprise, I could not shed it after I reached adulthood. I finally stopped trying while I was a law student at the University of Chicago. I began seeking out the comic books drawn by former Disney cartoonists like Carl Barks and Walt Kelly. I also started paying close attention to animated cartoons again, and I found that the best of them repaid serious study just as the best silent comedies did."

Barrier first became aware of fandom in his last year at the university, when he read the famous (or infamous) "Superfans and Batmaniacs" article about comicdom in *Newsweek* (February 1965). He contacted Jerry Bails who sent him printed information on fandom and fanzines. Barrier ordered zines, got on dealers' mailing lists, bought stacks of comics from Bill Thailing in particular, and became active by joining the comics apa *Capa-Alpha*. He named his apa-zine *Funnyworld*, which soon grew into a separate and very impressive fanzine. Michael became known to much of fandom when his original funny animal strip appeared in Bill Spicer's *Fantasy Illustrated* #7 (Spring 1967). Barrier's 20-page "Captain Egg" was quite accomplished, and demonstrated an understanding of the funny animal medium.

Michael's letters began appearing in *FI* and other fanzines, and he was well known by the time *Funnyworld* moved from *Capa-alpha* to become an entirely independent fanzine, with #12 in the summer of 1970. That issue sported a cover by George Metzger, an article on the underground comix scene ("Notes on the Underground"), an interview with Bob Clampett (producer, director and animator), and reviews (of such films as *Yellow Submarine*). All of it was written by Barrier. That an interview dominated the issue would become standard practice for the zine. *Funnyworld* appeared on an irregular schedule for the next ten years, selling several thousand copies of each issue.

Then Barrier shifted his attention to book projects such as co-editing with Martin Williams *A Smithsonian Book of Comic-Book Comics* (1981) and in the 1980s, *Carl Barks and the Art of the Comic Book* (1982), a biography and bibliography of the Disney comic book artist. His greatest achievements, however, took him almost 24 years to finish. First, his masterwork *Hollywood Cartoons: American Animation in Its Golden Age* (1999), and after that, his biography of Walt Disney, *The Animated Man: A Life of Walt Disney* (2008). If he wrote nothing else, these two books are an impressive culmination of Barrier's interest in animation and comic art.

Since writing books doesn't pay all the bills, Michael has worked as a journalist, a lawyer, and a political aide, analyzing important legislation for a U.S. senator. In later years, he was a senior editor of *Nation's Business*.

Fandom as well as the rest of the

Michael Barrier with Carl Barks

world have Michael Barrier to thank for interviewing hundreds of animators and comic artists who are no longer with us, and capturing their memories and perspectives. These interviews have given his books unique insights, which is a major reason why they are so complete and authoritative.

Tom Fagan
(1932–2008)

Tom Fagan was probably best known as the co-founder of the famous Halloween parade in Rutland, Vermont, which featured Batman as Grand Marshal, presiding over numerous floats ridden by fans dressed as their favorite comic book heroes or heroines. However, he is equally important in the history of comic fandom for his well-written articles that appeared in the early fanzines.

Born M. Thomson Fagan, Tom grew up in Rutland, the son of a physician. His love for Halloween began when he was little more than a toddler, when his parents brought him to a big Halloween party in Rutland for children of low-income families. (This was during the Great Depression of the 1930s.) Though he had just edged past his teenage years when James Dean became a star in *East of Eden* and *Rebel Without a Cause*, Fagan was a fan and deeply affected by the actor's tragic death in a car crash. Tom became known for wearing all-black and affecting a James Dean hairstyle for the rest of his life. He named his daughter Deana.

In 1960, Rutland had its first Halloween parade, a fairly modest affair; thereafter, Tom Fagan became the General Chairman of the event, and it began to grow. In 1961, Batman rode in a float for the first time, and was so popular that he was soon to be given the honorary title of Grand Marshal. Though it was supposedly a big secret, the Gotham Guardian was played by Fagan himself. Soon, more costumed comic book characters showed up on floats. Tom wrote an article called "The Big Parade" (*Batmania* #3, 1965) which made the parade known to fandom in general. It began, "Halloween! An evening when druids, denevers, vir-dulacs and other anthropophaghist hosts emerge from a world of midnight madness to cavort about on this, the highest of high holidays. And winging his way amongst them, straight from the pages of *Detective Comics* for a single night of mirthful merriment is the awesome figure of the mighty Batman. At least, that's what happens in Rutland, a Vermont community of some 18,000 souls, where Batman over the past few years has become the traditional trademark of the Rutland Recreational Department's annual Halloween Parade." Plugs in DC

(PHOTOGRAPH COURTESY *THE RUTLAND HERALD*)

Tom Fagan

letter columns brought the event's existence to the attention of a much larger audience, causing hordes of comic book fans to stream into the small New England town at October's end. The parade grew to the point where there were well in excess of 100 colorfully garbed comic characters on floats alone, and more in the crowds. Fagan hosted atmospheric parties for costumed revelers at the Victorian mansion on Grove Street (where he was caretaker). Rock bands played at the all-night celebrations, and numerous professionals from the New York comics industry were in evidence. The Rutland Halloween Parade and its chairman became immortalized in the pages of comic books from both Marvel and DC Comics in the 1970s. The parade continues to the present day, drawing crowds estimated at 10,000 in recent years.

Tom Fagan was regarded as a local eccentric in Rutland, for his all-black garb and often ghoulish sense of humor, but in the newsroom of the *Rutland Herald*, he fit in just fine alongside other colorful local characters. He earned his living as a reporter and editor of the paper, where he covered the police and City Hall beats for years. Over an ever-present cigarette, he often trained younger reporters, for he took the craft of journalism very seriously.

Tom Fagan's contributions to fandom as a writer of superlative articles began in 1963, with a piece on the Black Canary in *Comic World* #1, and a short piece for *Alter Ego* ("Warlock" in #6) that didn't appear until the following year. As the man who played Batman in the famous parade, and a big fan of the Caped Crusader, Tom naturally joined Biljo White's Batmanians, and became a writer for *Batmania*. When it came to his fanzine articles, Fagan took the opportunity to write in a more creative, poetic vein than he did in his day job, where journalistic principles and style were expected. When he linked up with Martin L. Greim, a fellow New Englander who published the highly popular *Comic Crusader*, Fagan had found a showcase for a series of top quality articles on the history of comics. *CC* was one of the most widely circulated fanzines of the late 1960s and early 1970s; while editor Greim presented work by the likes of Jim Steranko, Steve Ditko, Jack Kirby and others, there's no doubt that the publication's success was enhanced by offering something new by the talented Fagan in virtually every issue.

Comic Crusader #4 (1968) printed "And Did You Not Hear of a Hero Young?" by Fagan, the first of a three-part series on Airboy, the young ace who starred in *Air Fighters Comics* in the 1940s. Tom's articles were highly individualistic, featuring an oblique, nostalgic look at their subject matter, often with imaginative titles. There was "The Last Words of These Are!" about the "Lost World" series in *Planet Comics*, "Save Us Magician, Cried We and Came the Answer" on Mr. Mystic from "The Spirit" Section, and "05701" on the Lev Gleason Character "Thirteen." Clearly he was writing about his personal favorites, which were often less-celebrated features from comics' Golden Age. His work combined intelligence and a sense of wonder in a highly effective manner. As such, these pieces were a breath of fresh air after the large amount of coverage given the DC, Timely and Fawcett heroes. These memorable articles, and his role in turning a small-town Halloween parade into something special, are his fannish legacy.

"In some ways, he never stopped being a child," his daughter Deana told a reporter for the *Rutland Herald* upon the occasion of his death on October 21, 2008. "He enjoyed having fun. He didn't think he had to be a certain way just because of his age ... He's one of those people who made involvement in comics more likely for an adult. He made it legitimate."

Margaret Gemignani
(b. 1939)

Margaret Gemignani, one of the few women actively involved in fandom, also was known for her highly informative articles. Gemignani's articles were widely published, most notably by Gordon Love. Born in 1939, Margaret lived with her mother in Rochester, New York, and was attending Business College in 1964. In a short autobiographical piece called "The Feature" in *The Rocket's Blast* #25 (1963), she began with the obvious, "First of all, I am unique, being one of the few girls in comic fandom, and being a girl in a man's world is quite an experience." In comicdom's early days, Gemignani, Maggie Thompson and Pat Lupoff were the only female fans who can be considered founders of the movement.

In "I Remember This" in *The Rocket's Blast Special* #2 (1963), she wrote, "Many years ago a child read a comic. Today that child is a woman and that comic is gone but far from being forgotten. I am that child now grown but I still see it before me as clearly as if I still had it, the comic, *Human Torch* number 5. Anyone who is familiar with the fabulous Forties remembers why they were fabulous. Historians will say it was because of the nations whose events made those times so unforgettable. But if you were a kid at that time, it was the coming of the age of superheroes." She had collected comics off and on through the 1940s and 1950s, but became really serious about it "courtesy of Jerry Bails."

Left to right: Carole Seuling, unknown fan and Margaret Gemignani as Miss America.

Gemignani's favorite comics in the early 1960s were *Amazing Spider-Man, Fantastic Four, Justice League of America, Doctor Solar,* and *Magnus, Robot Fighter.* She admired the writing of Stan Lee, Otto Binder and Gardner Fox, yet she opined (in *RB #25*), "My most wanted improvement in comics is maturity. Some comics tend to talk down to readers and aren't even fit for 10 year olds and these give comics in a general a bad name."

Her enthusiasm for old comics combined with a sizable collection of those Golden Age treasures, gave her the impetus and ability to write articles for numerous fanzines. Though her talent wasn't exceptional, and her grasp of spelling was uncertain, editors gratefully accepted her many contributions, for the hunger to gain knowledge about the four-color wonders of that bygone era was great. However, when she launched her own fanzine, *Mask and Cape,* Gemignani's shortcomings as a writer became apparent. Moreover, the ditto printing in her issues of *M&C* was poor. She did fine as long as an editor with a sharp pencil was at hand.

Jeff Gelb, editor of *Men of Mystery* and *Flare Comics,* also lived in Rochester in the 1960s, and wrote of meeting Margaret Gemignani. "I was thrilled to find out that another comics fan lived in Rochester. The fact that she was a *girl* absolutely *stunned* me. Margaret invited me to her house, and we went to an attic where she kept her comics, and sifted through some of them. To be honest, I was hoping she'd look like Patty Duke or Hayley Mills, and found her to be much plainer: tall, lanky, glasses. My romantic fantasies flew out the window. She was also a very shy person with a strange lilt to her voice. She treated me (a 14-year-old kid) as an equal. I think I was a bit in awe of her knowledge of the field, which was on a par with fellow fan/historian Raymond Miller. And I was always pleased with the articles and fan fiction she wrote for my fanzines. It was concise, accurate and interesting."

No shrinking violet, Margaret attended the early New York comicons, as well as the 1964 World Science Fiction convention in San Francisco, where there was a large group of comic book aficionados on hand. (She was also a fan of SF and fantasy literature.) Gemignani gamely entered the masquerade competition at the 1965 New York Comicon garbed as the colorful Miss America, seeming to reinforce the notion that Timely Comics was her favorite Golden Age publisher. In the late 1960s, Margaret vanished from the fan scene, and nothing is known of her life since then, except that she may have moved to Florida.

Glen Johnson
(b. 1937)

If one of the most important functions of fanzines was the publication of informative, concise articles by writers who had direct knowledge of the Golden Age of Comics, it's no wonder Glen Johnson was sought after by the savviest fan-eds in the field.

Glen was born in 1937 in Mackintosh, Minnesota, the eldest of nine siblings in the Johnson clan. His father, who died when Glen was in his late teens, was a construction worker. By then the family was living in Superior, Wisconsin. Glen went to college at the University of Wisconsin, graduating with a major in Education and a minor in physical education.

As a child, Glen had begun reading comics in the mid to late 1940s, and became a firm fan of the Justice Society of America. He began as a superhero fan, and branched out into western comics too. Johnson credits comic books with encouraging him to read as a youth.

Glen's interest intensified in young adulthood, when, while working for the railroad as a relief clerk, he bought a copy of *Showcase* #4 featuring the return of the Flash in modernized form. He was still going to college when he linked up with comic fandom by writing to Jerry Bails in 1961.

By the end of 1963, Johnson had begun buying Golden Age comic books, not an especially expensive proposition at the time. The first time he tried his hand at writing was a Crime Buster article for G.B. Love's *The Rocket's Blast*. As a youth, he recalled, "I was a terrible writer. I would say that wanting to write about comic books really inspired me to become a somewhat better writer." Glen developed a clear, readable style, and never seemed at a loss for words. When he found himself drawn to the comics published by the Columbia Comics Group in the early 1940s such as *Big Shot Comics*, he wrote lengthy articles on

Glen Johnson

two of Columbia's biggest stars: Skyman and The Face. He found an eager publisher in Bob Jennings of *Comic World*. Johnson's "Skyman, America's National Hero" stretched 14 pages in *Comic World* #5 (February 1964), and was very well received by fandom. His follow-up in the next issue was an eight-pager on The Seven Soldiers of Victory, and "Presenting Tony Trent—The Face" in *CW* #7 filled 10 pages, including illustrations used merely to break up page after page of solid text. These efforts attracted the attention of Roy Thomas, who had taken over the helm of *Alter Ego* from Ronn Foss. This resulted in Johnson's piece "Two Cases of Conscience" about a pair of socially relevant issues of *All-Star Comics*, which finally appeared in *AE* #8 (March 1965). He wrote a piece on the two Injustice Societies from *All-Star* that saw print in the following issue.

On May 28, 1964, Glen Johnson traveled from Crown Point to Los Angeles and attended a fan meeting at the house of Russ Manning. Glen had sparked the meeting, asking if he could drop by Manning's place since he and his wife would be in L.A. When Johnson proposed the get-together, Manning decided to invite others who had also asked to visit him. Thus Russ hosted not only Glen Johnson, but Richard Kyle, John McGeehan, Bill Spicer and Rick Durell. The gathering lasted from 1:00 P.M. to 9:00 P.M., consisting of non-stop conversation, spiced by the examination of comic art brought by the various participants. Each of the visitors was given pages of Manning original art. Afterward, Johnson stayed with Rick at his home in El Segundo before returning home. This key fan meeting took place on the eve of Johnson being thrust firmly into fandom's forefront, as he took over the publication of *The Comic Reader*.

The Comic Reader had been spun-off from *Alter-Ego* by Jerry Bails mainly as a vehicle for disseminating news about the professional comic books and strips to a couple of hundred eager readers. By spring 1964, Bails was ready to move on to other projects. Recently Glen recalled, "Jerry Bails was going to give it up ... and there didn't seem to be anybody that was going to step up to the plate and do it. I thought, 'This is my chance to give back something to fandom.'" When he was editing *The Comic Reader* (from #26 in June 1964 to #41 in September 1965), Johnson lived with his wife in Crown Point, New Mexico, and taught school on the Navajo reservation. Glen received news reports of the pros from David Kaler in New York City, and also in short letters from Stan Lee, Steve Ditko and others. He published a beautiful drawing of Captain Atom that Ditko drew straight on a ditto master for him, as well as artwork from Fred Harmon of "Red Ryder" fame. After publishing 16 issues, Johnson passed *The Comic Reader* to Derrill Rothermich and Jim King. He shared an Alley Award with Rothermich in 1964 for the "On the Drawing Board" columns that appeared through the year in *TCR*.

Johnson contributed to other fanzines, of course, but his most sustained effort was as a charter member of *Capa-alpha*. His *Small Talk* fanzine ran in the apa for years, giving the voluble fan, who moved to Utah in 1967, an outlet for his writing. He attended the 1968 Gateway Comicon in St. Louis, appearing on a panel with Alan Hanley and Edwin Aprill, Jr. He also visited Biljo White in Columbia, Missouri.

As for his comic book collecting over the subsequent years, Glen recalled, "I was pretty much of a completist from about the time *The Fantastic Four* came out until 1975. I think I had every Marvel comic that came out from that period. I also bought most of the DCs. That's about it. In 1975, I got interested in old cars and I sort of put the comics aside. After that, I just collected what I liked. That's when I sold most of my original artwork and some of my comic books, so I could buy some old Hudsons. Now, car collecting is probably just a step above my interest in comic books. But I am still interested in comics. I collect anything that features the JSA." Glen was also a fan of comic book writer-artist Pete Morisi; he corresponded with Morisi until the end of the man's life, and visited Pete on three different occasions.

Richard Kyle
(b. 1929)

Best known for inventing the terms "graphic story" and "graphic novel," Richard Kyle was one of the most erudite and intelligent writers to contribute to the fanzines. His columns and articles appeared in *Xero*, *Alter Ego*, *Fantasy Illustrated* and *Graphic Story Magazine*. Kyle was the editor and publisher of *Graphic Story World*, a widely read publication that began in 1971.

Richard Kyle lost his mother when he was four years old, and left school to work at the age of 13. He educated himself by reading comic books, science fiction pulps and mystery stories. After serving as a combat infantryman in Korea, Richard Kyle read and enjoyed the innovative EC comic books, as well as science fiction (which was becoming more reputable) and mystery stories. His interest in comics waned with the advent of the Comics Code Authority, which made it much more difficult to publish comic book stories for mature readers. Then, in 1961, he discovered *Xero*.

Richard Kyle first appeared in comic fandom in spectacular fashion, with a much-lauded entry to the "All in Color For a Dime" series in Dick and Pat Lupoff's *Xero*. He penned "The Education of Victor Fox" which appeared in *Xero* #8 (April 1962). The longest of the series by far, this 27-page opus was not remarkable for its factual coverage of the Fox line of comics, though it did cover that aspect; it was simply a highly entertaining, humorous and often thought-provoking stroll through the sometimes bizarre world fashioned by the self-styled "King of Comics." After recounting some of the silly promotional gimmicks in

Fox's comics, Kyle got serious: "With the instinct of a man in the wrong business, he did the thing that has destroyed marginal publishers again and again and again. What Victor S. Fox did led directly to the establishment of the Comics Code Authority. Without Fox and the publishers like him, the Code would never have come into being. His magazines ... turned toward the sado-masochists, the fetishists, and the other hangers-on in the borderlands of sexual neuroticism. Like all promoters, [Fox] could never understand that you can't sell people entertainment—not with prize contests and premiums—they have to buy it. Nor could he understand what every good editor and publisher knows, and what the bad ones seem never to believe—that you can always sell sex, but you can never sell depravity, not in the long haul, not in the competitive market. The public only pays for what it wants. And most people have a mean streak of decency in them. This was Victor S. Fox's education."

Richard Kyle

Recently, Richard Kyle explained why "The Education of Victor Fox" was not among the AICFAD articles included in the Arlington Press book several years later. "I realized that the Fox piece was far too long in relation to the other articles. For proper balance, it would have to be cut about in half, which meant that I would have to effectively rewrite the entire piece. I didn't have the time. My own feeling is that the book benefits from the absence of the Fox piece. It wasn't in the tone of the other articles, and wouldn't have contributed to the nice comic-fan feeling in the final book, which was very enjoyable." It was reprinted in the *Comic Fandom Reader* book (Hamster Press) in 2002.

This was the beginning of Richard Kyle's well-regarded articles and columns for the comics zines. It was quickly followed by a second AICFAD entry, "Sparky Watts and the Big Shots" in *Xero* #10 (1963). Then he wrote "And That was the End of Solomon Grundy?" (billed as "The First of an Important New Series under the Direction of Jerry G. Bails, Ph.D.") which appeared in *Alter Ego* #7 (October 1964).

Kyle became a founding member of *Capa-alpha*, contributing for the first time to the second mailing, in November 1964. In that brief, four-page apa-zine titled *Wonderworld*, he coined the terms "graphic story" and "graphic novel." Kyle ended a one-and-a-half page essay called "The Future" as follows:

> As I read such stories as "Killer Hunt," in *Capt. Storm*, and admire the art of Joe Kubert, and re-read the Kurtzman and Krigstein stories in the old EC magazines ... I cannot help but feel that "comic book" and "comic book strip" are not only inappropriate and antiquated terms with which to describe these genuinely creative efforts and those of the even more fully realized productions which are bound to come, but are also terms which may easily prevent the early acceptance of the medium by the literary world.
>
> Charles Biro coined the word "illustories" to describe his attempts at adult "comic book strips." EC coined "picto-fiction" for a somewhat similar effort. But I believe there is a good

word, already in the dictionary, which does a far better job than either of these. My *Merriam-Webster* defines "graphic" as "of or pertaining to the arts (graphic arts) of painting, engraving, and any other arts which pertain to the expression of ideas by means of lines, marks, or characters impressed on a surface."

And so, in future issues of *Wonderworld*, when you find me using the terms "graphic story" and "graphic novel" to describe the artistically serious "comic book strip," you'll know what I mean. I may even use it on some that aren't so serious.

A number of reviewers and commentators were led to believe, by the mention of the term "graphic novel" on the paperback edition of *A Contract with God* published at the same time as the hardback edition, in 1978, that this was the first example of sequential art stories that merited the term. Some went further, based on statements from Will Eisner himself, to perpetrate the idea that Eisner had invented the term "graphic novel." Eisner has been quoted in saying that he was unaware that the term had already been coined, coming up with it independently. No one would expect him to be aware of the terms when they first appeared in *Wonderworld* #2 in 1964, but it isn't credible that he didn't become aware of it with the debut of Kyle's regular "Graphic Story Review" column in Bill Spicer's *Fantasy Illustrated* #4. Not only was *Fantasy Illustrated* one of the most popular and widely circulated fanzines of the day (with at least 1,000 copies printed of #4), Eisner himself was mentioned as the kind of artist whose work plumbed "the graphic story's potential." If he missed that essay in a gratis copy sent to him by Spicer, could he have been oblivious when the celebrated fanzine changed its name to *Graphic Story Magazine* with its eighth issue, in the fall of 1967? At this time, Eisner had been interviewed by John Benson for *Witzend*, was receiving complimentary copies of many of the best fanzines, and was aware of comic fandom. He may not have paid a lot of attention to such publications, but he could not have been unaware that the term "graphic story" was in use.

Richard Kyle's "Graphic Story Review" columns were some of the first, and certainly the most prominent, attempts to critically consider the aesthetics of the comic book story in intellectual terms. Fans appreciated these articles largely because they proclaimed that the humble, much-maligned medium was worthy of serious discussion. However, his theory that the graphic story is the editor's medium, similar to movies being a director's medium, was not met with much agreement.

In 1971, Kyle launched his own fanzine, *Graphic Story World*, which began as a comics news magazine, then became a more general comics fan magazine re-titled *Wonderworld*, which also carried new graphic stories by professionals, including Dan Spiegle and Alex Toth. With a circulation of almost three thousand copies per issue, *Graphic Story World / Wonderworld* was one of the most successful comics fan magazines published before the establishment of today's direct distribution system. That same year, Fred Patten introduced Kyle to European comics "albums," and they formed a partnership to import them, for sale through their mail-order store, the Graphic Story bookshop. By 1973, the mail-order bookshop had grown so quickly that a walk-in store was opened, later re-named Richard Kyle Books. In 1976, Kyle and Denis Wheary formed a company to publish *Beyond Time and Again*, by George Metzger. It was subtitled "A Graphic Novel" on the inside title page when it was collected as a 48-page black-and-white hardcover book, making it the first book self-identified as a graphic novel.

Fred Patten
(b. 1940)

Fred Patten was a prominent fan of science fiction and comic books whose writing often promoted comic art produced in Europe and other countries outside the United States. His articles appeared in *Alter Ego* and *Graphic Story World*, and he was Central Mailer of *Capa-alpha* from 1968 to 1971.

Frederick Walter Patten was born in Los Angeles, California. He learned to read from the comic strips in the *Los Angeles Times*. By age five, he had discovered *Walt Disney's Comics and Stories*, and was also a reader of the superhero comics of the Golden Age. Fred later wrote, "I don't recall when I discovered the superheroes, but I do know that my favorite was the Flash, from the moment I found him until he was discontinued. Captain Marvel was my next favorite, then Green Lantern. There was an old, dark drugstore near my home in those days ... where I used to stop with my grandmother coming home from Mass every Sunday. While she got something to eat, I'd sneak over to the corner with the comics and read as many as I could until she came over to warn me that I'd ruin my eyes reading in such bad light, and she'd buy me one if I'd just wait until I got out into the sunlight to read it." (*Heavy Water* #1, January 1965)

At nine, Patten was reading science fiction in book and magazine form, an interest that blossomed as the 1950s progressed. Fred entered the University of California in 1958, and its School of Library's graduate program four years later. In 1960, Patten discovered SF fandom, becoming involved in the Los Angeles Science Fantasy Society (LASFS), a prominent and active science fiction club. From there it was a short step to contributing to science fiction fanzines, which Patten did with enthusiasm. He received his Masters degree in Library Science in 1963.

It was as a member of the LASFS that Fred Patten became known to the burgeoning comic fandom movement. Dick and Pat Lupoff's sensational appearance as Captain and Mary Marvel at the 1960 World Science Fiction Convention in Pittsburgh led a number of the members of the Los Angeles Science Fantasy Society to decide to make a group appearance at the 1962 Worldcon in Chicago dressed as the Justice Society of America. The JSA contingent consisted of Flash (Fred Patten), Wonder Woman (Dian Girard), Dr. Fate (Bruce Pelz), Green Lantern (Ted Johnstone), Sandman (John Trimble), Hawkman (Jack Harness) as well as

Fred Patten as the Golden Age Flash

Black Canary and Dr. Mid-Nite. Also in attendance were Batman (Larry Ivie), Robin (Les Gerber), another Flash (Rick Norwood) and a Flash Gordon group. "Chicago was one of the badly run [costume] competitions," Bruce Pelz commented years later. "The costumes were put in a circular line to parade past the judges with no chance for announcement, no nothing. It was known as 'the Chicon Shuffle.' If they didn't know what the costume was, too bad. It was so bad that it set off George Scithers to invent what has turned into today's costume competitions." A feature on this masquerade, with excellent photos of Girard, Patten, Pelz and Johnstone appeared in *Alter Ego* #6 (Spring 1964) which brought Patten's name before the publication's large readership.

Once the *Alter Ego* connection was made, Fred cemented it with an article on foreign comics. Editor Roy Thomas, who had assumed the helm of *AE* with #7 (Fall 1964), had become interested in Mexican and Latin American comics when he vacationed in Puerto Rico in the summer of 1963, and collected more Mexican comics during a visit to Mexico the following year. This led to Roy's decision to run an article on Mexican heroes in *Alter Ego*. Patten volunteered to write the multi-part piece. "Supermen South!" appeared in *AE* #8 and #9, being cover-featured on the latter issue. As was characteristic of Fred, the articles were well written, informative and intelligent, and firmly established his reputation in comic fandom as a premiere writer about comic books.

Patten joined comics apa *Capa-alpha* about the same time he wrote "Supermen South!" His contributions, appearing under the name *Heavy Water*, began in *K-a* #4 (January 1965). He became Central Mailer from *K-a* #39 (January 1968) to #86 (December 1971). After #92, Fred was chosen to be an Honorary Member, receiving mailings through #275 (September 1987).

In 1972, Patten and Richard Kyle formed the Graphic Story Bookshop in Long Beach, California. When Kyle launched his fanzine *Graphic Story World* (May 1971), Fred had signed on to write a regular review column called "The Book World," which led to his enterprise with Kyle to import European graphic albums to the United States, where they had formerly been unavailable and largely unknown. At the same time, he became interested in Japanese comics (manga) and animation (animé), which would lead to his pioneering efforts to establish a fandom for these art forms. In 1977, Patten was a founder of the Cartoon/Fantasy Organization, the first American animé fan club.

From 1969 to 1990, Fred worked as a technical catalogue librarian at Hughes Aircraft in El Segundo, California. Then he became the first employee of Streamline Pictures, a pioneering animé specialty production company founded in Carl Macek and Jerry Beck in 1988. Over the years, he has written many articles and columns for comics and animation publications such as *Comic Buyer's Guide* and *Animation World.* Along the way, Patten also became a central figure in Furry Fandom, a group of fans who have an interest in anthropomorphic animals (sometimes referred to as "funny animals") and like any fandom, write and draw stories, dress up as their characters, do research, hold conventions, etc. He served as the Official Editor for the *Rowrbrazzle Amateur Press Association* until early 2005.

In March 2005, Patten suffered a stroke. He donated his mammoth collection of comics, animé, manga, books and fanzines to the J. Lloyd Eaton Collection at the University of California, Riverside. Despite being debilitated to the point of being forced to type with just one finger on his left hand, Fred continued to type his contributions to *APA-L* (a weekly L.A.-based apa) until January 2009. He had produced something for *APA-L* each week for more than 40 years.

Steve Perrin
(b. 1946)

Without a doubt, Steve Perrin was one of the best and most prominent writers in fandom's early days. His columns, letters and fan fiction appeared in most of the top fanzines. He was recognized as a superior talent, and was much in demand from fan-editors of the 1960s.

Perrin entered fandom early, while still living in Santa Barbara, California. He was enlisted by editor Parley Holman to script the third installment of *Spotlight*'s ongoing "Dimension Man" comic strip. Seemingly inspired by the experience to write his own costumed hero fiction, Steve launched his character Doctor Darkness and his partner Captain Liberty in Margaret Gemignani's zine *Mask and Cape*. By this time, he had become a drama major at San Francisco State College.

Doctor Darkness was actually a thinly disguised revival of the All-American Comics' character Captain Mid-Nite. Oddly enough, he debuted about the same time as another admitted Captain Mid-Nite revision, The Eclipse by Drury Moroz and Ronn Foss, which appeared in *Alter Ego* #5. These variations were required because DC editor Julius Schwartz had informed the fan community that they couldn't revive characters owned by DC, even if they were stuck in comic book limbo. When he took the helm of *Mask and Cape* with issue #4, Perrin proved his ability as a fanzine editor.

Meanwhile, Steve had gotten in touch with two other Bay Area comic book fanatics, Marty Arbunich and Bill DuBay. In an interview in 1994 about his days in fandom, Bill DuBay recalled, "He was attending classes at San Francisco State and just called one day. We got on well…. I liked who he was, his ideas, the way he wrote. He knew stuff we didn't, especially about Edgar Rice Burroughs. He introduced us to some awesome artists." Perrin readily wrote for their fanzines, most notably *Yancy Street Journal*. Perrin's "Courageous Captain" series found something new and interesting about Captain America to write about for the next half-dozen issues. His prose was always intelligent, well considered and well written. In an era when most amateur prose was often ungrammatical, Perrin's work stood out.

Steve Perrin was among the sizable contingent of comic book fans who attended the 1964 World Science Fiction Convention in San Francisco. Others in attendance were the Golden Gate foursome (Franke, DuBay, Arbunich, Bauman), Robert Metz, Margaret Gemignani, Jeremy Barry, Don Glut, Cat Yronwode (then Manfredi), Larry Ivie, Clint Bigglestone and at least a dozen more well-known fans, as well as pros like Edmond Hamilton, who wrote both science fiction and comics. Glut and Ivie played Captain America and the Red Skull in the masquerade, and Ivie

Steve Perrin

won a prize in the art show. In his con report ("Con Within a Con" in *The Comic Reader* #30, 1964), Steve concluded his report by stating, "Until comic fandom can support its own conventions, I suggest that comic fans make use of the facilities provided by the scifi [*sic*] fans to get together and build for the future of their own fandom."

With *Mask and Cape* #4, having ascended to the editorial helm in 1964, Steve Perrin showed what he could do as a fanzine publisher. In contrast to the first three Gemignani issues, which had ruined some good material (by Rick Weingroff and others) with poor reproduction, *M&C* #4 was one of the finest amateur publications among those that specialized in amateur fiction. It was here that Perrin introduced the Black Phantom and Wraith, the first black costumed heroes in fandom, accompanying it with superb (and beautifully drawn) artwork by Ronn Foss. The issue sported a nice offset cover by Bill DuBay, featuring Perrin's "Companions for Justice" super-team. The story itself, which featured Doctor Darkness, Captain Liberty, and other creations Night Rider, Medico and the Golden Comet, stretched over 15 pages, with many illustrations by the talented Hugh Surratt. Perrin had the knack of orchestrating a script for maximum effect, without the hoary clichés and amateurishness that hampered most scripters in comicdom. It is easy to admire the artistic highlights of the amateur comic strips of fandom's Golden Age, but one should not overlook the fine writing of Perrin and a handful of others.

Around this time, Perrin made another key connection in fandom, when he began an association with Bill Spicer, editor and publisher of the popular photo-offset fanzine *Fantasy Illustrated*. *FI* had begun as a quasi-EC homage zine, with amateur strips in the horror and SF genres. For a change of pace, Spicer decided to do an "all-costumed hero" issue, which ended up filling *Fantasy Illustrated* #4 (Summer 1965) and overflowing into #6 (Summer/Fall 1966). Three of the strips were scripted by one of the most intelligent and prolific writers of amateur comics, Steve Perrin.

While Perrin's "Who Is the Mystery Patriot?" boasted some of Buddy Saunders' better inked work, and the Dreamsman and Lucky in "Saviors from the Future" also benefited from Bill DuBay at his best, it was Perrin's "The Origin of the Black Phantom" in *Fantasy Illustrated* #6 that made a deep and lasting impression. This adaptation of the prose story from *Mask and Cape* #4 received much more attention than it had back in 1964, not only because Ronn's inked artwork was both incendiary and innovative, but because Spicer's fanzine had one of the largest circulations in fandom, at least 1,000 copies per issue. Of the "Battler Against Bigotry" and his encounter with "The Brothers of the Flaming Cross," author Perrin wrote (in that same issue of *FI*): "I do not intend the Black Phantom as propaganda ... but merely to use a conflict that is as real to our modern day as cops and robbers or spies and G-men. He's simply an adventure hero with a different menace than usual to work against—that's all, that's enough.

"I do hope readers enjoy this departure in fan fiction, and I hope to see more of it in times to come, for this is one thing that fans can do that pros cannot, or will not do. We have no restraint other than our consciences and the U.S. Postal regulations to what we wish to write about, so let's use this freedom. Not just for Civil Rights, but the hundred and one other issues that vitally concern the people of today." Perrin scripted a second Black Phantom script, "Death Trap in Harlem," for which Spicer did breakdowns, but it was never illustrated.

In addition to the high profile *Fantasy Illustrated*, Perrin continued contributing to the better ditto fanzines. One was *Action Hero*, published by Sherman and Wayne Howard of Cleveland, Ohio; another was *Intrigue*, the companion zine of *Super Hero*, published by Detroit-based Richard Buckler. In *Intrigue* #1 (1967), Perrin's Doc Darkness and Captain Liberty appeared in the strip "The Case of the Curious Crusader," which featured some nice Buckler-Surratt artwork.

By the late 1960s, Perrin began drifting away from comic fandom, becoming interested in the Society of Creative Anachronism. He continued writing in one form or another, and eventually moved into the role-playing game arena. In 1974, he got one of the first editions of *Dungeons and Dragons*, and by the late '70s Steve was the main author of *RuneQuest*, an award-winning role playing game. Steve worked full-time for Chaosium, Inc., the publisher of *RuneQuest*, and from there went to freelance game writing, eventually getting into computer games.

In the "real world" Perrin worked for Blue Shield and then Kaiser Permanente. Most recently, he has worked as a technical writer, usually for medical device firms. He wrote, "In my spare time I spend a lot of time playing superhero role playing games like *Champions* and *Mutants and Masterminds*. I generally use characters I created back in comics fandom for my characters, so heroes like Doctor Darkness and Captain Liberty are still swinging. And I still read comic books."

John T. Ryan
(1931–1979)

John Thomas Ryan was an Australian comic art scholar and writer, the most prominent fan from "down under" in comicdom of the 1960s and 1970s.

John had the distinction of publishing the first Aussie comic fanzine, *Down Under*, in November of 1964. He joined *Capa-alpha* early on, and titled his long-running apazine *Boomerang*. His primary interest in collecting was for American comic books prior to mid–1942, and Australian comics from all periods.

By the time Ryan discovered fandom, he was already past 30 and was a published writer, with articles relating to boxing, football and cricket appearing in *The Australian Ring* and *Sports Novels*. His love of Golden Age comics was the basis for the friendship between another far flung fan, John Wright of South Africa. Both were obsessed with this formative period in the history of comic books, and both were able to convey that enthusiasm to others, for they were fine writers: literate, articulate and knowledgeable. Wright recently wrote of Ryan, "I got the feeling that [his fanzine] *Down Under* had not been sufficient to satisfy his needs of expression. He had a great deal to tell and to share, and he found outlets for this in excellent articles for other fanzines...." (*Alter Ego* #79, July 2008).

John T. Ryan

John's Alley Award-winning "Bidgee" columns, which appeared in *The Comic Reader* and *Star-Studded Comics* offered intelligent histories of Australian comics, always with a good helping of accompanying artwork. His "Bidgee" piece on prolific Aussie artist John Dixon in *Gosh Wow!* #1 (1967) was cover-featured. In another installment, Ryan introduced Stan and Reg Pitt's "Gully Foyle," a proposed syndicated Sunday newspaper strip that adapted Alfred Bester's acclaimed SF novel, *The Stars My Destination*. "Gully Foyle" created a sensation in fandom, largely because of the spectacular art by Stanley Pitt, one of the greatest Australian comic artists (and a personal friend of John Ryan). Unfortunately, it never sold and so fans were left to drool over what amounted to a generous portfolio presentation of "what might have been."

John had a good working knowledge of older U.S. comics, and contributed a second part to the history of Will Eisner's career that began in the fanzine *Sense of Wonder* #11, and was completed in #12 (Summer 1972). It was this article that introduced Eisner's little-seen-until-then "Hawks of the Seas" comic strip to fandom. In addition, Ryan was a Contributing Editor and Australian sales agent for Richard Kyle's *Graphic Story World*.

In 1977, Ryan was approached by the publisher Collier Macmillan Australia to see if he would be interested in putting together a book on the history of Australian comics. Indeed he was, and the resulting book was titled *Panel by Panel: A History of Australian Comics* (Casell Australia Limited, 1979). The reception to the book was glowing, and the publisher received strong orders from the bookstores across Australia.

Unfortunately, John wasn't able to bask in the book's success for long. While on a business trip, he suffered a heart attack and passed away on December 11, 1979. He left behind his wife, Jan, and two children, Fiona and Sean.

Upon John's passing, his wife Jan donated John's collection of Australian comic books to the National Library of Australia: Manuscript Collection MS 6514. The cache of comic art consisted of 66 boxes containing over 500 different comic titles, over 600 titles of comic fanzines published between 1960 and 1979, and John's own research files. The donation was received by the library on September 9, 1980.

Larry Stark

(b. 1932)

Larry Stark was given the sobriquet "EC's Number One Fan" by the comic book publisher, due to the many letters of criticism he sent to publisher Bill Gaines and company during EC's heyday in the first half of the 1950s. He was editor of the EC fanzine *Potrzebie*, in collaboration with fellow editor Bhob Stewart and publisher Ted White, and was probably the most prominent writer in EC fandom. Stark's most celebrated piece is his "Elegy" to EC, published in Ron Parker's *Hoohah!*, which has been reprinted several times in the ensuing years.

Larry Stark was born in New Brunswick, New Jersey, in August 1932. His father was a linotypist and compositor at *The Daily Home News* in New Brunswick. He was drafted in 1951, spending just 18 days in the Army before receiving a medical discharge for asthma. Having missed the beginning of classes at Rutgers University College in New Brunswick, he spent the academic year in Glen Falls, New York, in another night-school division of Skidmore College. Already an SF fan, Stark had begun reading ECs with *Weird Science* and become an EC enthusiast; while in Glen Falls, he began his "career" as an EC Fan-Addict. Early in 1952, Stark formed the habit of writing a letter of comment to the "editor" of every issue of every EC title. Those letters were kept and collected by Bill Gaines, though they were inexplicably stolen from Gaines' desk in a mysterious break-in. Stark's letters then, and his critiques in the following years, were almost exclusively focused on the structure and content of the stories, rather than the artwork or other related matters.

Because of his serious attention to their comic books, Gaines conferred on Stark a "free life-time subscription to everything we publish," and gave him the nickname "EC's Number One Fan." Gaines and Feldstein were impressed when SF fan Stark compared their sto-

Larry Stark

ries to the originals in SF story anthologies being published at the time. The life time subscription shrank to consist solely of *Mad* magazine when the comic books died, and the issues continued arriving at Larry's residence—even following him to various new addresses—until about 1982 or 1983.

Larry Stark entered EC fandom upon receiving a copy of *The EC Fan Bulletin* #1 in April 1953, which began a voluminous correspondence with Bhob Stewart. According to John Benson in "The EC Fanzines—Part Two" in *Squa Tront* #7 (1977), "Larry's capacity to write letters during this period is legendary. It was not unusual for Bhob, and Larry's other correspondents, to get letters of 12 pages and even longer. These letters were often like little essays, and were not limited to EC, but covered subjects as diverse as 3-D movies, poetry, 'The Spirit' and censorship." Upon the unknowing instigation of Dr. Fredric Wertham in his notorious book *Seduction of the Innocent* (1954), Stark was given a fan forum for his critiques and opinions by publisher Ted White and editor Bhob Stewart in a second generation EC fanzine. *Potrzebie* was conceived as a vehicle for Larry's writing, and the first issue was mainly comprised of two lengthy pieces by Stark. It was a literate, intelligent fanzine, patterned after the SF zines of the day. Unfortunately, there would be only one White-Stewart-Stark issue, because White and Stewart were appalled and discouraged by the juvenile quality of the inquiries they received from a plug in the fourth issue of EC's *Fan-Addict Club Bulletin*, and the paucity of cash orders.

Eventually, Larry Stark's letters to the new *Potrzebie* editor Larry Clowers saw print, most notably a lengthy missive in #4 decrying the fact that a certain dealer was charging more than cover price for back issue EC's, which Stark called "scalping." At this time, no one in EC fandom was attempting to make money on the fanzines or back issues. When the capitalist spirit reared its head, Stark was upset. He correctly ascertained that this would change the character of fandom. It did.

Larry spent six years in the 1950s commuting from home to New Brunswick's Rutgers University, earning a fully accredited Bachelor's Degree in English. He also spent one semester in the Rutgers Graduate School of Library Service before moving from New Jersey to Cambridge, Massachusetts. Larry privately mourned the death of EC's comics in 1955, and when he received an invitation from Ron Parker to write something for Parker's fanzine *Hoohah!*, chose to write of that loss. Stark penned "Elegy" (*Hoohah!* #7, 1956), his best-known comic book essay. Editor Parker later stated (in his "best of" *Hoohah!* book in 1984) that the essay "is generally regarded as the best single effort to appear in any of the EC fanzines of the '50's, and is probably the best of any article about the EC comics era outside of any purely technical exercise." It begins:

> EC is gone.
>   Nothing remains but a memory, and the tattered copies yellowing in the closets of collectors.
>   For EC death was long and cruel in coming, and almost as undeserved as it was inevitable.
> The meteor of its genius was hot and brief, yet flashed with such a brilliance as to make forget-
> ting difficult.

"Elegy" was reprinted in full as recently as in *Tales of Terror!* (2000) by Fred von Bernewitz and Grant Geissman.

The end of the EC comics caused Larry Stark to "quit comics" until underground comix and *Elfquest* reawakened his interest in the medium. Between 1963 and 1972, he reviewed plays for the local arts-newsletter called *Boston After Dark* (now called *The Boston Phoenix*). When asked how he has made his living, Larry recently explained, "Mostly I pushed books at the local Paperback Booksmith chain in Cambridge and Boston. In 1994, I retired to get my left knee replaced by a metal one, and in October 1995 started a web-site called *The Theater Mirror* which is still in existence. I see about four to seven plays every week, write reviews when I can, see to it that other people's reviews get featured, and I'm trying to make the world aware that any city that has 93 theater companies working every year deserves to be called a Theater City."

Roy Thomas
(b. 1940)

Roy Thomas served as Jerry Bails' co-editor of *Alter Ego* for its first four issues, and became sole editor and publisher (after two issues helmed by Ronn Foss) for *AE* #7 through #10. He originated the basic concepts of the Academy of Comic Book Fans and Collectors, and the Alley Awards. In 1965, he became much less active in fandom when he became a professional comic book writer at Marvel Comics.

When Roy first established contact with Jerry Bails, he was an English and history major in his senior year at Southeast Missouri State College in Cape Girardeau, a hundred miles south of St. Louis on the Mississippi River. Thomas, though several years younger than Bails, had learned to read in the pages of *All-Star Comics*, and was so taken with the "new JSA" (i.e., the Justice League) that he'd written his first letter to editor Julius Schwartz. When Roy inquired about obtaining back issues of *All-Star*, Schwartz gave him Gardner Fox's name and address. Fox in turn referred Roy to Jerry Bails, informing him that Jerry had purchased all his back issues a couple of years earlier. Though disappointed, Roy immediately dashed off a letter to "Mr. Bails" on November 21, 1960, the day before his 20th birthday. Bails responded at once, and the two *All-Star* enthusiasts entered into frequent correspondence. Jerry was plotting ways to support *Justice League of America* and, near the

Left to right: Biljo White, Jerry and Sondra Bails, Linda Rahm and Roy Thomas, at White's home in Columbia, Missouri, 1963.

end of 1960, informed Thomas of his idea to publish a "JLA Newsletter" to be distributed to contacts made through the letter pages in Julie's comics. Schwartz had decided, toward the end of 1960, to begin running complete addresses in his letter columns. Full addresses appeared in *Brave and Bold* #35 (May 1961) with pre-publication comments on the Hawkman revival from Jerry, Roy and others. *The JLA Subscriber* concept soon evolved into a fanzine devoted to the revival of superheroes that was then taking place at DC and other companies. Bails came up with a title he liked better: *Alter-Ego*.

By early March 1960, Jerry had outlined tentative contents of the first issue. He would write the first part in a history of the JSA and an article on the Comics Code Authority; Roy would contribute his proposed ideas (in short story form) for a revival of the Spectre, as well as Part I of his *JLA* parody strip "The Bestest League of America" (which would become the zine's cover feature). The issue would include ads for the sale and trade of comics, and news of coming events at DC. By March 28th, the masters for *Alter-Ego* #1 were completed; it was printed via a portable spirit duplicator that Jerry had purchased. Copies were in the mails by the end of the month. When Roy received the first issue, consisting of 22 pages, he had a pleasant surprise: Jerry had given him the title "co-editor," something he had never discussed with Roy. Jerry apparently considered it fitting because Thomas had been so much a part of the initial planning of the fanzine, including the type of editorial content that could be included.

Roy's contributions to *Alter-Ego* #2 (June 1961) included another cover, this time a drawing of the Spectre and Count Dis from "The Reincarnation of the Spectre—Part 2," a piece about Timely-Marvel's 1946 All Winners Squad, and Part 2 of the "Bestest League of America." For *A-E* #3 (November 1961), Thomas wrote a piece on the Hal Jordan Green Lantern, and the final chapter of the BLA parody, with Wombatman and Superham. There was also a humor piece by Roy's girlfriend at that time, Linda Rahm. By the time *A-E* #3 saw print, comicdom was growing at an astounding rate, and there were a host of potential contributors who were both knowledgeable and talented to help Jerry and Roy carry the ball.

When Bails launched *The Comicollector* in September 1961, the first issue set the precedent for running articles as well as ads, with a review of *Fantastic Four* #1 ("Four of a Kind") by Thomas. It had been submitted to Jerry for inclusion in *A-E*, with the cover note from Roy reading, "Yesterday I discovered a new comic called *Fantastic Four*, which just might turn out to really be something. Have you seen it?" In his review, Thomas wrote (in part), "Despite its faults … *Fantastic Four* holds promise of becoming one of the better comics now on the stands. One interesting aspect of this comic … is that the Thing is a rather rebellious creature who is often at the point of fighting to the death with the leader, Mr. Fantastic… . This feature alone, especially if and when the Torch begins to get in on this running feud, would make it well worth any super-hero fan's dime."

Roy came up with two ideas that caught Jerry's imagination: the Alter-Ego Awards, a sort of "Academy Awards" for fandom, giving fans an annual opportunity to vote for their favorite comic books and comic book creators, and the notion of calling the nominating committee "the Academy." Bails expanded this simple idea into an organization designed to add respectability to the hobby, and to unify and organize fandom—the Academy of Comic Book Fans and Collectors—and the awards swiftly metamorphosed into the Alleys, named after the comic strips' Alley Oop, who as a caveman could be considered the earliest adventure hero.

One of the most significant trends in 1963 was fans traveling to meet their correspondents in nearby cities—and sometimes not-so-nearby cities. In March, a significant meeting took place at the home of Biljo White in Columbia, Missouri, when Roy and Jerry both traveled there to meet each other for the first time.

In 1964, a year of restless shifting of plans and fanzine publishing responsibilities, most of them fortuitous, one of the happiest turned out to be Roy Thomas's ascension to post of full Editor and Publisher of *Alter Ego* (the hyphen had been dropped during Ronn Foss's interim issues as Editor/Publisher). Two issues had been enough for Foss, who wanted to focus his energy on his artwork. Actually, Foss offered the fanzine to Biljo White, who accepted, then quickly realized it would be too much work, and asked Roy for help. When the dust settled, it was Roy who became Editor and Publisher, and Biljo a chief contributor, with the title Art Editor.

Roy, who had been working as a high school English teacher in Missouri since fall of 1961, hurtled headlong into the task in the late summer of '64 in an effort to beat the Alley Award deadline of October 31st. As a writer, Roy brought to his work the kind of literary approach that one found in *Xero* and *Comic Art*. For *AE* #7, utilizing Biljo's vast collection, he wrote a Marvel Family article he'd been planning since 1961. "One Man's Family," with many illustrations by White, expertly recounted the origins of the Marvel Family, discussed the Sivanas and other villains, and highlighted some of the more memorable adventures. Thomas's fine piece undoubtedly introduced a whole new generation of younger fans to the magic and mirth of the Fawcett Captain Marvel, Captain Marvel Jr. and the rest. (It won a 1964 Alley for "Best Article in a Fanzine," in a tie with Rick Weingroff's "Lee" from *Slam-Bang*.) Augmenting Thomas's article was a long letter from Otto Binder, writer of many of the Golden Age adventures of Captain Marvel and the Marvel Family. Other top-notch features in this issue included a strip by Biljo ("Alter and Captain Ego"), a JSA article on Solomon Grundy by Richard Kyle, and a piece ghosted by Thomas on the Human Torch. All helped make *AE* #7 one of the best fanzines of the 1960s. "*Alter Ego* #7 was printed by Cashbook Printing in my home town of Jackson, Missouri, though I was teaching in the St. Louis environs at the time," Roy recalled. "I was both amused and annoyed when I heard … that Mr. Beatty [the pressman at Cashbook] had grumbled, 'The best printing job I ever did, and it was for a goddam *comic book*!'"

Roy Thomas had perfected the *AE* formula, and followed the excellent #7 with two more fine issues. Issue #8 sported a spectacular Blackhawk cover by Biljo. The Blackhawk article "When Hawkhood Was In Flower" by Derrill Rothermich and Roy Thomas started things off, followed by a Doc Savage piece by Robert Hopkins, a high school teacher and colleague of Roy's from Sullivan, Missouri. A JSA piece by Glen Johnson and the second Eclipse strip by Moroz & Foss ("The Mystery of Malimoor!") were top-notch. "I'd become interested in Mexican and Latin American comics when I spent a few weeks on the west coast of Puerto Rico in the summer of 1963," Roy recently wrote. "Then, the next summer, I had gone to Mexico with a girl friend for a month, and amassed more Mexican comics there, as well. This inspired me to try to get an article on Mexican heroes for *Alter Ego*." Fred Patten offered to pen such an article, and the first part ("Supermen South!") rounded out *AE* #8.

AE #9 maintained the standards of previous issues in terms of contents, with a photo feature titled "Otto in Binderland" (photos of Binder and other Fawcett pros) and samples of the unsold "Tawky Tawny" syndicated strip by Binder and Beck. Also on hand was the second part of "Supermen South!" This was Roy's last issue (for some time), delivered to the printer just days before he moved to New York. *Alter Ego* under Roy's editorship won Alleys for "Best Fanzine" in 1964 and 1965 (and there was strong competition in both those years).

In May 1965, Charlton editor Pat Masulli offered fans a chance to write for that company (in the form of an "Open Letter," which ultimately appeared in *RBCC*, *TCR* and elsewhere) for either *Son of Vulcan* or *Blue Beetle*. In the end, he bought scripts from three fans: first Roy Thomas, then David Kaler and Tom Fagan. Thomas, who had submitted "The Second Trojan War" for *Son of Vulcan*, was asked to try his hand at a *Blue Beetle* script. But, though Roy complied, in the interim he'd received a more intriguing offer. Superman line editor Mort Weisinger had been looking for a replacement for E. Nelson Bridwell, a lesser-known fan from Oklahoma who had moved to New York to work for Weisinger a year earlier, and he offered Roy a try-out. Thomas completed his teaching year at Fox High School in Arnold, Missouri, and flew to New York at the end of June, having no idea he was to replace Bridwell. Roy's tenure at DC proved to be short-lived; within two weeks he had jumped ship to Marvel following a personality clash with Weisinger: "I found to my surprise that I reacted unfavorably to his particular methods and personality." Roy spent the July Fourth holiday with the Lupoffs in Poughkeepsie, his mind in a quandary. "When I returned to my hotel room [at the George Washington Hotel on 23rd street] after my next day back at work [a Tuesday] ... I found a request to phone Stan Lee at his office." Lee, to whom Roy had written a letter from his hotel, asked if Roy wanted to try his hand at a writing test that Lee had devised. Could Roy adapt to the "Marvel method" of adding captions and dialogue *after* the penciling was done, when nearly 100 others had tried it unsuccessfully? Thomas took the test overnight on Wednesday, turned the pages in to Sol Brodsky (Marvel's production manager) on Thursday, and on the following morning received a phone call at DC from Marvel secretary Flo Steinberg informing him that Stan wanted to see him. Lee offered him a job after about ten minutes of conversation. That very afternoon Roy gave notice at DC, and was back at Marvel a few minutes later, looking over art for a *Modeling with Millie* issue he was to dialogue.

"I ... moved in with Dave Kaler in East Greenwich Village," Thomas concluded his tale in the pages of *Capa-alpha*, "where we live pretending to be starving writers and wearing our Dr. Strange t-shirts in the coffee-houses." Kaler's two-room studio apartment, located on Avenue A near 2nd Street, on the ground floor, was nicknamed "Kaler's Kave." (Eventually, both Denny O'Neil and Gary Friedrich would join them in that apartment, albeit briefly, both fellow Missourians having come to NYC at Roy's behest.)

In one respect, making the adjustment to pro-dom offered a unique difficulty for Roy. His friends in comicdom naturally asked him questions about developments at Marvel, but

Stan Lee specifically "requested" that he not reveal future plots or other Marvel news to the fanzines. Thomas's active participation in the fanzines thus came to an abrupt end, though he did keep his "Roy's Ramblings" contributions to *Capa-alpha* going for some months. Although he became a professional, Roy never lost his basic point of view as a fan, at least of Golden Age and Silver Age comics published before 1965. *Alter Ego* #10, published in 1970, had a similar pro-fan duality. (An eleventh issue, published by Mike Friedrich in 1978, offered a kind of final coda to the original run of *AE*.)

Roy Thomas proved to be an excellent writer in a quasi-Stan Lee style, adapting to the Marvel style (scripting pages by pencilers who worked from a written plot) with ease, and developing a real enthusiasm for Marvel's characters. Fans did more than accept him in Stan's stead: after turning pro, Roy first came in second to Stan for "Best Writer" in the 1968 Alley Awards, then bested Stan to become fandom's favorite pro writer in 1969, the final year of the Alleys. Thomas ended up being the first person to succeed Lee as Editor-in-Chief of Marvel Comics in 1972, though in truth he didn't covet the position.

Thomas also "gave back to fandom" by helping some of his friends get work published in professional comics. Grass Green and Gary Friedrich were able to place work at Charlton after a boost from Roy, and Gary went on to become a popular Marvel writer in the late 1960s and 1970s. Even Biljo White and Ronn Foss managed to gain a professional credit, when Roy was able to find spots for them.

Of his professional comics credits, Roy is perhaps best known for his adaptation of Robert E. Howard's hero *Conan the Barbarian* to comic books. He is also known for long runs on *The Avengers* and *X-Men*. In 1981, Thomas returned to DC Comics for several years. After moving to California, Roy met his wife and sometime writing partner Dann. While living on the west coast, Thomas worked on numerous projects for the television and movie industry.

Today, Roy lives a semi-idyllic existence on his estate in South Carolina. He and Jerry Bails maintained their close friendship and passion for comic books until the end of Jerry's life, via letters and emails. One of the last times they met in person was at "Fandom Reunion 1997" in Chicago. Soon afterward, Roy established contact with John Morrow of TwoMorrows Publishing and Jon B. Cooke, editor of TwoMorrows' projected magazine *Comic Book Artist*, which led to the return of *Alter Ego* as a professional magazine in 1998—first as a flip section of *Comic Book Artist*, and then on its own in what Roy dubbed "Vol. 3" of *Alter Ego*. Focused on the Golden and Silver Ages of comics, mostly in the form of interviews with the professionals who were still living, the new *Alter Ego* has made an incalculable contribution to the recorded history of the comic book industry. In addition, Roy has edited a four-volume *All-Star Companion*, his exhaustive tribute to his beloved Justice Society of America.

Rick Weingroff
(b. 1946)

With the proliferation of fanzines came a need for writers to fill their pages. Rick Weingroff proved to be one of the best, authoring the long-running "Rocketeer Gossip" column in *RBCC* and publishing his own fanzine, *Slam-Bang*, beginning in 1964.

Richard Weingroff grew up in Baltimore, Maryland. His father, a salesman by trade, wasn't into comics, but was supportive of his son's hobby and encouraged his writing aspirations. "I became involved in comic fandom after a letter of mine appeared in the Letters to the Editor column of *The Flash* in the early 1960s," Rick recently recalled. "Based on that letter, I received a flyer in the mail from Jerry Bails advertising *Alter-Ego* #3 (if memory serves) and I subscribed. That was my introduction to the world of fanzines." That would have been in the second half of 1961.

Rick began writing his "Rocketeer Gossip" column to G. B. Love's *The Rocket's Blast* in 1962 (almost from the fanzine's beginning) and continued regular installments well into 1964. By then, *The Rocket's Blast* had merged with *The Comicollector*, and had the then-enormous circulation of 750 copies per issues. Thus, Weingroff was widely known and read, and recognized as being one of the most intelligent commentators on the comic book scene of the day. "Rocketeer Gossip" covered the

Gil Kane and Rick Weingroff

gamut, from a discussion of a single classic comic book (*Mystery in Space* #1) to second-tier publishers like Charlton, Gold Key and Archie, to Batman's "New Look" in 1964.

In April 1964, Weingroff launched a fanzine of his own called *Slam-Bang*. In the first issue, he announced "A Statement of Policy" that began, "My philosophy in publishing this fanzine has been formulated over a period of three years. In this period, I have seen many zines, most of which were not worth the money I paid for them." He then broke his philosophy down into three main points: (1) articles, which should include "a series of valid opinions/ideas" and should also have good grammar; (2) story narration would be minimal, and (3) "an editor should publish what he believes in—what he enjoys publishing." Also, the letter column would consist not of commentary on the prior issue (which he considered "a personal evaluation"), but the writer's own ideas and opinions. The fanzine was printed by Rick's father at his office via the fairly exotic "multilith" method, which looked more or less like high-quality mimeography. The art, that was there only to break-up the monotony of all-text, consisted of fairly skillful tracings by Weingroff himself.

The main article in *Slam-Bang* #1 was titled "Lee, Part One." It was one of the first serious attempts to explain and understand the special appeal of Marvel Comics, which had arisen to become fan favorites by that time. This article, which was continued into subsequent issues, ended up sharing an Alley award for "Best Article in a Fanzine" in 1964 with Roy Thomas's "One Man's Family" in *Alter-Ego* #4. Fans signaled their continued enthusiasm for Rick's fanzine when they voted it "Best All-Article Fanzine" in 1965, along with Biljo White's *Batmania*.

In the summer of 1964, Weingroff was one of about 50 fans who attended the first comic-con held in New York City. The Tri-State Con (its actual name) was spearheaded by Bernie

Bubnis, and wasn't exactly an impressive, well-organized affair. Rick was invited by Bubnis to write a review of the convention for a souvenir fanzine published in August (after the con) called *The 1964 Comicon Booklet*. He did, and didn't pull any punches, pointing out the event's flaws and advancing ideas that would be largely adopted for the 1965 New York con. In a note attached to his article, however, he added to Bernie: "Anyway, I had a great time … despite my article." In fact, Weingroff was in evidence at the 1965 New York comicon, which in many ways can be considered the first "full service" comicon. He appeared on a panel entitled "Comics and Fandom: Where Do We Go From Here?" which was perhaps the highlight of the official program, for it tackled issues close to fans' hearts. The fans and pros on the panel sparked fireworks with their candor and occasionally opposing views. Con organizer David Kaler moderated the panel, which consisted of Weingroff and Roy Thomas (for the fan point of view) and Jim Warren, Murphy Anderson and Bill Harris (representing the professionals' viewpoint). In the audience, and very vocal, were also Gil Kane, Leonard Darvin (of the Comics Code Authority) and others. A lively, spirited discussion ensued, proving just how interesting and important such comicon programming could be.

In the fall of 1964, Rick entered the University of Maryland, where he would major in English. Nevertheless, he continued to write and publish *Slam-Bang* (and even the occasional "Rocketeer Gossip" column) for the next two years. These issues contained major articles on Fawcett's *Gift Comics*, Doctor Fate ("Behind the Spectre") and Superman ("Inner or Other: A Theory on Superman"). This was heady stuff, perhaps a bit too academic to appeal to fans across the board, but demonstrated that the hobby could be considered in serious academic terms.

For the sixth and final issue (September 1966), Weingroff changed the title to *Tint, A Quarterly Journal of Comic Art*. The opening editorial began, "Comic fandom has long needed an outlet for the expression of a serious interest in the comics as a media, rather than as an idol upon which to lavish adulation. Hopefully, *Tint* will serve as such an outlet on a fairly regular basis." Tint contained two main articles, "Super-Heroes as Folklore" and "Psychoanalysis and Superman," both heavily footnoted like college themes.

As it turned out, Rick Weingroff's plans to publish *Tint* with some frequency were derailed. In his junior year at the University of Maryland, the demands of school (among other things) caused Rick to drop out of comic fandom altogether. "I made it a clean break," he remembered, "because I think that's easier, when it's from something you love."

After graduation in 1968, he entered the U.S. Air Force, serving at Lackland Air Force Base in San Antonio, Texas, from 1968 to 1972. He was an instructor in the "Proficiency Reading School," an extension of the Jobs Corps designed to teach reading skills to basic trainees so they would be able to succeed in technical training schools. He joined the Federal Highway Administration (FHWA) in 1973 as a Technical Correspondence Writer in the Office of Engineering. Over the years, Weingroff's primary work has involved preparing replies to the congressional, citizen, and other inquiries the FHWA received.

Weingroff credits the fanzines with giving him an opportunity to increase his proficiency as a writer. "My experience in fandom was entirely positive, and led to a career that I've enjoyed for over thirty-five years." Meanwhile, his enjoyment of comic books has transferred to following (and collecting the DVDs of) nearly all the superhero-themed movies. He also is a fan of the television show *Smallville*.

John Wright

(1933–2008)

John Oliver Wright owns the unique status of being the only active comics fan in the 1960s who lived in South Africa. Of Welsh and Irish stock, Wright was the perfect age to read the comic books of the Golden Age, the first he can remember being *Superman* #4 (1940). This opportunity was interrupted once the U.S. was fully involved in World War II. "During the war, the only comics I saw were those that drifted my way from American warships that had stopped at Port Elizabeth to take on supplies," he recalled in an interview in *Alter Ego* #35 (2004). "Then, with peace returning, American comics began filtering back to this side of the puddle. Life changed from then on. Marvelous discoveries were made. The very early versions of Batman we'd never seen before, characters until then unheard of. We'd ride our bikes for miles seeking out new sources of supplies, selling empty bottles for a penny each, and old newspapers for a penny a pound in order to earn money for additional purchases. Wonderful times."

Against his parents' wishes, Wright quit school at fourteen, and began working at a succession of jobs: nightclub photographer, trainer at a judo school, racing stock cars, and in construction management. Though he sold his first attempts at professional writing as a teenager, he didn't seriously apply himself to a writing career until he married his wife, Coral, and was facing monthly mortgage payments. Then, he wrote his first novel, a pastiche of American detective fiction called *Suddenly You're Dead*. He assumed the pen name "Wade Wright," which began a pattern of using differing pen names for the numerous subsequent books, articles and radio shows he wrote in the coming years.

In the early 1960s, while checking out a copy of *The Writer's Market*, he found a listing for *Sick* magazine, citing Joe Simon as editor. Recognizing the name from classic comic books by Simon & Kirby, Wright wrote Simon. Simon's quick response mentioned an amateur journal about comic books called *Alter-Ego*, and provided Jerry Bails' name and address. Soon Wright had a sample copy of *A-E* #1 in his hands, and discovered the existence of comic fandom in America. This immediately inspired the South African to plan his own amateur publication.

Wright's *The Komix* #1 (1962) was printed by ditto machine, and quite well considering it was his first experience with the primitive printing process. Of necessity, lacking sufficient data to write informative articles about comics, John published his own fiction in that first issue, introducing his character, The White Dragon. The second issue, in 1963, carried contributions from John's correspondents Ronn Foss, Mike Vosburg, Rick Durell, Larry Kopf and

John Wright

Biljo White. His local "staff" was himself under various pen names. Wright's story featuring his own character, The Black Panther (pre-dating the character of the same name at Marvel Comics), won a 1963 Alley Award for "Best Fanzine Fiction." John Wright was profiled by Biljo White in *Batmania* #1 (July 1964).

His writing proved fairly lucrative over the years. Including *Suddenly You're Dead,* he wrote six "Bart Condor" books in something like a Mickey Spillane style, all by "Wade Wright." There were also five books featuring a private investigator named Paul Cameron, set in Southern California, beginning with *Shadows Don't Bleed.* These were also written in the American idiom, like most of Wright's books. Both the Condor and Cameron series were published by Robert Hale, Ltd., London. There were also eight western novels by "Ray Nolan," including *Trouble in Twilight* and *Hang-Rope at Harmony,* among others. Despite his success as a professional wordsmith, however, John occasionally augmented his income with stints working as a consultant to businesses, as a sort of troubleshooter, trainer and efficiency expert. This from a fellow who had dropped out of school at 14!

Wright remained second to none in his enthusiasm and affection for comics of the Golden Age, and managed to obtain the new comics in the early 1960s by a special arrangement with Jerry Bails. He often wrote to his heroes, the folks behind the comics he enjoyed in his childhood, and ended up having a long-running correspondence with Mart Bailey, creator of The Face from Columbia's *Big Shot Comics.* His writing and involvement in fandom also brought him into contact with such celebrities as Mickey Spillane, Gene Autry and Sax Rohmer.

John planned *The Komix* #3, which he was going to retitle *Ace High Fantasy,* and it was to feature a strip called "Crime Crasher vs. the Flying Dragon" by Richard "Grass" Green. One thing after another delayed it, until finally Wright dropped the idea. He would never publish another issue. His memories of fandom of that decade remained positive, especially in terms of the people he met through the mails. "Back then few were thinking of making big bucks from collections," he recounted in a late-in-life interview in *Alter Ego* magazine (#36, 2004). "Instead each tried to help the other. Ronn Foss, Grass Green, Raymond Miller, Howard Keltner, Capt. Biljo, and Jeremy A. Barry—none were ever slow in offering a helping hand. Why, there were even guys like Alex Almaraz, God bless him, who sent me dozens of Golden Age titles. We were also pretty naïve about future values, I guess. I recall Roy Thomas offering a copy of the pulp magazine *Black Hood Detective* for 25 cents! I've been fortunate to have been a part of it all."

In later years, Wright carried on correspondences with Howard Siegel, Dwight Decker and John A. Pierce. His story, "The White Dragon Strikes Back!," which had appeared in *Star-Studded Comics* #8 (March 1966), was reprinted in *The Best of Star-Studded Comics* (Hamster Press, 2005) along with the same artwork by Buddy Saunders that had accompanied the original. John Wright passed away on November 14, 2008.

SECTION VI: ARTISTS

How can artists be considered founders of comic fandom? An artist may be able to create an image on paper or canvas, but that seems a far cry from laying the building blocks of a self-sustaining society of fans. One might better ask how a fandom based on an appreciation of an art-based medium could possibly have flourished without the contributions of those who could provide the visual accompaniment to the many fannish activities that would make up the very fabric of the movement. Or ask how fanzines could have appealed to comics fans without accompanying illustrations. Simply reproducing images from the comic books wouldn't work.

Fanzines, newsletters and apas were initially printed by technology that was incapable of such reproductions. Hectograph, mimeograph and spirit duplication were hand-typed on various kinds of stencils, and any drawings that were to be included had to be drawn on those same stencils. There wasn't any way to use a camera image. Photocopiers didn't come into much general use until the mid to late 1960s, and they were initially too expensive for fanzine printing. Professional photo-offset printing was also beyond the budget—and need—of most zine publishers. You needed to have 300 to 400 paying readers to make offset cost-effective. As we've seen, the earliest fanzines often had circulations under 50 copies, and were commonly in the 200 copy range. Even by 1965, few could garner enough orders to engage a professional printer.

How did early fanzines approach this challenge? Fortunately, fandom was rife with aspiring artists. Many of those who loved comics had doodled and drawn their favorite characters as youngsters, and a large percentage dreamed of some day being able to draw Superman or Prince Valiant or Donald Duck for a living. Of that group, a lot of them had both talent and drive, and were eager to get published. Receiving financial compensation was not an immediate concern for these fans. They just wanted to put their work out there, and gain experience in the process.

By 1963, a number of artists had emerged from the field. Many of them were showcased in the stunning *Super Hero Calendar* published near the end of that year by Bernie Bubnis. Bernie's line-up included, in order (one for each month): Jack Kirby, Raymond Miller, Bubnis himself, Buddy Saunders, Alan Weiss, Ronn Foss, Ken Tesar, Howard Keltner, Bill Ryan & Jim Elliott, Biljo White, Grass Green and Russ Manning. Quite a line-up!

Fanzine editors were quick to utilize the talents of these amateur artists, and so did convention organizers, when conventions became a factor. Some fan artists gained substantial followings. Most of them provided not only spot illustrations and covers, but their own comic strips, sometimes done solo and other times in collaboration with popular fan writers. Certain fanzines were devoted mostly or completely to such amateur graphic stories, such as *Star-Studded Comics*, *Fantasy Illustrated*, *Fighting Hero Comics* and *Comic Book*. Thus began the first "small press" comic books, welcome alternatives to the sometimes limited works available from DC, Marvel and the others.

In time, many of the artists graduated to the pages of the pro comics that had been their destiny. Others for a multitude of reasons—not just artistic limitations—did not make that leap. Certainly there were some who did not aspire to break into New York publishing, or whose hearts and minds, in the final analysis, lay in the world of fandom. This in no way diminishes the significance of their services and talents in aiding in the establishment of comic fandom.

D. Bruce Berry
(b. 1924)

D. Bruce Berry was an artist in SF fandom who was drawn into comic fandom by Bill Spicer, editor and publisher of the prominent comics fanzine *Fantasy Illustrated*. Berry illustrated Spicer's superb sequential art adaptation of Otto Binder's "Adam Link's Vengeance."

Douglas Bruce Berry was born in 1924 in Los Angeles, California, the son of a former Marine who was a technical adviser and sometime stuntman in silent films. Later, Bruce's father was a policeman in the Los Angeles Police Department. In the early 1930s, the Berrys moved to Stockton in Northern California. Bruce was a promising artist from the beginning and showed writing talent as well. The appearance of "Flash Gordon" as a Sunday strip in the early 1930s inspired him to develop his artwork. By the time he was a teenager, his work was exceptional. While still in school, he was writing and drawing a Sunday-style science fiction strip in the full-page "Flash Gordon" format as a projected submission to a newspaper syndicate. Bruce's pre-war editorial cartoons for *The Stockton Record*, the city's principal newspaper, also showed great promise.

After high school, Berry took a commercial art job in Chicago, with plans to move on to New York when he felt seasoned enough. However, he was soon drafted, and served his tour of duty in Europe. In an interview in *The Jack Kirby Collector* #17 (November 1997), Berry recalled, "Shortly after the war, I wandered into a bookstore in Oakland in search of science fiction reading material. That was where I met Richard Kyle. He was the clerk behind the counter. After I visited the store a couple more times,

D. Bruce Berry

he offered to introduce me to some other people who were interested in science fiction. That was the beginning of a somewhat erratic connection with science fiction fandom. What made it erratic was the fact that I had no idea what the group really was. It was not actually a 'fan' group in the accepted sense of the word; it was a 'literary' group."

In the 1950s, Bruce Berry moved to Chicago where there was more work in the advertising field. In the Windy City, in his spare time, he began to illustrate for local magazines, including the Hamling SF and fantasy digent-size magazines, *Imagination* and *Space Travel*, as well as *Rogue*, Hamling's *Playboy*-esque title. Bruce also contributed to a number of SF fanzines. He and Bill Spicer began corresponding, which led to his acceptance of doing the art for a very ambitious comic strip for Spicer's fanzine, *Fantasy Illustrated*. Bill had received Otto Binder's permission to adapt a chapter of his successful SF story from the pulp magazines of the early 1940s, "Adam Link's Vengence," part of Binder's saga of a sentient robot that asked the question, "Can a robot have feelings?"

A fan of the Kurtzman school of comics creation, Bill broke down the prose story into graphic story form, even going so far as to do basic layouts and lettering the pages in advance. He had a vision for the story, but recognized that a more accomplished artist was needed to do the actual illustration. That's when he brought Bruce Berry onto the project. Berry later recalled, "I read the stories of Adam Link when they first appeared in the pulp magazines, and enjoyed them tremendously. But the original illustrations of Adam Link did not satisfy me. They looked like something out of *The Wizard of Oz*. They were definitely not the impression I got from reading the stories. I pictured Adam Link as being a creation of human dignity, who just happened to be a machine. When I had the opportunity to draw the cartoon version, I reconstructed the image of the robot from my own point of view. I redesigned the robot on a higher technological level. To the best of my ability, I tried to depict human emotion in an entity that was made of metal."

The resulting 29-page comic strip, presented in *Fantasy Illustrated* #1 and #2 (1964), was one of the most accomplished, impressive feats of graphic story construction to appear in any fanzine. Comicdom in general loved it, voting it "Best Fanzine Strip" in the 1964 Alley Award Poll. Spicer reprinted it in *Graphic Story Magazine* #13 (Spring 1971) with a new painted cover by Berry. (The strip was also reprinted in *Fandom's Finest Comics*, Vol. 2, Hamster Press, 1998.) "Adam Link's Vengeance" put D. Bruce Berry on the "fandom map," and showed the heights that the amateur comic strip could achieve. Also, it showed that the fanzines could present adult-level stories that had no outlet in the professional comics industry of the early 1960s.

As the decade wore on, Berry found advertising work drying up in Chicago, and moved back to Los Angeles. Soon after, he found work as an assistant to Mike Royer, who was inking all the Jack Kirby comic books for DC. When Royer moved on, Bruce inherited the account. Berry inked many issues of *Kamandi*, *Omac* and "The Losers" in a style that was similar to that of Royer. When Kirby returned to Marvel, they decided they wanted the inker to live in the New York City area, and Berry didn't want to move. Therefore, he only inked a smattering of Marvel issues as he began looking for other work. Bruce worked outside the comics field, writing a novel in collaboration with Andrew J. Offutt called *Genetic Bomb* (Warner Books, 1975), and later he illustrated a series of children's books. In 1990, Berry contributed artwork to *Argosy* magazine.

Richard Buckler

(b. 1949)

Among the amateur artists in comicdom, Richard Buckler was obviously talented enough to break into professional comics. His determination to get there was apparent in the rapid improvement displayed by his fanzine artwork in his own publications, and those fanzines of many others in fandom.

Richard "Rich" Buckler, known in the early days to family and friends as "Rick," was born in Detroit, Michigan, in 1949. His family moved to upstate Michigan during his boyhood, where he didn't have much access to comic books. It wasn't until the Bucklers returned to the Motor City around 1961 that he discovered those four-color wonders. Rick plunged into the comic books featuring new and revived superheroes, and never looked back.

Buckler remembered, "I started out reading the *Superman* titles, and then I discovered Marvel Comics. That's when I started to collect comics as a hobby." He and his friends scoured second-hand stores and barber shops in their hunt for back issues, sometimes venturing for miles on their bicycles. Within a year, as he began junior high school, Rick started copying pictures from the comic books after he read them. He preferred reading comics to watching television "because the comic books fired up my imagination more than anything on TV or in the movies." Then, after writing to some of the addresses he found in comic book letter columns, he discovered fanzines such as *RBCC* and his favorite amateur comics zine, *Star-Studded Comics*. He caught the fanzine publishing bug, just as he was beginning to make connections with active fans in the Detroit area.

According to Mike Tuohey, editor of *Super-Hero*, "Buckler had been in touch with Jerry Bails and wanted to publish his own comic book fanzine. Jerry felt there were plenty of fanzines around already, and suggested he get in touch with me to see what was going on with *Super-Hero*. Rick called me and we started to get together to discuss comics and movie serials and comic fanzines. He showed me his artwork and I was, needless to say, impressed." Rick began helping Mike finish up what would be Tuohey's last issue of *Super-Hero* (#3), since the fan editor was heading to college where he didn't think he would have the time to continue it. "Mike's energy and enthusiasm were incredible," Buckler recollected. "He inspired me a lot. We had only known each other for a few short weeks, yet he trusted me enough to hand over all his contacts and editorial material." Though he hadn't even considered publishing until he met Tuohey, Rick Buckler became the new editor of *Super-Hero*.

Other fans entered his life who were eager to contribute to Buckler's zine. Gerry Sorek, a school teacher in a nearby district, was probably one of the fans Rick had contacted through the comic book letter columns. They immediately began collaborating on the "SuperSix," a costumed hero team that would be cover-featured on Buckler's first issue at the helm (*Super-Hero* #4). "I guess he was willing to try anything back then," Sorek recently

Richard Buckler (left) with Jerry Bails

explained. "Like most of the comic fans of the time, I had come up with several ideas for superhero characters, among them the "SuperSix." I shared those ideas with Rick, he did a few sketches, and our collaboration began." *Super-Hero* #4 appeared in late 1966 or, perhaps, the very beginning of 1967.

Buckler, who now introduced himself to fandom as "Rich" not "Rick," proved immediately that he was a capable zine editor. What really set him apart was the quality and quantity of the artwork, which was always given great emphasis. He had the knack of drawing on ditto masters, and was able to accurately trace artwork of various professionals to go along with the articles. But more than anything else, Buckler was able to produce some of the best-drawn amateur comic strips that ever appeared in the ditto fanzines. With each issue—and especially in a sister fanzine, *Intrigue*, entirely devoted to ama-strips—Rich's artwork improved noticeably. Like the work of another fan artist, Grass Green, Buckler's stylistic approach was heavily influenced by art of Jack Kirby, who had become the definitive artist of Marvel Comics.

What attracted Buckler to Kirby's work? "It was the sheer dynamics and boldness of the storytelling," Rich explained. "Jack Kirby seemed to have it all, and in a relatively simple and straightforward cartoon style that I could analyze and imitate, very crudely at first. I learned a lot of my drawing 'chops' from Curt Swan's Superman, but definitely most of the storytelling skills I developed in those early fanzine days came from studying Kirby. I never had any formal art training." The second "SuperSix" tale in *Super-Hero* #5 was a major improvement over the origin story, and the adventures of Buckler's "Ghost" in *Intrigue* #1 and #2 show further development.

Hugh Surratt, another Detroit fan who became a Buckler collaborator, stated, "As I'd imagine was true with any fanzine publisher, his room was filled with random work-in-progress ditto masters, comics, pencils, pens, artwork and stacks of fanzines. Rich worked his tail off on honing his artistic skills. He was *extremely* focused on his craft. Man, that kid could draw!" Surratt was also an aspiring artist, and contributed a number of excellent spot illustrations to *Super-Hero*. For *Intrigue* #1, Surratt "inked" Buckler's pencils on a Captain Liberty and Doc Darkness strip "The Case of the Curious Crusader," scripted by Steve Perrin. "Inking on ditto is a bit of a misnomer," Surratt explained, "since it really meant just pressing down hard with a ball point pen over Rich's pencils. This was a little intimidating for me, since I was light-years behind Rich in my own artistic development." The quality of Buckler's ama-strips was creating a following for his work.

Shortly after his nova-like introduction onto the fan-scene in early 1967, Buckler began receiving invitations from other fan-eds. He complied with as many requests as possible. He drew two high-profile assignments for *Star-Studded Comics*. The first was assisting Grass Green in the completion of the all-Human Cat issue (*SSC* #12), and then providing the artwork for Larry Herndon's Defender story "The House Where Terror Lived!" (*SSC* #13). He also contributed illustrations and strips to *On the Drawing Board, Dolphin Comics, Bombshell* and a multitude of other ama-zines. At the same time, Buckler managed to publish *Super-Hero* #6 and #7, the last issue, which appeared in 1968. In addition, Buckler created the wraparound cover for Jerry Bails' *Collector's Guide: The First Heroic Age* index, and was paid for the work. All during this period, Rich was a regular attendee of the Detroit Triple Fan Fair, becoming co-chairman at one point, and is credited with helping to shift the emphasis toward comic books, over fantasy literature and movies.

When he started high school, Rich Buckler realized "that high school was simply a review of junior high, wherein we are all indoctrinated into a system that deplores imagination and rewards mediocrity." He knew that he would never fit into the mold of "civilized culture," working in a job he hated just to survive. The creativity involved in drawing comics was, he felt, necessary to maintain even his sanity; thus, he would redouble his efforts to break into professional comics. In those days, that meant going to New York City, where nearly all the comic book companies had their offices.

Rich Buckler's first foray East was on the occasion of the 1969 New York Comic Art Convention. He met Alan Weiss, who became a frequent correspondent, as well as Marv Wolfman, Len Wein, Mike Kaluta, Berni Wrightson, and Jeff Jones. He became part of the network of aspiring young artists trying to break into pro comics, all fighting the fact that DC and Marvel weren't looking for new artists. This would change in a few years, but in 1969 the young artists—Buckler included—felt as though they were pounding their heads against a brick wall. "In those days nobody was looking for new talent," Buckler confirmed. "The comic book industry was a 'closed shop' and the companies didn't think they even needed anybody new. This was entirely new territory, and it was only opened up by new guys like Jim Steranko and Neal Adams." Buckler was able to make an early sale to King Comics' *Flash Gordon* #10 (November 1967), a four-page backup strip with the "Freedom Fighters." Then, nothing until Neal Adams finally took pity on him, and offered to ink his pencils on a short strip for DC if Murray Boltinoff would give Rich the assignment. It was "The Symbionts" from a Marvin Wolfman script, which eventually appeared in *House of Secrets* #90 (February–March 1971). It took moving to New York City, and a period of near-starvation while staying week-to-week at the 34th Street YMCA in Manhattan, for Buckler to make a realistic attempt to break into the industry. A letter of recommendation from Jack Kirby to Stan Lee opened the door a crack at Marvel. Soon Rich began wrangling some modest assignments. He was on his way to making a regular living drawing comics, and living his dream.

Before long, Buckler was doing most of his work for Marvel Comics, including a high profile run on the *Fantastic Four* in the mid–1970s, and co-creating the character Deathlok with writer Doug Moench in *Astonishing Tales* #25. He is remembered also for his collaboration with writer Don McGregor on the 1970s "Black Panther" series in *Jungle Action*. In the early '80s, he drew *All-Star Squadron*, written by Roy Thomas. As the years progressed, Rich Buckler had occasion to draw nearly all the major characters of Marvel and DC Comics, often as a cover artist. Since the year 2000, Buckler has been doing both Surrealistic and comic book character paintings. He has had shows in numerous galleries, including a solo exhibition in Paris in 2002. He is the author of *How to Be a Dynamic Comic Book Artist* (Vanguard, 2008).

Landon Chesney

(1938–2001)

A top amateur artist influenced by the horror and humor comics of EC, Landon Chesney created an indelible impression on fanzine readers of the early to mid 1960s. His work for *Fantasy Illustrated*, done in association with Bill Spicer and Bob Overstreet, is among the finest amateur artwork to appear in this era.

Landon Columbus Chesney was born in 1938 in Knoxville, Tennessee. In 1944, his father's work required a transfer and the Chesneys moved to the much smaller Tennessee town of Cleveland. In a later interview, Chesney recalled, "Even in the isolated backwater that the old hometown was in those days, there seemed to be an enormous pool of second-hand comics, constantly in circulation, from which innocent babes could draw fresh reading material. I didn't make a practice of buying comics new off the stands until I was well into my teens.... That was when I started saving the EC's ... and I've been an EC fan ever since."

Writing of his youth as a comic collector, and his boyhood friendship with Landon Chesney, Bob Overstreet recalled meeting Chesney in the eighth grade at Arnold School in Cleveland. ("Bob's Bizarre Tales," *Overstreet Comic Book Price Guide* #30, Gemstone Publishing, Inc., 2000). "Chesney invited me over to his house

Landon Chesney

one day to look at his EC collection, which was a stack of comics carefully stored in a small cardboard box," Bob wrote. "These comic books were special." Overstreet instantly became an EC fan, and the two became fast friends. Though Landon didn't participate in the EC fanzines of the 1950s, he did send letters of comment to EC, and some saw print.

Chesney had many interests, often shared with Overstreet: his love of magic and admiration for Harry Houdini, and amateur photography. Later, he and Bob would pose for photos used as art reference when they were collaborating on drawing comic strips together. Landon's art talent was already well developed by the time they met. He had created hundreds of short gag strips featuring his humorous character "Frank Fearnot." Overstreet wrote, "He once said that he had enough of these to run as a daily in a newspaper for two years. His flare for cartoon art was inspired, and it came easy for him."

In a late-in-life interview, Landon Chesney spoke of his favorite comic book artists and influences. Jack Burnley was his favorite Superman artist. Landon's humor work was influenced by that of Walt Kelly, Harvey Kurtzman and Bill Elder; his serious drawing shows a noticeable similarity to that of Johnny Craig. While Chesney loved drawing images of haunted houses and frightened faces similar to the style of EC, it was a humor strip that introduced Chesney to fandom. After finishing his Air Force enlistment in 1960, Landon saw his first issue of Richard and Patricia Lupoff's fanzine *Xero*. "The first sight of *Xero*, which featured a carefully stenciled figure of Batman ... hit me with an impact not unlike that described by Jerry Bails on beholding *All-Star Comics* for the first time," he remembered. Such was his inspiration that Chesney impulsively concocted a parody of "The Flash of Two Worlds" entitled "Two Flashes Meet The Purple Slagheap," and sent it to *Xero*. The Lupoffs loved it, and enlisted Bhob Stewart and George Scithers to help with color overlays and offset printing. The result (in *Xero* #10) was the first multi-colored offset strip in the fanzines, and one that gained a lot of attention for the young Tennessean. This led to Chesney's early connection with Bill Spicer, who was preparing the first issue of a new amateur comic book in an EC vein called *Fantasy Illustrated*. Landon's first artwork for *FI* was drawing the cover of issue #1 (1964).

Shortly afterward, Spicer received permission from Otto "Eando" Binder to adapt his short story "The Life Battery" into comic strip form for his fanzine, and enlisted Chesney to draw it. The result qualifies as one of a handful of true classic amateur strips. "The Life Battery" is about a scientist who discovers a way to animate dead things, like a museum mummy, only to realize firsthand that there is more to life than simply consciousness. On this ambitious story canvas, Chesney meticulously fashioned a series of images of stunning craft and detail. His mastery of the interplay of light and shadow, as well as his excellent feel for heightened drama, made him the perfect artist for the story. When it appeared in *Fantasy Illustrated* #2, "The Life Battery" created a sensation. Spicer later commented, "Chesney made the most of static scenes replete with wordy captions and talking heads until you saw some semblance of action toward the finale. A good argument might be made that artwise he never again quite reached this same level of expertise." (*Alter Ego* #22, March 2003) In a letter that appeared in *Fantasy Illustrated* #3, Dick Memorich, an artist in his own right, wrote, "if you will study Chesney's art you will discover that he is an exceptional cartoonist who 'feels' what he puts down in pen and ink. He isn't just 'drawing pictures.' It is evident that he has a deeper association with the imagination, a deeper understanding of human emotions ... the ability to create a mood. This is the quality which makes one cartoonist stand out over another, a handful stand out over hundreds. Chesney strikes me as being this type of cartoonist."

Landon Chesney's subsequent strips for Spicer's magazine ("A Study in Horror," in collaboration with Bob Overstreet, and an adaptation of Ambrose Bierce's "One Summer Night") didn't disappoint, though they along with "The Life Battery" comprised the sum total of all the horror strips Landon drew for the fanzines. His other work was either in the pulp or comic hero genre, or humor. Unexpectedly, "One Summer Night" was framed by three pages of hilarious work featuring Chesney's Misbourne, the gnomish assistant to a miniature man in a cage who draws comic books known as the Master. Reminiscent of Kurtzman and Elder's "Outer Sanctum" in *Mad* #5, "Misbourne and the Master" was a hit with the readers, who demanded more.

Chesney wrote, "The early sixties was an optimum time for me to get involved in fan activity. I was in my first year in college, and I had all my classes scheduled for the morning. That way, I could devote my afternoons to the really important things in life, like doing amateur comic strips!" For *Star-Studded Comics*, he illustrated two stories featuring Howard Keltner's character Dr. Weird, in a looser, less dense style than he had used on his horror tales. He created a Shadow-like protagonist, "The Cloak," for a continuing feature in *Voice of Comicdom*, and inked a pair of "Xal-Kor the Human Cat" strips written and penciled by Grass Green. Around 1970, he began working on a graphic novel featuring "The Cloak" for Bill Spicer's Graphic Story Press, and though it was announced, it never came to fruition. The existing pages of penciled lay-outs are tantalizing, but Chesney found himself stymied by the sheer ambition and size of the project. In fact, this proved to be the death knell of the writer-artist's participation in fanzines.

Grass Green, who remained a friend, became frustrated with Chesney's lack of interest in building a career as a professional in the comics field. Landon later explained, "I stopped doing comic strips when the fun went out of it. I was, essentially, never anything but a fan. Don Thompson once said that he got involved in fandom to make friends with people of like mind. That was my principal motivation." He took a job in advertising in the early 1970s, still in his hometown of Cleveland, still living in the little red house at the same address that had accompanied his letters in early issues of *Fantastic Four*. "After spending eight or nine hours on a drawing board all day, the last thing I wanted to do was 'relax' by sitting down to more of the same at home. I continued to get ideas. I continued to make notes and I would get sufficiently inspired to occasionally sit down and start on a project. But I never saw any of these latter-day efforts through to completion because the venue, the forum, was gone. I felt like I'd be playing to an audience of phantoms."

Chesney's work did appear in the pages of some underground comix, and he was involved as a lay out artist for the covers of the adzine *Comics Source* as late as the early 1990s, but mainly drew for his own pleasure, and at the request of his nephew, Jason Gillespie. Chesney was always ready to entertain or instruct young Jason with a sketch. The boy was in awe of his uncle's talent, and learned a lot from the soft-spoken, thoughtful man. "I've always said to people he's probably about the most intelligent person I've ever met," Gillespie wrote in his remembrance of Chesney in *Alter Ego* #22. "He had a very ... calm and thoughtful demeanor. You always get this feeling that there was something below the surface, and I'm sure there was.... But, at the same time, once he started talking about something that he was very interested in, there was just this wealth of information. If he didn't have his art ability, he probably could have gone into many different areas."

Landon Chesney died on December 19, 2001. He had suffered for many years from Chronic Fatigue Syndrome and other physical maladies, and died in his sleep from an apparent heart attack. A tribute with reprints of "The Life Battery" and other rare Chesney work appeared in *Fandom's Finest Comics* Vol. 1 (Hamster Press, 1997).

Bill DuBay
(1948–2010)

Bill DuBay (who didn't capitalize the "b" in his last name when he was involved in early fandom) was a highly energetic and prolific fanzine publisher from 1963 to 1967, but is probably best remembered for his effective, carefully rendered fanzine artwork. He contributed to nearly all of the top fanzines, doing covers, pin-ups, spot illustrations and complete comic strips.

William DuBay was born in 1948 in San Francisco, California, the first of seven siblings. During the summer of 1963, a copy of Ronn Foss's *Alter Ego* #5 had found its way to the mailbox of Bill DuBay, a recent "graduate" of St. Paul's grammar school in San Francisco, California. "When I got that, it blew my mind," DuBay recently remembered. Suddenly realizing that there were old comic books and superheroes published long before his current favorites, Bill immediately began treasure hunting for old comics in the Bay Area, and planning to publish his first amateur magazine. DuBay was joined in this effort by his friend since first grade at St. Paul's, Marty Arbunich.

Immediately bitten by the fanzine bug, Bill put together the first issue of *Fantasy Hero* and published it in September 1963. It was printed on a ditto machine at Sacred Heart High School (another all-boys Catholic school), and offered three amateur comic strips. The

Bill DuBay

first, which demonstrated Bill DuBay's penchant for putting himself (and Marty) into his strips, was "Billy De," a 14-page opus that showed the influence of Infantino on DuBay's budding art style. It also demonstrated Bill's knack for working in the ditto medium. Bill drafted Marty to help on *Fantasy Hero*, and it wasn't long before they formed Golden Gate Features (with Rudi Franke and Barry Bauman) and launched the two fanzines for which they would be best remembered: *Yancy Street Journal* and *Voice of Comicdom*.

Although Bill did most of the ditto art for *Yancy Street Journal*, he was more engaged in the production of *Voice of Comicdom*, mainly because he was responsible for creating the lay outs and pasting up the pages for offset printing, but also because *VoC* carried first daily-style and then Sunday-style newspaper strip installments. His creation, "The Web" (apparently inspired by Will Eisner's "The Spirit"), was the first he drew in ink on Bristol board for professional printing, and enabled him to gain confidence using ink pens, zip-a-tone and approximating professional lettering. Two of his best-known amateur comic strips were done in pen and ink: "The Dreamsman and Lucky" in *Fantasy Illustrated* #4 (1965) from a script by Steve Perrin, and "The Crimes of the Transmuter" starring Powerman in *Star-Studded Comics* #9 (1966). He also played a big part in the production of *Fandom Presents*, a 100-page publication featuring a "who's who" of the amateur superheroes who were appearing in fanzines at that time.

Though he co-published *Yancy Street Journal*, DuBay wasn't as big a fan of Marvel in 1964 as he was of other companies. He enjoyed the Kirby and Ditko-drawn pre-superhero Marvel monster titles, but wasn't especially impressed by the Marvel characters. "I loved the Julie Schwartz edited books," he remembered. "I always loved anything produced by superior artists. So, when I discovered the EC line, a decade after they were no longer published, I went out and found them all." He also collected original art, and owned pages of Sgt. Rock stories drawn by Joe Kubert, and "Sky Masters" by Jack Kirby and Wally Wood.

His fannish days ended abruptly in 1966 when he was drafted into the U.S. Army. DuBay found himself editing an Army newspaper called *The Ft. Bragg Paraglide*. "It was a good training ground," he recalled. "I got to see all my mistakes in print instantaneously. That was always helpful and humiliating. It was hard work, but sported major benefits. Newspapers teach you to perform quickly and accurately and to respect a deadline." He had been doing that for more than a year when Roy Thomas of Marvel Comics invited him to contribute something to their humor title *Not Brand Ecch*. He wrote and drew a four-page satire of Stan Lee and Jack Kirby's creative process, which was his first professional writing and drawing assignment. (His first professional work of any kind was artwork for Charlton's *Go-Go Comics* in his senior year of high school in 1966.)

After finishing his military stint, Bill studied journalism in college, while moonlighting for Warren Publishing's *Creepy* and *Eerie* magazines as a writer and artist. As he was completing his college education, Jim Warren called and asked him to become his Art Director if he was willing to move to New York City. With the promise that he would likely advance to the full editor job at Warren if he worked out, DuBay accepted. He spent the next decade in Manhattan editing and designing *Creepy, Eerie, Vampirella, The Spirit* and *The Rook*. After that, he worked as an editor and writer for Western Publishing and Red Circle (an Archie imprint), and did occasional assignments at DC and Marvel.

Bill moved into the animation field, and was involved in various creative aspects (writing, storyboarding, directing, producing) on more than a 100 TV and film projects, including "The Simpsons," "Ghostbusters," "Jem," "GI Joe," "Transformers," "Peter Pan," and "The Incredible Hulk." In recent years, he launched a venture called Time Castle Books, republishing his work on "The Rook" and other series.

John Fantucchio
(b. 1938)

Perhaps as a result of its relatively large circulation, *RBCC* attracted a staff of some of the most talented cover artists in fandom. By 1967, when its conversion to photo-offset printing was complete, the magazine began running a series of outstanding covers by a new breed of fan artist. Two were mainstays of the magazine: one was Don Newton, and the other was John Fantucchio.

John G. Fantucchio was already a professional illustrator by the time he came to fandom. Born in Massachusetts in May 1938, about the same time *Action Comics* #1 hit the stands, John was the son of a shoemaker. Growing up, Fantucchio particularly admired the work of C. C. Beck, Alex Raymond, Mac Raboy, the team of Meskin and Robinson, Harold Foster and Dick Sprang, as well as the great artists of EC comics, such as Wally Wood, Al Williamson and Frank Frazetta. While still in junior high and high school, John's parents paid for a correspondence course, and he graduated from Art Instruction, Inc. in 1955. A short time later, he enrolled in a course put out by the Cartoonist Exchange in Ohio, and was creating a comic strip and comic book covers that he submitted to the Scholastic Art Awards. John won several "Gold Keys," the top prize back then. He attended The School of Practical Art in Boston full time, and graduated in 1962. His instructor was Harry Habblitz, who was a big fan of Edgar Rice Burroughs, and would draw a celebrated adaptation of ERB's "The End of Bukawai" for *Fantasy Illustrated* #3 (1964).

After his graduation, Fantucchio moved to Arlington, Virginia, and in 1963 found employment with the CIA (Central Intelligence Agency) as an illustrator. He later explained, "The title at that time was called 'Illustrator General,' which encompassed creative illustrations, all of which were classified and were for internal use only. Very interesting!" Not long after, he saw an advertisement in a comic book by The S.F.C.A., which was for *RBCC*, and he subscribed. On the bottom of his subscription form, as was his wont, he drew a small sketch. Publisher G. B. Love asked him to do a cover for the fanzine. "Back then the stuff was mimeographed so I drew an accented line which I knew would reproduce well in the method he was using," John said. That first cover, featuring the Golden Age hero Fighting Yank, appeared on *RBCC* #44 (1965). Love admired Fantucchio's work, and gave him a standing invitation to produce more covers, sometimes of subjects suggested by the editor. John and Gordon developed a good working relationship, and the results were some of the most spectacular and admired covers to appear on the popular publication.

John's interest in comics had continued unabated from his childhood. During the

John Fantucchio

Silver Age, his favorite artists were Wayne Boring, Carmine Infantino, Joe Kubert, Steve Ditko, John Buscema and Neal Adams, who was a special favorite. He also greatly admired other artists in fandom who appeared in *RBCC* and elsewhere. Fantucchio recalled, "There were a few fan artists who were unique. I admired Don Newton's knowledge of creating a solid form, Bob Kline for his action figures, Martin Greim for his use of lines. The one I feel stood out was Jim Jones, who had a very personal look to his work…. Great use of solid blacks and a good understanding of positive and negative shapes."

In the summer of 1969, Phil Seuling gave John Fantucchio space at the annual New York Comicon at Statler-Hilton Hotel. Jim Warren viewed John's work and asked him to draw a strip for *Vampirella* magazine. This was "Ghoul Girl, 1969" (written by Don Glut), which appeared in the fifth issue. Fantucchio illustrated a second story for Warren, "Minanker's Demons" (from a script by Buddy Saunders) in *Creepy* #34, but that was the end of it. John was busy with commissions from fans and was preparing to start his own art school. The Fantucchio School of Art was established in 1973. John taught four evenings a week and all day Saturday. The school continued until 2001. After leaving the CIA in 1988, he also created his own commercial and fine art studio.

Of the early days of fandom, John says, "I thoroughly enjoyed this era and tried to produce the best possible work I could. I enjoyed working with the many talented young entrepreneurs." Fantucchio's artwork appeared in many of the top, high-circulation fanzines of the late 1960s and early 1970s, such as *The Collector* and *Fantastic Fanzine*. His decorative style was utterly unique, and he used zip-a-tone brilliantly. It was only the time commitment involved in starting his school that caused him to lessen his participation in the fan scene.

John is still interested in comics, and continues to do comics-oriented art commissions. He creates works in every medium: oil, acrylic, watercolor, casein, gouache, pastel, ink and pencil. In his studio, he has created custom art from caricatures to logo designs, portraits, paintings and murals. "Every morning and evening, I feed the squirrels and birds around my house," he explains. "Then I sharpen my pencils and wash my brushes to get ready for the next day. I get up at 4:00 A.M. and go to bed at 9:00 P.M.

Ronn Foss
(1939–2001)

Ronn Foss was a ubiquitous artist, writer and fanzine publisher in comicdom of the 1960s, known for his sophisticated artistic style and "man who reads *Playboy*" look, and was often depicted smoking a pipe.

He was born Ronald Eugene Foss in 1939 in Defiance, Ohio, and grew up in various small Midwestern cities in Ohio and neighboring Indiana. Ronn (who added the second "n" to his first name when he reached adulthood, though never changing it legally) had been drawing his own comics as early as 1949. Thin of frame, bespectacled Foss was a dreamer who grew up on the comics of the late 1940s and early 1950s. As such, while he loved superheroes, he also cultivated a taste for westerns, SF and many of the other genres who had crowded out the heroes at that time. His favorite artists were Mac Raboy, Al Williamson, Joe Simon and Jack Kirby, and Joe Kubert, who became his biggest influence. He and writer/artist Richard Green were best friends in junior high and high school in Ft. Wayne, Indiana, where they created and collaborated on dozens of amateur costumed heroes. Both showed promising art ability, and aspired to draw comic books professionally as adults. As a teenager, Foss won art awards and gained visibility doing various forms of art-for-hire in his local community.

In 1957 he left high school to join the U. S. Air Force, spending part of his hitch in the Middle East. Foss recounted in a 1991 interview, "In 1958 through 1960, I was stationed at Travis Air Force Base in Fairfield, California, which is 45 miles from San Francisco. I spent lots of my free time in the North Beach area, digging jazz and poetry and more expressive arts

Biljo White (left) receives an Alley Award from Ronn Foss.

than cartooning. I was really caught up in the beatnik scene." He wrote and published his own booklet of beat poetry entitled *Far Gone: Like Lost and Looking Back*. Foss was introduced to comic fandom with *Alter-Ego* #2, which began his correspondence with Jerry Bails. Bails put him in touch with Ron Haydock, Roy Thomas and others. Little did he know that in just two years he would take over the helm of *A-E*, as well as its companion magazine, *The Comicollector*, when original editor Jerry Bails wanted to focus on other projects.

Foss came to the forefront because of his great enthusiasm, which he conveyed in flurries of handwritten letters to the most active fans, always accompanied with a colorful illustration or two. His facile artwork gained him many fans, after it appeared in such early fanzines as *Spotlight* ("Dimension Man," written by Parley Holman), *Headline* ("Little Giant," written by Steve Gerber) and *Masquerader* ("The Cowl," scripted by Mike Vosburg), as well as in *Alter-Ego* itself. At first, Ronn seemed to be feeling his way, perhaps because this was the first time he had drawn on ditto masters. Fortunately, he had a strong command of the syntax of comic strip construction, and soon the famous "Foss fluidity" emerged. His panels expressed his sophisticated design-sense, with figures springing into dynamic action. This was no legacy from Kubert or other influences; Foss brought to his strips an individuality that made his work instantly recognizable. His origin of "The Eclipse," scripted by prison guard Drury Moroz, won an Alley Award as "Best Amateur Strip" in 1963. In 1963 and 1964, he was much in demand, with "The Viper" for *Komix Illustrated* #5 (1963) and a second "Dimension Man" strip in *Fighting Hero Comics* #12 (1964), featuring a sexy adversary named "Velvet of Venus."

All but "The Eclipse" and the first chapter of "The Liberty Legion" in *Star-Studded Comics* #4 (1964) were drawn on ditto masters, reproduced in purple printing, for amateur publications printing 100 or 200 copies. Foss's ditto work was more skillful than most, and the medium's informal quality had a way of obscuring some of his artistic weaknesses. When he worked in ink on Bristol board, his inattention to detail, lack of solid anatomical knowledge, and sketchy backgrounds somewhat belied the promise of his superficially sophisticated, eye-pleasing style. Nonetheless, he was and would remain an inventive stylist with a unique "look" that was always interesting, if not ascending fully to professional quality.

The Foss issues of *Alter Ego* (#5 and 6) carried on the standard set by Jerry Bails (and his co-editor Roy Thomas), and he managed to publish six issues of *The Comicollector* in the span of a year. *The Comicollector* #8 introduced its hostess, Joy Holiday, whose name was suggested by the Christmas season. Joy was a figure drawn by Foss, ostensibly a beautiful woman in a colorful costume, like a superheroine. Instead of appearing in strips, she acted as a mascot for *CC* and *AE*. An actual costume was sewn, and three women posed in it for photographs that were published in *AE* and elsewhere: Ronn's sister Beverly Ann Foss, Roy Thomas' girlfriend Linda Rahm, and another female friend of Roy's named Pauline Copeman. The photos appeared in *Alter Ego* starting with #5.

By mid–1964, however, Ronn Foss was approaching burn out. He handed the fanzines over to others, and focused his attention on drawing comics with pen and ink on special drawing paper, like the pros. He tackled a second Eclipse strip (which appeared in *Alter Ego* #7, under Roy Thomas's editorship) with excellent results, and then did the art for the first African American amateur hero.

Writer Steve Perrin had submitted a script to Bill Spicer, publisher of *Fantasy Illustrated*, starring The Black Phantom and his teenaged sidekick Wraith, two black Americans who donned costumes to fight injustice. The "Battler against Bigotry" first appeared in *Mask & Cape* #4 (Fall 1964) in text form, with a splash page and spot illustrations by Foss. Now the Black Phantom would appear in full-blown comic strip form in one of the most widely circulated fan publications of the day. The strip, which appeared in *FI* #6 (1966), came alive with incendiary imagery and a message of universal brotherhood. It proved to be the last strip that Foss drew during his early period of fan activity.

On October 1, 1965, Ronn married Coreen Casey, an Illinois fan with whom he had carried on a passionate correspondence. The newlyweds moved to Fort Lauderdale, Florida (where a brother-in-law had a sign-painting business), and it was there that "The Origin of the Black Phantom" was drawn. A projected adaptation of Gardner Fox's *Warrior of Llarn*, with Roy Thomas, never came to fruition, and he didn't pursue the dream of drawing comics professionally, perhaps because it involved (at that time) living and working in the Greater New York City area. He and Coreen became active in the Society for Creative Anachronism. By the end of the decade they drifted into a counter-culture lifestyle, and became increasingly political. Politics came to the fore in Ronn's fanzines *Pandora* and *Issues*, as the 1970s arrived.

Thanks to Roy Thomas, who had become the second-most-important writer at Marvel Comics by the early 1970s, Foss was given the opportunity to draw a feature for the then-popular parody title *Not Brand Ecch!* This gave Ronn Foss a genuine Marvel Comics credential, but the result was unimpressive, and he didn't do more. Unlike his best friend Grass Green, Foss never was published by Charlton, nor did he get into underground comix during their heyday. Most of his published work in later years appeared in counter-culture newspapers and magazines.

In 1975 Foss moved to a cabin in the Ozarks, where he spent the rest of his life raising two children with Coreen, and later on his own. He eked out a meager existence doing art commissions, and worked for a time in the mid–1980s for Russ Cochran in West Plains, Missouri, opaquing negatives for the large EC reprint books. He was interviewed at length only once, for *The Ronn Foss Retrospective*, an amateur publication that appeared in comics amateur press alliance *Capa-alpha*, in 1991. (The interview was later reprinted in *Comic Fandom Reader*, Hamster Press, 2003.) Many of his strips from the early fanzines were reprinted in various books by Hamster Press in the 1990s.

Foss maintained that he never regretted his decision to live a rural, almost hermit-like, existence. "I've always simply enjoyed nature, like Thoreau, since my childhood on the farm," he mused, late in life. "I've discussed this with many who think I have it hard, living without lots of conveniences and creature comforts, while to me the nine-to-five is the hard way to live." A lifelong smoker, Ronn suffered from emphysema in the last decade of his life. He passed away in his rural home, alone, on September 14, 2001.

Rudi Franke
(b. 1939)

Artist, writer and fanzine publisher Rudolf Franke grew up in Oakland, California. His father was a baker. "I have the same first name as my father, but our middle names are different," he explained in a recent interview. "I'm not a Jr., but to avoid confusion I was called 'Rudi.' Also, 'Rudolph' is a bit too formal. Most people spell 'Rudi' with a 'y' at the end of the name. I started with an 'i' just to be different, and I liked how it looked when I signed my art."

He began drawing as a way to improve his vision. "During my elementary school years, I had trouble with my eyes crossing. I started wearing glasses from age four. My parents found a doctor who could correct my crossing eye problem. He used machines where you looked through a viewing end and traced drawings. Many of these drawings ... were cartoons of Walt Disney characters. I traced Mickey Mouse hundreds of times in an attempt to strengthen my eyes." He continued to draw on his own.

The comics of his youth were those of the late 1940s, especially Fiction House when he found out a friend had saved hundreds of copies of *Jungle*, *Wings* and other titles. Franke was introduced to the work of Wally Wood in *Mad* #4, which proved a life-changing event. "From there I discovered the EC science fiction comics.... I was hooked. I had to have every EC that I could get my hands on. I finally completed my collection just as I was graduating from Fremont High School in 1957." He did this by sending postcards to the members of the EC Fan-Addict club, since their addresses were printed in full in the club newsletters. By this time, he was also an avid fan of "Prince Valiant" by Harold Foster, and other strips with an illustrative quality. He learned by copying his favorite artists.

Although his grades were good enough for the University of California, all his friends were going to Oakland City College, so that's where Rudi began his higher education. Soon he realized he wanted to be a teacher, and transferred to San Francisco State in 1960. He studied Art and, as a minor, drafting in Industrial Education. "They had some great teachers [but] if you wanted technique and drawing skills ... you were on your own. That was one of the reasons I got into fandom. I used the fanzines as a place to learn how to draw." In fanzines he learned to deal with deadlines, working from the ideas of others, found out about printing techniques, and to listen to the critique of the fans. "I was on a journey," Franke recalled. "Each time I contributed to a fanzine, it would help me improve."

A key event in Rudi's fannish life occurred in 1961 when he met Barry Bauman. Though eight years younger, Bauman was a young comic book collecting wheeler-dealer who helped Franke amass a sizable collection of Golden Age comic books. The two began

Rudi Franke

combing the Bay Area used bookstores for old comic books. It was Bauman who showed Franke the first issues of *Alter-Ego*, introducing Rudi to comic book fandom.

A visit to Ronn Foss in Fairfield, California, prior to the publication of *Alter-Ego* #5 in March 1963, proved to be pivotal in two ways. First, it inspired Rudi to publish his own fanzine, and it was Foss who tipped the two collectors off about a large collection of Golden Age comics for sale in the Liberty Book Store on Folsom Street in Sacramento. Bauman and Franke cleaned out the store's closet of thousands of vintage comic books—an incredible find—for just 40 cents per copy! Fortified by the Liberty Book Store windfall of vintage comic books, which would serve as a basis for drawings of Golden Age heroes and articles about their adventures, Rudi decided to launch his own fanzine. *Heroes Hangout* #1 appeared in November 1963, with more issues popping up in 1964. A fan meeting around Christmas-time 1963, probably engineered by the ever-enterprising Barry Bauman, dramatically impacted Franke's fanzine plans.

Marty Arbunich and Bill DuBay, two other teenage comics enthusiasts who were responsible for the amateur *Fantasy Hero* fanmag, invited Rudi and Barry over to Bill's home in nearby San Francisco. The foursome formed a publishing "consortium" grandly dubbed Golden Gate Features, and joined forces to produce a mega-fanzine called *Fantasy Heroes Hangout*. Together and individually, the four were responsible for dozens of fanzines over the next several years. One of the most long-lived was the continuation of *Fantasy Heroes Hangout*, which morphed into a newspaper format under the banner *Voice of Comicdom* with its second issue. Franke contributed artwork to nearly all of the Golden Gate endeavors, though he didn't care for drawing on ditto masters.

Rudi's artistic style, as evidenced in "The Sorceress" and "Johnny Doom," two early syndicated-style strips that appeared in *Voice of Comicdom*, proved to be florid and emphasized decorative elements. He relied on brush more than pen for his inking, achieving subtle effects seldom seen in other amateur illustrations and strips. Sometimes this technique overwhelmed the storytelling, indicating that Franke was more suited to single illustration than narrative sequential art.

Comic book fans in the Bay Area came together at the 1964 Science Fiction World Con in San Francisco. Their "con-within-a-con" included such personages as Don Glut, Larry Ivie, Steve Perrin, John Chambers, Mike Friedrich, Jeremy Barry and others. Soon they were looking for other ways to meet for the purpose of trading comics and experiencing the camaraderie of like-minded individuals. On January 8, 1966, Franke hosted a gathering of some 28 fans at his house, with the garage serving as a mini-theater, where the Captain America serial was shown. Later that same year, the group was invited to Mike Fredrich's place for a similar gathering, where original art pages donated by DC Comics editor Julius Schwartz were door prizes. The first giant California comic book convention wouldn't take place until 1970 in San Diego.

In 1965 Franke received his teaching credential and began his classroom career at William C. Overfelt High School in San Jose, California, after completing his Navy training. It proved a felicitous beginning, as Rudi would continue teaching in the East Side Union High School District up to his retirement in 2002.

While on the East Coast for military training, Rudi attended the 1965 New York Comi-con, and at other times spent time with Larry Ivie and professional comic strip artist John Belfi. Between his Navy training, beginning teaching and getting married during one frantic year, Franke's contributions to the fanzines dwindled, but it wouldn't be long before he would re-enter the fan scene as a prominent fanzine publisher.

First, Rudi revived *Heroes Hangout* for a few digest-sized issues. Then, after Marty and Bill moved on from *Voice of Comicdom* in 1967, Rudi picked up the Golden Gate Features mantle. He edited and published the popular publication into the next decade. As a parting gift, DuBay jump-started Rudi's tenure at the helm by giving him a number of pages for *VoC* that were already laid out and ready for printing. When Franke visited local fan Dennis Cunningham, editor of *Weirdom*, he was shown artwork by Richard Corben that was slated to appear in Cunningham's mag. However, Rudi claims that Corben's "Monsters Rule" strip in *Voice of Comicdom* was the first to actually appear in a fanzine, and may be Corben's first published work anywhere. *VoC* also had "From the Lower Depths," a strip by the new fandom sensation, George Metzger. The only major comic strip Franke did for fandom appeared in *Star-Studded Comics* #16 (1969), featuring the zine's amateur hero Doctor Weird. "The Castle on Demon Mountain!," scripted by Larry Herndon, showed the influence of the psychedelic posters that Franke admired.

After the demise of *Voice of Comicdom* with its seventeenth issue in 1971, Rudi continued to do occasional art pieces for comics publications. In the 1980s, he drew a number of covers for *The Buyer's Guide to Comic Fandom*, and various spot-art and logo assignments for *The Comics Journal* and *Amazing Heroes*. Around this time, Franke stopped teaching art and instead taught ongoing high school courses in photography at Independence High School, which he continued for the rest of his career.

After retiring in 2002, Rudi and his wife, Bettie, moved to Lincoln, California. "It's a small little town with some really great people," Franke said. "I haven't contributed to fanzines for a number of years. I am doing art now as well as photography. I have a darkroom and still work with film. I am also learning digital. There is just so much to learn. The journey has been an interesting and enjoyable one, and I hope I'll be able to continue it for some time." He is still interested in comic art, but finds the computer coloring and art styles of recent comics unappealing. Instead, he focuses his attention on the numerous books that reprint the great comics of the past.

Richard "Grass" Green
(1939–2002)

Richard Green was known in fandom almost exclusively by his nickname "Grass." He was a popular writer/artist in the fanzines of the early 1960s, known for both his humorous and serious illustrations and comic strips. His work appeared in all the major fanzines, including *Fantasy Illustrated*, *Star-Studded Comics*, *Alter Ego*, *RBCC*, *Komix Illustrated*, *Super Hero* and more. He was the first prominent member of comicdom who was African-American.

Richard Edward Green was born in Ft. Wayne, Indiana, one of eight siblings (three sisters and four brothers). One of the few memories he had of his mother, who died when Richard was only six, was of a suggestion she gave him to improve a childhood caricature he had drawn of his eldest brother, Sam. "My interest in comics started when I was a tot," he recalled. "When I learned to read, Batman was my first fave, then Captain Marvel, then almost any comic I could get my hands on. I loved comics!"

As he got older, Richard began to discern the differences in the artists' styles, and developed favorites. At age 13, he discovered Simon and Kirby's *Fighting American*, and the boy's admiration for the artwork of Jack Kirby led to a heavy Kirby influence on his own art, especially his straight superhero strips.

In 1954, in ninth grade, Richard Green met another budding young cartoonist who gave him the nickname that he adopted for the rest of his life. That fan was Ronald E. Foss, later better known as Ronn Foss. They called each other "Spider Foss" and "Grasshoppa Green." Ronn shortened the nickname "Grasshoppa" to just "Grass," and later introduced his pal to fandom using that distinctive moniker. It stuck. The two of them became best friends, with the racial difference (Foss was Caucasian) of no consequence. The two of them created many, perhaps hundreds, of amateur heroes and heroines together, drawing their own one-of-a-kind comics, which Grass would color. On November 4, 1955, Green drew a hero they called The Eye, remarkable because he wore a helmet covering his head that was shaped like a huge eyeball. Later, upon seeing the 1955 drawing, another writer/artist named Biljo White developed the strange-looking character into the protagonist of a popular series of amateur comic strips in fanzines of the mid–1960s.

Like Foss, Green enlisted in the U.S. Air Force after high school, and the friends entered into a period of heavy correspondence until they were both civilians again. Ronn was the first of the duo to hear about comic fandom, but soon both of them were furiously drawing amateur strips on ditto masters for various fan editors who were desperate for material. Although Grass could draw straight superheroes, he had a special flair for humorous artwork and cartoons, which had a contagious playfulness that reflected his own personality. Because it was a humorous strip that introduced Grass Green's work to fandom, he quickly became known as a humor artist of remarkable ability. That strip was a superb spoof of Marvel's *Fantastic Four* called "Da Frantic Four" by Green (with some plotting and gags by Foss). It saw print in Foss's *The Comicollector* #8 (1962), introducing readers to an issue of "The World's *Greatless* Comic Magazine," featuring the Human Scorch, Thang, the Invisibubble Girl and Mister Frantic. Green's parody work sometimes resembled *Mad* and *Panic*, and like Kurtzman, there was little subtlety to Grass's figures, facial expressions and general approach. Instead, there was wild abandon. Green became the "Clown Prince of Comicdom."

Thus, the team-up of Roy Thomas and Grass Green on "Bestest League of America meets Da Frantic Four" in *Alter Ego* #6 (March 1964) was a true fandom event. The collaboration worked wonderfully, with characters drawn by Thomas and Green interacting together in the same panels. (Green finally had the chance to draw the Bestest League characters, along with numerous Marvel characters, when the BLA crossed over to pro comics in Charlton's *Go-Go* #5 and #6 in 1966, with scripts written by Roy's friend Gary Friedrich. Da Frantic Four also appeared there, as the Fantabulous Four—with the characters pretty much as they appeared in *A-E* and *CC*. These were the first known instances of an ama-strip's heroes making it into professional comics.)

Green did provide examples of his ability to handle straight superhero material in a number of the early ditto fanzines. For Biljo White's *Komix Illustrated*, he did "The

Richard "Grass" Green

Blade" in #3 (October 1962) and "The Fog" in #6 (December 1962); for Mike Vosburg's *Masquerader*, Green provided "Action Ace and Thrill Boy." In the Texas Trio's *Star-Studded Comics* #2 (December 1963), Grass drew a strip starring The Defender written by Larry Herndon. Still, humor strips like "Speed Marvel" and "Gizmo the Ghost" in *Komix Illustrated* offered further proof that Grass's talent as a humorist set him apart. Green's ability to handle both straight and humorous comic strips could also be seen in the first two issues of Bill Spicer's *Fantasy Illustrated* in 1964. *FI* #1 offered Green's artwork on the parody "Will the Real Lance Lightning Please Sit Down?" *FI* #2 featured the suspense strip "Someone Please Help Me!" with excellent pencils and inks by Green.

If Grass Green had drawn no more than the stories listed thus far, his place as one of the best and most important artists in fandom of the early 1960s would be secure. The fact that he was one of just 19 fans to attend the historic Alley Tally Party at Jerry Bails' house in March 1964 further demonstrates the depth of his fannish participation. But it was the multiple adventures of his character "Xal-Kor the Human Cat" in the pages of *Star-Studded Comics* that cemented him as a fandom superstar in a category all his own. Only Biljo White's tales of "The Eye, Underworld Executioner"—adapted from a character design by Green himself—rivaled the Human Cat in quality and popularity in the fanzine firmament.

The idea for the Human Cat came to Green in a nightmare when he was about 14 years old. It involved Grass being chased by a man who had transformed from a human into a "cat man." Inspired to create a character based on this idea, Grass named him "Cat Man" until he realized there was already a professional character by that name. Then he renamed him "Zal-Kor," and finally "Xal-Kor the Human Cat." The character's origin was told in *Star-Studded Comics* #5 (September 1964). Xal-Kor was a warrior from the planet Felis, who has pursued his ratlike nemesis Queen Roda to earth. Both could transform themselves into human form, or take on the form of a cat or rat, respectively. Xal-Kor's task was to stop the Queen and her minions on Earth from marshalling forces to launch a surprise attack on his home planet. When he took a job at the Linton *Daily News* as photographer Colin Chambers, Xal-Kor didn't realize that his co-worker Ann Rhoden was really the nefarious Queen Roda in disguise. Green played out this "cat-and-rat" story with an assurance and level of technical accomplishment that no other ongoing ama-strip series had attained. Green wrote and drew (with some inking assistance) a total of seven Xal-Kor strips for *Star-Studded*, with the highlight appearing in #8 (March 1966). "Operation Big Move" was one of the most enjoyable, satisfying strips produced in any fanzine of this era.

Landon Chesney, another important artist in fandom, later wrote:

> Grass Green's concept of comic art ... totally blew me away at the time ... and continues to impress me today. I can't get over how good this guy is. There's more to it than his affinity for doing a credible reading of Simon and Kirby. I was hard-pressed at the time ... to put into words just what set Grass apart from the herd. But, more recently, I read a line by C. C. Beck that gave me a clue. Beck said, "if you don't know who Roy Crane is, you aren't in the comic book business."
>
> It hadn't occurred to me, until that moment, that Beck had been inspired by Crane's "Captain Easy." And the thing that comes through is not the similarity in styles, but Crane's facility for interweaving humor with straight adventure conventions, without the seams showing. C. C. Beck could do that as well. And so could Richard Green. Rich was probably the most gifted (the guy most in touch with Roy Crane) of anyone else active in those days [*Fandom's Finest Comics*, Vol. 1, 1997].

Given the quality of his work, one wonders why Green didn't make it into professional comics in a big way. He penciled "The Shape" in *Charlton Premiere* #1 (September 1967), and other humor strips for Charlton's *Go-Go*, but was unable to break into Marvel or DC. Grass said, "Charlton was about as close as I came. Roy Thomas tried several times to get me in at Marvel, but it was always squashed by somebody higher up. I think I never made it as a big-time pro because I've never disciplined my art style, never quite pinned it down until I got older, and by then I'd said to hell with pro comics." If there was a weakness in his work, Green's backgrounds (buildings, cars and other real world objects) weren't as convincing as his figure work.

In the 1970s, Green made inroads into underground comix, and in the 1980s he produced a series starring his humorous superhero team "Wildman and Rubberoy" for Miller Publishing. Oftentimes, Xal-Kor showed up in backup strips. Green also collaborated with Michael Vance, Howard Keltner and others on various projects over the years, and even did some "adult comics" for Eros and Rip Off Press. In 1997, he attended the Fandom Reunion at the Chicago comicon, meeting Keltner for the first time.

Green explained, "In the 1990s, something always came up to keep me from working on Xal-Kor. I was more focused on selling my REGco blue-line drawing paper," a product to help save comic book artists and letterers production time, which Green designed, manufactured and sold beginning in 1967. In 2000, Grass began scripting and penciling "Xal-Kor in 2013!," a grand Human Cat saga that would run 92 pages in finished form. With the help of inkers Angel Gabriele and Ron Fontes, it was completed in the summer of 2001. Just about this time, Green was diagnosed with terminal lung cancer. He lived long enough to see his "Xal-Kor in 2013!" published as a stand-alone comic book by TwoMorrows Publishing in spring of 2002. He passed away August 5, 2002.

Alan J. Hanley
(1939–1980)

Alan James Hanley was born the last of seven siblings of Irish and Canadian-Ukrainian parents in Chicago, and grew up in a milieu he later described as "a poor Italian immigrant neighborhood, Catholic schools, complexes, general misery, gang fear, cowboy movies, radio programs and comic books." His first cartoons to see print appeared in his high school newspaper, which also printed comics and various articles by the creative teenager. He attended one semester at the Chicago Art Institute, then went into the U.S. Army for two years, where he was stationed in Missouri, Korea and Texas.

After his military hitch, Hanley decided to continue his education. He attended city colleges, graduating in 1964. Alan created a strip for the college paper called "Bite-Size." He became a teacher and taught elementary school for three years, becoming convinced during that process that he wasn't cut out for that profession. In 1966 he discovered fandom through Chicago fan Ross Kight's *Trading Post* fanzine. As in the case of so many others, fandom changed Hanley's life, for it gave him a place to express his creativity and hone his skills for what he hoped would be a career in the art field. As he put it in a short autobiography in Ron Kraus's *Enterprise* #2, "I was very starved for creative outlets and Fandom was a veritable lifesaver." Alan immediately began working on a fanzine he titled *Comic Book*, which would be printed photo offset, and contain three or four self-written and drawn comic strip features per issue.

Although amateur strip fanzines never sold as well as good article-zines, a substantial number of fans recognized and enjoyed Alan Hanley's cartooning talent and ability as an entertainer. *Comic Book* #1 introduced his "Goodguy" feature, Alan's thinly veiled revival of the Fawcett Captain Marvel. Hanley's choice of the name "Goodguy" reveals a lot about his creative approach; it conveys simplicity, an emphasis on innocence, and has a tongue-in-cheek, gently humorous quality. Virtually every one of the writer-artist's fanzines featured a new adventure of Goodguy, or Major Marvel as he was sometimes called, versus such villains as The Rotten Egg and Czar Castic. Hanley was also known for frequently illustrating tales of a funny animal-superhero group called the "Mitey Buggers," featuring members including The Green Hornet (an actual hornet), Ladybug, Capt. Bat and Marvel Mouse, among others. Alan also presented straight, non-humorous strips such as Fawcett-type feature "Captain Thunder" and "The Spook," a takeoff on The Spirit, one of Hanley's chief inspirations. But the Chicagoan's obvious major influence was the artwork of Clarence Beck, chief artist of the adventures of Captain Marvel in the 1940s. Beck's charming, cartoony style belied a craftsman of exceptional talent and intelligence; the same could be said for the work of Alan James Hanley. However, this anachronistic style—which made him a fan favorite—proved his undoing when he tried to break into the professional cartoon arena. Tastes had changed. The 1960s and 1970s were a time of social unrest and great cynicism, a climate that was the antithesis of Hanley's style and innocent characters.

Hanley made a trip to New York City in 1967 to see if he could find work. He was able to show his work to Carmine Infantino

Alan J. Hanley

at DC Comics and Roy Thomas at Marvel. Both received him respectfully, but had no place for his work. (This was six years before DC would revive the original Captain Marvel, which might have been something that could have provided assignments for Hanley.) The artist returned to Chicago, and continued to produce issues of *Comic Book*. In *Enterprise Monthly* #2, two years later, he wrote, "I don't know what the secret to success is. Salesmanship. The right moment. Who knows? All anyone can do is hope that through his efforts and ability, he will find that place in the sun that says, 'Here's some work. Do your thing, receive your pay, and live happily ever after.'" There was nothing to do but produce more issues of *Comic Book*, and contribute to a fair number of other fanzines, hoping to get noticed or break through somehow. He contributed a "Mitey Buggers" strip to *Sense of Wonder* and to *Enterprise Monthly*. By his count, Hanley did over 500 pieces of art for his own and other fanzines.

In 1973 Hanley made another foray to New York City, on the occasion of the New York

Comic Art Convention. *Comic Book* #6 featured a photo of Alan with his idol, the venerable C. C. Beck, as well as with other fans. Some fans who met him on this occasion commented that he seemed remote, perhaps preoccupied with making connections that would lead to professional assignments. Little apparently came of this networking, except perhaps (eventually) a number of two-page text features in Charlton's *Blondie* and *The Great Gazoo* in 1975. His "big foot" style was not in fashion, and he was doomed to disappointment in the comics industry. When he billed himself as "America's Number One Starving Artist," it was a case of humor overlaying frustration and very real disillusionment.

Aside from *Comic Book*, Alan Hanley is probably best known for his numerous covers for the widely circulated *The Buyer's Guide for Comic Fandom*. Alan Light's weekly adzine reached just about everyone interested in collecting comic books, and Hanley's covers were some of his most impressive single illustrations.

Hanley died on his way home from a convenience store December 24, 1980, when he lost control of his Volkswagen van on an icy road and plowed into a tree.

Alan Hutchinson
(b. 1948)

With his solid drawing skills, neat inking and attention to detail, Alan Hutchinson became a much-sought-after artist by fanzine publishers in the mid to late 1960s. In many ways, his work approximated the look of professional comic book art, thus providing an important element to fanzines as they increased their print runs and appearance by switching to photo offset (lithographic) printing.

Born in St. Louis, Missouri, Alan Hutchinson grew up in St. Petersburg, Florida, where his father was a tile contractor. Just as he graduated from high school in 1966, Alan was contacted by two comic book fans attending the University of South Florida in nearby Tampa, Gary Brown and Wayne DeWald. "They had seen my name in either a comic book letter column or a fanzine, and both wrote me letters asking to get together," Hutchinson recently recollected. "It was sometime that summer that they drove over in Gary's broken-down, unsafe-at-any-speed Corvair. They must have taken a wrong turn because they told me after arriving that they ended up in some rural area and wondered if I lived on a farm." It wasn't long before Alan was contributing covers and other artwork to Brown's and DeWald's fanzine *Comic Comments*. Soon, other fan-eds were requesting the young man's artwork, and he became a welcome presence in numerous fanzines, including the best in the field.

Alan Hutchinson

Some of the fanzines that bore Hutchinson's distinctive artwork were *Comic Comments*, *Gremlin, Sense of Wonder, Comic Crusader, On the Drawing Board* and *Bombshell*. He participated in the creation of two of the best strips to appear in *Star-Studded Comics*. The first was "War of the Weaponer" featuring Powerman, scripted by Leonard Tirado, Jr., and Larry Herndon (*SSC* #13, June 1968). The second was an adaptation of Robert E. Howard's "Gods of the North" story, with the script adaptation by Herndon and pencils by Steve Kelez, with Hutchinson inking Kelez (*SSC* #14, December 1968).

After that, Alan focused his concentration on contributing to the comics apa *Capa-alpha*, which he joined in 1968. For a few more years, he continued to do artwork for just about every fanzine publisher who asked him, then relegated his creative energy to his apa zine. He also contributed often to *Ibid*, the *Capa-alpha* zine of Gary Brown, who remained his closest friend in fandom. Hutchinson never tried to become a professional comic book artist. "I suppose I just lacked confidence in my ability, and the drive necessary to push yourself in front of people who could judge your work," Alan explained recently. "I was happy just doing my little fanzine covers and cartoons." He did collaborate with Doug Potter on a panel gag cartoon for newspaper syndication, but it failed to sell.

To earn a living, Hutchinson worked with his dad in the tile business. Construction in Florida was booming in the 1970s, and there was plenty to keep them busy. When the economy declined and the tile business slacked off, he took the test for employment with the U.S. Postal Service, and was hired in 1979. Alan continues to work at the Post Office to the present day. Though not enamored with the work itself, Alan Hutchinson is philosophical: "The pay and benefits are good, and have enabled me to purchase many more old comic books than I could have as a tile-setter."

Hutchinson feels the early years of fandom were unique. "I don't think the 1960s can ever be duplicated as far as fan activity goes. There's no way to explain to a young fan today what it was like to open the mailbox and find a ditto or mimeo zine with hand-traced copies of comic book covers you'd only heard about, and articles by 'old' collectors—who were probably 25 years old—about superheroes as much as 20 years ago that had yet to be reintroduced to comics. There are no mysteries left. We've covered it all. I hope young fans are grateful to us pioneers of the Golden Age of fandom."

Steve Kelez
(b. 1947)

Steve Kelez was an artist and fanzine publisher best known for his comic strips in *Star-Studded Comics*, as editor of *The Gotham Gazette*, and as a columnist in the *Yancy Street Journal*.

Kelez was born and raised in San Francisco until 1964, when his family moved north to the small town of Ukiah, California. "I had been reading and saving comic books from at least the middle 1950s," Steve remembered. He became active in fandom around 1962, most likely when he saw a fanzine plug in a professional comic book. He began ordering as many fanzines as he could afford. One of them was *Fantasy Hero*, published by Bay Area fans Bill DuBay and Marty Arbunich. "Instead of sending the zines they showed up at my home with them," Kelez recalled. "Soon I was contributing to their various fanzines and learning how to draw on ditto masters. I dove headfirst into fandom, and started to contribute to other fanzines around the country, gaining a lot of new friends along the way." Steve was an artist, and also an able writer—both skills fanzine editors valued, as they searched for ways to fill the pages of their homemade publications. Living in a small town like Ukiah was no drawback, since most fan relations at this time were conducted through the postal system.

In 1965, Steve's fan activity exploded on the scene. First, he began his long-running column in *Yancy Street Journal* called "The Yancy Street Walker." In this humorous but rather strange feature, Kelez assumed the persona of Levram (Marvel spelled backwards), a mysterious denizen of New York City's Yancy Street, the fictional location which had been made famous in Marvel's *Fantastic Four* comic book. Each installment consisted of Levram's misanthropic, offbeat commentary on the latest developments at Marvel Comics. It proved popular, and would appear in every issue of *YSJ* until the fanzine's demise in January 1966.

Next, with the help of Marty and Bill's ditto machine, Kelez launched a companion fanzine to Biljo White's popular *Batmania* called *The Gotham Gazette*. With Capt. Biljo's support, occasional illustrations and free plugs in *Batmania* (which had a large circulation), *GG* offered six pages of news, commentary, ads and other miscellaney for a mere dime. It lasted four issues, ending just as 1965 drew to a close.

Then, in August, came *Magnum Opus* #1, which Kelez co-published with Mickey Schwaberow. Schwaberow was a talented, facile and prolific amateur writer and artist who visualized a publication similar to *Star-Studded Comics* to feature his amateur characters the "Ace of Spades," "Ultro" ("Man or Machine?") and others. For the first issue Kelez inked a sword & sorcery tale written and penciled by Schwaberow called "Son of the Sabre." Presumably he would have contributed more to subsequent issues, but the response to the photo-offset *Magnum Opus* was disappointing, and it never reached #2.

In addition to being a regular columnist for the first Marvel fanzine, publishing or co-publishing two comic book fanzines of his own, and being an early member of comics apa *Capa-alpha*, Kelez's part in fandom's first decade is significant because he helped enlarge the concept of what an amateur comic strip could be. The first case was his collaboration on the first authorized adaptation of a Robert E. Howard short story into graphic story format.

"Gods of the North" in *Star-Studded Comics* #14 (December 1968) was adapted from Howard's story by Larry Herndon, penciled by Kelez, and inked by Alan Hutchison. The nine-page result was extremely effective, and the adaptation was much talked about at the time. Steve also pushed the boundaries of ama-strips when he wrote and drew "King of the Hill," which was the first war-themed story to appear in the fanzines. The five-pager saw print in *SSC* #15 (May 1969).

Along with his interest in comics, Steve Kelez was equally interested in film. He recently recalled, "Along with comics I loved movies and spent too much of my time in the movie theater and reading *Famous Monsters of Filmland* and *Screen Thrills Illustrated*. I found serials to be like reading comics, since they

Steve Kelez

featured so many of the same characters. I started collecting movie stills, and some poster material. It was all so very cheap in those days, but then I was all so very poor too. I would have bought everything in sight if I could afford it."

After he started college, Kelez was forced to cut back on his fan activities. When he got married, he sold his collection, retaining only a couple of boxes of comics and miscellaneous books. He became interested in writer Raymond Chandler and channeled a lot of energy into collecting anything to do with the author and his prime creation, "Philip Marlowe." This was before the market for Chandler's work exploded, and one could still hunt down obscure little book stores and find many old pocket book editions of Chandler novels and various hardcover first editions. In that sense, it was like collecting comics in the late 1950s and early 1960s.

"I went to school to become an artist," Kelez stated. "I ended up designing magazines while living in Southern California. This was self taught; much of it based on my earlier fanzine endeavors. I did some freelance illustration, but that never went anywhere. I had originally planned on doing comics, then pocket books, and finally movie posters. Oh, you dreamer!" Today, Steve works at refurbishing and repairing computers, while designing websites and writing code for backend website applications. He has augmented his income since 1983 by selling Old-Time Radio recordings, though in recent years the introduction of MP3 and portable MP3 players has made that business much less profitable.

Don Newton
(1934–1984)

One of the best, most popular artists from fandom of the 1960s, Don Newton proved that it was possible to graduate to the professional ranks without moving to New York City. Before he did so, however, his beautifully penciled and inked drawings appeared on the covers and interiors of many of the most popular fanzines, including many issues of *Rocket's Blast-Comicollector.*

Donald L. Newton was born November 12, 1934, in St. Charles, Virginia. When he was four years old, he developed asthma, forcing his family to move to the warmer climes of the American southwest. After living in New Mexico, California and Colorado, the family put down roots in Phoenix, where Don grew up.

As a boy during the Golden Age of comics, Don's favorite characters were Batman, the original Golden Age Daredevil and especially Captain Marvel. In an interview conducted by Bill G. Wilson in *The Collector* #17, Don recalled, "I was getting 'Golden Age' comics even before I could read and by the time I was nine or ten I had

Don Newton

a fabulous collection. By high school, however, my interests changed and I dumped out a huge collection for the garbage man. Almost complete runs of *Captain Marvel, Whiz, Batman, Daredevil, Planet* and *All-Star*."

Newton was a high school athlete, setting a record for shot put, and was also the middleweight weight-lifting champion of Arizona at one point. A back injury caused him to shift his focus to his artistic development, though he would continue to stay in good physical shape. In later years, he was still muscular, and when he attended convention masquerades as Captain Marvel, he made an impressive figure. Nevertheless, his emphasis turned to the art field. He drew the "Sports Star of the Week" panel for *The Mesa Tribune* while a sophomore in high school. Newton also painted in oils, earning money doing specially commissioned paintings. Don attended Arizona State University in the early 1950s, earning a teaching degree. While in college he continued to take classes in oil painting, and also sculpted. His favorite non-comics artists were N. C. Wyeth, the great illustrator, and Gustave Doré, who did etchings of the *Bible* and *Dante's Inferno*. When he graduated, he became the art teacher at Mountain View school in Phoenix. One of his favorite lessons was having his students each create their own comic strips.

Newton married but became a widower, raising his son, Tony, on his own. In the mid–1960s, Don's interest in comics flamed anew. He began thinking about creating an original Sunday comic strip to submit to the newspaper syndicates. For reference and inspiration, he began scouring the Phoenix area for old comic books. "I had been scouting for comics for about six months and finding little," Newton told Bill G. Wilson. "Then a collector friend showed me a copy of *RBCC* and I decided to get a copy. Looking *RBCC* over, I figured here was a logical place to get a start in comic work. I sent Gordon Love an illo called 'The Great Comic in the Sky.' He liked it, and shortly after I did a *Star Trek* back cover for him." Then Newton proposed a comic strip for the fanzine, and "The Savage Earth" debuted in *RBCC* #60 (October 1968) and ran for the next nine issues.

"The Savage Earth" showed the influence on Alex Raymond's classic "Flash Gordon" strip of the 1930s and 1940s, as well as Don's appreciation of Aldous Huxley's *Brave New World*. As *RBCC* had a circulation of 2,300 copies at this time, Newton became a "superstar fan artist" almost overnight. Gordon Love knew a good thing when he saw it, and essentially made Don the "official artist" for *RBCC* over the next few years, featuring his work on the covers and interiors of not only *RBCC*, but other fanzines Love published, such as *The Golden Age*. Along with John Fantucchio, Love's other artistic mainstay, Newton fulfilled an essential role in the days before professional artists began doing fanzine work from time to time. Don's painted color covers for *RBCC* featuring Flash Gordon, Superman and others, are among the finest to appear on any fanzine of the 1960s. His mastery of human anatomy, page composition and design were, in fact, superior to that of many professionals. Love credited Don's work with helping propel the success of *RBCC* into the 1970s. He contributed to many other zines, among them *The Collector* and *Sense of Wonder*.

Like many artists in the fanzines, Don Newton aspired to become a professional comic book illustrator. At this time, however, Marvel and DC generally gave assignments only to those living in New York City and its environs. There were exceptions, such as Jack Kirby who moved to California in the late 1960s, but new artists without a proven track record for meeting deadlines weren't considered. Then, in 1974, Newton submitted samples to low-rung Charlton, and found sudden acceptance. Editor George Wildman and Nick Cuti were so impressed with Don's work that they gave him a try, which began a happy association for all concerned. Newton's artwork in *The Phantom* and *Ghost Manor*, among many other titles, was excellent, and the many painted covers he did for them were among the most beautiful ever to grace a comic book. All this work was done in Newton's spare time, sandwiched between classes and grading assignments, for the rates at Charlton were insufficient to allow him to give up his teaching position.

As it turned out, Charlton was just the beginning of Don Newton's illustrious career in comic books. By the early 1980s, he was working mainly for DC Comics. He concentrated on penciling during this period, often ably inked by Dan Adkins and Alfredo Alcala. He drew "Captain Marvel" in *World's Finest* and "Aquaman" in *Adventure Comics*; a long run on Batman is perhaps his greatest achievement in the field, and proved that he had made it to the top. Many fans rank Newton as one of the top five artists to ever draw the Caped Crusader. It would be the keystone of his legacy in the medium.

Tragically, Don Newton's career was cut short when he suffered a massive heart attack and died on August 19, 1984. According to his longtime friend, Howard Siegel, "Don … had a long history of heart problems. During his last five years he suffered from several mini-attacks which were borderline critical. At the end, he suffered a massive coronary occlusion, and while in the hospital in intensive care, had another one which killed him." He was just 49 years old.

Mike Vosburg
(b. 1947)

Fandom's top artists—Landon Chesney, Biljo White, Ronn Foss, D. Bruce Berry—were adults, in their 20s (or even older) in the early 1960s. Their styles had matured. Fandom's second tier artists—obviously talented and extremely active—were still teenagers in those early days of comic fandom. Among them was Mike Vosburg, an artist whose work evolved and improved before fans' eyes, in the pages of his well-known fanzine *Masquerader*, and also in the many zines that bore his work, including *Voice of Comicdom*, *All-Stars* and *Fandom's Special*. By the decade's end, Vosburg—sometimes called "Voz" by his friends—was ready to graduate to the ranks of comic book professionals, becoming especially adept at his ability to delineate the female form.

Michael Vosburg was born in 1947 and grew up in Pontiac, Michigan. Of his earliest encounters with comic books as a boy, Mike recalled, "I had a cousin about my age. By my Aunt's back door, there were always three or four foot-high piles of comic books, all the latest comics that came out. Not ECs—this was probably 1955 or 1956—but things like *Buzzy*, *Fox and Crow*, *Classics Illustrated*, Archie titles and also a lot of *Superman*, *Batman* and *Superboy*. When we got ready to go home, my Aunt

Mike Vosburg

would always go through a stack of comics that my cousin had read and give a bunch of them to me." Pre-teen Mike responded to the visual aspect of the medium (he's called it "instant gratification"), though he wasn't one of those artists who was drawing as soon as he could hold a pencil. It wasn't until he met his friend, Fred Jackson, who created little comic books for his own amusement, that Vosburg tried his hand at drawing. By 1959, when he was entering junior high school, Mike had discovered the work of Joe Kubert on "Viking Prince" in *The Brave and the Bold*. Kubert would become his chief artistic inspiration and influence in the ensuing years.

Mike discovered fandom in late 1961 or early 1962. By September 1962, he launched his fanzine *Masquerader* with the help of Fred Jackson. It headlined an amateur character that Vosburg and Foss had been grooming for several months, though it was essentially Mike's concept: "The Cowl," a costumed character (with no superpowers) who was an ex-cop, forced to don a mask to fight crime because he was wrongly accused of murdering his partner. Future issues of *Mask* offered "Action Ace and Thrill Boy" by Grass Green (#4), "Astro Ace" strips by Biljo White, and more Vosburg characters.

As an aspiring artist, Mike received considerable tutelage by the older and more accomplished Ronn Foss. That led to a close friendship between the two, with extensive correspondence, punctuated by a few in-person visits. Both being Kubert fanatics, they spearheaded the "Save Hawkman!" campaign that swept fandom in the wake of the *Brave and Bold* issues featuring the Winged Wonder. In fact, Hawkman appeared on the cover of all six issues of *Masquerader*, and several issues contained features exhorting readers to "save the Kubert Hawkman" by writing to DC editor Julius Schwartz. When asked what he remembered most about fandom, Voz answered without hesitation, "Getting mail! I was this nerdy little kid, terrified of girls, very quiet, not an athlete, but yet when I got home I had this massive correspondence waiting for me."

Probably because he had visited Jerry Bails in Detroit some time in 1963, and was a fanzine publisher, Mike Vosburg was invited to the Alley Tally Party at Jerry's house in March 1964. Of this event, Voz commented, "You know that expression in the 1960s, 'blowing your mind'? These were people that I was writing to, and in a sense when you write to someone, it's a cerebral thing, because they don't really exist. Basically you're sending them words, they're sending you words. Suddenly all these people were coming together. This was a first! As far as I knew, no one had ever done this for comics before! To gather at one place all these guys who were into comics, and more or less make a statement about how they felt about the books that were being done. You've got to give Jerry credit, because he was able to organize and put something like that together. The other thing I remember about it was the generation gap. Mike Tuohey, myself, Jim Rossow, we were all like 15 and 16. I remember talking to Grass [Green] and Ronn [Foss] for awhile, and joking around, but basically the older guys had their own things they were interested in, that I couldn't have related to at the time. Jerry had a bunch of original art at this point. He had a Hawkman page, he had a Jack Kirby page, and those were things that fascinated me."

Vosburg's fanzine *tour de force* was *Masquerader* #6 (1964), which was printed by photo offset, and contained a great deal of work by Foss and Green, as well as some outstanding artwork by Dick Memorich, an article on Ace Publications by Raymond Miller, a piece on Disney comics by Richard West, and the only inked strip featuring his character, "The Cowl." While he sold 300 to 400 copies, Voz had 1,000 copies printed because it cost very little for the overage; this may be the reason why *Masquerader* #6 is easier to find than other vintage publications from this era. It was of *Alter Ego* quality.

As the 1960s progressed, Mike's artwork improved. His "Star Master of Navola 5" in *All-Stars* #1 (1965) and "Dave Gypsy" in *Fandom's Special* showcased his transition from ditto to photo offset, working with India ink in pen and brush. About 1965, when he was about to graduate from high school, Vosburg met a very young Jim Starlin and Al Milgrom who influenced him into thinking in terms of breaking into professional comics, rather than continuing in the fanzine milieu. When these and others in Detroit fandom came into Voz's life (Terry Austin, Mike Nasser, Arvell M. Jones, Keith Pollard, Rich Buckler), he was attending college at Oakland University in Rochester, Michigan. Trying to think practically, he obtained a teaching degree, but by the early 1970s, his desire to draw comic books could no longer be denied.

Works for underground comix (*Bizarre Sex*), other small press comics (*Star*Reach*), and creations such as *Split Screen*, written by Tom Veitch, presaged assignments for horror books from Gold Key and Charlton. Then Mike did some strips for the DC ghost comic books edited by Joe Orlando, and finally landed at Marvel doing "Master of Kung Fu" in the black and white magazine version. There was also *John Carter of Mars*, *Ms. Marvel*, *She Hulk* and *G. I. Joe*. Vosburg worked for Valiant Comics on *Archer & Armstrong* and *Bloodshot*. He also did a lot of *American Flagg!* and books featuring his self-created character Lori Lovecraft.

Like many of his fellow artists, Mike Vosburg moved into animation and storyboarding. In 1984, he moved to California with his wife, Anna, and eventually found perhaps his highest profile project on the TV series *Tales from the Crypt*. Voz drew the faux-EC comic book covers for all of the show's 93 episodes, from 1989 to 1996. He created storyboards for the first *Chronicles of Narnia* movie directed by Arthur Adamson. Mike explained, "So often a great deal of the design work I've done for films ends up being ignored, usually by directors who have their own ideas. But with *Narnia*, I could see my work in scene after scene, and it was tremendously satisfying."

Alan Weiss

(b. 1948)

Of the younger artists to make an impact in the fanzines of the early to mid 1960s, Alan Weiss had perhaps the most sophisticated, developed understanding of both human anatomy and sequential storytelling than any of them. He was a young teenager when he drew a comic strip that appeared in Bill Spicer's *Fantasy Illustrated* #1 (1964), an adaptation of Eando Binder's Jon Jarl story titled "The Ancient Secret." He went on to contribute to G. B. Love's *The Golden Age*, and the Texas Trio's *Star-Studded Comics*, among several others, mostly top-run fanzines. He didn't restrict himself to just illustrating superheroes, but also western strips, science fiction, and humor.

Alan Weiss was born in Chicago, Illinois, the eldest of two brothers. When he was seven years old, his family moved to Las Vegas, and his father made his living in the gambling business. Alan recalled, "My father wasn't only a terrific artist, but he was a fan of artwork and he liked all kinds. He mostly did fine art, himself, all the way up and including abstract. But he would show me the Sunday comics. We would look at 'Prince Valiant' and various strips, whichever ones had the good artwork at the time." Alan's early motivation to create art came from his efforts to draw Superman and The Lone Ranger because he was watching their adventures on television.

Discovering fandom around 1962, Weiss began sending drawings to many of the fanzine editors of the day. At first, he worked on ditto masters, and then he had an opportunity to

draw the pencils to the Eando Binder adaptation "The Ancient Secret" for *Fantasy Illustrated.*
Bill Spicer had been sufficiently impressed by young Alan's sample drawings—he was only
fourteen at the time—that he sent Weiss the breakdowns with all the panels bordered and
the lettering completed, for the artist to fill the panels with penciled and inked artwork.
"The first inked stuff I did ... was Jon Jarl," he said. "I didn't even know how to really use
a brush and it was very crude. I was just winging it, really. I had no idea what a page of
original comic book art looked like. When I first saw an original, I couldn't believe how big
it was ... because as far as I knew, everything was done the same size." The resulting strip,
published in *FI* #1, was a respectable first attempt.

Alan distinguished himself from many of his teenage peers who were drawing amateur
comic strips at the time by seriously studying human anatomy. He spent an entire summer
learning all the Latin names for the muscles, and poring over the drawing books by George
Bridgeman, Andrew Loomis and Burne Hogarth. Others were content to imitate the way
their favorite comic book artists portrayed musculature and anatomy, and lacked the solid
foundation of knowledge that Weiss brought to his art. As his work progressed, this knowledge of figure drawing and anatomy would become one of Alan's greatest strengths. In addition, the well-conceived and effective storytelling techniques he honed while working on
strips for *Star-Studded Comics* demonstrated his understanding of the importance of narrative
flow and composition in the sequential art arena. "Satan's Hirelings!" in *SSC* #6 (from a Phil
Liebfred script, with inks by Alan's friend Scott Bell) was the first, but the real standout was
"The Curse of Skullwing!" in #9, from a rather grisly script by Larry Herndon. In this one,
which appeared in July 1966, a considerably more mature Weiss both penciled and inked,
rendering the battle between the Golden Ghost and the evil Skullwing in dramatic high-
contrast black-and-white. He had a confidence that allowed him to bring a certain looseness
to the inking, which created a highly exciting result.

Weiss proved to be one of *Star-Studded Comics'* most prolific contributors in its later
issues, and also perhaps its most versatile. While he had few peers in the fandom milieu
when it came to drawing superheroes, Alan was fascinated with other genres, including west-
ern-themed strips which were virtually non-
existent in the fanzines. His western strips
"Boy, You Sure Don't Look Like a Hero!" in
SSC #13 (1968) and "The Battle of Credibility
Gap!" in #15 (1969) are the kind of outstanding
tours de force that put him in the very first rank
among the amateur artists. As such, Weiss contributed significantly to the side of fandom that
could be said to be the forerunner of later
"small press comics."

Given his energy and ability, it was a fore-
gone conclusion that Alan Weiss would graduate to professional comic book assignments,
and he did along with several of his other com-
patriots in the early 1970s. His first published
story was penciling "It's Better to Give" in
House of Secrets #92 (June–July 1971), the same
issue that introduced Swamp Thing. The strip
was inked by Tony DeZuniga. Alan did more
miscellaneous ghost stories for DC, as well as
western strips, *Shazam* and *Batman*. He found

Alan Weiss

work at Marvel doing *Warlock*, *The Avengers*, *Captain America* and many others. He created "War Dancer" for Defiant Comics, worked on "Tom Strong" and many other comic book projects over the ensuing years. Alan Weiss lives in New York City with his wife, Pauline.

Biljo White
(1929–2003)

Biljo White was a talented writer/artist who created many of the finest amateur comic strips produced in fandom's early years, and a fanzine publisher whose production was prodigious. His fanzine *Batmania* was a classic of the form. White also published *Komix Illustrated, The Stripper* (about comic strips), and was Art Editor of *Alter Ego* during Roy Thomas's tenure as Editor/Publisher.

Born William Joseph White on June 4, 1929, in Columbia, Missouri, he was the perfect age to read and collect the comic books of the late 1930s and 1940s. The somewhat introverted youth grew up loving aviation pulps and strips, as well as the ubiquitous superheroes of the era. He demonstrated cartooning ability early in life, creating many of his own characters during his childhood.

After his discharge from the military in 1952, he made some halfhearted attempts to break into pro comics. Being turned away by *Batman* editor Jack Schiff, and not wanting to live in New York City or its environs, ended that dream. Nevertheless, Biljo penciled and inked numerous strips in the 1950s for his own pleasure, among them "The Fog," "The Blade," and "Gus Gunn."

Biljo White

Discovering comic fandom and fanzines was like an answer to a prayer for the young Missourian. Suddenly there was an audience—however small—for White's homespun heroes. In July 1962, he launched a fanzine showcase for them called *Komix Illustrated*, which was well-received due to the quality and charm of Biljo's writing and artwork. His simple style, somewhat reminiscent of that of C. C. Beck, worked well within the limitations of the ditto medium. White drew little caricatures of himself as "Capt. Biljo," and the nickname stuck.

White's artwork displayed confidence in every line. There was no uncertainty, no sketchiness, no awkwardness. Later, Biljo explained, "I pretty well know what I want. I can draw the strip on the Brisol board with very little pre-sketching. I see it in my head, and can draw it very much as I envision it." His work had a kind of perfection, achieved by an artist who knows just how to deftly translate the images in his head directly to the page. White fan and fanzine publisher Jeff Gelb aptly stated, "What's amazing is how his work remained so true to his childhood influences without being affected by time. Reading a comic strip by Biljo White is like finding a great, quintessential Golden Age comic book I've never seen before, but always hoped to find." Prominent underground cartoonist and Topps card designer Jay Lynch put it succinctly: "Biljo White was a genius."

In addition to his remarkable talent, Biljo was known for having a large comic book collection. It was housed in an out-building on his property that he named "the White House of Comics." Visitors were often let down when they found out it was merely a small, cinder block building, which didn't match the grandiose images that its nickname conjured up. He had complete runs of *Batman* and *Detective Comics*, and nice runs of the Fawcett Captain Marvel comics, among many other Golden Age treasures. These would provide excellent reference for his fanzine contributions.

Komix Illustrated also published strips by Ronn Foss ("The Viper"), Ken Tesar and Grass Green, and a popular feature called "Profiles of Collectors." After turning out ten issues in quick succession, and experiencing some printing problems, he passed the *Komix Illustrated* name to a California-based fan named Mickey Martin, who published three more issues. This fanzine is also known as the first to carry an advertisement for old comic books from legendary dealer Howard Rogofsky.

Sometime in early 1963, Biljo White was visited by Ronn Foss, who showed him a drawing of an amateur hero named "The Eye," designed by Foss's friend Grass Green. Captivated by The Eye's "eyeball helmet," White developed a storyline and milieu for the character, whom he gave the sobriquet of the "Underworld Executioner." Biljo offered the first Eye strip to the Texas Trio for their new fan-mag *Star-Studded Comics*. Upon its acceptance, he prepared a four-color cover for *SSC*, and The Eye made a flashy debut in #3 (1964). Just as the weird-looking character had intrigued White, fans were captivated by the image of a man's body with a huge eyeball for a head. White quickly prepared a followup, but by that time *SSC* was switching to professional printing; therefore, it was submitted to Gordon Love for his *Fighting Hero Comics*, appearing in #10 (1964).

Capt. Biljo had bigger plans for The Eye. He had always wanted to break into the newspaper syndicated strip market, and decided The Eye was different enough that it just might catch on. White produced a half-dozen sample Sunday strips which featured his most accomplished artwork, but there were no takers. The strip featured the character in a Cold War story, ostensibly an attempt to add relevance. All six installments saw print in the first professionally printed solo comic book starring an amateur hero, *The Eye* #1 (1965). That issue presented a redrawn, more fully realized version of the hero's introductory tale.

Recovering from fanzine burnout with alacrity, Biljo White commenced publication of what would be his most important fanzine: *Batmania*, subtitled *The Fanzine Especially for Batman Fans*. The first issue was dated July 1964. It ranks as his most important in several ways. First, there were more issues of it than any of his other zines, a total of 17. Second, it was his most popular, with a circulation that eventually reached as high as 800, an astounding number for a mimeographed publication. Third, it created connections between the fans and the editors at DC, as well as the creative people behind the Dynamic Duo. The fanzine had input from Julius Schwartz, Bill Finger, and a famous "Open Letter" from Bob Kane, the creator of Batman and Robin (though Kane's "sole creator" status would be debated in the pages of the fanzine). Fourth, probably due to appearing while the Batman TV show was broadcast, *Batmania* was mentioned in many newspaper articles about the show, and some about the magazine itself. Such articles appeared in foreign countries, too. The readership of *Batmania* was international.

In a late-in-life interview, Biljo opined, "I believe my work on *Batmania* should be regarded as a blueprint for producing a fanzine." That is, it had just about a perfect mix of articles and features, art and text, and the right price and page count. Issues sold mostly for 30–40 cents, in the days when all that was needed was a six- or eight-cent postage stamp to send them through Third-Class Mail. At about 30 pages in length, it was enough to give the reader plenty of material, but not so long as to cause the available editorial material to be padded. The features themselves ranged from fairly long articles, to fan profiles, to punchy "Bat-Facts" and "Comic Oddities" columns made up of little tidbits of information. There would be a letter column that was always intelligent and interesting, and a certain amount of advertising matter. Finally, there would be items geared toward the "Batmanians" club, which was made up of anyone who bought the fanzine: lists of members and their locations, pieces urging fans to write letters to Julius Schwartz about the "New Look" of Batman, and promos for get-togethers of "Batmanians" at comicons or otherwise. All of it was accompanied by Biljo's charming tracings and original illustrations, which he managed to do even in the difficult-to-illustrate mimeograph medium. (Mimeograph resulted in black printing; ditto appeared in purple.) Ditto was no good when he had to print more than 300 copies, and photo offset was too expensive and elaborate for a frequently published fanzine, at least from White's point of view. The funky printing process added to the homemade charm of the finished product, which had undeniable eye appeal.

However, the sheer physical task of keeping track of orders, printing and collating the pages, and then affixing addresses and stamps was enormous, when done by hand with little help. Capt. Biljo inevitably needed a break after about three years. In 1967, he briefly tried to convert the zine into an apa (amateur press alliance) with multiple outside contributors, but this didn't work. *Batmania* #17 was the last, until Rich Morrissey continued the title a few years later, with White's blessing. (However, the 1970s issues feel like a very different fanzine.)

Concurrently with the publication of *Batmania*'s early issues, Biljo White also served as Art Editor of *Alter Ego* after it passed from Ronn Foss to Roy Thomas. White's artwork was a major plus for the three issues that Roy published before becoming a professional writer. Biljo produced a cover featuring the Marvel Family for *AE* #7 (October 1964) that is one of the iconic fanzine covers of the era. His covers for *AE* #8 and #9 were almost as good. Inside, the magazine was filled with White's assured spot illustrations. All three issues appeared in the space of ten months. Then Roy Thomas moved to New York City to take his place as a writer of professional comic books, and White was freed from his commitment to *AE*.

In the later 1960s, Capt. Biljo decided to publish more fanzines utilizing photo offset printing, so that he could print more of the inked comic strips he'd kept in his files from the 1950s, as well as a brand new "Origin of The Eye." In 1968, *Capt. Biljo Presents* #1 appeared with material from White's archives of original creations, and the following year, *Capt. Biljo Presents* #2 offered that long-awaited origin story of the "Underworld Executioner" which did not disappoint. He only did two more adventures of The Eye after that, one in 1977 and another for *Fandom's Finest Comics* Vol. 2 (Hamster Press, 1998), which was a book that reprinted many of the amateur comic strips of the 1960s fanzines.

Biljo was also a big fan of newspaper comic strips, which led to the last fanzine that he published: *The Stripper*, which appeared in the late 1960s and early 1970s. Though he gradually played a less active role in fandom, disappearing completely from the scene by the 1980s, his memories of those past times were warm ones. "Without being a part of comicdom, I would never have met and corresponded with such wonderful fans, artists and writers— and a goodly number of professionals," he stated. He continued to visit his local comic book store, and do artwork in his local community, often as a part of his job as a firefighter. Biljo White passed away early in 2003, eight days after being diagnosed with Burkett's Lymphoma.

SECTION VII:
ACTIVE FANS AND COLLECTORS

Fans of comic books and strips come in many stripes. That's true today, and it was certainly true during fandom's genesis. Some of the most active fans contributed greatly to the formation and development of comicdom, yet don't fit easily into any of the other sections in this book. Those folks have been included in this catch-all category that is titled "Active Fans and Collectors."

Most of them published fanzines. However, if their fanzines had been their main claim-to-fame, they probably wouldn't have qualified as founders of comic fandom. They are here because, *in addition to their very worthwhile fanzines,* their other activities were equally or more notable. For example, Paul Gambaccini's only fanzine was *Forum,* the newsletter of the Executive Board of the Academy of Comic Book Fans and Collectors. However, it's the fact that he succeeded Jerry Bails as Executive Secretary of that organization that his bio warrants inclusion in this book.

Similarly, the other folks here have dual or triple or multiple credits, with no single area taking precedence. Was Mark Evanier's role in the development of fandom in Los Angeles primarily that of a fanzine publisher? Comic book club instigator? Writer? He, like others here, straddles several categories, which together create a portrait of a significant mover and shaker.

Finally, there is the late Rick Durell, who was one of the most prominent collectors of Golden Age comics when fandom was young. Rick was an important figure in California fandom of the early 1960s, by virtue of sharing data gleaned from his collection, meeting others in the area (including his participation in a key gathering at Russ Manning's home in 1964), as a contributor to *Capa-alpha,* and other, almost intangible, ways. Designating him an "active fan and collector" is highly appropriate.

One could argue with the inclusion of certain fans into this or another chapter. Since such editorial decisions are subjective, there is room for disagreement. However, by the definition established earlier, everyone profiled in this book can truly be considered a founder of comic fandom no matter what section includes their biography.

Roy Bonario
(b. 1934)

Roy Bonario was one of a core group of comic book fans living in Houston, Texas, who formed the "Houston Comic Collector's Association" (HCCA) in 1966. The HCCA organized the first Houstoncon in 1967, and subsequent Houston conventions throughout the 1970s.

Roy Bonario was born in Houston, Texas, in November 1934. A comic book reader as a boy, he had given them up when he reached adulthood. Bonario remembered, "In 1965, at age 30, I owned a phonograph record shop near a high school in southeast Houston. One day, a high school student, David Eddings, introduced me to comics fandom. He overheard me talking about Captain Marvel, and informed me that he had some comics with the Big Red Cheese. The next day he not only brought in *Captain Marvel* comic books to my shop, but a copy of the *RBCC* and a list of old comics for sale from Howard Rogofsky. I was completely hooked."

Ray Bonario

Roy shared this discovery with Marc Schooley, his close friend who was also a comic book fan. After searching for old comics from magazine exchanges, used bookstores and *RBCC*, they decided to see if they could find others in town who shared their interest in comics. "Having read an article in one of the local newspapers about Gene Arnold, a radio newsman who collected old comic books, we decided to start with him. After recruiting Gene, and used bookstore owner Fred Van Cleave, we compiled a list of about a hundred comic books fans." Bonario and Schooley set up a meeting in June at the Houston YMCA and were astonished when 60 or 70 comics fans showed up. Their ages ranged from teenagers to men in their forties. One was renowned writer Larry McMurtry (*Lonesome Dove*) who collected Fiction House comics. That meeting was a big success, and the Houston Comic Collector's Association was launched.

With the help of the HCCA members, Bonario and Schooley organized the first Houstoncon in June of 1967. "Marc and I had attended the first Southwesterncon in Dallas in 1966," Roy recalled. "We made arrangements with the Dallas club, headed by Larry Herndon, to alternate the cons between the two cities." In that fashion, each city only had to gear up for a convention in alternate years, and an annual competition between Houston and Dallas could be avoided. The HCCA, whose membership fluctuated from 25 to 35 members, put on many more conventions throughout the late 1970s. Two other important forces in Houston fandom had a lot to do with the conventions: Earl Blair, Jr., and *RBCC* publisher Gordon Love, after he relocated to Houston in 1974.

Roy Bonario had three main interests: Golden Age comic books, old records and vintage movie posters. In November 1970, he opened Roy's Memory Shop, which dealt in both old and new comics, records, film posters and related items. Some consider it the first direct sales comic shop in Texas. The store continued under various name changes and new locations until 1996, when Roy retired. "Over those 26 years, I went to numerous conventions and shows all over the country dealing with all three of my interests, and made many lasting friendships," Bonario explained. "However, times have changed, the shows are fewer and bigger now, and I don't find them as much fun. I now sell some comics, records and movie items on eBay, but nothing on a larger scale. My collecting tastes have never changed, but because of the prices, I have to settle mostly for reprints now."

Roy especially misses one fan, his friend Marc Schooley. Bonario wrote, "Marc, who was like a younger brother to me, passed away from cancer in 2007. He was the first president of the HCCA and a guiding force behind all the conventions we hosted. He was an extremely likable guy with a great sense of humor and we shared many happy 'adventures' together. He is certainly missed by his family and by all who knew him."

Bart Bush
(b. 1951)

Bart Bush is a comic book fan who has been a ringleader in Oklahoma fandom since 1967. A founding member of OAF (the Oklahoma Alliance of Fans), he published the *OAF* newsletter for several years, founded the first comic book specialty store in the Sooner state, and helped mount the first major nostalgia show (Multi-Con 1970) in Oklahoma.

James Bart Bush was born in 1951 in Ponca City, Oklahoma, ten miles south of the Kansas border. He grew up in the town (population: 25,000) and lived there all through the 1960s. Bart heard of fandom first through a plug for *Alter-Ego* in Forrest J Ackerman's *Famous Monsters of Filmland*. Then a notice in *Justice League of America* #30 (September 1964) led him to order *RBCC*, revealing a source for back issues. (That mention in the letter column of *JLA* #30 was responsible for a major influx of fans, which can be judged by the steady climb in circulation for *RBCC* from 600 to 850 copies over the course of the next year.)

Amazing Spider-Man was Bart's favorite comic book in 1964, but he had been collecting

Bart Bush

every comic book published by Marvel, DC, and most other publishers starting in 1963. Other favorites were *Fantastic Four, Daredevil, Avengers* and Dr. Strange. He was also a fan of *T.H.U.N.D.E.R. Agents, Herbie, Mad* and *Creepy*. He became interested in old movie serials after reading *Screen Thrills Illustrated*, and seeing the 90-minute serial compilations that appeared on television starting in 1966. He collected SF pulps, Doc Savage paperbacks, and the Ace books featuring the stories of Edgar Rice Burroughs. Bush recalled, "When I entered fandom and met other collectors, we were all connected by the same reading and movie material. We were comic fans first, but the Shadow, Sherlock Holmes and Tom Swift were all part of us too!" Later Bart would become interested in Old-Time Radio and dime novels.

In March 1967, a group of 14 Oklahoma fans met to form a comic book club. Bart related, "On this cold March day, the garage where we met held the esteemed beginnings of a group that would call themselves the Oklahoma Alliance of Fans, or OAF."

They planned to publish their own monthly newsletter to keep members informed about future monthly "garage meetings." The original 14 OAFs were Robert A. Brown, Bart Bush, Wilt Conine, Jim Elsey, Steve Fears, Danny Hutton, Larry Latham, Paul McSpadden, Charles Rice, Bruce Shults, David J. Smith, Matt Waldroop, Lee Whittlesey and John Wooley. "We all felt a bond develop when as a group we attended the Houston Con in 1967," Bart said. "Nine of us were driven down by Wilt Conine. We became closer friends just by the sharing of stories, knowledge and passing around the comics we had brought with us. Even when the return trip was beset with car troubles, our morale never faltered. To indicate the level of enthusiasm, our *OAF* newsletter stuck to a monthly publication schedule for the next three years." Bush edited the *OAF* zine from May 1968 to September 1970. It featured photo offset covers by Reed Crandall, Vaughn Bodé, Virgil Finlay and other such luminaries. In addition to the fan club newsletter, Bush edited and published *Comic Detective*, a fanzine devoted to the comic strip detectives, which lasted three issues from 1970 to 1973, as well as *The Harvey Collector* (1977), *Betty Boop Funnies* (1975), the *Lou Fine Index* (1985) and *The Merriwell Collector* in the 1990s.

Bart Bush was a pioneer in the field of comic book and nostalgia retailing. He and Don Maris started the first Oklahoma comic book store called Down Memory Lane in Norman, Oklahoma, in 1974. He had just graduated from Oklahoma University. They were able to obtain comics from Phil Seuling and have them on sale weeks before the local news agents would release them. The store has continued under various retail names for 35 years.

Bart and other members of OAF (such as chairmen Robert A. Brown and Don Maris) launched Multi-Con, the first major nostalgia show in Oklahoma, in 1970. This was an ambitious affair, featuring special guests Buster Crabbe, R. A. Lafferty and Jim Harmon, that was a resounding success. Attendance was 511 people, the largest for any convention outside of a New York con. It paved the way for a string of conventions that were the equal of shows in major cities across America.

A 40-year reunion of the members of OAF was held in 2007 at the Biltmore Hotel in Oklahoma City. The event which was coordinated by Bart brought together members of the group from a multi-state region, including some who hadn't been in touch for decades. The emotion-laden affair was attended by many of the original OAFS, as well as dozens of others who had joined later, including such fans as Mark Lamberti, Jerry Weist, Rick Kelsey, Larry Bigman and Brett Weiss (who wrote an account of the event for *Alter Ego* #87). Similar conventions were held in 2008 and 2009, catering mainly to fans and collectors of items dating before 1975. These shows, though modest in scale, had active dealer rooms, auctions and other special events, and harkened back to the spirit of fandom in the 1960s.

Bart's interest in current comics isn't what it used to be, but he still reads many independent comics and non-superhero titles. He is a big fan of the comic strip reprint books and Golden Age reprints of classic comic books. "It's a great time to be a collector," he avowed. "There's so much to choose from!"

Bob Butts

(1947–2008)

Bob Butts was a voluminous writer of letters to pro comics, many of them appearing in the DC and Marvel letter columns of the early 1960s. He was a talented writer, a fanzine publisher and attended several important early fan gatherings, including the Alley Tally Party in 1964.

Robert (Bob) Butts grew up in South Bend, Indiana. His parents were divorced at an early age, so Bob assumed a "man-of-the-house" mantle early on. He met Jim Rossow, his best friend in fandom, in junior high school. Bob was nearby when Jim opened up a locker and took out some comic books he'd bought, and shortly thereafter a lifelong friendship in and out of fandom was established.

Bob Butts gained his first recognition as a familiar name from the DC letter columns. For one of his letters he was awarded a complete Flash story, featuring Abra-Kadabra, the magician from the future. Letter columns were where fans got the names of people who shared their passion, and Bob maintained regular correspondence with over 20 other fans, longest with Larry Herndon of the famed Texas Trio. The daily contents of the mailbox were one of his joys in life.

Around 1963 both Bob and Jim decided to publish fanzines. They threw in their resources together and bought a used Rexograph spirit duplicator, a gallon of fluid, several reams of paper and a box of spirit masters. Bob decided to call his zine *Fan-to-Fan*; Jim titled his fanmag *Countdown*. Editorial offices were in a cramped section of the basement of Bob's house. The two shared the duplicator and a typewriter Bob owned, and also the skills they had acquired in preparing masters and printing pages. Contributors such as Grass Green, Ronn Foss, Biljo White, Steve Perrin, Mike Vosburg and other fandom notables were contributors to *Fan to Fan*. When Ronn Foss gave up *Dateline: Comicdom* after 12 issues, Butts published #13 and #14, before it was passed on to another South Bend fan and friend, Robert "Keith" Greene.

In 1964, owing to his reputation in fandom and as a fanzine publisher, Bob was invited by Jerry Bails to attend the first Alley Tally at Bails' home in Warren, Michigan. Too young to drive, it was arranged to have Ronn Foss drive from Van Wert, Ohio, to Ft. Wayne, Indiana, and pick up Grass Green. The two then drove to South Bend to pick up Bob and Jim Rossow, who was also invited to the Tally. The four-hour drive to Warren was filled with non-stop comic conversation.

After high school Bob enlisted in the Army, serving for a year in Vietnam. Always an excellent student, he used his G.I. Bill educational benefits to attend Indiana University, where he was awarded a BA degree in Psychology. After kicking around at a few odd jobs after graduation, he took a position with the State of Indiana as a welfare caseworker, and later a casework trainer. He was employed by the state for almost 35 years.

By 1980 Bob was no longer actively involved in fandom or collecting comics. When his longtime friend, Jim Rossow, decided to start his own comic book convention in 1983, Bob lent his support. He traveled to Chicago to attend Fandom Reunion 1997. He assisted at every Michiana Comicon until its demise in 2005.

Bob Butts

Bob developed health problems

later in life, most notably diabetes (which ran in his family). On November 16, 2008, he suffered a stroke in the laundry room of his apartment, and fell into a coma. He never regained consciousness and died peacefully in the hospital three days later.

Rick Durell

(1932–1982)

At a time when Golden Age comics were often difficult to obtain but not yet out of the price range of an adult with a middle-class income, Rick Durell avidly built what was surely one of the finest collections ever to exist in the world.

Richard Durell lived in El Segundo, California, not far from the Los Angeles Airport and worked in the petroleum industry in one capacity or another for many years. He was a typical middle-class family man during the 1960s, when he began to recapture his childhood love of comic books. Like so many collectors of the era, he would lament how his mother threw out his beloved stash of Golden Age issues of *Batman*, *Captain America* and *Captain Marvel Adventures*.

What distinguished Durell from other collectors was his boundless enthusiasm for old comics. Few collectors have ever loved Golden Age comics more than Rick Durell, and he loved to share that enthusiasm with other collectors. He wasn't a fanzine writer, editor or comic book indexer. He wasn't a comic book dealer. He wasn't a convention organizer, although he supported the early San Diego Comic-Cons after they began in 1970. He was simply a friendly, handsome fellow— very much a "man's man"—who never tired of talking about the old comics he loved so much.

Durell especially loved collecting the iconic characters of his youth from the major comic book publishers. Unlike most collectors of the 1960s, however, he stressed comics in the finest condition and thus preferred to buy his comics in person rather than through the mail. During the 1960s, before the creation of the *Overstreet Comic Book Price Guide* and the resulting condition standards, most mail-order dealers did not grade their comics, at least in the way the price guide ultimately forced them to do.

Had Durell lived long enough to see the era of Comics Guaranty grading and slabbing, his collection would have been worth millions. He had complete runs of titles like *Action Comics*, *Superman* and *Captain America*, and almost every issue was fine

Rick Durell

or better; many were what today would be 9.0 or better near-mints. He was one of the earliest collectors who would passionately upgrade his issues.

Early fanzine writer and editor Glen Johnson, in an interview in *Alter Ego* #51 and #52 (August and September 2005), couldn't have been more impressed when he met Durell in person for the first time during a trip to Southern California in 1964. That was the trip that resulted in the famous photo of a meeting at artist Russ Manning's home, with Manning flanked by Johnson, Kyle, Durell, fanzine collector John McGeehan and fanzine editor Bill Spicer.

"I don't think anybody had a collection as huge as Rick Durell did at that time," Johnson recalled. "I remember he brought out all these bound volumes of newspapers that had been discarded when the papers had been transferred to film. His garage was just *filled* with bound volumes of newspaper editions. He was taking out the comic strips he wanted and then selling the rest of the stuff to somebody else. His mother had thrown out his comic book collection while he was in the service. So when he came back, he had to start *re-collecting*. He went out to all these used bookstores in small towns and bought back his collection. I had been corresponding with Rick Durell quite often, and after we left Manning's, we drove back to El Segundo and stayed at his place. He had a vast comic collection."

Durell was fortunate enough to live within driving distance of dozens of used-book stores, which were the prime sources of old comics and magazines in the 1960s, but his main supplier was the Cherokee Book Store on Hollywood Boulevard. The Cherokee Book Store, with Burt Blum running the comic book department, had even more comics than Durell could possibly have purchased. Durell didn't want them all. He was primarily interested in the classic Golden Age superheroes. Blum, knowing how serious a collector Rick was, would often purchase comics with this super collector in mind.

In the mid–1960s, when even the oldest Golden Age comics were only three decades old, condition wasn't close to being the factor it is today in the price of a comic. Thus, Durell could pick up a fine or near-mint *Captain America* for only a buck or two more than a "good" copy. Although he was aware the value of his comics would inevitably go up, he didn't buy fine or better copies with an eye to investment. Instead, he simply wanted his comic books to look as fresh as possible, as close as he could find to their condition on his childhood newsstands of the 1940s.

"It would have taken me a lot longer to do my indexes for Timely, MLJ and Nedor (1968–1969) had Rick not been unfailingly willing to help," said Michelle Nolan. "He and his wife, Ann, would welcome me into their home and let me spend hours indexing Rick's comics during several visits. He had such a large percentage of them, it was simply amazing. When I met Rick in 1967, I had already seen a couple of large collections, but nothing of the quality or magnitude of the comics on his shelves. When he would bring out a stack of a Timely title, most of which I had never seen, it was simply mind-boggling. I met lots of dealers with lots of old comics, not to mention a few collectors, but there was simply nobody like Rick.

"Collectors didn't come any friendlier than Rick. He was a wonderful conversationalist and he really knew the books and the artists. He was also well liked by the professionals who lived in Southern California and he knew most of them. I'll never forget the evening Rick took me to dinner with Alex Toth in 1968. The Green Lantern was my favorite Golden Age character along with Wonder Woman and Flash Gordon, and here I was, a 20-year-old college student, enjoying conversation with one of artists who drew the Golden Age Green Lantern and one of the collectors who not only owned every issue, but remembered reading the books when he was a kid."

Rick lived long enough to see his comics increase substantially in value during the first decade of the existence of the *Overstreet Comic Book Price Guide.* Fortunately, he had already obtained almost everything he needed by the time the price guide first appeared in 1970.

"Rick was regarded very highly by people in collecting, dealers as well as fellow collectors," comics historian Richard Kyle, for many years one of Durell's best friends, stated. "Attendance at his memorial service was extraordinary. He was a devoted, enthusiastic collector of comics and magazines. He wasn't an actor, but he had the easy presence of one, and somehow managed to look like a middle-period Alex Raymond drawing. An unforgettable person."

Mark Evanier
(b. 1952)

Mark Evanier was president of the Los Angeles Comic Book Club, the first known organization of comic book fans in California. He had numerous letters published in the letter columns of DC and Marvel comics, and contributed articles and opinion pieces to fanzines in the late 1960s.

Mark Stephen Evanier was born in 1952 in Santa Monica, California. His desire to make his living as a writer was a reaction to the way his father supported his family. Mark recently commented, "My father had the worst job in the world. He worked for the Internal Revenue Service and hated every minute of it." This lifestyle was in sharp contrast to the happy life of a professional writer as portrayed on *The Dick Van Dyke Show* that Evanier watched avidly.

Evanier was reared on Dell Comics that featured characters he loved in cartoons on television like Bugs Bunny and Woody Woodpecker. By the mid–1960s, Mark was buying everything that came out that wasn't romance, Harvey or Archie. He heard about fandom through the letter columns in DC comics edited by Julius Schwartz; when he had letters published, he received sample fanzines and ads. Evanier began buying and reading such fan publications, and entered into correspondences with other comics enthusiasts, such as Tony Isabella and Dwight Decker.

In 1967, Mark became involved in the Los Angeles Comic Book Club (LACBC), the first known organization of comic fans in California. Core members were Rob Gluckson, Jeff Gluckson, Rob Solomon, Bruce Schweiger, Craig Miller, Mike Rot-

Mark Evanier

blatt, Barry Siegel, Steve Finkelstein, Bruce Simon, Herb Robaire, Jon Yost, Gary Lowenthal, Peter Backus, Randy Cunningham, Jim Shull, Warren Somers, Steve Sherman, Gary Sherman and about 20 others. According to Rob Gluckson, there was some interaction with the Los Angeles Science Fantasy Society (LASFS). "Just how the group got started was one of the topics that could provoke fist fights," Evanier recalled. "About eight members all had their stories about how they started the group, which seemed to have evolved out of a couple of different informal gatherings. It was a fun organization while it lasted." Evanier was president during most of the club's three-year existence.

In 1969, Mark made a connection that would have a profound effect upon his life and future career. That year, Jack and Roz Kirby attended a science fiction convention in Santa Monica. They were new in the state and looking to connect with local writers and artists. A couple of the officers of the LACBC were at the con—not Evanier—and they met Jack and Roz, whereupon they were invited to visit the Kirbys at their home, which was then in Irvine. As president of the club, Mark was included in that trip. He gave Jack some fanzine articles he had written, and Kirby liked them. Not long afterwards, Evanier got a job working for Marvelmania, which was an L.A.-based company that was producing Marvel posters, decals and other mail-order items. As Mark later wrote, "The company proved to be crooked and I soon got out but by then, Jack was impressed with the work I'd done for the firm and asked another employee (and former LACBC member) Steve Sherman and me to become his assistants." Evanier and Sherman created editorial matter for the Kirby "Fourth World" comic books at DC Comics, and Mark's relationship with the Kirbys proved to be long lasting.

While apprenticing under Kirby, Evanier began writing foreign comics for Disney, and from 1972 to 1976 scripted Gold Key comics. At this time, he also found success writing as part of a team with Dennis Palumbo for such television comedy shows as *Welcome Back, Kotter*. From there Mark began writing for Hanna-Barbera's comic book division and other television shows, including animated cartoons such as *Scooby Doo* and *Thundarr the Barbarian*. His greatest success in that field was on *Garfield and Friends*, a popular Saturday morning cartoon series which lasted seven seasons. Evanier wrote or co-wrote every episode.

In the comic book arena, Mark has written *Blackhawk*, *Fanboy*, *DNAgents* and *Crossfire*. He has shared multiple Eisner awards for collaborations done with cartoonist and friend Sergio Aragonés on projects such as *Groo the Wanderer*. Evanier has contributed immeasurably to the appreciation of Golden Age comics, and to the historical record of the industry, by hosting annual panels at Comic-Con International featuring professional writers and artists who created comic books. Mark's illustrated Jack Kirby biography, *Kirby: King of Comics*, was published in February 2008 by Abrams Books. It won a Will Eisner Comics Industry Award, and whetted fans' appetites for the exhaustive biography of Kirby that Mark is currently writing.

Paul Gambaccini

(b. 1949)

Before succeeding Jerry Bails as Executive Secretary of the Academy of Comic Book Arts and Sciences, Paul Gambaccini was known for writing letters that frequently appeared in the letter columns of DC and Marvel comics of the early 1960s. He later became a columnist for *RBCC*.

Gambaccini was born in the Bronx, New York. It was in the Bronx, where his family lived before moving to Westport, Connecticut, in 1955, that he saw his first comic books. With the publication of *Superman Annual* #1 in 1960, and the revivals of the characters the Flash and Green Lantern at that time, Paul became a fan of superhero comic books. He bought every DC comic book except the war comics, with the help of a friendly retailer. In *Alter Ego* #10 (2002), Gambaccini recalled, "I am deeply indebted to the woman of this mom-and-pop shop because every Tuesday and Thursday, which were the new-comic days, she would set aside one copy of each new comic for me to have dibs on." When *Fantastic Four* came along, Paul added Marvel comics to his purchases.

When he was 12 years old, Gambaccini began writing letters to comic book editors. His first published letter appeared in *The Flash* #122 (August 1961), and was accompanied by his full address. Thus, he was one of the recip-

Paul Gambaccini

ients of *Alter-Ego* #1 that Jerry Bails was sending out for free at the time. Because Paul was a good typist, recipients of his letters and postcards—whom he hadn't met in person—thought he was much older than 12 or 13. He loved the comic books of the day, especially those edited by Julius Schwartz, and wrote to express his appreciation and offer suggestions. "What nobody who did not go through it could ever understand is how exciting it was for readers of [Schwartz's] books in '60 and '61." (*Alter Ego* #10.) His letters were so well known at DC that the recurring character Paul Gambi, introduced in *The Flash* #141, was named after him. Gambaccini maintains that the Marvel title *Not Brand Ecch* took its name from a comment he made in the letter column of *Amazing Spider-Man* #7 (1963).

Soon Gambaccini was contributing to the fanzines. One of his biggest projects was writing the *Rocket's Blast Special* #3 (1964) on All-American Comics. He also wrote a review of the book *Seduction of the Innocent* that appeared in the *RBCC Annual* #1 (also 1964). Paul wrote other things for Gordon Love's publications, and was chosen to succeed Rick Weingroff on the widely read "Rocketeer Gossip" column in *RBCC*. Gambaccini's prose was always intelligent, concise and demonstrated a grasp of the English language that was better than the run-of-the-mill writers in comicdom.

In 1964, Jerry Bails asked Paul Gambaccini to take over as Executive Secretary of the Academy of Comic Book Arts and Sciences. This was the umbrella organization designed to administer the Alley Awards and other projects, and lend a certain respectability to the hobby. Paul, who had a great deal of regard for Jerry, agreed to take on the job, and launched a newsletter called *Forum* (October 1964) for the 20 or so members of the organization's Executive Board. The newsletter was a hornet's nest of controversies, suggestions, voting deadlines and squabbles over the charter and by-laws. The attempt to organize and mobilize fans in any particular direction was beginning to reveal itself to be an exercise in frustration, if not futility. After serving for a year, and editing numerous issues of *Forum* during that period, Paul's term in the job ended. (The position of Executive Secretary was passed on to David Kaler.)

Gambaccini essentially dropped out of fandom when he graduated from high school in 1966. He graduated from Dartmouth in 1970, then went to Oxford. While in his senior year at Dartmouth, he had begun submitting record reviews to *Rolling Stone* magazine. They were accepted, and before long he was a contributing editor to the publication. When he moved to England after graduating from college, he would go to London several times a week for *Rolling Stone* purposes. This activity led to him being given a regular slot on the BBC in 1973. He was the presenter of a long-running BBC arts radio show called *Kaleidoscope*, which was on from 1974 to 1999, and he was able to interview comic book people such as Julius Schwartz, Stan Lee and Neil Gaiman on the show. He also interviewed Carl Barks on the *Good Morning, Britain* show. Gambaccini currently has two programs a week: *The American Hits* on BBC Radio 2, and *The Classic Countdown*.

Don Glut
(b. 1944)

Don Glut (pronounced gloot) was prominent in the earliest days of comic fandom in Chicago, but was best known then for making his own amateur superhero movies, which were featured in *Famous Monsters of Filmland, Castle of Frankenstein, Fantastic Monsters of the Films* and other publications. He co-published the fanzine *Shazam!* and was an invited attendee at the famed Alley Tally Party in 1964.

Photograph of Don Glut in 1965 when he was a member of The Wicks, a rock group.

Donald F. Glut was born in 1944 in Pecos, Texas, and grew up in Chicago, Illinois. Bitten by the movie bug at an early age, he made 41 amateur films in the 1950s–1960s. These movies featured his own versions of the classic Universal horror films starring Frankenstein's monster, Dracula, the Wolfman, *et al.*, as well as comic book characters such as Spider-Man, Captain America and Spy Smasher. When Forrest J Ackerman published stills from Glut's amateur films in the pages of *Famous Monsters of Filmland*, the Chicagoan became something of a fan sensation.

There were numerous fans of comic books, fantasy films and pulp magazines in the Chicago area. Having linked up with this loose network of aficionados in 1962, Glut hosted get-togethers in his family's basement, where old serials were shown and many a comic book was sold or traded. Some of the key members of this group were Alex Almaraz, Ed Navarette, Billy Placzek (who had an amazing collection of Golden Age comics), Ross Kight and Doug Moench.

With his trusty 16mm movie camera in hand, Don attended the 1962 World Science Fiction Convention in Chicago (known as Chicon). As numerous members of the Los Angeles Science Fiction Society appeared costumed as members of the Justice Society of America, Glut filmed them. His are the only films that capture what is widely considered an event that gave early comicdom a much-needed boost.

"There were at least two fandoms that started about the same time," Glut recounted in a 1992 interview. "One was the organized comic book fandom, and the other was monster movie fandom. And of course there was science fiction fandom, which had been going since the 1930s." In late 1962, Don decided to publish a fanzine that would appeal to fans of many different interests. He and his friend Dick Andersen called it *Shazam!*. He explained, "*Shazam!* was our attempt to do something better than *Fantasy Journal,* a horror magazine put out by our friends Bob Greenberg and Jim Hollander, and *Screen Thrills Illustrated,* which was being filled up with a lot of things we weren't interested in. I figured a lot of people who were interested in old movie serials and monster movies were also into the comics and pulps. We tried to accommodate them all within the covers of one fanzine."

In March of 1964, Don Glut was an attendee at the invitation-only Alley Tally Party at Jerry Bails' home in Detroit, Michigan, which is widely considered the first sizable gathering of comic book fans. Later that year, Glut moved to Los Angeles to attend the film school at UCLA. By this time his amateur films had become near-professional, and he attempted to perfect his filmmaking skills at the university. In later years, he would start his own film company, and produce and direct films that would find national distribution. Attending the 1964 World Science Fiction Convention in San Francisco, he met Marty Arbunich, Bill DuBay, Steve Perrin and reconnected with his old pal, Larry Ivie. While living in California, he and Forry Ackerman became even closer friends, and Ackerman would become Glut's literary agent. Don also pursued his interest in music at this time, as part of the band "Penny Arkade," which was produced by then–Monkee Michael Nesmith.

In the 1970s, Don became a successful freelance writer. He created the comic book titles *The Occult Files of Dr. Spektor, Dagar the Invincible* and *Tragg and the Sky Gods* for Gold Key, and scripted Marvel comics for much of the 1970s. Glut penned tales starring such characters as Captain America, Thor, The Invaders, Kull the Destroyer, 3-D Man and Solomon Kane. He also wrote for *Creepy, Eerie* and *Vampirella* for Warren Publishing, and for DC, Red Circle, Skywald and Charlton comics. Following his comics career, Glut wrote numerous scripts for TV childrens' shows, both live action and animation.

As his long-time interest in paleontology (especially dinosaurs) grew stronger, Glut wrote extensively on the subject. His *Dinosaur Dictionary* (1972) and *Dinosaurs: The Encyclopedia* (1997) are two of the best known, but there are many others. His most successful book was his novelization of the movie *The Empire Strikes Back* (1980), which sold over three million copies. He also wrote a well-received series of novels starring his own version of Mary Shelley's *Frankenstein*.

"I'm not really that much into comics anymore," Don stated. Instead, he continues to pursue movie-making (Frontline Entertainment), both as script writer and director, and a variety of writing projects. Recently he produced the DVD *I Was a Teenage Movie-Maker,* which recounts his experiences along those lines, with film clips of the movies he made. (There are a few clips from the footage he shot at the 1962 Chicon.) He also wrote a book by the same title. More recently, Glut found a new career as a voice-over actor, dubbing Japanese animé movies into English.

Mark Hanerfeld

(1944–2000)

Mark Hanerfeld was known in fandom as a writer who contributed to numerous fanzines, as the last editor of *The Comic Reader/On the Drawing Board*, and as the final Executive Secretary of the Academy of Comic Book Fans and Collectors. He was also widely known for his fan-oriented news columns in DC Comics of the late 1960s and early 1970s.

Mark Hanerfeld of Flushing, New York, was a knowledgeable comic book and strip fan who was an active member of the fan community in the Big Apple. A grown man in 1964, the rotund, bearded Hanerfeld brought a mature presence to the scene, and emerged as a key helper on the con committees formed by David Kaler to mount the 1965, 1966 and 1967 New York Comicons. In an interview that appeared in *Comic Book Artist* #7 (2000), Hanerfeld recalled that he met Marv Wolfman and Len Wein in 1965, and was part of the group that would repeatedly go on the DC tours: "We used to go up there together into the DC office every Thursday when they would have a tour and within a couple of weeks, I started hosting the tour myself and got very used to being with the people around there." Mark was also part of a group dubbed "The Illegitimate Sons of Superman" (abbreviated TISOS) that had their initial meeting over Christmas vacation in 1966. In attendance were Mark Hanerfeld, Marv Wolfman, Len Wein, Andy Yanchus, Rich Rubenfeld, Ron Fradkin, Eliot Wagner and Stan Landman. (Other members not at that first meeting were Andy's sister Pat, and Irene and Ellen Vartanoff.) In 1968, the TISOS group traveled to Rutland, Vermont, for the annual Halloween Parade, and made a spectacular appearance in costumes at the post-parade party held by Tom Fagan at the mansion-like Clement House, where Fagan was caretaker.

Mark Hanerfeld

TISOS members were frequent attendees at Fagan's annual costume shindigs in Rutland.

Mark Hanerfeld came to prominence in fandom-at-large when he succeeded Dave Kaler as the primary source of comics news for Bob Schoenfeld's *On the Drawing Board*. He went to every company to get news: DC, Tower, Archie, Gold Key, Marvel, even Milson, making many contacts in the business along the way. When Schoenfeld was ready to shed *OTDB*, Mark took over. His first issue was #65 in 1968. Hanerfeld kept the issues coming through the end of that year. In September of 1971, after an almost three-year hiatus, Paul Levitz (along with Paul Kupperberg at first) continued *The Comic Reader* with Hanerfeld's blessing (and subscription list). The first Levitz issue picked up the original numbering of *The Comic Reader* with #78, and he later claimed to have reached a peak circulation figure of 3,500 copies per issue. The news-zine continued into the 1980s.

Also in 1968, Hanerfeld became the last Executive Secretary of the Academy, after Bails, Gambaccini and Kaler. The Academy had fallen into disarray during the latter part of Kaler's tenure. About all that Hanerfeld was able to salvage was conducting the last two Alley Award polls. In the last one, in 1969, fandom voted *Fantastic Four* as the "Best Adventure Title," Dick Giordano at DC Comics as "Best Editor," Roy Thomas as "Best Writer," Neal Adams as "Best Pencil Artist" and Tom Palmer as "Best Inking Artist." In terms of the "Popularity Poll" portion, *Amazing Spider-Man* was most popular, and *Superman* was judged "Strip Most Needing Improvement."

As a frequent DC visitor, Mark Hanerfeld found opportunities to assist the editors there in various capacities. He wrote two "floater" columns that appeared in every title, "The Wonderful World of DC Comics" and "Fact Files." From there he became assistant editor to Joe Orlando. He was heavily involved in selecting stories for the DC reprint comics of the early 1970s, such as the *100-Page Super Spectacular Weird Mystery*, a task he really enjoyed. He was something of an expert on the holdings in the much-vaunted DC back-issue library. Interestingly, Hanerfeld served as the reference model for *House of Secrets* host, Abel. In that same *Comic Book Artist* interview, he recalled, "Abel in *House of Secrets* is based on me and I have Joe's original sketch. He took two rolls of film just shooting me with every expression that I could come up with. I became a vaudevillian, mugging all the emotions and nuances of facial language. The strange thing is that I could never portray fear!" Hanerfeld appeared in costume as Abel at subsequent Rutland masquerade parties.

Mark was an editor and writer for DC for several years, then had to leave in order to take care of his ailing father. His efforts at collecting bits of original art from an unpublished Golden Age Justice Society of America strip, "The War of William Wilson," are credited by Roy Thomas with contributing mightily to its eventual partial reconstruction—an important historical achievement. Hanerfeld remained an avid behind-the-scene comics aficiando until his passing from a heart attack in 2000.

Rick Norwood

(b. 1942)

Rick Norwood was active as a fanzine publisher, contributor to numerous fanzines, member of *Capa-alpha*, attendee at many early conventions, and a letter writer whose missives appeared with frequency in DC and Marvel comics of the early-to-mid 1960s.

Frederick Norwood was born in Franklin, Louisiana, in 1942. His father was a Chevrolet dealer. In the 1950s, Rick's favorite comics were *Captain Marvel Adventures*, *Tarzan*, and *Superboy*. He loved everything 3-D, and his favorite comic book published using that process was *Tor* by Joe Kubert. He became interested in science fiction fandom in the early 1960s, and wrote a letter plugging the National Fantasy Fan Federation (N3F), an entry-level nationwide SF club, which was published in *Mystery in Space* in 1961. Since many comic book fans were also science fiction fans, and the plug appeared in a comic book, it had the effect of bringing a lot of comics fans together.

When Norwood went to college at the Massachusetts Institute of Technology in 1960, he was active in the M.I.T. Science Fiction Society. He contributed to *The Twilight Zine*, the M.I.T. fanzine, and in 1962 began publishing his own zine called *So What?* A fan of the revival of the characters Green Lantern (which had many SF elements), Rick got the idea of writing a new story featuring another DC hero from the 1940s called Dr. Mid-Nite, and obtained permission to do so from DC editor Julius Schwartz. Schwartz gave him the go-ahead, and also showed Norwood some art from Golden Age stories that were never published. In an odd coincidence, Rick found himself recreating Dr. Mid-Nite at the same time as three other fans launched their own versions: Steve Perrin with Doctor Darkness in *Mask and Cape*, and Drury Moroz and Ronn Foss with The Eclipse in *Alter Ego*. Of course, at this time DC itself was retooling many of its Golden Age costumed heroes.

Another memorable fanzine published while Norwood was at M.I.T. was *God Comics*, a collaboration between Rick, Al Kuhfeld and others. In this sardonic amateur comic, "God" was portrayed as a shapeless energy being who was a superhero, and wore a cape. The first issue began, appropriately, with an origin story: "We all know of the mighty powers of God," the opening caption read. "But what happened when he was just learning to use them? For the first time, we give you the full story of ... The Super-Powers of God." The splash panel featured humans staring up at God (wearing his cape) saying "Look! Up in the Sky! Is it a bird? Is it a plane? It's God!" Billed as "The World's Most Blasphemous Comic Fanzine!" *God Comics* lasted for five issues, and became known far beyond the limited number of copies that were produced (using ditto printing) at the time. Norwood's part was to contribute to the writing.

While at M.I.T., living in the East Campus Dorm, Rick Norwood corresponded with numerous comics and SF fans, including Jerry Bails. He was on the mailing list of the first issue of Bails' seminal fanzine *Alter-Ego*, and had a letter published in an early issue. Rick's involvement in fandom had consequences for his educational career. He recently wrote, "I was at M.I.T. from 1960 to 1962. I was having so much fun—it was the first time I had real friends who shared my interests—that I stopped going to class." However, after leaving that esteemed university, Norwood nevertheless earned a Ph.D. in mathematics, and has made his living as a math professor.

Rick had letters published in *Fantastic Four*, *Green Lantern*, and many other comics of the 1960s. He was known for his intelligent observations and commentary. Many of his letters were published as "Rick Wood," some as "Rick Norwood," and a few as "Frederick Norwood." In his apa-zine in *Capa-alpha*, he wrote a novella called "The Adventures of Superhero," which portrayed what it would be like for a real person to suddenly gain a super power. He also helped organize conventions, wrote articles for other fanzines, and was one of the most active fans in fandom's formative years.

In 1976, Rick Norwood founded a small press publishing company called Manuscript Press. It was formed when Rick met SF writer Hal Clement, who mentioned that he couldn't find a publisher for his latest novel. Clement's *Left of Africa* was the first book of many to be published by Manuscript Press, which is now located in Mountain Home, Tennessee. Norwood recently wrote, "Since then I've published *Archipelago* by Ray Lafferty, *The Magic Talisman* (A Rick Brant Science Adventure) by Hal Godwin (John Blaine), three volumes of *Prince Valiant, An Amer-

Rick Norwood

ican Epic, two Buz Sawyer books, one Alley Oop book and one Flash Gordon book." Norwood also founded *Comics Revue*, which reflects his interest and appreciation of newspaper comic strips. In its ongoing monthly issues (over 275 published thus far), *CR* reprints comic strips such as "Alley Oop," "Modesty Blaise," "Tarzan," "Gasoline Alley," "Flash Gordon," "Amazing Spider-Man," "Star Wars," "Hagar the Horrible," "Peanuts," "Batman," "Barnaby," "Steve Canyon," "Casey Ruggles," "Krazy Kat," "Little Orphan Annie," "Mandrake the Magician," "The Phantom," "Latigo," "Rick O'Shay," and "Buz Sawyer."

These days, Rick Norwood's interest in comics is as strong as it ever was, though his focus is mainly on comic strips, which he feels usually have better stories and artwork than comic books. He collects works by Neil Gaiman, Alan Moore, Carl Barks, Will Eisner, Phil Foglio and Joe Kubert, but mainly comic strips. He was on the comic strip panel at the 2009 New York Comic-Con.

Jim Rossow
(b. 1948)

In the early 1960s, there was an east-west corridor that linked comics fans. It ran from Cleveland to South Bend to Chicago. In Cleveland, there was Don and Maggie Thompson, Bill Thailing and Larry Raybourne. Chicago was home to Don Glut, Alex Almaraz, Billy Placzek, Ed Navarette, Ross Kight and many more. Midway were the "South Bend crew," consisting of Bob Butts, Bob "Keith" Greene and Jim Rossow. They were the ones—along with fans in Michigan, such as Jerry Bails, Shel Dorf and Edwin Aprill, Jr.—who made up the nucleus of the earliest sizable gatherings of comic book fans in the United States. These get-togethers, precursors of regional and national comicons, began in the spring of 1964. Jim Rossow, who later organized comicons of his own, was an active participant at the most historic of these proto-conventions.

Jim Rossow

At 15 years old in 1964, Jim Rossow had already formed the beginnings of a lifelong friendship with fellow South Bend collector Bob Butts, whom he had met in junior high school. An enterprising soul with incipient writing ability, Jim decided to publish his own fanzine shortly after seeing his first issues of *Alter-Ego* and *The Rocket's Blast* in 1963. *Countdown* became another example in the surge in amateur publishing that occurred that year, that included first issues of *Star-Studded Comics, Action Hero, Brave Adventure, Comic Caper, Dateline: Comicdom, Fantasy Hero, Fighting Hero Comics* and *Heroes' Hangout*. Each would make itself known in an advertisement in *The Rocket's Blast*, imploring fans to send their hard-earned dimes and quarters. *Countdown*, like most zines, only lasted a short time, but its three issues were worthy, offering some sterling ditto art by Howard Keltner, Biljo White, Ronn Foss, Grass Green and text features by Paul Gambaccini and Steve Perrin. Copies of *Countdown* sold at a good clip, owing to a plug in DC's *Challengers of the Unknown*.

In *Countdown* #3 (1964), Jim wrote an account of the first time Richard "Grass" Green visited him in South Bend. He began the account with "I doubt that I'll ever forget October 19th 1963 as long as I live. On that day, I was fortunate enough to meet one of fandom's best artists, Grass Green." In those days, Big Name Fans were almost considered celebrities to fandom's rank and file, and Green had already achieved that status by dint of the artwork and strips he had drawn for *The Comicollector*, *Komix Illustrated*, *Super Hero* and more. Jim's meeting with Grass may have led to an even more exciting opportunity for the teenager, the formal invitation by Jerry Bails to attend a fan-gathering on March 21–22 at Bails' home in Detroit. Bob Butts was also invited. In any event, the "South Bend crew" rode to the Alley Tally Party with Grass and his pal, Ronn Foss. Rossow later recalled, "I was amazed that my father agreed to let me go to Detroit with two people he was not familiar with. But he had met Grass once before and he had made an excellent impression on my father. Years later, he would ask if I'd ever heard from Grass again."

Jim was active in all phases of fandom for many years, and in 1983 founded a comic book show in South Bend called the Michiana Comicon. It continued until 2005, offering something like the simpler cons of an earlier era, where old comics were still king, and one could spend hours going through the quarter boxes of comics books from the 50 or so dealers who were there. His friend Bob Butts helped out for all 23 years. In 1992 Jim had reestablished contact with Grass Green, and invited him to be a guest at the show. Almost 30 years after they had first met, Jim, Bob and Grass were back together again.

To earn his living, Rossow has worked mostly as a technical writer; in the last several years, he's been in technical support and customer service. When asked about his current level of interest in comics, Jim wrote, "I am no longer actively collecting comics, and can't remember the last time I bought one. There used to be 20 comic book stores in the area; now there are only two. There are some great stories being written with a new generation of impressive artists, but they've become too expensive to collect all that I'm interested in, and they don't hold the same joy of those simpler times. I have been slowly auctioning off my collection, and salting away the proceeds for retirement. The fond memories will always remain."

Len Wein

(b. 1948)

Len Wein was a writer, artist and fanzine publisher who, in the late 1960s, began a highly successful career in pro comics. While in high school, he became best friends with Marv Wolfman, and together they were among the most active fans in New York City fandom.

Len Wein was born in New York City in 1948. A sickly child, Len fell in love with comic books when his father brought him a stack of comic books to keep him occupied during a hospital stay. He was about 14 years old when he discovered comic fandom. He was part of a bunch of teenage comic book enthusiasts in and around New York City, a group

Left to right: Mark Hanerfeld, Marv Wolfman and Len Wein.

also consisting of Paul Vizcarrando, Rick Bierman, Ron Fradkin and Marv Wolfman. He was an aspiring artist in these early years, though his ability in that area was later overshadowed by his writing and editing talent. The writers who inspired him were Ray Bradbury, Paddy Chayefsky and Rod Serling. The only comic book writer whom Wein counts as an influence was Robert Kanigher.

Like many a young fan at this time, Len plunged into fanzine publishing after seeing the products of others. His *Aurora* appeared on the leading edge of a flood of new zines appearing in 1963, with #1 hitting the mails in March. Len was able to publish three more issues before year's end, an impressive achievement. *Aurora* was a garden-variety ditto fanzine, featuring a mix of articles and amateur comic strips. Len's original hero, The Prism, appeared in strip form, with art by Len and fellow New Yorker Bernie Bubnis. Wein managed to attract contributions by Margaret Gemignani and Mike Vosburg, though the majority of the zine was the work of his local pals, Wolfman, Fradkin and others. Jack Kirby and Steve Ditko contributed covers which Wein traced onto ditto masters with considerable skill. *Aurora* was a fanzine of higher quality than one usually produced by a fan in his mid-teens. Len's enthusiasm attracted contributors, making it a real team effort. Issue #5, in November 1964, was the last issue.

In late 1964, Wein acquired his own spirit duplicator, and formed plans for a "next generation" fanzine to be called *Trident*. He was to be chief artist of the endeavor; his co-editors were Paul Vizcarrando and Rick Bierman. However, the fanzine was delayed for over a year when Wein became ill. When *Trident* finally appeared in March 1966, co-editor Paul Vizcarrando wrote, "Co-editor, chief artist, and owner of the ditto machine, Len Wein, took seriously ill with a staphylococcus infection which brought him very close to death. Work on the zine came to a virtual standstill for the three to four months during which he was seriously incapacitated." However, the fanzine itself was worth the wait. In addition to able art by Wein throughout, the front cover was an excellent Batman piece by Johnny Chambers, and Frank Brunner contributed a Doctor Fate illustration for the back cover. Paul McSpadden wrote an article on EC's *M.D.* title, Tom Lauria expounded on the Golden Age Hourman, and Rick Bierman penned a piece on the 1950s hero, Captain Flash. Then, in contrast to these articles, Vizcarrando and Wein created a strip starring their amateur hero, The Prism.

In "The Man Who Replaced The Prism!," Lumpy Wott (who was reminiscent of Plastic Man's sidekick Doiby Dickles) tries to take over for the hero whom he thinks has died beneath a fallen meteor. Wein acquitted himself quite well in his artwork on this humor-tinged tale. *Trident* was a step up from *Aurora*, especially in terms of its focus on informative articles. However, by the time it came out, Len was on the verge of graduating from high school.

In college, Wein majored in Advertising Art and Design. He worked on honing both his writing and drawing skills, generally seeing his amateur work appear in Wolfman's *Super Adventures*. At this time, DC was holding weekly tours of their New York offices, which Len took frequently along with Marv and others in their group. This demystified the world of pro comics, so that Len and Marv ended up submitting samples to DC. Editor Joe Orlando was willing to look at short scripts for *House of Secrets*, *House of Mystery* and other "weird" comics he was editing. Orlando did buy some scripts by Len, and with that, Wein was off and running. (However, Wein's artwork did not receive the same acceptance, and he soon concentrated fully on his scripting.) A chance collaboration with Bernie Wrightson in 1971 led to the co-creation of the character Swamp Thing, which became an enormous fan favorite.

Len Wein became a mainstay scripter of comic books at both DC and Marvel, going on to co-create Human Target, Nova, Wolverine and the rest of the 1970s X-Men. Over the ensuing years, he's written many, if not all, of the major characters from DC and Marvel, including Spider-Man, Fantastic Four, Justice League of America, Batman, Superman and many others.

Wein has successfully worked in comic books, animation and film, and has received numerous awards for his work. He won a Shazam Award in 1972 for *Swamp Thing*, an Inkpot award in 1979, and a *Comics Buyer's Guide* award as Best Editor in 1982. He was nominated in 1999 for the Bram Stocker Award, given by the Horror Writers Association, for the one-shot *The Dreaming: Trial and Error* from DC's Verigo Comics imprint. In 2008, Len was inducted into the Will Eisner Comic Book Hall of Fame.

Marv Wolfman
(b. 1946)

Marv Wolfman was a prolific fanzine publisher, writer and sometime artist who was a key member of New York City fandom. His friendship with another New Yorker named Len Wein led to a number of fan projects together. They both broke into pro comics about the same time, and both became important creative forces in the comics industry as writers and editors.

Marvin A. Wolfman was born in Brooklyn in 1946, the first year of the post-war baby boom. His favorite comics as a child were *Superman, Batman, Strange Adventures, Mystery In Space* and others. Marv quickly became a fan of The Flash, Green Lantern and the other Silver Age heroes introduced in the books edited by Julie Schwartz. Marv picked up *Fantastic Four* #4 off the newsstands, but it wasn't until a few issues later when Sub-Mariner met Doctor Doom that he became a Marvel fan. At the same time he was an avid reader of *Amazing Adult Fantasy*, Marvel's O'Henry-ish comic and wasn't happy when the mystery stories were supplanted by another superhero with the unlikely name, Spider-Man. He bought the adventures of Spidey starting with issue #1 and quickly became a fan of that

book, too. As much as he loved the DC characters, the Marvel brand of high-octane storytelling quickly won him over.

Even as he began to gravitate toward the
older-appealing Marvel comics, Marv
remained a die-hard fan of Julie Schwartz's
superheroes and he wrote enthusiastic letters
that occasionally appeared in letter columns.
One that appeared in *Mystery in Space #75*
(May 1962), the issue featuring the Adam
Strange story, "The Planet That Came to a
Standstill!," led to him meeting a fan named
Ron Fradkin. By this time, Schwartz had
begun running complete addresses with the
letters, which greatly facilitated contacts
among fans. Marv recently recalled, "Ron
Fradkin called me after seeing that letter I
wrote printed in *Mystery In Space*. Ron said
he lived in Levittown, Long Island, and by
the kind of coincidence writing schools will
tell you never to commit to print, I was heading out to Levittown the very next day to
spend a week with my sister and brother-in-
law. Ron and his friend rode their bikes over
to my sister's house and we spent the day
talking comics." That friend of Fradkin was
14-year-old and later fellow professional, Len

Marv Wolfman

Wein. Marv also became friends with Ron Fradkin, and soon the other stalwarts of New
York fandom including Dave Kaler, Mark Hanerfeld, Stan Landman, Eliot Wagner, Andy
Yanchus and more.

In 1964, when Wolfman was attending New York's High School of Art and Design,
hoping to become a cartoonist, he made another important fan connection; he met a talented
young writer-artist and comics fan by the name of Dave Herring. Marv introduced Dave to
fandom, and showed him examples of the popular fanzines of the day. Herring was a fan of
the Kurtzman *Mad*, and launched his own version called *Odd*. Wolfman, also a Kurtzman
fan, was publishing his humor fanzine, *The Foob*. Herring was also publishing a second
fanzine, *Super Adventures*, but he preferred the humor fanzine to the superhero zine, and
turned over *Super Adventures* to Wolfman. *Super Adventures* lasted ten issues, with the last
one appearing in 1969. Marv published a third fanzine called *Stories of Suspense*, a horror
fanzine which had five ditto issues also through 1969. *Super Adventures* was Marv's version
of *Fighting Hero Comics* and *Star-Studded Comics*, crammed full of amateur strips. Dave Herring and Len Wein were frequent contributors; Marv and Len teamed up to create a 16-page
photo offset strip called "Who Can Defeat a God?" in a later issue which introduced the
character of the Black Nova, later adapted in *The Man Called Nova* for Marvel. The horror
fanzine, *Stories of Suspense*, had both horror comic strips and prose stories, and has the distinction of reprinting the first published story by a very young Stephen King (the story had
originally appeared in the obscure fanzine *Comics Review*, edited by Mike Garrett). In *SoS*,
"I Was a Teenage Graverobber" was retitled "In A Half-World of Terror." Marv also published a fourth fanzine, an opinion, article zine titled *What Th—?*

During these years, Wolfman was a ball of energy, finding time for fan activities beyond being one of the most prolific fan publishers of the day. He contributed to other fanzines, penning several strips for Dave Herring's *Odd*, such as "The Man from C.O.U.S.I.N.S." in #9 and "How To Get Lost in Space (Without Really Trying)" in #10, both featuring sterling Herring art. Marv had long before realized his art would never be up to the same level as his writing and pretty much stopped drawing. He also was part of the army of young volunteers who helped Dave Kaler mount the New York Comicons of 1965 and 1966. He enthusiastically appeared in the costume masquerades at these conventions, portraying Tower Comics' No-Man, as well as Herbie, The Fat Fury and Aquaman. Since DC Comics offered a weekly tour of its offices each Thursday, another frequent fan activity for those "in the know" in the mid to late 1960s was to take the tour repeatedly, which Wolfman, Hanerfeld, Alan Kuperberg, Steve Mitchell and others did. In this way, Marv became known to many of the DC editors and staff at this time, which led to him becoming a summer intern for the company by the decade's end. Marv's art background came in handy as he worked on DC's cover color-separations under the guidance of Jack Adler. He was also a member of the fan group TISOS dubbed "The Illegitimate Sons of Superman."

Due to his talent, persistence and proximity, Wolfman became one of the first fans to penetrate the "closed shop" barrier that DC comics presented to fandom at that time. (Marvel had scarcely been more open, despite the high profile case of Roy Thomas being brought in to become the number two writer.) His breakthrough took place in 1967, with a script he wrote on spec for *Blackhawk*, one of his favorite comics that had fallen on hard times. Although he mailed it to the editor at the time, that editor never got back to him. Marv thought the story had been lost, but a year later Dick Giordano took over the editor's job, found the script (in its unopened envelope), and bought the story. Simultaneously, Joe Orlando had Marv re-dialog a script that another writer had written. Wolfman had scripts published in both Dick Giordano's and Joe Orlando's mystery-oriented comic books.

Marv wrote comics while attending college to become an art teacher. He taught junior high school art for one year before heading back to full-time comic writing. In 1970–71 he became an assistant editor to Joe Kubert. After the famous DC Implosion, Marv moved to Warren Magazines as editor of *Creepy*, *Eerie* and *Vampirella*. At the same time, Marv was writing both for DC ("John Carter, Warlord of Mars") and Marvel (*Tomb of Dracula*), among others. After about eight months editing Warren's magazines, in 1973, at the urging of Roy Thomas during a Rutland Halloween Parade vacation, Marv moved to Marvel to become editor of their impending black and white magazine line.

Marv Wolfman's achievements in professional comic books in the ensuing years are numerous and impressive. Among the highlights during this time were his lengthy run on *Tomb of Dracula*, the creation of the character Blade for Marvel Comics, and *The New Teen Titans* for DC Comics. He conceived and scripted the classic "limited series" *Crisis on Infinite Earths*. He served as Editor-in-Chief for Marvel Comics in the 1970s, Senior Editor at DC Comics in the '80s, and founding editor for *Disney Adventures Magazine* in the '90s. In the course of his long, successful career in comics, he received many awards, including the Shazam Award in 1973, the Inkpot Award in 1979 and the Jack Kirby Award (a precursor of the Eisner Awards) in 1985 and 1986. For his 2007 book, *Homeland, The Illustrated History of the State of Israel*, he won a National Jewish Book Award. Today, he continues to write comics for DC, animation, video games, novels and more.

SECTION VIII: PROFESSIONALS

Professional comic book publishers, writers, artists and editors all have had one primary goal in entering the comics industry: making a living. In the early days, when the comics were young, most of them fell into it along the way toward hoped-for careers in illustration, writing for pulps and slick magazines, and other loftier vehicles for their talents.

After the strips and comic books had been around for awhile, there were those who were exposed to them in their youths, and wanted to try their own hand at it. Many of the successful comic strip artists of the 1950s grew up on the wonderful strips of the 1930s, and those who didn't make it found a certain satisfaction in working in the humbler comic book medium. The great artists of EC—Wood, Williamson, Craig, Davis, Frazetta—grew up on the newspaper strips, but were unable at first to break into the tough syndicated markets.

Whether in it just to make a buck, or to make a buck at something they loved, the professionals—especially those who wrote and drew comic books—toiled with little thought of receiving recognition for their efforts beyond a paycheck. Often, they worked in semi-isolation, in basements or tiny home studios, banging typewriter keys or filling large sheets of heavy-duty paper with drawings, shut off from the world day after day. Sometimes, if they were able or required to work in the publishers' offices, they received commentary on their work from their colleagues; the editors who bought the work seldom did more than nod their heads as they examined the work. They were there to give out assignments, not compliments.

Though comic books in the 1940s sold to plenty of teenagers and young adults, publishers in those years rarely ran letter columns, perhaps feeling that hardly anyone would have much to say about the kind of light reading offered, or care enough to put pen to paper. With a few exceptions, the comic book letter column didn't become an important component until William M. Gaines, publisher of EC comics, began receiving such letters, and decided to publish them regularly. The EC professionals suddenly realized there were people who especially loved their work. Not only did fans exist, they could be quite eloquent in their expressions of appreciation for the stories and artwork.

The existence of comic book fans led, inevitably, to the potential for a "fandom"—a recognizable group of such aficionados coming together to share their enthusiasm for the medium. How would they be able to find each other and connect? The solution was simple, once Gaines took a leaf from the SF magazines which printed full addresses along with the names of the letter writers.

This section of *Founders of Comic Fandom* is made up of bios of those comic strip and comic book professionals whose efforts concretely and significantly helped boost the formation and sustenance of comic fandom. It took the pros to help the fans find one another, and there were many things they did to make the sparks of the smoldering tinder of early connections burst into flame.

In helping the fans come together, the life of the comic book professional opened up into something quite different than it had been. As the fan world came into being, the world of the pros was commensurately enlarged. Now there were two hands clapping, and the applause was resounding.

Otto Binder

(1911–1974)

Otto Binder holds the distinction of being a famous and accomplished writer in both comic books and science fiction. Binder wrote about 3,000 comic books stories during his career, including hundreds for the character Captain Marvel and the Marvel Family during their heyday and an equal amount for Superman in the 1950s and 60s. He also wrote hundreds of science fiction short stories, novels and UFO books from 1932 until his death, some with his brother Earl under the name "Eando Binder." Their most important story appeared in *Amazing Stories* in January 1939: "I, Robot," about a human-like robot called Adam Link, who stands trial for killing its creator (not to be confused with the novel of the same name by Isaac Asimov). The unique character was hailed as an SF classic and led to a series of other Adam Link stories and novels.

A Bill Spicer-D. Bruce Berry adaptation of Eando Binder's "I, Robot" won the "Best Fan Comic Strip" honors in the 1964 Alley Awards. Binder was posthumously inducted into the Comic Book Hall of Fame in 2004.

As a youth in the 1920s, Binder enjoyed popular radio programs and movies, but it was his discovery of pulp magazines, especially *Weird Tales* and *Amazing Stories*, that got him hooked on science fiction and fantasy. These magazines were not only a delight to Binder, but helped spur his ambition to write on a professional level. A few years later, the Eando Binder brother-team sold its first story, "The First Martian," to *Amazing Stories,* appearing in their October 1932 issue. Binder began to read several of the fan publications of the day, including the SF fanzine *Time Traveller*. Otto and Earl became celebrity-like fans in the Chicago area, being published professionals who attended small fan gatherings and contributed to fanzines. At one of these meetings, they met Jerry Siegel and Joe Shuster, two SF fans from Cleveland who traveled to Chicago. They also met Mort Weisinger, who, along with Julius Schwartz, was running a writer's agency called Solar Sales, to help get stories sold for SF authors. Solar Sales represented the Binders for a while.

Otto's brother, Jack, was an accomplished artist who worked in the early days of comics, eventually becoming a permanent fixture at Fawcett Comics and with the *Captain Marvel* line of books. It was Jack who helped get Otto into the comic book writing business and later into a job at Fawcett. After realizing he had a knack for writing comic books, Otto left the SF pulps and concentrated exclusively on the four-color medium. He wrote more than half of all the comic books featuring Captain Marvel and the Marvel Family, and then switched to becoming chief writer on the Superman family of comics in the 1950s.

Then, in 1960, while editing the magazine *Space World*, Binder received a package that contained a copy of Richard A. Lupoff's SF fanzine *Xero* #1. Inside, he found an article by Lupoff called "The Big Red Cheese," an appreciation of Captain Marvel, which was the first of what became a celebrated series called "All in Color For a Dime." Otto was surprised and obviously pleased and wrote Lupoff a letter that saw print in *Xero* #3: "Let me commend you for a remarkable résumé of the Cap'n's adventures. This all seems of a remote past that itself seems part of another world." The letter was printed in the next issue of *Xero,* thus beginning Binder's involvement with, and encouragement of, the nascent comic fandom movement.

"It never occurred to me that there could be such a thing as comics fans," Binder said in a later interview in *Comic Crusader* #15 (1973). "I know there were science fiction fans and movie fans and such, but—I just assumed people read [comic books] for what they were and threw them away." In an October 18, 1964, letter to comic fandom founder Jerry Bails, Binder asked if comics fans had considered annual comic book conventions similar to the "very successful and colorful Sci-Fi-cons." He suggested such gatherings could attract as many as 10,000 fans.

Binder continued his newfound popularity in the emerging comic fandom when he appeared at the 1965 New York Comicon, one of those conventions he advocated less than a year before. He and comics writer Gardner Fox were on the first event of that convention, a panel at which Bails interviewed the two popular comics writers. At one point in the panel discussions, Binder livened up the crowd when he said, "To be a writer in the comics, you don't have to be a nut—but it helps!"

In the same manner he and Earl had attained a celebrity-like status in the Chicago SF fandom of the late 1930s, Binder became one of the pros who acknowledged and welcomed comics fans' numerous questions and inquiries. He often would invite them to his home and talk comics for hours with these young, enthusiastic fans. "The really surprising thing was how big the movement got," Binder said in the 1973 interview in *Comic Crusader*. "And then all the fanzines. I felt like I was suddenly doused by fans."

Otto graciously contributed to fanzines like *Xero, Fantasy Illustrated, Alter Ego, Shazam* and *Fighting Hero Comics* in one form or another. Binder was the focus of a feature in *Alter Ego* #9 called "Otto in Binderland." It discussed Binder's writing stint at Fawcett's *Captain Marvel*, including photos of folks like C.C. Beck. The piece also printed samples of a "Tawky Tawny" comic strip that Binder and Beck created but were unable to sell.

In 1963, California comics fan Bill Spicer contacted Binder about adapting some of his SF stories in a new fanzine he was planning, *Fantasy Illustrated*. Unfortunately, Spicer had a big problem; he couldn't pay Binder to use them. Understanding how fandom worked, Binder agreed to allow Spicer adaptation rights for some of his stories. Spicer himself drew a Jon Jarl of the Space Police story "World of Vampires" for *Fighting Hero Comics* #3, then in the first issue of *Fantasy Illustrated*, a young Alan Weiss drew "The Ancient Secret," another Jon Jarl story. Perhaps the story that had the biggest impact was the Spicer-D. Bruce Berry adaptation of a chapter in Eando Binder's "I, Robot" saga from the pulps. "Adam Link's Vengeance" appeared as a two-parter *in Fantasy Illustrated* #1 and #2. It proved to be very popular and forged a link between comics and their distant cousin, science fiction.

There is no doubt that Binder, as a long-time professional comics writer, provided comic fandom with a big boost by his participation and endorsement of the growing group. Early fans craved input from their heroes and had many questions they wanted to ask about how comics were made and the thought behind their favorite characters and stories. Binder graciously provided that link between professionals and fans, as well as the past and the present. Binder rightly can be named one of the heroes who helped found comic fandom. Without him, the rise of fandom may have been slower and certainly not nearly as fun.

Steve Ditko

(b. 1927)

Ask fans to describe Steve Ditko and they'll most certainly say he co-created Spider-Man and Doctor Strange for Marvel, but it would be a surprise if they didn't also mention tales of his elusive and hermit-like existence. That perception isn't entirely accurate. While Ditko has protected his privacy for many years, in the early days of fandom he was as encouraging and cooperative as any professional in the business. He attended a convention, answered fan letters, offered free drawings to fans, gave interviews to fanzines and even welcomed fans into his home during a time when many of his peers were leery of those enthusiastic youngsters who seemingly popped up out of nowhere.

In his early years, Steve Ditko reportedly gained a love of newspaper comics partly inspired by his father, who was a fan of Hal Foster's "Prince Valiant." He found he had a talent for drawing and soon the youngster graduated to comic books like *Batman* and *The Spirit*. While in the Army, he drew for various base newspapers and, after his discharge, he went to New York to seek work as an artist. His first comics work was published in 1953 in *Daring Love* #1, a story called "Paper Love." He got the break of being employed by the Jack Kirby/Joe Simon shop, where he worked with famed comics artist Mort Meskin. Ditko had some work published through the Simon and Kirby shop, then began to freelance to such companies as Marvel and Charlton. Ditko ended up working for decades at Charlton, drawing such popular heroes as Captain Atom, Blue Beetle and The Question, as well as hundreds of science fiction and mystery stories. He also had legendary stints at Marvel and DC, where he created or co-created (and drew) such titles as *Amazing Spider-Man*, "Doctor Strange" in *Strange Tales*, *Speedball*, *Hawk & Dove*, *The Creeper* and *Shade, The Changing Man*. All the while, he wrote and drew his own pieces or strips that he self-published or had published in fanzines, many of them featuring a character called Mr. A, inspired by the objectivist philosophy of Ayn Rand that Ditko had been following. Whether he was always understood or not, Ditko has been a principled artist, not afraid to walk away from a project when he believed he was being compromised.

In the early 1960s, when fans began to make contact with one another and professionals (mostly through the mails), Ditko wasn't the reclusive person he became in later years. Along with Lee and Kirby, he was one of the "big guns" at Marvel, attracting a lot of praise and attention. Fans wrote him and he wrote back. He also appeared at the 1964 New York Comicon, the first and only appearance Ditko has made at a fan event. He even contributed an illustration to the program book. Fanzines Ditko drew covers or inside artwork for in the 1960s included an incredible cover for *All-Stars*, and contributions to *Alter Ego*, *Aurora*, *Champion*, *Comic Crusader*, *Comic Fan*, *Comic Fandom Monthly*, *The Comic Reader* (five covers), *Gosh Wow*, *Gremlin*, *Inside Comix*, *Komix Heroes of the Future*, *Rapport*, *Realm*, *Sense of Wonder*, *Super Adventures*, *The Collector* and *Yancy Street Journal*. That is hardly the output of someone who wanted nothing to do with fans. In *Voice of Comicdom* #4, April 1965, Ditko wrote a letter disagreeing with using the phrase "Best Liked" when talking about comics or fanzines. "What is Best Liked by readers is what they are most familiar in seeing, and any policy based on readers likes has to end up with a lot of look-a-like strips," Ditko wrote. "You have a great opportunity to show everyone a whole new range of ideas, unlimited types of stories and styles—why *flub* it!"

He also gave a few interviews to fanzines, the first in 1965 in Larry Herndon's *Comic Fan* #2 and then in Bob Greene's *Rapport II* in 1966. In the *Comics Fan* interview, conducted by Gary Martin, Ditko was asked what he would recommend to a young artist wanting to break into comics. "Learn what is right and wrong about drawing or art. Practicing bad habits is an awful waste. Everything today, whether it's a light bulb or the English language—or a car—is the result of people building on the knowledge of people before us. Everyone adding something of their own." In *Marvel Main* #4, 1968, Mark Canterbury interviewed Ditko. In the piece entitled, *Steve Ditko, Man of Mystery*, Canterbury asked Ditko why he had become so elusive. "It just happens because I'm a cartoonist in the comic-book business, not a performer or personality in show business. When I do a job, it's not my personality that I'm offering the readers, but my artwork. It's not what I'm like that counts, it's what I did and how well it was done. I produce a product, a comic art story." At the end, Canterbury asked Ditko for some personal information like where he was born and about his family. Ditko cleverly responded, "Like you said, man of mystery."

Ditko is a well-decorated creator, writer and artist who was inducted into the Jack Kirby Hall of Fame in 1990 and also into the Will Eisner Hall of Fame in 1993. He and Stan Lee won the 1962 Alley Award for Best Short Story, "Origin of Spider-Man" in *Amazing Fantasy* #15. Spider-Man garnered at least ten additional Alleys over the years. He also was presented the Inkpot Award at the Comic-Con International in 1987, and Renegade press publisher Deni Loubert accepted it on his behalf. According to Blake Bell's *Strange and Stranger: The World of Steve Ditko*, Ditko had her return the award and say: "Awards bleed the artist and make us compete against each other. They are the most horrible things in the world. How dare you accept this on my behalf?"

Despite anyone's opinion on how forthcoming Steve Ditko needed to be with fans interested in what made him tick, the fact is he's chosen to be who he is, and he's more than earned that right. Yet, he provided a crucial link to fans in the early 1960s, and considerable encouragement, when comic fandom was taking root. He reached out on many occasions, and provided an example that other professionals undoubtedly saw and, perhaps, followed.

Jules Feiffer
(b. 1929)

Jules Feiffer played a most curious role in the development of comic fandom. While he is an internationally known, award-winning cartoonist and cut his teeth working on "The Spirit" in Will Eisner's shop, Feiffer's importance to the development of fandom mainly revolves around a book he wrote reminiscing about the popular superheroes of his youth. Feiffer's *The Great Comic Book Heroes* (Dial Press, 1965) was one of the key elements in giving comic books credibility in the eye of the public.

Like other cartoonists, Feiffer was seen to have an ability to draw as a young child. He won a gold medal at the age of seven from a New York department store for his drawing of movie cowboy hero Tom Mix arresting an outlaw, according to Feiffer's introduction in *The Great Comic Book Heroes*. He loved the comic strips and read them in the pages of the *World-Telegram*, which his father brought home. He wanted to read "Terry and the Pirates," but that strip appeared in the *Daily News*, which his family wouldn't allow in the house because of his parent's political beliefs. Jules attended the Art Students League at the age of 15 and later went to the Pratt Institute. Shortly after leaving school in 1946, he found a job working for Will Eisner's comics shop. "He said I was worth absolutely nothing, but if I wanted to hang out there, and erase pages or do go-fer work, that was fine," Feiffer recounted in an interview in the August 1988 issue of *The Comics Journal*. Soon Feiffer was assisting Eisner in writing and laying out "The Spirit" Sunday strip. He also was able to create a comic strip called "Clifford" that was included with "The Spirit" comics sections. Feiffer worked for Eisner until 1951, when he was drafted into the Army. After his discharge, he focused on his cartooning career and began contributing to *The Village Voice*, a job that lasted 42 years and resulted in fame and more than 20 books. Along the way, he wrote the highly successful play *Little Murders*, illustrated the childrens' book *The Phantom Tollbooth*, and wrote screenplays for Mike Nichols' film *Carnal Knowledge* and Robert Altman's film *Popeye*, among other non-cartooning endeavors.

There are many reasons Feiffer's *The Great Comic Book Heroes* is so effective, and one of them is clearly that he was there as a young kid when comic books with all-new material like *Detective Comics* and *Superman* were beginning to appear on the newsstands. In his introduction, Feiffer describes his reaction to those first "real" comic books: "*Detective Comics* was the first of the originals to be devoted to a single theme—crime fighting. And it looked different. Crime was fought in larger panels, fewer to a page. Most stories were complete in that issue (no more of the accursed 'to be continued'). And a lot less shilly-shallying before getting down to the action." Feiffer also said that these new comic books "didn't have the class of the daily strips but, to me, this enhanced their value."

The Great Comic Book Heroes featured story examples—in full color—of all the icons of the Golden Age of comics: Superman, Captain Marvel, Batman, Human Torch, The Flash, Green Lantern, The Spectre, Hawkman, Wonder Woman, Sub-Mariner, Captain America, Plastic Man and The Spirit. In his text, he also compared these heroes to other comic book features of the time. Yet, the most important thing was that he named names. He talked about the writers and artists of the time like Jerry Seigel, Joe Shuster, Bob Kane, Joe Simon, Jack Kirby, and Will Eisner. He also wrote about some of the creators who were, as yet, little-known to many of the young fans in the 1960s: Charles Biro, Fred Guardineer, Creig Flessel and Will Ely.

Feiffer compared the various heroes and put their uniqueness into perspective. "Superman had only to wake up in the morning to be Superman. Clark Kent was the put-on…" and "What made Batman interesting, then, was not his strength but his story line. Batman, as a feature, was infinitely better plotted, better villained, and better looking than Superman."

One cannot overestimate the impact of Feiffer's book on the birth of the comic book industry. It not only brought these old heroes (some of whom were being revived) to the public attention, but also gave comics fans of the 1960s a source of pride that their favorite medium was now being held up as a hardback book listed on best-seller lists everywhere. Fans also appreciated the book's high-profile defense of comics against the long-time dreaded charges from Dr. Fredric Wertham. Feiffer was aware of fans and described them in the Afterword of the book: "…surprisingly, there are old comic book fans. A small army of them. Men in their thirties and early forties wearing school ties and tweeds, teaching in universities, writing ad copy … who continue to be addicts who save old comic books, buy them, trade them, and will, many of them, pay up to 50 dollars for the first issues of *Superman* or *Batman*; who publish and mail to each other mimeographed 'fanzines'—strange little publications deifying what is looked back on as 'the golden age of comics books.'"

The Great Comic Book Heroes was a literate, colorful book that sang the praises of the wonderful comic books of the past, written by an accomplished cartoonist and thinker. There is no doubt that if Feiffer hadn't written a book like this, someone else would have. However, it would have been unlikely to bear the personal touch and imprimatur of someone with Feiffer's credentials and credibility. In any case, its reprinting of complete Golden Age strips in full color struck like a lightning bolt out of the blue, and made a thundering impact.

Feiffer is one of the most decorated cartoonists alive. Most importantly, he won a Pulitzer Prize for editorial cartooning in 1986. He was elected to the Will Eisner Comic Book Hall of Fame in 2004 and also has been awarded a special George Polk Memorial Award, a Newspaper Guild Page One Award, an Overseas Press Club Award, and a Capital Press Club Award, among many others.

Gardner Fox
(1911–1986)

Gardner Fox was one of the most prominent, prolific writers in comic book history. He was one of the main creators when comic books were born in the late 1930s to begin comics' Golden Age and provided some of the best stories when DC's superheroes were recreated in the early 1960s for the Silver Age. Along the way, Fox wrote for virtually every publisher in the business, including DC, Marvel, Dell, and EC.

Fox began writing for DC Comics in the late 1930s, sometimes under a variety of pseudonyms, beginning with *Detective Comics* #4. Some of the early characters he worked on included Speed Saunders and Batman, where he came up with the idea for the Batarang. Fox is credited with co-creating some of the most enduring superheroes in the industry. Some of those include The Flash, Sandman, Starman, Dr. Fate, Hawkman and Hawkgirl, and Johnny Thunder. He also was one of the main writers on the Justice Society of America comic book, *All-Star Comics*. Fox was versatile as a writer, so when the superhero books waned in popularity in the late 1940s, he felt comfortable writing everything from science fiction and westerns to romance and teen comics. He didn't limit his writing to comic books. He wrote novels beginning in 1944, turning out about one a year until 1984, and in 1974 alone he produced 12 novels. Fox estimated he wrote more than 4,000 comic book stories during the course of his career, and well over 50 million words in all.

Gardner Francis Cooper Fox became smitten with the worlds of science fiction and fantasy at an early age. During an interview session with Phil Seuling at the 1971 New York Comicon, Fox said he was about 11 years old when he received two Edgar Rice Burroughs books, *The Gods of Mars* and *The Warlord of Mars*. He told Seuling those books opened up a complete new world for him. He went on to read all of Burroughs books and just about anything similar he could get his hands on. In 1935, Fox graduated from St. John's College with a law degree and was admitted to the New York state bar. However, with the Great Depression putting great restraints on job opportunities, Fox turned to writing professionally to help pay the bills. He wrote a variety of stories for the pulp and SF magazines of the day, then hooked up with Vin Sullivan at DC Comics. He was off on a very busy and successful writing career.

In the 1950s, he began a lengthy correspondence with Jerry Bails, a dedicated fan of the Justice Society of America, who wanted to know as much as possible about his favorite comic book. Fox eventually sold Bails his personal back issues of *All-Star Comics*. Later, Jerry would state that the values of egalitarianism, fairness, the quest for justice and team spirit of the JSA were an inspiration to him as a youth, and attributed those aspects of the comic book to Fox.

Fox also played a crucial role in the evolution of comic fandom in 1960 when he introduced two of the most prominent names in fan history to each other, Jerry Bails and Roy

Thomas. Working together, the two fans launched *Alter-Ego* in 1961. Fox continued to offer them encouragement in the coming years.

Perhaps one of the scripter's greatest contributions to comic fandom was a huge creative shot-in-the-arm for the comic book industry as a whole. In *The Flash* #123, September 1961, he wrote "Flash of Two Worlds," introducing the concept that the Golden Age Flash and other superheroes from the past still existed on a parallel planet, Earth-2, and could interact with their Silver Age counterparts. He expanded on that theory in the two-part "Crisis on Earths 1 and 2," in the *Justice League of America* Alley Award–winning story. Through the parallel Earth theory, Fox gave fans what they had been clamoring for all along—a chance to see some of the great Golden Age heroes in the current issues of their favorite Silver Age comic books. It also gave comics publishers a hook to not only use older popular characters, but also to create new ones on what has become a bevy of parallel worlds in their various universes.

Fans appreciated Fox's work, who was generally their favorite writer from DC comics in the early 1960s. He won Alley Awards in 1962 for "Best Script Writer" and "Best Book-Length Story" ("The Planet That Came to a Standstill" in *Mystery in Space* #75); "Favorite Novel" ("Crisis on Earths 1 and 2" in *Justice League of America* #21 and #22) in 1963; and "Best Novel" ("Solomon Grundy Goes on a Rampage" in *Showcase* #55) in 1965.

Fox did more in fandom's early days than write exciting stories and answer fan letters. He appeared at several early conventions, most notably the 1965 New York Comicon and the 1971 New York Comic Art Convention, and was interviewed on panels at both. When asked by a member of the audience in 1971 what advice Fox would give to someone who wanted to break into comics as a writer, he replied he would recommend not choosing comics as a career. He said if one really wanted to get into the business, "…study the way the script goes, in terms of dramatics." In the transcript published in the 1972 New York Comic Art Con program book, he said, "Concentrate on telling the story the best way you can—what is the most interesting way, what is your approach, your viewpoint."

In 1998, Fox was posthumously inducted into the Jack Kirby Hall of Fame and given the Harvey Award for his career body of work. In 1999, he was also posthumously inducted into the Eisner Hall of Fame. He was the honored guest at the 1971 New York Comic Art Convention and received an Inkpot Award in 1978 at the San Diego Comic-Con. He also was given the Jules Verne Award for "life-time achievement" in 1982 at Skycon II.

His fan legacy can best be seen in the continuing existence of *Alter Ego*, a magazine that started when Mr. Fox introduced Mr. Thomas to Mr. Bails. The rest is history.

Bill Gaines
(1922–1992)

Leave it to the eccentric genius of the comic book industry to create an open-door policy for fans, seeking their support and approval for his comics. William Gaines understood that his readers appreciated quality stories and art in EC Comics and *Mad* magazine and trumpeted that philosophy wherever he went. Alternately viewed as a cheapskate and a generous soul, Gaines was one of the smartest, most unique and successful publishers in comic book history.

Gaines was born into comic book royalty. His father, Max Gaines, who began packaging premium comics in 1933, put together *Famous Funnies* #1 several years later, and then *Popular Comics*. Max saw the rejected "Superman" daily strip, had Sheldon Mayer paste it together in comic book form, and presented it to Harry Donenfeld, head of DC Comics. That interaction led Max Gaines to create All-American Comics, which was financially linked to DC, then formed Educational Comics (EC) that published among other titles, *Picture Stories from the Bible*. Max was killed August 20, 1947, in a boating accident, leaving the EC Comics business to his son, a reluctant Bill Gaines. By the end of 1949, EC was publishing just six titles and going nowhere. In his book, *The Mad World of William M. Gaines*, Frank Jacobs tells the story of how during a crisis at the company at that time, Gaines rang the doorbell of Sheldon Mayer at three A.M., looking for advice. Mayer, who thought Gaines was taking the business lightly, said he would go nowhere unless he stopped treating the company like a toy. It was a scant few months later that Gaines and editor Al Feldstein came up with a plan to change EC and enter the market with a unique brand of horror comics.

As EC grew in popularity and *Mad* (first the comic book, then the magazine) burst onto the scene, Gaines, took pride in forming a "family" of writers and artists working for him. Jacobs wrote that when the National Cartoonists Society honored *Mad*'s writers and artists in 1972, Milton Caniff asked Gaines how the quality at *Mad* was kept so high year after year. Gaines answered, "The same way you keep doing it—talent." The Internet Movie Database quoted Gaines humbly defining the success of EC: "My staff creates the magazines; all I provide is the atmosphere." In the 1950s, when many magazines were published monthly, Gaines had *Mad* rolling out just eight times a year, or every 45 days. Gaines wanted to put out a quality magazine, and concluded his staff "could not do their jobs efficiently if it was published more frequently."

If EC's writers and artists talked fondly of Gaines' treatment of them, the fans were off the charts in their embracing EC's comics and *Mad*. Beginning when EC's comic books were riding high, fans showed up unannounced at the EC offices just to say "hello" and talk to their favorite artists. Editors and contributors to the EC fanzines of that era visited Gaines' office, generally by appointment, to get some information or gossip for their publications. One reader, Larry Stark, wrote critical letters that so impressed Gaines, he gave him a lifetime subscription. Stark later became a well-known Boston theater critic.

In addition to an open-door policy, Gaines appealed to fans by starting the EC Fan-Addict Club. For 25 cents, a reader could become a member, get a newsletter and an occasional surprise in the mail. Membership included a $7\frac{1}{2} \times 10\frac{1}{2}$ full-color framable membership certificate, a wallet-sized ID card, a patch for a shirt or jacket and a membership pin. In the club newsletters, Gaines printed names and addresses of fans so they could correspond with one another and trade back issues. Profiles of EC's top artists that often were published on the inside front covers of the comics and letter pages became an important component to the books. What was unique was EC treated its fans like they were buddies who lived down the street. They kidded them, laughed with them and allowed them to be in on the joke, most of the time. So, it is no surprise that amongst this mutual admiration society, EC fanzines proliferated. There was Jimmy Taurasi's *Fantasy-Comics*, which began in late 1952 and lasted 15 issues; it contained news of all the SF-theme comic books being published, including those of EC. Bhob Stewart's *EC Fan Bulletin* was the first fanzine devoted totally to EC comics, appearing in the summer of 1953. Soon, there was a bevy of EC fanzines being mailed out to loyal fan subscribers, many of them dedicated to and modeled after *Mad*.

On April 19, 1953, the Fan-Vet Convention was held by the Fantasy Veterans Association. Gaines and most of the EC staff were there, including popular artist Wally Wood, who displayed the original art to *My World*, which had not yet been published. Almost 20 years later, in 1972, the EC Fan Addict Convention was held in New York, drawing a large number of fans, Gaines and many of the EC bullpen. Jacobs wrote that when Nostalgia Press's large reprint of the best of EC stories was published in the early 1970s, Gaines was not only proud, but felt vindicated from the many complimentary letters he received about the book, mostly from former readers during the 1950s.

However, with all the adulation and quality aside, it was Gaines' stand against censorship and the U.S. Congress when comic books came under fire that is most appreciated by all fans. Even though it was his horror comics that were front-and-center and his company that was on the line, Gaines appeared before the Congressional panel to fight the demonizing of comic books. He spoke eloquently in defense of comics, forcefully attacked their critics and spoke out against censorship. However, the publicity surrounding the hearings hurt Gaines and led him to change the lineup of EC to the New Direction books which didn't catch on, and then the Picto-Fiction titles that also failed. In the end, Gaines only had *Mad* left—but what a leftover it turned out to be. *Mad* was so successful that it more than carried the company until it was sold for tax purposes in the 1970s. When the Comics Code Authority was formed, Gaines joined, but quit after less than six months. Jacobs said Gaines' detested the Comics Code because it represented censorship.

He was posthumously inducted into the Eisner Hall of Fame in 1993 and the Kirby Hall of Fame in 1997. He also received the Inkpot Award in 1990.

As a man who owned the company that published some of the finest comic books ever sold and battled tirelessly for the independence of the industry, Gaines is certainly atop the mountain of heroes for comics fans. However, it is his active encouragement of fans and fanzines that guaranteed him an entry in this book.

Stan Lee

(b. 1922)

Stan Lee is the perfect pitchman for not just Marvel Comics, but every thrilling, super, adventurous, hyperbole-filled comic book ever printed. Whether it was from behind his desk in the Marvel offices in the 1960s or through the thousands of interviews he's given over the years, Lee has proven that he loves the comics with all his heart and, even more so, the legion of fans who read them. Lee has become more than just a writer and editor who created or co-created some of the most enduring superheroes and villains in comic book history. He became the public face and spokesman for all the superhero comics and the fun that they bring. His lifetime of accomplishments and awards would overlow the Baxter Building, the headquarters of the Fantastic Four.

As a young teenager in New York, Stanley Lieber helped his struggling family by working an array of part-time jobs, including writing press releases and obituaries for a news service. At the age of 17, he got help in finding a job with Timely Comics as an assistant editor under Joe Simon. Lee's cousin was married to Martin Goodman, publisher of the comics and pulp magazine line. Young Stan began writing text features, stories and eventually co-created his first superhero, The Destroyer, in 1941. It was around this time that he decided to use a pen name on his comics work, choosing the easy-to-remember Stan Lee. "I felt someday I'd write the great American novel and I didn't want to use my real name on these silly little comics," Lee has often said.

After the boom of the early years of comics, Timely went through alternating good and bad times. During the 1950s, the business model of the company was to seize on the latest "hot fad" in the industry and quickly publish their own version of it. Lee wrote and edited many hundreds of comic books ranging from teenage hijinks to funny animal adventures and war comics. In the late 1950s, Timely was known for its comic book monsters that sported a litany of strange, unpronounceable names. As legend has it, during a golf game in 1959, Goodman heard of the success of DC's *Justice League of America* comic book and suggested his editor give the superhero genre another try. The small publishing firm exploded into success behind Lee's co-creations of such characters as the Fantastic Four, the Amazing Spider-Man, Iron Man, Thor, Doctor Strange, X-Men, Ant Man, Sgt. Fury and so many more. Lee didn't just write about regular superheroes. Marvel's twist was that its heroes argued, had financial troubles, weren't always popular and struggled with the frustrations of life, despite their superpowers. It not only proved successful, but young fans loved these stories of heroes who had as many problems as they did. Lee was smart enough to incorporate the growing Marvel fan base into his plans.

Stan Lee used the letter columns to relate to the fans personally, just as he did in captions and asides throughout the cover and story itself. The "Fantastic Four Fan Page" published many letters from members of fandom, and a few plugs for fanzines such as *The Comicollector*. These text features, which quickly were instituted in every Marvel title, reflected Stan's happy-go-lucky approach to fans, cracking jokes and even identifying his staff with friendly nicknames like "jolly" and "dashing." Lee credits boys books author Leo Edwards' style in his *Jerry Todd* and *Poppy Ott* books he read as a kid for influencing Marvel's style. In an interview with *ZineZone*, Lee said: "At the end of the book ... the author had pages where he would talk to the reader and he would print some letters. In fact, that's what gave me the idea to do the Bullpen pages in the comics years later." Until it became too costly, Marvel sent postcards from "Stan & the Gang," thanking readers for their letters and sometimes giving a short answer to a question.

When the comicons began in New York City, Stan initially seemed reluctant to attend. There was great disappointment at the 1964 and 1965 New York Comicons when, although Marvel had a presence, Lee did not show up. He learned from that and made a point at attending the 1966 event and many of the future New York fan gatherings, even if only for a panel or a short visit to talk. Talk to the readers in the Bullpen he did! As the 1960s progressed, Marvel added his "Stan's Soapbox" column to the "Bullpen Bulletin" page that ran through all their titles. The bulletin provided items of news, notes and announcements. In "Stan's Soapbox," he alternately pitched new projects, answered fan questions, and occasionally offered opinions on the current issues of the day. In a 1968 "Soapbox," Lee used his familiar pitch-personality to tell readers about a forthcoming *Amazing Spider-Man* magazine (all exclamation marks are Lee's): "Okay, we admit it! We just can't keep a secret! We're so excited about our newest and most ambitious project that we've GOT to tell you about it, or we'll just plain bust!" A year later, Lee took a more serious tact in answering questions about how ideas are formulated at Marvel: "Strangely enough, the answer usually proves surprising. The point is, ideas are no problem ... the big hangup is getting the time to develop the ideas ... to polish them, and refine them...." The effect of the letter columns, "Bullpen Bulletins" and "Stan's Soapbox" was to employ Stan's friendly, conversational style to make readers comfortable and enthusiastic about all things Marvel. This made fans feel a part of the process and therefore important. Lee treated the fans with respect.

When Stan hired Roy Thomas as a writer and assistant editor in 1965, fandom sat up, took notice, and followed Roy's progress at Marvel closely. Thomas made good, and was soon writing many of their favorite books. Though Lee's decision to hire Thomas had to do with the younger man's energy and talent, as well as his credentials as a former English teacher, Stan got points with fandom for giving one of their own such a terrific opportunity. He also gave other young writers a chance (such as Larry Ivie and Gary Friedrich) which gave aspiring young writers (and artists) in fandom reason to believe they could break into Marvel some day.

Without question, the Marvel characters and style brought more fans to comic books and fandom than any other event. They liked what Marvel offered and how they presented their comics, so they latched on and many of them stayed for the long run. Perhaps Lee put it best in his *Comic Book Artist* interview with Roy Thomas in 1998: "I had done my best to build up Marvel, and as much as I may have contributed to Marvel's success with any stories, editing, or creating characters, I think equally as valuable was the advertising, promotion, publicity, and huckstering that I did, traveling around the country and talking about Marvel, trying to give it the right image."

Stan Lee has received dozens of fan awards through the years and has won virtually every comics-related honor available. He was inducted into the Will Eisner Hall of Fame in 1994 and the Jack Kirby Hall of Fame the next year. He received his own star on the Hollywood Walk of Fame in 2008 and later that same year was awarded the National Medal of Arts. On his certificate for the Medal of Arts, it reads, "His complex plots and humane superheroes celebrate courage, honesty, and the importance of helping the less fortunate, reflecting America's inherent goodness."

Russ Manning
(1929–1981)

Russ Manning is best known for his comic book and comic strip work on two literary icons: Tarzan and Star Wars. A third, which he created, *Magnus, Robot Fighter*, has also garnered passionate fans. Manning's beginnings are clearly linked to Edgar Rice Burroughs' famed Ape Man.

Young Russell Manning learned to draw by copying various characters in books and newspaper comic strips. Manning's first exposure to Tarzan came with the Big Little Book, *The Beasts of Tarzan*, according to Bill and Sue-On Hillmans' *ERBzine*. He began reading the Tarzan series of books by Burroughs and soon found such offshoots as the "Tarzan" Sunday comic strip, the Tarzan movies and eventually science-fiction novels. His design of a "bus of the future" earned him $100 in a high-school art contest. Manning attended the Los Angeles County Art Institute and, while in the Army, he drew for the base newspaper in Japan.

Manning was a fan of both of ERB novels and comic strips, joining the National Fantasy Fan Federation (N3F) and contributing some of his first fan drawings to Vern Coriell's *Burroughs Bulletin* in July 1947. His work was instantly popular, so he gladly provided a number of drawings to various fan publications. He teamed with friend and artist Jerri Bullock to publish their own fanzine, *Fan Artisan*, in May 1948. The fanzine included a biography of Manning, in which he listed Lawrence Sterne Stevens, Edd Cartier, and Robert Gibson Jones as his favorite artists.

He began working for the west coast office of Western Publishing in 1953, drawing a wide assortment of comic book stories for Dell Comics throughout the 1950s. His first main feature was "Brothers of the Spear," a backup strip in the *Tarzan* comic book. When Western cut off its association with Dell in the early 1960s and began publishing its own comics under the Gold Key symbol, Manning blossomed as an artist and writer. He began drawing the main stories in *Tarzan* and, in 1963, co-created *Magnus, Robot Fighter*, writing (for the most part) and drawing the first 21 issues. One thing Manning was noted for was hiding his name or initials in his Dell Comics work, since they did not allow artists to sign their work. Fans enjoyed searching for familiar names throughout Manning's work, often times discovering his name on signs, buildings, pieces of paper and storefronts.

Manning contributed to a number of comics fanzines, including an illustration for the month of December in the *Super Hero Calendar* (1963), an illustration for *Alter Ego* #6 (March 1964), and an essay about Jesse Marsh, "Model T to T-Bird" in *Batmania* #1 (July 1964). He also had letters in *Alter Ego*, *Comic Art* and *Dateline: Comicdom*. He went as far as hosting a fan gathering at his home in California in 1964, attended by such big-named fans as Bill Spicer, Richard Kyle, Glen Johnson and Rick Durell.

To his great delight, Russ was chosen in 1967 to draw the "Tarzan" daily and Sunday comic strip, which curtailed much of his comic book work. He later drew comic book stories for the ERB overseas publishing unit. Manning began the "Star Wars" daily and Sunday comic strip in 1979, and drew it until he fell ill in 1980.

Russ was happy with his life as an artist, he told reporter Cheryl Addams for an article about his comics career in the January 27, 1971 issue of the *Register*. "There are other things I could do to make more money, probably ... [but] this is what I always wanted to do." In an interview with Shel Dorf in *Menomonee Falls Gazette* (vol. 4, #186, July 7, 1975), Manning said he learned about his strengths and weaknesses while in high school. "I have always drawn, of course, and being the 'best' artist in high school tilted me toward a career in art ... as opposed to music, say, where several classmates out blew me," he told Dorf. Later, he realized the limitations he faced as an artist. "I found out in art school and college that I wasn't fad- [or] chic-oriented enough to make it in advertising art ... and I was still buying comic books long after my buddies had switched to beer."

For the most part, Manning was one of the most accessible artists in the business for fans, probably because in many ways, he stayed a fan at heart. Plus, he grew up working for fanzines and publishing his own, so he understood how fans needed to know all about their favorite writers and artists.

Manning was posthumously inducted into the Comic Book Hall of Fame in 2006. Shortly after his death, the West Coast Comics Club and Comic-Con International in San Diego created the Russ Manning Promising Newcomer Award for the best new comics artist. In 1982, one of Manning's former assistants, Dave Stevens, was given the first award.

Julius Schwartz
(1915–2004)

Of all the professionals who helped jump-start comic fandom, none was more influential than DC editor Julius Schwartz. He brought back the Golden Age heroes in high style, plugged the fanzines that celebrated them, and gave fans a means of contacting one another by printing full addresses in his letter columns.

Julius Schwartz's young life in the 1920s in New York City was filled with SF pulps and dime novels. Then he saw a letter from Mort Weisinger in *Amazing Stories* announcing the formation of The Scienceers, an SF club in the Bronx. Schwartz was thrilled and jumped at the chance to join, sending in a penny postcard, only to be turned down by the club because he was not yet 16 years old. He had to wait a year to join, eventually becoming close friends with Weisinger. He eagerly offered to help with the club's fanzine, *The Time Traveller* (subtitled "Science Fiction's Only Fan Magazine"). The first issue appeared in January 1932 and is considered the second fanzine in SF fandom. It was six pages long and printed on a mimeograph. Schwartz was managing editor, Weisinger was associate editor and Forrest J Ackerman, who lived in Los Angeles, was contributing editor. Like all good fans, Schwartz and Weisinger visited the New York offices of the SF magazines and pulps, gathering news, receiving advance copies of their publications and getting to know the editors and staff members. Eventually, Schwartz and Weisinger formed Solar Sales Service, an agency that would promote stories by SF writers to the various New York publications. The agency allowed them to visit writers around the country and attend SF conventions. At the 1939 World Science Fiction Convention, Schwartz brought a number of Solar Sales clients as guests. Schwartz continued reading fanzines and going to SF fan meetings while operating the literary agency until he joined the All-American Comics Group.

Schwartz was the archetypal fan turned pro, moving from joining Mort Weisinger in an agency selling SF writers' stories to becoming an editor at All-American Comics. DC Comics eventually took over the All-American group and Schwartz remained with that company for 42 years, retiring in 1986. He edited a variety of comics ranging from SF to superheroes, but his claim to fame was being at the head of the revival of characters like The Flash, Green Lantern and other Golden Age heroes at the dawn of the Silver Age of comic books. After a tryout comic book named *Showcase* floundered with its first three issues, Schwartz suggested reviving The Flash, a character he edited in the Golden Age. It was a success, and more followed.

As a long-time SF fan, comics editor Schwartz didn't have to be schooled in the basics of fandom and how devoted readers can become fully absorbed in the books he was editing. Comic fandom founder Jerry Bails sent him a number of letters early on about the newly revived *Justice League of America* and *The Flash*, making suggestions and asking questions. When he asked about purchasing back issues of *All-Star Comics*, Schwartz gave Gardner Fox's address to Bails, which led to a long correspondence between the fan and the writer. Likewise, it was Schwartz who put Roy Thomas in touch with Gardner Fox, who in turn put him in touch with Jerry Bails. That act alone set into motion a friendship that would help cement a cornerstone of comic fandom. During a fateful visit to New York City in February 1961, Jerry Bails received Schwartz's support for what he found out was called a "fanzine," and was shown copies of *Xero*, which encouraged Bails to think bigger than just putting out a sheet promoting the Justice League of America. Thus was born *Alter-Ego*. Later, it was Schwartz who suggested that Thomas plug *Alter-Ego* in the letter column of *JLA* #8. The response was such a success that Bails and Thomas's first issue was sold out and then some. Such an assist to fans was typical in Schwartz letter columns. Miami fan G.B. Love helped get *The Rocket's Blast* off and running through a plug in *Mystery in Space*, and a later one in *Justice League of America*. When Hawkman was to be revived in *Brave and Bold* #34, Julie went so far as to send advance copies of the first issue so that he would be able to get letters from the new, mature fans he was meeting for a letter column with the second Hawkman issue.

Julius Schwartz was, in fact, going against existing policy at DC Comics. In an earlier contact with DC, a youthful Roy Thomas had been informed that trading and selling old comics could not be officially sanctioned by the company, for it might spread disease. They didn't run full addresses in their letter columns until Julie broke the policy, no doubt because they feared their young readers might receive unwanted mail. Schwartz brushed these concerns aside, to the benefit of fandom. After all, wasn't the ring leader of the new comic fandom a college professor, and his associate a college student-cum-schoolteacher? And wasn't that how he, Schwartz, had gotten involved in SF fandom so many years ago, through a letter column? Julie understood that giving true fans a way to communicate not only helped the sales of his books, but created a base to work with for future projects. In fact, he took pride in it. In his biography, *Man of Two Worlds*, Schwartz wrote: "So, not just being satisfied to be one of the founding fathers of science fiction fandom, I can also claim the honor of having been a seminal part of the founding of comics fandom, as well." In fact, Schwartz never lost his fan "sense of wonder" and so described one of his first meetings with various SF editors in New York City in his biography: "Here were Mort (Weisinger) and I, in touch with all the editors of the professional science fiction magazines in the world. I personally knew the men behind not only *Amazing Stories*, but *Wonder Stories* and *Astounding* as well. They were my idols!"

The most interesting letters in the DC letter columns generally appeared in Julie's books, not only because he catered to the more mature readers, but because he instituted the unheard-of policy of giving away original comic book art to the reader who wrote the most interesting letter. While in retrospect, fans realize that this art should have been returned to its creators, at the time it was accepted that these originals were DC's to dispose of as they pleased, and since the company didn't value them, why shouldn't fans have them? After all, the official policy at the time was to destroy or trash the art since it was just part of the process to achieve the final product, the comic book itself. To think that Schwartz went to the trouble and cared enough to have this art packaged up, and have the company pay the postage, just so that readers would be given these remarkable gifts, bespeaks a generosity of spirit in the man. These early Silver Age originals have sold for huge sums in Sotheby and other auctions, though usually the artwork had long since passed into other hands.

Fandom loved the comic books edited by Julius Schwartz. Every one of the ten awards given in the first Alley Awards poll was given to a Schwartz titles. Though this dominance couldn't last long with the rise of Marvel comics, a number of the books and stories Julie edited won additional Alley honors over the years. As the years rolled on, and Schwartz took on the editing chores first on the Batman, then the Superman titles, he received many honors. He won a pair of Eagle Awards; the 1972 Shazam Award; the Inkpot Award in 1981; and the First Fandom Hall of Fame Award by the SF community at the 1986 WorldCon. Schwartz also has been voted into both the Will Eisner Hall of Fame and the Jack Kirby Hall of Fame. And in 1986, the Atlanta-based DragonCon created the Julie Award in his honor for achievement in multiple genres. Ray Bradbury was the first recipient.

In later years, as Julie regularly worked the comicon circuit, he was continually reminded how his decisions in the late 1950s and early 1960s had such great impact. He met a continual stream of fans, many of them extremely active and having done a lot for fandom themselves, who were brought into the fold by the plugs he ran and through the letter columns he edited.

Jim Steranko

(b. 1938)

Jim Steranko is the renaissance man of comics. He is a creator, publisher, magician, editor, painter, musician, movie storyboard artist, entrepreneur, idea man, graphic designer, colorist, comics historian, and—above all—one of comicdom's legendary writers and artists. He has played a key role in moving fandom from a mimeograph-fanzine culture to one with professionally produced publications that attract interest from all genres.

Born in Reading, Pennsylvania, Steranko, like many artists, found he had a desire and talent to draw at an early age. He studied and copied comics strips by such greats as Hal Foster, Milton Caniff, Alex Raymond and Chester Gould, as well as Disney and Superman comic books. An uncle helped by providing him with boxes of comic books to read. He combined his love of comics with the adventure and mystery films and radio programs of his youth, setting himself on the road to a lifetime passion. By the mid–1960s, he was art director of a small advertising agency and found he had a desire to break into comics. In 1965, he attended the New York comic book convention where he had a table selling comics from his own collection. He submitted some art samples to Marvel Comics, which were turned down. After creating some new superheroes for editor Joe Simon at Harvey Comics, Steranko prepared new samples and made a second trip to Marvel later that year which turned out to be more successful. He was given the Nick Fury, Agent of SHIELD assignment.

Steranko's entrance into the world of professional comics was unusual at the time. The big-time comics companies were essentially a closed-shop in the 1960s, with editors often turning to proven pros or longtime friends to dole out assignments. Steranko's emergence into the comics big-time proved to be an inspiration to young fan artists dreaming of working within the industry. However, he remained modest. During the 1972 Benson interview, Steranko said he didn't classify himself as an artist. "I've said this many times—I do not consider myself an artist. When I think of people who are really artists, I think of Reed Crandall and Neal Adams and maybe a half dozen other people in comics who draw amazingly well. If I had to categorize myself, I would probably say that I belong in the class of the storyteller."

After a four-year, high-profile run on *SHIELD*, *Captain America*, *X-Men*, Marvel's horror titles and an array of covers, Steranko left regular comics to work on his comics history books and pursue other interests including painting and publishing. One project would become especially significant to comic fandom, *The Steranko History of Comics*. Jim interviewed comics legends such as Otto Binder, Stan Lee, Mort Meskin, Chuck Cuidera, C.C. Beck, Jack Binder and Wendell Crowley, among others, putting a personal touch to the chronological history he was writing. The first volume appeared in 1970 and a much larger second volume appeared two years later, both published by Supergraphics, Steranko's publishing firm. These history books represented a quantum leap ahead in fandom's understanding of the way comic books were produced in their early years, how they evolved partly from the pulps and comic strips, and what it was like for the creators to be involved in the field at that time.

Steranko was well aware of how fandom was growing, hiring such fans as Gary Groth and Ken Bruzanek to assist him as his publishing ambitions came into focus. In the summer of 1972, Steranko contacted Miami, Florida, fan Gary Brown about plans to begin a comics newspaper. Brown had been publishing *Comic Comments*, a popular fanzine that reported on comics industry news and reviewed current books. Steranko offered to takeover the subscription list of *Comic Comments* and bring on Brown as editor of the new publication, *Comixscene*. The first issue appeared in November 1972, cost 50 cents and featured a Doc Savage cover drawn by Steranko. It contained 24 pages of news from DC Comics, Marvel, underground, other publishers and even Tarzan news. In his editorial, Steranko wrote: "It seems like there has long been a need for a high-quality news publication designed especially for the comics fan. Some have come close with acceptable material, but were typed by hand and run off on basement mimeo machines." *Comixscene* was going to be something different, Steranko wrote. "Its function is simple: to inform the comic reader of the latest developments in the comic

world, to give him an accurate, concise picture of all the happenings in the industry...."
Comixscene did all that and more, also serving as a device to publicize new Supergraphics projects such as calendars and books. In 1973, Steranko and Supergraphics also published the first four issues of Marvel's fan magazine, *FOOM*. *Comixscene* lasted six issues before morphing into *Mediascene*, which expanded its content to include science fiction, movies, music and television. After issue #40, *Mediascene* became *Prevue*, a slick magazine targeting the adventure movie industry.

Steranko's contributions to fandom are many, but he certainly upped the ante on what fans should expect from the books, magazines and newsletters they buy. He brought better design, crisper writing and a huge upgrade in printing to fandom, all while continuing his career as one of the most talented writers, artists and thinkers in the industry.

Jim Steranko has been the recipient of numerous fan awards. He won three Alley Awards in 1968, including "Best Pencil Artist," "Best Feature Story" ("Today Earth Died," *Strange Tales* #168), and "Best Cover"(*Nick Fury, Agent of SHIELD* #6). He also won 1969 Alleys for Best Feature Story ("At the Stroke of Midnight," *Tower of Shadows* #1) and Best Cover (*Captain America* #113). Also in 1969, he earned Alley Award Hall of Fame honors for his work on *Nick Fury, Agent of SHIELD*. He won a Shazam Award for Outstanding Achievement by an Individual in 1970 for *The Steranko History of Comics* and won the Julie Award at the 2003 DragonCon. The culmination of these awards occurred in 2006 when he was inducted into the Comic Book Hall of Fame, fandom's most prestigious honor.

Wally Wood
(1928–1981)

"Hooray for Wally Wood, he's everybody's favorite, Wally Wood." That "Hooray for Hollywood" song parody by *Mad* magazine's Frank Jacobs says it all. Nobody doesn't like Wally Wood. The versatile artist who plied his talents in all corners of the comics industry for more than four decades made his mark as not just a fan favorite, but also as the ultimate pro's pro.

Wood produced memorable work not just in comic books and comic strips, but in advertising, trading cards, record-album covers, product packaging, gag cartoons and posters, as well. His pro fanzine, *Witzend,* pioneered the melding of comics professionals and comics fans. Despite all his success and talent, Wood dealt with demons in the latter part of his life. In an article in the *EC Fan-Addict Convention Book*, Harvey Kurtzman described Wood this way: "Wally had a tension in him, an intensity that he locked away in an internal steam boiler. I think it ate away his insides, and the work really used him up. I think he delivered some of the finest work that was ever drawn, and I think it's to his credit that he put so much intensity into his work at great sacrifice to himself."

As a young child, Wood read comic strips and began copying them and drawing his own versions. Roy Crane was a favorite artist of his, but he listed Alex Raymond, Hal Foster, Will Eisner and Milton Caniff as influences. In Bhob Stewart's biography of Wood, *Against the Grain: Mad Artist Wallace Wood*, the artist said as a young child he would dream about finding a magic pencil that could draw anything. Wood's mother recognized his talents and collected his early drawings into a book, binding them together on her sewing machine. After his discharge from the Army in 1948, Wood moved to New York, where he worked odd jobs while showing his art portfolio to every publisher he could. A chance meeting with artist John Severin gave Wood a lead on a job Will Eisner had inking backgrounds on "The Spirit." Wood was hired on the spot. It was the beginning of an illustrious career that included work for EC, DC, Marvel, Harvey, Tower, Archie, Gold Key, Warren, Wham-O and numerous others. Wood inked Jack Kirby's pencils on the "Sky Masters" comic strip, did the concept drawings for the cult favorite *Mars Attacks!* Topps trading cards, and did hundreds of random illustration jobs and advertising artwork, not to mention pouring all he had into his own comic stories and projects.

During the comics explosion of the mid–1960s, something began bubbling inside Wood. He long had realized that as a work-for-hire artist, he was inventing characters and visuals for a fee and not sharing in the eventual profits when those creations proved popular and successful. Well aware of the growing comic fandom phenomena through letters, attending conventions and receiving fanzines, Wood realized there was a market out there not tapped by the regular comics publishers. In an attempt to start down the road that might correct this problem for him and other artists and writers, Wood decided to publish his own magazine dedicated to comic art. Inspired by an incomplete publishing project by Dan Adkins (his assistant at the time) called *Outlet Science Fiction*, he conceived of a magazine he first called *Et Cetera* and later changed to *Witzend*. The first issue appeared in 1966, was 40 pages long, printed in black and white, and cost one dollar. He used the goodwill of enthusiastic fanzines to advertise his effort and sold it through the mails. It wasn't distributed in the regular manner by a news dealer. *Witzend* featured four comics stories, including Wood's "Animan," illustrations by a variety of artists and several other features. He wrote about contributors to future issues of *Witzend*, but cautioned readers not to subscribe to the magazine, but just order the second issue in advance. The first issue began with an editorial by Wood offering the magazine's "Statement of NO Policy." "This first issue may be a bit misleading," Wood wrote. "It is a comic book—and it is not. Neither is it a Science Fiction, Fantasy, Monster, Satire or Girlie Book. It is a platform, a vehicle, for any idea in any form." Wood said making money wasn't the aim of his publishing venture, but he and others wanted to own the rights to what they created. "It is … the culmination of a lot of futile fantasies which date back almost 20 years to student days at [Burne] Hogarth's [school] when there was a lot of loose talk about pooling our meager resources and putting out a comic book as sort of a co-operative."

Wood continued *Witzend* and in the fourth issue wrote, "I am going to continue publishing *Witzend*, possibly indefinitely. But definitely up to and including #8." But those plans quickly faded and he soon sold the magazine to fan Bill Pearson for a dollar. Wood continued to contribute to *Witzend* and Pearson published a very good magazine through #13 in 1985. Wood continued working on various publishing projects consisting of his own, original material, but espousing the intent of *Witzend*. Wood's effort produced two results: It led to the glimmer of a dream of a direct market in which comic books and other magazines could be sold independently of regular newsstand distribution; and helped produce a thaw in the cautious approach many pros took to fans and fanzines.

Over the years, Wood hired a number of fan artists as assistants, including Adkins, Roger Brand and Wayne Howard. Adkins went on to work as an inker for Marvel; Brand also worked for Gil Kane and created his own underground comix; Howard had a significant career with Charlton. Howard, who along with his brother Sherman, published the fanzine *Action Hero*, was the most Wood-like of all his assistants. Wood also wrote many of his fan and fanzine editors letters, giving his opinions of the comics industry and his own works. In Stewart's biography of Wood, Nick Cuti and Paul Kirschner, during a meeting of Wood's former assistants, fans and friends, talked about the one comment from fans that always would get Wood defensive: "Your old stuff was better," meaning his more cluttered EC work was better than what he did later in his career. "He used to resent that tremendously, because he felt he was a much better artist," Cuti said. "And he learned to simplify his art and really make it good. He resented that a lot when the fans said that."

Wood was posthumously inducted into the Jack Kirby Hall of Fame in 1989 and the Will Eisner Hall of Fame in 1992. He won Alley Awards for "Best Pencil Artist" in 1965 and "Best Inking Work" in 1966; he was named winner of the National Cartoonist Society's Comic Book Division in 1957, 1959 and 1965 and won the "Best Foreign Cartoonist" honors at the Angouleme International Comics Festival in 1978.

It would take literally hundreds of pages to do justice to all of Wood's work and accomplishments over his career. Ask any of his fans what their favorite Wood story or drawing was and they would offer you a many different answers, all of them correct. Without a doubt, Wood was a man with innumerable visions, far too many of them left unrealized. However, his concept of and participation in comics fandom opened crucial doors that down the line made this hobby better and a lot more fun for everyone.

Afterword: Fandom's Founders— The Next Generation

During the early years of fandom, there were dozens, probably hundreds, of young fans who wrote an article or a fan fiction story or assisted (either writing, drawing or "inking" onto ditto masters) on an amateur comic strip for their own limited distribution fanzine or one published by a friend.

However, the majority of fans supported the birth of early comic fandom merely by purchasing fanzines, attending fan gatherings or just with their overall enthusiasm. Even the early incomplete list from Jerry Bails in 1964 indicates well over a thousand fans existed and yet only the smallest handful of them are profiled in this book.

The fans spotlighted in *Founders of Comic Fandom* are the ones who set the standards and blazed the trails that those others tried to match or exceed even in those early days. They were the inspiration for their peers as well as the next generation of fans who got involved with fanzines and conventions. Often the choice of which fanzine to buy from the many that were advertised was influenced by the presence of a contribution by one of the names highlighted in these pages.

I was one of the "next generation" of fans described above, one of hundreds—nay, thousands—who joined the movement in the 1960s and early 1970s. In my case, I entered fandom in the fall of 1964, about six months too late to be listed in the *Who's Who in Comic Fandom*. I was one of those fans who ordered those early fanzines and published my own, inspired by the fan-friends I only met through the U.S. mails or in their publications but who I felt I knew as well as the kid next door. Like so many others, I felt part of that community when I joined fandom. I ordered old comic books through the mail, wrote letters to the names that appeared in letter columns, and eagerly joined into any activity to celebrate my love of comic books and strips. My best-known fanzine, *Sense of Wonder*, worked its way up to becoming a worthy if unspectacular publication by the time I was in college. Others who weren't interested in the zine scene found other ways to participate. Trading, selling and buying back issues were probably the most universal activities.

I reiterate this book's dedication to everyone who became a part of that wonderful, crazy, enthusiastic world of fandom in those halcyon days. The memories remain vivid, and the echoes of those days will never die.

APPENDIX: THE 1964 *WHO'S WHO* LIST

When Jerry Bails and Larry Lattanzi prepared the *Who's Who in Comic Fandom* in 1964, they listed everyone who was known to them in comicdom at the time. I felt it was appropriate to include that list in this book, for the historical record. However, keep in mind that this is merely a reproduction of the 1,683 names that appeared in the two or three editions of the *Who's Who* (all published in the same year). There were certainly members of fandom who weren't listed, either because they didn't have dealings with Bails, or they didn't make the deadline (June) or simply through errors of omission.

Acciavatti, Jodene
Ackerman, Forrest J
Acord, Gary
Adams, Tony
Ahlstrand, Ken
Ahrens, Ed
Alderson, Daniel
Allaire, Jay
Allan, Ed
Allebson, Mike
Allen, Barry
Allen, Spence
Allensbach, Marilyn
Allison, Terry
Almaraz, Alex
Almasy, Allen
Altshuler, Thomas
Alusick, John
Anderson, Danny
Anderson, Elwood
Anderson, Sgt. R.
Andrews, John
Andrews, Randy
Angell, John
Angelos, John
Anthony, R. C.
Antolick, George Jr.
Apostal, Chris
Aprill, Edwin M. Jr.
Arbunich, Marty
Armstrong, David
Arndt, Leroy
Arnold, Jimmy
Arseneault, Bob
Arundale, William
Asher, James

Astin, Ronald
Atteberry, Jane
Auerbach, Reuben
Austin, Dick
Austin, Doug
Azbell, Fred
Baber, Michael
Baca, John
Bachman, Clifton
Backer, Alan
Baes, Allen
Bails, Jerry G.
Baker, Bruce
Baker, Scott
Baldyga, William
Balfour, Allen
Ball, Russell
Balnicke, Craig
Balthis, Walter
Bammer, George
Banks, Harold
Banks, R. Jeff
Banzhof, Donna
Barbas, Joe
Barber, Robert
Barber, Roger
Barker, K.
Barkey, Charles
Barnhill, James
Barnowitz, Elliot
Barr, Stephen
Barron, Bob
Barron, Jon
Barry, Jeremy
Bartel, Ray
Bartels, Ken

Bartholomew, Richard
Bastie, Steve
Batiuk, Thomas
Battersby, Timothy
Bauman, Barry
Baxter, David
Baxter, Jim
Beair, Rickey
Beane, Connie
Beard, Walt
Beaudet, Leopold
Beaverson, Jim
Becher, Art
Beck, Bob
Beck, Martha
Beck, Marti
Beckley, Dennis
Beer, Morris
Behymer, Gary
Beinish, Roger
Bell, Daniel
Bennett, Billy
Bennett, Dean
Benson, Charles
Benson, John
Berg, Steve
Bergeron, Richard
Berglund, Ronald
Beriner, Mrs. J. L.
Berkeley, Sidney
Berkowitz, Gerald
Berman, Leonard
Berrier, Philip
Berry, D. Bruce
Berry, Richard
Bertram, Hal

Beschita, Ken
Bestard, Ricky
Bianculli, Joseph
Bibby, David
Bibby, G. A.
Bibby, George
Bieger, Peter
Bierman, Rick
Bilewich, Buddy
Birenbaum, Preston
Bixler, Charles
Blackburn, Jay
Blackburn, Mark
Blackwell, Nick
Blanck, Debby
Blanck, Larry
Blatt, John
Bleckley, Thomas
Bleimister, Willie
Bliss, Ted
Block, Royce
Bluedorn, Allen
Blumenthal, Alan
Boehmler, Chuck
Bogash, Irving
Boggs, Hiram
Boggs, Red
Bolay, W. E.
Bomboy, Susan
Bond, Jerry
Borbas, Joseph
Bossard, Bruce
Boullier, Gerald
Bourgeois, Bruce
Boylan, Owen
Boyle, John

Bradley, David
Brady, Alan
Brady, Dennis
Brady, Douglas
Brainin, Perry
Braitman, Barry
Brand, Roger
Bratetic, Donald
Breen, Kevin
Brennan, Casey
Brenner, Howard
Bridwell, E. Nelson
Brier, Royce Jr.
Brierley, Jack
Briggs, Lucinda
Brill, Louis
Brim, Greg
Britt, Anne
Broad, G. Richard
Brodnik, Charles
Bronson, Fred
Brooks, Richard
Brosch, Robert
Brosnan, John
Brothers, Ranken
Brown, Dannie
Brown, Jim
Brown, Larry
Brown, Len
Brown, Leonard
Brown, Mike
Brown, Robert
Brown, Steve
Browning, Kenneth
Bruesch, Bill
Bruscato, Bruce
Brynjolfsson, Per
Bubnis, Bernard
Buchanan, David
Buchman, Edwin
Budd, Dennis
Budnick, John
Bunn, William
Burdick, Loraine
Burke, Timothy
Burridge, Scott
Burrows, Thomas
Burt, Dick
Burton, Joseph
Bury, Greg
Buscato, Bruce
Buser, Jim
Buset, David
Bush, Bart
Butterworth, John
Butts, Robert
Byer, Robert
Byrd, Larry

Byrne, Frank
Byrne, Joe
Byrne, Joseph R.
Byrne, Terry
Cadmus, Eddie
Cafferata, Mike
Caiazza, Saba
Cain, Tim
Cajero, Michael
Caldwell, Robert
Calise, David
Campbell, Jim
Campbell, Mike
Campbell, Steve
Camper, Kenton
Camus, George
Cannon, Gene
Cannon, Jack
Capes, Reggie
Caplan, Daid
Carberry, Robert
Carey, Mark
Carlson, John
Carmo, Jackie
Carpenter, Kent
Carroll, John
Carver, Butch
Casal, Bob
Casey, Coreen
Cassel, Alan
Cassello, Christine
Cassidy, Danny
Castora, Phil
Castronuovo, David
Catchings, John
Catena, David
Cavalier, Bill
Cazedessus, Camille
Celestri, John
Celi, Louis
Centner, Arthur
Cetrone, Phil
Cevalina, Stephen
Chamless, John
Chan, Stanley
Chance, Kenneth
Chandler, Keith
Charet, Larry
Cheesman, David
Chesney, Landon
Cheves, Jack
Chiselbrook, Craig
Chiselbrook, Wayne
Christie, George
Christman, Dale
Christman, Harry
Christoff, Steven
Christophes, Thomas

Christpherson, Lee
Church, Ginger
Churchill, Robert
Cibelli, Kenneth
Circosta, Anthony
Civarra, Jim
Cizevskis, Maris A.
Clark, Allan
Clark, Robert
Clark, Steve
Clark, Wayne
Clemens, Mark E.
Clinton, Jack
Cockrum, David
Cocorelis, Ricky
Coderre, William
Cohen, Edward
Cohen, Lee
Cohen, Louis
Cohn, Steven
Cole, Donald
Cole, M.
Coleman, David
Collier, Chris
Collins, Jack
Collins, Spencer
Colossi, Joseph
Conant, Sherwood
Conkright, Jim
Connally, Garth
Connell, Gary
Connor, Jim
Consolian, Thomas
Conte, Johnny
Cook, Fred
Coons, Jim
Cooper, Noel
Cooper, Wayne
Corbett, Ed
Corda, Anthony
Coriell, Vernell
Cornell, Steve
Corogana, Richard
Corrsin, Steve
Coryell, Charles
Cosby, Douglas
Cosgrove, Patrick
Costello, Sidney Jr.
Cox, Marsha
Crawford, Ralph
Crilly, Larry
Crim, Michael
Crissey, Paul
Crocke, Albert
Crockett, Jim
Crowdus, Gary
Crowe, Dan
Crowe, Kenny

Crum, Charles
Crump, Harold
Csaszar, Joe
Cucchiara, Andrew
Culkowski, David
Cummings, Ralph
Czarnik, Stan
D'Amico, Vincent
Dagenais, Kurt
Danehy, Thomas R. A.
Danehy, Tom
Dang, Lucas
Daniels, Danny
Darcy, Stan
Darcy, Stanley
Darjean, Bob
Dassinger, Warren
Davey, Daryl
Davey, Scott
Davidson, John
Davidson, Sol
Davis, Alan
Davis, Robert
Davis, Scott
Davis, Wendell
De Andrew, Bill
De Chenne, Tim
De Maio, Mrs. Joseph
De Michele, Alfonso
De Muccio, John
De Paul, Carter, Jr.
De Sipe, Larr
De Vere, Danny
De Vincenzo, Victor
De Vore, Howard
Dean, Charles
Dean, Larry
Dean, Michael
Dean, Ward
Debelo, Nick
Debes, Vern
Delger, Clem
Delich, Craig
Delph, Grant
Del-Val, Rick
DePaul, Carter Jr.
Deranleau, Dan
Des Georges, Doug
Deshotel, R. W.
Desrosiers, Gerry
Detrow, George
Devere, Danny
Devolas, Peter
Devries, John
Di Fonzo, Andy
Di, Paolo
Diamon, Alec
Dickman, Kenny

Diekmann, Richard
Diethert, Brett
Diettinger, Bill
Dietz, Tom
Diglio, Jim Jr.
Dill, Earl Jr.
Dirks, Dianna
Dirzulaitus, Mike
Dismukes, Jim
Dixon, Ken
Dobbins, Steve
Doerner, Norman
Dohler, Don
Dolinar, Frank
Dolner, John
Dolph, Herbert
Dombkowski, Tom
Donehower, Bruce
Dorchak, Edwin Jr.
Dorf, Sheldon
Dorn, Mark
Draper, Kevin
Drapkin, David
Duarte, Dennis
DuBay, Bill
DuBay, Chick
DuBay, Harry
Dugha, Charles
Duncan, Bob
Duraj, John
Durell, Richard
Dusek, Sharon
Earl, Larry
Eastin, Steve
Eberts, Glen
Echtinaw, Harold
Edmonds, Mark
Edmund, Larry
Egan, Robert
Einziger, Ronald Eis-
 giuber, Frank
Ellberger, Simon
Ellis, Patrick
Ellis, Robert
Engates, Leon
Engel, Leslie
Engle, Jay
Enrico, Gerald
Ensign, Donald
Epperson, Winston
Epstein, Joe
Erickson, Donald
Erickson, Stephen
Essig, James
Estleman, laren
Ethell, Jeff
Evans, Mike
Evans, Sidney

Evans, Tim
Eyck, Lynn
Facciole, Jay
Fagan, Tom
Fahey, John
Fallis, Michael L.
Farrell, Erin
Farrell, Joseph
Farrell, Mary Ann
Farrell, Richard
Favareau, John
Feder, Robert
Feil, William
Feldman, Gregory
Felipe, Edward
Femia, Vincent
Feola, Paul
Fergus, George
Ferguson, Johnny
Fernandez, Joseph
Ferrazzano, Johnny
Fetta, Patrick
Fetters, Robert
Fick, Alvin
Fiedler, David
Fielding, Wayne
Fields, R. C.
Figueroa, Anthony
Finger, Paul
Fink Douglas
Finley, Joe
Finley, Mike
Finnerty, Kenneth
Fireman, Richard
Fischer, Robert
Fisher, Tommy
Fitch, Harry
Fitzpatrick, Dave
Fitzpatrick, Joseph
Fitzsimmons, Dave
Fiyalka, Arthur
Flagg, Gordon Jr.
Fleming, Dan
Fleming, Richard
Flesher, Mike
Flowers, Brady
Folse, Mike
Foote, Donald
Ford, Charles
Forrest, Robert
Foss, Ronn
Foster, John
Foston, Stephen
Fowler, Dave
Fox, Doug
Fox, John
Foy, J.
Fradkin, Ronald

Fraknoi, Andrew
Francis, Steve
Franke, Rudi
Frankland, Laura
Franklin, Bill
Fraser, Jerry
Frassetti, Michael
Frawley, Tim
Frazier, Richard
Frederick, Scott
Fredericks, Harold
Free, Ken
Freeman, C.
French, Donald
Friedman, Jim
Friedman, Murray
Friedman, Stephen
Friedrich, Michael
Frisson, Joseph
Frith, Norman
Fritter, Stephen
Froehlich, Greg
Fromm, Eric
Fuerschbach, Raymond
Fulco, Barry
Fuller, Lana
Furek, John
Gaines, Robert
Gainor, Sam
Gaither, Mickey
Galaburri, Joseph
Galeas, Gary
Gallagher, Kenneth
Gallegos, Pablo
Galvanin, Robert
Gambaccini, Paul
Gander, Don
Garbark, Paul
Garber, Clifford
Garbett, Craig
Garcia, Bill
Garcia, Fred
Gardner, J. H.
Gardner, Lytt
Garlinger, Douglas
Garofalo, Vincent
Garrett, Joe
Garrou, Randy
Gee, Edward
Gee, Judy
Gelb, Jeffrey
Gemignani, Margaret
George, Bob
Gerber, Steve
Gerhardt, Paul
Gianino, S. R.
Gibbons, David
Gibbons, Fred

Gibbons, George
Gibson, Jim
Gibson, Lawrence Jr.
Gigliotti, Joseph
Gilbert, Jack
Gilchrist, Jeffrey
Giles, Marvin
Gilman, Roger
Gilmour, William
Girard, Dian
Glass, Charles
Glassel, Curtiss
Glassman, Marc
Gleeson, A.
Gleeson, Paul
Gleeson, Tony
Glenn, Ken
Glidden, Russell
Glut, Don
Gobeil, J. A.
Goepfert, Eric
Goff, Roand
Goggin, Glenn
Goldberg, Alex
Golden, Jay
Goldman, Ronald
Goleas, Gary
Gombarcik, Tom
Gonzalez, Efrain
Gonzalez, Ricardo
Gordon, Jeffrey
Gordon, Mark
Gore, Sharon
Gould, Neil
Gowan, Kenny
Grace, David
Graham, Ronnie
Gramazio, Guiseppe
Grant, Mark
Grant, Steve
Gray, Steve
Green, Gordon
Green, Richard
Green, Thomas
Greene, Keith
Greenspoon, Yale
Gregor, Charles
Gregory, Donnie
Greilich, Ronald
Grenn, Marlin
Grey, Mike
Griffin, Robert
Griffin, Steve
Grimes, Charles
Gruenwald, Mark
Gualtiere, Nick
Guastello, Michael
Guthrie, William

Guzman, Agustin Jr.
Haas, Bruce
Haefele, John
Haendiges, Mike
Halcums, Bob
Hale, Albert
Hall, Bruce
Halligan, Mike
Halprin, Robert
Hamilton, Jim
Hamm, John
Hannifen, Oven
Hannus, Hans
Hanson, Michael
Harmon, Jim
Harner, Bob III
Harp, Duncan
Harris, Gerald
Harris, Jack
Harris, Wayne
Harris, Wm.
Harry, Daniel Jr.
Hartman, Donald
Hartman, Lane
Harvey, Eric
Haryes, Art
Hasson, Jerry
Hauptman, Bill
Hauptman, Don
Hawk, Douglas
Haworth, Allen
Hawthorne, Robert
Haydock, Ron
Hayes, Arthur
Hayner, Raymond
Haynes, Joe
Haynes, Richard
Haynes, Robert
Hayward, Harry
Hayward, Steve
Headlee, Jeff
Hecht, Joseph
Hegenberger, John Jr.
Heineman, Kenneth
Held, Claude
Henault, Maurice
Henderson, Arnold
Henerson, Eugene
Henri, John
Herbers, Melvin
Herink, Curtis
Hernández, Raphael
Herndon, Larry
Hertel, Harry
Hertel, Ted
Hess, Roger
Hewetson, Alan
Hildebrand, Bruce

Hill, Tim
Hjortness, Chuck
Hofbauer, Bill
Hoffman, Mary
Hoffman, Rebecca
Hogan, Edward
Hogan, Kathleen
Hogle, Mac
Hollander, Jim
Holman, Parley
Holt, Judy
Holtzman, Arthur
Hooper, Ched
Horn, Marshall
Horner, John
Horowitz, Harvey
Hosmer, Dave
Howard, Bill
Howard, Sherman D.
Howe, Richard
Hruska, Dianna
Hubbard, Gary
Hubbard, Rick
Hudson, John
Hughes, Morton
Hughes, Terry
Humberstone, Fred
Humphrey, Walter
Hunneman, D. H.
Hunt, Ralph
Hurst, James
Hurwitz, Dan
Husick, Patricia
Hussey, Jon
Hutcheson, Jim
Hute, Ralph
Hyde, C. D.
Hyland, Jim
Iacopelli, Sal
Iacovone, Pat
Inzer, George Jr.
Iurato, Paul
Ivie, Larry
Jackson, Bill
Jackson, Don
Jackson, Frederick F.
Jackson, John
Jackson, Pete
Jackson, Terry
Jacobs, Bob
Jacobson, Steve
Jam, Steve
Janes, Robert
Jankoski, Richard
Jason, David
Jean, Gerard Jr.
Jehle, John
Jein, Gregory

Jenkins, Vernon
Jennings, Robert
Jeong, Gordon
Jerome, Lawrence
Johns, Kevin
Johnson, Bradley
Johnson, Christopher
Johnson, Frank Jr.
Johnson, Frederic
Johnson, Gaylan
Johnson, Glen D.
Johnson, James
Johnson, John
Johnson, Kevin
Johnson, Larry
Johnson, Richard
Jonas, Gerard
Jones, David
Jones, David (II)
Jones, Gerard
Jones, Jeff
Jones, Jerry
Jones, Jim
Jones, John
Jones, Mike
Jones, Randy
Jones, Ron
Jones, Thomas
Jones, Waring
Jones, William
Joseph, Robert
Joss, Mark
Judd, Donald
Kaler, David
Kaltenbach, Thomas
Kalwasinkski, Jerome
Kantor, Karen
Kanus, Myron
Karl, John
Karl, Stephen
Katz, Arnold
Kaufman, Richard
Kaufman, Stuart
Kawicki, Dennis
Kay, Jerry
Kaye, Lenny
Keefer, Don
Keeling, David
Kehayias, George
Keis, Stephen
Kekola, Kenny
Kelez, Steve
Keller, Henry
Kelly, John
Keltner, John Howard
Kennedy, Bob
Kent, Richard
Keonte, Reed

Kettle, Lucien
Kettle, Ronald
Key, Tommy
Keyes, Steve
Keyser, Dorothy
Kight, Ross
Kiloh, Wayne
King, Adam
King, Antone
King, Eric
King, Harvey
Kinney, Jay
Kirkness, Jack
Kiser, Frank
Kitchen, Dixie
Kitchen, George
Klein, Jonathan
Klein, Robert
Kleinstein, Phyllus
Klimcheck, John
Klotz, Marshall
Knee, Helmut
Knobloch, Rick
Knowles, David
Knowles, Jim R.
Knudsen, Kerry
Knuth, Dennis
Koch, John
Kochanowski, Bob
Koen, Wayne
Koerper, Jim
Kohl, Gary
Kolky, Hank
Komesshok, Stephen Jr.
Kon, Leo
Koorhan, Leslie
Kopf, Larry Jr.
Kopp, George
Kovers, A.
Kowalewski, David
Kozel, Ronnie
Kracalik, Allen
Kramel, Kim
Kreienkamp, Gerard
Kreisher, Michael
Kremberg, Marvin
Krey, Gene
Kridel, Richard
Kristiansen, Ralph
Krizek, Earl
Kuhfeld, Albert W.
Kulicke, Dieter
Kunkel, Jim
Kurtz, Loretta
Kyle, Richard
Lahmann, Edward
Lamb, Earl

Lancaster, David	Love, Gordon B.	McAllister, Forrest	Mitchell, David
Landesman, Fred	Lowry, Bruce	McCague, Bob	Mitchell, Lon
Langguth, David	Lowry, Joseph	McCall, Bob	Mitchmich, Milta
Largaespada, Ricky	Lucas, Kathlyn	McCall, Jerry	Mockido, David
Laroe, Mark	Lucci, Jerry	McCance, Bob	Moen, Richard
Lash, Jonathan	Luczak, Anthony	McClain, Mary Ann	Moench, Douglas
Lasors, Dom	Ludwig, Larry	McCollom, Douglas	Moldenhauer
Lasruk, John	Lum, Glenn	McConville, John	Molenda, Joe
Latona, Robert	Lundgren, Carl	McCord, Bill	Montanarello, Leonard
Lattanzi, Larry	Lupoff, Patricia	McCormich, Mike	Montgomery, David
Lauria, Thomas	Lupoff, Richard	McCoy, Kathleen	Montgomery, Larry
Lawinski, Russ	Lyles, Duke	McDaniel, Jim	Montgomery, Randy
Lawler, Steve	Lynn, Richard	McDaniels, Ellis	Montoya, Phil
Lawson, George	Lyons, Patrick	McDonald, Kevin	Moore, Danny
Leary, Warren	Madine, Chuck	McElroy, James	Moore, Hollis Lynn
Lebar, John	Madr, John	McGee, Ernest	Moore, William
Lee, Hong	Maguire, Dennis	McGee, Jerry	Moorefield, David
Lee, Robert	Maher, Christopher	McGeehan, John G.	Moothart, Mervin
Lee, Robert (II)	Mahinka, Stephen	McGeehan, Thomas	Morehead, James
Lee, Robert (III)	Malisani, Bob	McGinnis, Don "Red"	Morone, Leon
Lee, Stan	Malisani, Robert	McGlade, Kevin	Moroz, Drury S.
Leet, John	Malone, Eddie	McGough, Michael	Morris, Chris
Lehner, Frank	Malson, Mike	McGregor, Donald	Morrison, James
Leibfred, Philip	Maltin, Len	McGriffin, Carey	Morse, Lalrry
Leibowitz, Kenny	Manbeck, Steven	McIlhany, Billy	Moser, Brian
Leiffer, Paul	Mangen, Patricia	McKeever, Michael	Moslander, Paul
Leigh, Robert	Mangus, John	McKesson, David	Moss, Chuck
Levin, Frank	Mannheimer, Steven	McKnight, David	Mossmann, Ronald
Levy, Bruce	Manning, Ken	McKnight, Pat	Motta, Miguel
Lew, George	Manning, Russ	McLean, Anne	Motto, Kenneth
Lewandowski, Dennis	Manson, John	McLean, William	Moy, Steven
Lewis, Stefan	Mantione, Merc	McMullan, Larry	Much, Romona
Liberman, Larry	Mapelli, Mark	McQueeney, William	Mudrick, Bob
Libraro, Philip	Marden, Douglas	McWalter, Keith	Mueller, Bud
Lichtman, Charles	Mark, Larry	Medeiros, Jerry	Muhlberg, Neal
Liebfred, Philip	Markstein, Donald	Meed, Mark	Mulero, Domnic
Lien, Dennis	Marshall, Bob	Meier, James	Mulinski, Thomas
Light, Richard	Martin, Bill	Meisner, Dwayne	Mullen, Robert
Lighter, Jonathan	Martin, Gary	Melnichok, James	Mullins, Gary
Lightner, W. T.	Martin, George	Memorich, Dick	Murano, Mike
Lillian, Guy	Martin, Michael	Mendelson, Phil	Murphy, Daniel
Linge, Ailsa	Maruzo, Mike	Merkin, Richard	Murphy, James
Lipniski, Frank	Marzano, Peter	Metz, Robert	Murphy, Michael
Lisiecki, Peter	Mask, Ace	Miaso, John	Murphy, Milt
Litziner, Lew	Masloski, Daniel	Michell, Lon	Murray, Joe Jr.
Lloyd, James	Mason, Bruce	Midyett, Rocky	Murray, Ken
Lodi, Jon M.	Massey, Philip	Milewski, Robert	Murrell, Jerry
Lodi, Mike	Matthies, Ronald	Milgrom, Allen	Musich, Joe Jr.
Logan, Allen	Mattingly, Dale	Millan, Freddy	Mustic, Lewis
Logan, Phillip	Mattingly, Greg	Miller, Bob	Mysinek, Al
Logue, Gerald	Mattson, Ed	Miller, Ray (Ontario)	Nadel, Marc D.
Loiselle, Diane	Maves, Tom	Miller, Raymond	Nass, John
Loiselle, Marc	Maxim, Mike	Milliken, Don	Navarrete, Eddie
Long, Rodney	May, Richard	Mills, James	Nessel, Vickie
Loper, Jerry	May, Thilola	Millsap, Barry	Nevares, Andy
Lortie, Arthur Jr.	Mayer, Gerry	Millsaps, Alan	Nevins, Williams
Loudani, Robert	Mayo, Britt	Minter, R. H.	Newman, Brett
Louie, David	Mayr, Billy	Mitchell, Bill	Newman, Dean

Newman, Dennis
Newton, Jerise
Nichls, Cecil Jr.
Nicholson, Alexander, Jr.
Nicholson, David
Nickerson, Joe
Noble, Larry
Nodtvedt, John
Noga, Robert
North, Dick
Northern, Dennis
Norwich, Gary
Norwood, Frederick
Nowicki, Thomas
Nuessel, Frank
Nuttleman, Fred
Nygard, Tom
O'Brien, George
O'Brocta, Joseph
O'Connor, Ross
O'Connor, Thomas
O'Leary, Howard
O'Neill, John
Occhipinti, Joseph
Ogden, Peter
Ogden, W. D.
Oliver, Michael
Olivieri, Ray
Olkowski, Joey
Olsen, Richard
Oppenheimer, Israel
Organek, Mike
Orlicki, Wayne
Ortiz, Michael
Osborn, Pell
Osten, William
Ostfeld, William
Ovshinsky, Harvey
Owalina, Stephen
Owen, Rita
Oxford, Beth
Oyerly, Dave
Pachon, Stanley
Pacinda, George
Packer, Noreen
Page, John
Pagel, Robert Jr.
Painter, Frank
Painter, Ralph
Palazey, Kathie
Palermo, Nick
Palmer, Chris
Palmer, James
Palmerme, Nick
Parent, David Jr.
Parise, Michael
Parry, Roy

Paskow, Al
Paskow, David
Pasternik, Norman
Patten, Fred
Patterson, Bob
Patterson, Kenneth
Paul, William
Pavlac, Ross
Payne, Bill
Pearson, Dan
Pearson, Durk
Pearson, William E.
Pelz, Bruce E.
Pelzel, Bob
Pender, Rick
Pennig, Jeff
Penovich, Norman
Perkowski, Ron
Perrin, Steve
Peters, Terry
Petroc, Richard
Petrone, Donald P.
Pfannerstill, Robert
Phelan, H. C.
Phillips, Carl
Phillips, Jerry
Phillips, Peter C.
Phillips, Ricky
Phillips, Victor
Phillipson, Phil
Philobsky, Mike
Philpott, Julian
Piccirillo, Mrs. P.
Pickard, Al
Pierce, John
Pierce, Lenny
Pike, James
Pilati, Joe
Pines, David
Piranio, Robert
Plachta, Dan
Placzek, Bill
Player, Judith
Plott, Billy
Pobst, Jim
Polk, Gary
Polozola, Joey
Pontello, Jeff
Poone, Airman
Poreleski, James
Potts, Allen
Poupard, Ian
Powell, David
Powers, Don
Powers, Kathie
Poyer, Richard
Praschak, Paul
Prather, Dave

Prestone, Dave
Price, Mike
Primavera, Robert
Pritchett, Darwin
Pritchett, Jerry
Prouty, Tom
Prouty, Tommy
Pryor, Dick
Ptacels, Harry
Puhan, Frederic
Puhr, James
Pujol, Rich
Pujol, Robert
Purinton, Robert
Putnam, Liz
Pyles, Bradley J.
Pylypun, Richard
Radzikowski, Gerard
Rafferty, Gary
Rajca, John
Rakun, R.
Raleigh, Daniel
Ramos, Jose
Rampine, Michael
Randall, Clay
Randolph, George
Rankins, Rudy
Raub, Mike
Raven, Jon
Ray, Larry
Raybourne, Larry
Reddish, John
Ree, Gerry De La
Reed, Larry
Reed, Lesley
Reed, Mike
Reed, Ted
Regier, Bill
Reich, Dick
Reinsel, Charles
Renner, Rodney
Renzoni, Mike
Renzoni, Robert
Ressegiue, Philip
Rey, Michael
Rhodes, R.
Ribbio, Anthony
Ribisi, Joseph
Ricci, M.
Rice, Marya
Rich, Lawrence
Richard, Dennis
Richards, Brent
Richardson, Darrel
Richardson, Fred
Richardson, Michael
Richendollar, James
Richey, Terry

Richter, K. H.
Riddle, Charles
Riddle, Lee
Rigali, Richard
Riley, Charles
Rintz, Billy
Riske, Marty
Roach, Stuart
Robbins, Bill
Robbins, Bobby
Roberts, Dan
Roberts, Ethan
Roberts, John
Roberts, Phil
Robertson, Duncan
Robertson, R. J.
Robertson, Randy
Robinson, Sammy
Rochrig, John
Rockwell, Dick
Rodriguez, Leonard
Roeserg, Richard
Rogofsky, Howard
Rollins, Bob
Romanek, Fred
Romer, Jean-Claude
Rosa, Paul
Rosenfeld, Jeffrey
Rosenfeld, Neill
Rosner, Brian
Ross, Ira
Ross, Martin
Rössel, Carol-Lynn
Rössel, Gregory
Rosskopf, Marvin
Rossow, Jim
Rostron, Bill
Rothenberger, Larry
Rothermich, Derrill
Roy, Vicki
Rubenfeld, Richard
Rubin, Murray
Rudnick, Howard
Rudolph, Jerry
Ruffin, Gardner
Rulli, John
Rummell, Jimmy
Russell, Allen
Russell, Kent
Russell, Kent R.
Rutschman, Siefried
Ryan, Bill
Ryan, John T.
Ryan, Johnny
Ryan, Kevin
Rybarczyt, Paul
Rypel, Ted
Sabo, Steven

Sagisser, Tom
Saint John, Danny
Salerno, Joey
Saliba, Samuel Jr.
Salvagni, Richard
Sammutt, Vincent
Sampson, Bernard
Sanders, Ala
Sanders, Joe
Sanderson, Steve
Sandhaus, Stuart
Sandler, Marvin
Sands, Robert
Sansing, Rob
Santino, John, Jr.
Sarett, Stuart
Sarill, Bill
Sarti, Randy
Sassaman, Richard
Satenstein, John
Saunders, Buddy
Sauvage, David
Savage, Mark
Sawyer, Charles
Sawyer, Robert
Saxe, Howard
Scarfo, Patrick
Schank, Donald
Schardt, Kathleen
Scheifer, Stewart
Schenker, Larry
Schiff, Richard
Schisesiger, Vernon
Schlobin, Sue
Schmulawitz, Paul
Schnieber, Robert
Schommer, Donald
Schottenstein, Gail
Schotz, Paul
Schueftan, Oliver
Schulftan, Oliver
Schultheis, Stephen
Schultz, Richard
Schurman, Kelly
Schuster, Al
Schwartz, Mark
Schwer, William
Sciabica, James
Scollo, P. A.
Scorzelli, Mike
Scott, Eddie
Scott, Noel
Scruggs, Roger
Searles, Michael
Secrest, Arnold
Seger, Eugene
Segroves, Mike
Seidman, Cory

Seldman, Greg
Selig, Bob
Sell, Barry
Sepansky, Mark
Sessions, Will
Seuling, Phil
Sevonty, Robert
Sewell, Richard
Seydor, Paul
Shapiro, Jerrold
Shaw, Bill
Shaw, Wayne
Shea, Joseph
Shelby, Mrs. Jo
Sheppard, Shari
Sheridan, Bob
Sheridan, Susan
Sherman, Joseph
Shields, Bob
Shoap, Richard
Shoemaker, Joseph
Sidney, Joe
Siegel, Philip
Sikes, Mo
Sikorski, Bill
Silver, Merle
Silverman, Harold
Simon, Jim
Simpson, Edward III
Simpson, Lowell L.
Singer, David
Sipe, Jeff
Sipe, Larry
Sizemore, Danny K.
Skinner, Tom
Skube, Michael
Smallidge, Donald
Smart, Morris
Smith, Billy
Smith, Charles
Smith, Dave
Smith, David (II)
Smith, David (III)
Smith, David H., Jr.
Smith, Douglas
Smith, Gideon
Smith, Gregg
Smith, Harold
Smith, Harold (II)
Smith, James
Smith, Jerry
Smith, Jim
Smith, Jimmy
Smith, Joe Allen
Smith, Joseph Jr.
Smith, Kenneth Jr.
Smith, Marcus
Smith, Pat

Smith, Ryle
Smith, Walter
Smoke, Linda
Snell, Michael
Snider, A. B.
Snowden, Lee
Snyder, Robert
Sohrweide, Robert
Sollenberger, Roy
Solof, Bruce
Solomon, David
Sondreal, John
Sorek, Jerry
Soricelli, Leo
Sosnaud, Jeff
Spann, Bob
Spence, Mike
Spencer, Bob
Spencer, Ellie
Spicer, Bill
Spino, Sandra
Spitz, Jay
Spitz, Lonny
Sponder, Marshall
Spotch, Robert
Spotts, John
Stallings, Alden
Stanfield, Charles
Starlin, Jim
Steele, Jimmy
Steinborn, Mickey
Steingasser, Susan
Stephens, John
Sterling, Michael
Stern, Stephen
Sternschein, Manas
Stevens, Mark
Stewart, Bhob
Stewart, Bob
Stewart, Corliss
Stock, Craig
Stockman, John
Stockman, William
Stodolka, Frank
Stokes, Gerard
Stone, Bob
Stone, John
Stoner, Joe
Storer, Doug
Stough, Steve
Streck, Chris
Strickland, Linda
Strickling, Johnnie
Strnal, Jim
Stroud, Jon
Stuard, David
Stuart, Sebastian
Stuart, Vincent

Sturm, Jeff
Stutson, L.
Suratourec, Kenneth
Suriano, Greg
Surratt, Hugh
Sustaita, Manuel
Sustar, Jim
Sutton, Gail
Swanson, Carl
Swanson, Michael
Swartz, Jon D.
Sweeney, Martin
Sweet, Charles
Sweet, William
Swetland, Variety
Swiatower, Ken
Swink, Alan
Switzer, Larry
Synder, Glen
Szczepanski, Mark
Szczuka, Michael
Szidik, Le Roy
Szurek, David
Tamerius, Steve
Tanner, James
Tapper, A.
Tatge, Richard
Taurone, Michael
Tavares, Tom
Taylor, Dan
Taylor, David
Taylor, Walt
Taylor, William
Tedor, Dick
Tenney, Dennis C.
Terwilleger, Guy
Tesar, Ken
Teske, Edward
Tewksbury, John
Thailing, Bill
Tharp, Gary
Thomas, Harry
Thomas, John
Thomas, Michael
Thomas, Roy
Thompson, Donald
Thompson, Keith
Thompson, Margaret
Thompson, Paul
Thompson, Paul Jr.
Tillman, Geoffrey
Tillotson, Alan
Tingle, Bill
Tirado, Leonard
Tomyama, Jiro
Tong, Richard
Toren, James
Torrance, Clifton

Tragno, Joseph
Trimble, John
Tripp, Arthur
Trotter, David
Trotter, Frederick D.
Trout, David
Tucker, Larry
Tung, Victor
Tuohey, Francis
Tuohey, Michael
Turner, Danny
Turner, James III
Turner, Peter
Tverdak, Joseph
Unger, Robert
Urbanski, Joseph
Urrutia, Benjamin
Utley, Steve
Valdes, Mane
Valentine, Tom
Vasily, Gerald
Verhagen, Jim
Vernig, Peter
Versandi, Robb
Vincent, Darryl
Vincent, Richard
Virgin, Mike
Visser, Randy
Vizcarrondo, Paul
Von Bernewitz, Fred
Vosburg, Michael
Vucenic, Joe
Waage, Michael
Wachter, John
Wagner, Eliot
Wagner, Harvey
Wahl, Allen
Wahl, Mike

Walczak, Laurence
Wald, R. F.
Waldrop, Howard
Walker, Dave
Walker, Donald
Walker, Freddie
Wallace, George
Walsh, Gene
Walsh, Steven
Walters, Larry
Wampler, Billy
Ward, Denny
Warfield, Wayne
Warner, Mark
Warner, Mark A.
Warren, Bill
Warren, Harry
Was, Leonard
Watson, George
Watts, Ron
Way, Gregg
Wayne, Robert
Weber, Darrell
Weck, Bob
Weidig, Mike
Weidner, Harry
Weidner, Harry Jr.
Wein, Len
Weingroff, Richard
Weinstein, Jerry
Weinstein, Paul
Weinstock, Ronald
Weisberg, Mitchell
Weiss, Alan
Weiss, Ed
Weiss, Jeffrey
Wells, Anne
Wells, Charles

Wells, Curtis
Werder, Paul
Wermers, B. F.
West, Richard C.
Weston, James K.
Weston, Robert
Wheeler, Alan
White, Bill
White, Charles
White, John
White, Ted
Whittlesey, Lee
Whitzker, George
Wichman, Keith
Wickstrom, Andy
Wild, Waren
Wilde, Jim
Wilhelm, Charles
Williams, Bruce
Williams, Jim
Williams, Larry
Williams, Mike
Williams, Tim
Williamson, Christo-
    pher
Willits, Malcom
Willoughby, Henry
Wilson, Bill
Wilson, Charles
Wilson, Danny
Wilson, Pete
Wilson, Steve
Wilson, Thomas
Wilson, William
Wimperis, Bruce
Winsel, Ricky
Wirtanen, Donald
Wirth, Dan

Witham, M.
Withers, Robert
Wittits, Dennis
Wolfendale, Eva
Wolfman, Marvin
Wolfram, David
Wolinsky, Howard
Wolz, Richard
Wong, Harvey
Wood, Mel
Wooley, Carl
Woolley, Gary
Worley, Mike
Wright, James
Wright, John
Wright, Mrs. Beryl
Wright, Sidney
Yakey, William
Yanchus, Andy
Yankowski, Stanley
Yee, John
Yonenson, Barry
York, Henry
Youhouse, Robert
Youman, Eugene O.
Younkins, Jerry
Yourshaw, Michael
Yow, Gordon
Yunker, Bruce
Zack, Paul
Zak, James
Zeltzer, David
Zerbe, Andy
Zidarevich, Rudy
Zimmerman, Jimmy
Zuchero, John H.

BIBLIOGRAPHY

Books

Schelly, Bill, ed. *Best of Star-Studded Comics*. (Includes interview with Alan Weiss.) Seattle: Hamster Press, 2005.

_____. *Comic Fandom Reader*. (Includes interviews with Marty Arbunich, Jerry Bails, Bill DuBay, Ronn Foss, Dick Lupoff, Pat Lupoff, Raymond Miller, Bill Thailing, and Roy Thomas.) Seattle: Hamster Press, 2002.

_____. *Fandom's Finest Comics*. (Includes interview with Langdon Chesney.) Seattle: Hamster Press, 1997.

_____. *Fandom's Finest Comics, Vol. 2*. (Includes interview with Biljo White.) Seattle: Hamster Press, 1998.

_____. *Giant Labors of Love*. Seattle: Hamster Press, 2000.

_____. *Golden Age of Comic Fandom*. Seattle: Hamster Press, 1995.

_____. *Sense of Wonder*. Raleigh: TwoMorrows Publishing, 2001.

Thomas, Roy, and Bill Schelly. *The Best of Alter Ego*. Seattle: Hamster Press, 1998.

Emails, Letters, Interviews and Questionnaires Received or Conducted by the Author

Arbunich, Marty, questionnaire returned in July 2009.

Barrier, Michael, questionnaire returned in summer 2009.

Bonario, emails received in 1997 and summer 2009.

Bubnis, Bernie, emails in April and September 2009.

Buckler, Rich, email interview in July 2009.

Bush, Bart, emails in October 2009.

DuBay, Bill, questionnaire returned in May 2009.

Evanier, Mark, emails in September 2009.

Fantucchio, John, letters in March and September 2009.

Franke, Rudi, letter received in spring 2009.

Glut, Don, telephone interview in June 1, 1992.

Hill, Roger, emails in August 2009.

Hutchinson, Alan, questionnaire returned in March 2009.

Ivie, Larry, letters in spring 2009.

Jennings, Robert, questionnaire returned in August 2009.

Kelez, Steve, questionnaire returned in April 2009.

Keltner, Howard, telephone conversations in 1994.

Kyle, Richard, letters in spring and summer 2009.

Lupoff, Richard, questionnaire returned in May 2009.

McGeehan, Tom, questionnaire returned in May 2009.

Nolan, Michelle, letters in March and April 2009.

Norwood, Rick, questionnaire returned in July 2009.

Parker, Ron, questionnaire returned in March 2009.

Perrin, Steve, questionnaire returned in September 2009.

Rogofsky, Howard, letter in September 2009.

Rothermich, Derrill, questionnaire returned in spring 2009.

Spicer, Bill, emails in spring and summer 2009.

Stark, Larry, questionnaire returned in February 2009

Stewart, Bhob, emails in March 2009.

Tuohey, Mike, questionnaire returned and emails in August 2009.

Von Bernewitz, Fred, telephone conversation in February 2009.

Vosburg, Mike, telephone interview in January 1992.

Wein, Len, emails in September 2009.

Weingroff, Rick, questionnaire returned in April 2009.

White, Ted, emails in March 2009.

Wolfman, Marvin, emails in June and September 2009.

Interviews in Alter Ego Magazine

(Note: All interviews in *Alter Ego* magazine from TwoMorrows Publishing are ©William Schelly.)

Bibliography

Schelly, Bill. "Claude Held, Pioneer Comic Book Dealer." (Interview conducted February 19, 1998.) *Alter Ego* vol. 3, no. 23, April 2003.
_____. "Fandom Across the Puddle, Part I." (Interview with John Wright.) *Alter Ego* vol. 3, no. 35, April 2004.
_____. "Fandom Across the Puddle, Part II." *Alter Ego* vol. 3, no. 36, May 2004.
_____. "Finding the 'Inner Bud,' Part I." (Interview conducted on July 26, 2004.) *Alter Ego* vol. 3, no. 47, April 2005.
_____. "Finding the 'Inner Bud,' Part II." *Alter Ego* vol. 3, no. 48, May 2005.
_____. "Gary Brown, Comic Book Reporter." *Alter Ego* vol. 3, no. 37, June 2004.
_____. "Gary Brown, Comic Book Reporter Part II." *Alter Ego* vol. 3, no. 40, September 2004.
_____. "Paul Gambi—Tailor to the (DC Super-Villain) Stars!" (Interview with Paul Gambacini.) *Alter Ego* vol. 3, no. 16, July 2002.
_____. "Tales Calculated to Drive You ... Odd! (Part I)." (Interview with Steve and Dave Herring.) *Alter Ego* vol. 3, no. 42, November 2004.
_____. "Tales Calculated to Drive You ... Odd! (Part II)." *Alter Ego* vol. 3, no. 44, January 2005.
_____. "A Talk with John Benson, Part I." *Alter Ego* vol. 3, no. 27, August 2003.
_____. "A Talk with John Benson, Part II." *Alter Ego* vol. 3, no. 28, September 2003.
_____. "A Talk with John Benson, Part III." *Alter Ego* vol. 3, no. 29, October 2003.
_____. "A Talk with Writer, Educator, & Comics Fanatic Glen Johnson, Part I." (Interview conducted January 16, 2005.) *Alter Ego* vol. 3, no. 51, August 2005.
_____. "A Talk with Writer, Educator, & Comics Fanatic Glen Johnson, Part II." *Alter Ego* vol. 3, no. 51, August 2005.
Schelly, Bill, and Jeff Gelb. "The Don and Maggie Thompson Interview." *Alter Ego* vol. 3, no. 11, November 2001.

INDEX